Social and Economic Life
in Second Temple Judea

Social and Economic Life
in Second Temple Judea

Samuel L. Adams

WESTMINSTER
JOHN KNOX PRESS
LOUISVILLE · KENTUCKY

© 2014 Samuel L. Adams

First edition
Published by Westminster John Knox Press
Louisville, Kentucky

14 15 16 17 18 19 20 21 22 23—10 9 8 7 6 5 4 3 2 1

Book design by Sharon Adams
Cover design by Dilu Nicholas
Cover illustration: Ruth Gleaning. James Tissot (1836–1902 French)
Jewish Museum, New York, USA © SuperStock/SuperStock.com

Library of Congress Cataloging-in-Publication Data
Adams, Samuel L., 1970– author.
  Social and economic life in Second Temple Judea / Samuel L. Adams
    p. cm
  ISBN 978-0-664-23703-5 (alk. paper)
  1. Jews—History—586 B.C.–70 A.D. 2. Jews—Social life and customs. 3. Jews—Economic conditions. 4. Jews—Social conditions. 5. Judaism—History—Post-exilic period, 586 B.C.–210 A.D. I. Title.
  DS121.65.A33 2014
  933'.4903—dc23

2013049521

Most Westminster John Knox Press books are available at special quantity discounts when purchased in bulk by corporations, organizations, and special-interest groups. For more information, please e-mail SpecialSales@wjkbooks.com.

Contents

List of Figures   vii

Acknowledgments   ix

List of Abbreviations   x

List of Ancient Sources Quoted   xiii

Introduction   1

1. Family Life and Marriage   **8**

Basic Household Structures   10

Household Size and Larger Population Estimates   15

Life in the Household   18

Marriage   22

   Finding a Partner   23

   Marriage Gifts and Dowry Arrangements   29

   The Economics of Divorce   34

Summary   40

2. The Status of Women and Children   **41**

Roles and Responsibilities of Women   42

The Status of Widows   51

Children   58

   Roles and Responsibilities of Male Offspring   61

   Roles and Responsibilities of Daughters   65

Responsibilities toward Parents   72

Inheritance   74

Debt Slavery   77

Summary   80

3. **Work and Financial Exchanges**   **82**
   Occupations   82
      The Challenges of Farming   82
      Animal Husbandry   90
      Other Occupations   91
   Financial Exchanges   99
   Borrowing and Lending   103
      Interest   104
      The Practice of Surety   114
      Bribery   121
   Summary   126

4. **Taxation and the Role of the State**   **128**
   Taxation in an Advanced Agrarian Economy:
      Anthropological Perspectives   129
   Persian Period   130
   Ptolemaic Period   145
   Seleucid Period   155
   The Hasmoneans   165
   Roman Period   171
   Summary   181

5. **The Ethics of Wealth and Poverty**   **183**
   Ethics of Wealth and Poverty in the Wisdom Literature   184
      Contradictions in the Book of Proverbs   184
      Skepticism in the Books of Job and Ecclesiastes   189
      Ben Sira and Social Ethics   192
      Second Temple Instructions and Question of an Afterlife   194
   Apocalyptic Eschatology, Economics, and Social Ethics   196
      4QInstruction and the Dead Sea Scrolls   197
      The Epistle of Enoch and the Gospel of Luke   198
      Wisdom and Apocalypticism   201
   The Question of Social Location   202
   Summary   205

Conclusion   206

Bibliography   209

Index of Ancient Sources   223

Index of Subjects   233

Figures

1. Persian period gold daric 132
2. Satrapy of Beyond the River 136
3. Ptolemy II, AR tetradrachm, struck at Gaza (225/4 BCE); bust of Ptolemy I/Eagle 149
4. Ptolemy II, AR tetradrachm, struck at Joppa; bust of Ptolemy I/Eagle 149
5. Demetrius I, AR tetradrachm struck at Akko-Ptolemais; head Demetrius I/Tyche on throne 156
6. Alexander Jannaeus, AE prutah; Paleo-Hebrew/two cornucopias 169
7. Alexander Jannaeus, AE prutah; anchor/sunwheel within diadem 169
8. The growth of Herod's kingdom, 40–4 BCE 175

Acknowledgments

This study emerged from an ongoing interest in economic issues in the ancient world, and initial research began in the midst of the global financial crisis that started in 2008. I am grateful to Jon Berquist for helping me formulate the topic and for his kind encouragement. John Collins read through the manuscript and offered his usual array of helpful suggestions. I continue to be thankful to have him as a mentor. Here at Union Presbyterian Seminary in Richmond, Virginia, my dean, Stan Skreslet, and president, Brian Blount, have supported my research and teaching. Megan Strollo has been my excellent research assistant for this book, and she offered substantive feedback in the process. I thank Westminster John Knox for publishing this volume, with deep gratitude to my editor, Marianne Blickenstaff. Her knowledge of the field and passion for this topic have energized my work. Bridgett Green at WJK guided me through the final steps of the process, along with Dan Braden, and I have appreciated their helpful suggestions. Special thanks also to members of the Society of Biblical Literature unit on "Economics in the Biblical World," especially my co-chair Richard Horsley, Roland Boer, Catherine Murphy, and Roger Nam. This unit has been a fruitful venue for conversation on the topic. Finally, my wife, Helen, and two children, Virginia and Charlie, are my greatest joy and source of support. I dedicate this book to Virginia and Charlie, whose creativity and love for family continue to inspire me.

Abbreviations

AB	Anchor Bible
ABRL	Anchor Bible Reference Library
ABS	Archaeology and Biblical Studies
AE	*aes*, bronze/copper/brass
AIL	Ancient Israel and Its Literature
AR	*argentum*, silver
AYB	Anchor Yale Bible
AYBRL	Anchor Yale Bible Reference Library
BBB	Bonner biblische Beiträge
BJS	Brown Judaic Studies
BASOR	*Bulletin of the American Schools of Oriental Research*
BI	*Biblical Illustrator*
BInt	Biblical Interpretation series
BTB	*Biblical Theology Bulletin*
BZAW	Beihefte zur Zeitschrift für die alttestamentliche Wissenschaft
BZNW	Beihefte zur Zeitschrift für die neutestamentliche Wissenschaft
ConBOT	Coniectanea biblica: Old Testament Series
CBQ	*Catholic Biblical Quarterly*
CHANE	Culture and History of the Ancient Near East
CRINT	Compendia rerum iudaicarum ad Novum Testamentum
DEJ	*The Eerdmans Dictionary of Early Judaism*. Edited by John J. Collins and Daniel C. Harlow. Grand Rapids: Eerdmans, 2010.
DJD	Discoveries in the Judaean Desert (Oxford: Clarendon Press, 1955–)
enl.	enlarged

EvT	*Evangelische Theologie*
FCB	Feminist Companion to the Bible
Gk.	Greek
Heb.	Hebrew
Hen	*Henoch: Studies in Judaism and Christianity from Second Temple to Late Antiquity*
HTR	*Harvard Theological Review*
HUCA	*Hebrew Union College Annual*
IEJ	*Israel Exploration Journal*
IRT	Issues in Religion and Theology
JBL	*Journal of Biblical Literature*
JBS	Jerusalem Biblical Studies
JHS	*Journal of Hellenic Studies*
JJS	*Journal of Jewish Studies*
JNES	*Journal of Near Eastern Studies*
JPS	Jewish Publication Society Torah Commentary
JR	*Journal of Religion*
JSJ	*Journal for the Study of Judaism in the Persian, Hellenistic, and Roman Period*
JSJSup	Journal for the Study of Judaism in the Persian, Hellenistic, and Roman Period: Supplement Series
JSOT	*Journal for the Study of the Old Testament*
JSOTSup	Journal for the Study of the Old Testament: Supplement Series
KTU	*Die keilalphabetischen Texte aus Ugarit*, edited by M. Dietrich et al. (Neukirchen-Vluyn, 1976; 2nd enlarged ed. [= CTU], Münster, 1995)
LAI	Library of Ancient Israel
LCL	Loeb Classical Library
LEC	Library of Early Christianity
LHB/OTS	Library of Hebrew Bible/Old Testament Series
LSTS	Library of Second Temple Studies
LXX	Septuagint (Greek)
MT	Masoretic Text (Hebrew)
NICOT	New International Commentary on the Old Testament
NovTSup	Supplements to Novum Testamentum
NRSV	New Revised Standard Version
NTL	New Testament Library
NTS	*New Testament Studies*
OIP	Oriental Institute Publications
OTG	Old Testament Guides

OTL	Old Testament Library
PEQ	*Palestine Exploration Quarterly*
QR	*Quarterly Review*
repr.	reprinted
SAHL	Studies in the Archaeology and History of the Levant
SBLDS	Society of Biblical Literature Dissertation Series
SBLSP	*Society of Biblical Literature Seminar Papers*
SJLA	Studies in Judaism in Late Antiquity
SOFS	Symbolae Osloensis: Fascicle Supplement
SHBC	Smyth & Helwys Bible Commentary
STDJ	Studies on the Texts of the Desert of Judah
SUNT	Studien zur Umwelt des Neuen Testaments
TAD	Bezalel Porten and Ada Yardeni. *Textbook of Aramaic Documents from Ancient Egypt.* 4 vols. Jerusalem: Hebrew University Department of the History of the Jewish People, 1986 (*TAD* A), 1989 (*TAD* B), 1993 (*TAD* C), 1999 (*TAD* D).
TDOT	*Theological Dictionary of the Old Testament.* Edited by G. Johannes Botterweck and Helmer Ringgren. Translated by John T. Willis. 15 vols. Grand Rapids: Eerdmans, 1974–2004.
Transeu	*Transeuphratène*
VT	*Vetus Testamentum*
VTSup	Vetus Testamentum Supplements
ZPE	*Zeitschrift für Papyrologie und Epigraphik*
ZTK	*Zeitschrift für Theologie und Kirche*

Ancient Sources Quoted

Except as otherwise indicated, translations of ancient sources are from the following works:

Bible: New Revised Standard Version (NRSV), with its verse numbers. Alternate parenthesized or bracketed numbers show versification of the Masoretic Text (MT).

Josephus and other Greek sources: Loeb Classical Library editions (LCL) (Cambridge, MA: Harvard University Press).

The Mishnah: Herbert Danby, *The Mishnah: Translation from the Hebrew with Introduction and Brief Explanatory Notes* (Oxford: Oxford University Press, 1933).

Qumran-related texts: Florentino García Martínez and Eibert J. C. Tigchelaar, *The Dead Sea Scrolls Study Edition*, 2 vols. (Leiden: E. J. Brill, 1997–98).

Introduction

And there were those who said, "We are having to borrow money
on our fields and vineyards to pay the king's tax."

Nehemiah 5:4

This short verse from Nehemiah addresses a seemingly mundane set of circumstances: taxation, borrowing, and the challenges of farming. The complaint that a particular group lodges to Nehemiah, the governor in Judah
working under the Persians (fifth century BCE), does not offer lofty theological concepts or purple prose. Yet the issues at stake in this verse were pivotal
for those trying to preserve their households under trying conditions. How
would these persons retain their land? Were the lending arrangements fair,
or did exorbitant interest rates place them at great risk? What was the nature
of their tax obligations? Would God protect the righteous believer or allow
such a person to reach desperate straits? Such questions are actually far from
mundane: they point to critical realities for those living in Judah during the
Second Temple period.

Those who study the Bible are becoming increasingly attentive to the significance of economics when examining ancient texts and the cultures that
produced them. Although exegetical studies often touch on economic matters, it is also necessary to focus specifically on the economics of the historical
context that ancient sources address or from which they arise. From the restoration of the temple in the sixth century BCE to the context out of which the
Jesus movement arose, it is difficult to overstate the importance of economics for understanding the cultural dynamics of ancient Judah. In a stratified
economy, with difficult farming conditions and a succession of foreign rulers,
wealth and poverty concerns pervaded every aspect of life.

This book examines the socioeconomic landscape of Judah/Judea in the Second Temple period, from the end of the Babylonian exile to the destruction of the temple by the Romans (532 BCE to 70 CE). No previous study has focused specifically on economics when analyzing this time frame, and the current discussion will engage in a close reading of key sources, consideration of relevant archaeological evidence, and theoretical analysis. By taking up topics like marriage gifts, borrowing and lending, and taxation, our discussion will provide an overview of economic life, with fresh insights from relevant biblical texts, including passages and entire books that do not receive enough attention in this regard (e.g., Ruth, Ezra–Nehemiah).

Discussion will proceed according to theme, with special attention to family life and the status of women and children, along with marketplace practices and taxation. Our thematic focus will allow for innovative analysis and conclusions. For example, interpreters often take the sayings on wealth and poverty in Proverbs, Ecclesiastes, and Ben Sira as a timeless set of abstract principles, rather than as a response to actual dynamics on the ground. Yet when the author of Ecclesiastes rails against bribery (Eccl. 7:7) or Ben Sira urges his listeners to stand as guarantors for their neighbor's loan (Sir. 29:14), these sapiential figures are responding to financial realities and the expectations of their sacred tradition. The thematic arrangement also allows us to consider the implications of living under a succession of foreign powers. Burdensome taxation policies and stratification confronted most Judeans during this period; in every chapter this study details the financial impact of colonization.

Our study will begin at the household level and work outward to the larger marketplace and state level. Chapter 1, "Family Life and Marriage," will survey basic issues like household structure, family size, and population levels during the Second Temple period. We will highlight the importance of the patriarchal kinship grouping, or "house of the father," that persisted into this period. The bulk of this chapter will take up the topic of marriage and its economic implications. Our discussion will point to the endogamous understanding of marriage (i.e., marrying within one's kinship group) in many of the extant sources and conflicts that developed over proper matches. Economic issues are often at the center of decisions in this regard (e.g., Ezra 9–10). This chapter will also address the custom of marriage gifts as a component of the betrothal process and how divorce might have worked during this period. Information about marriage customs appears in the biblical texts and also in such extracanonical sources as the Elephantine papyri and the Babatha archive.

Chapter 2, "The Status of Women and Children," will consider the roles for women and their offspring in the household structure and how they contributed to the viability of their kinship group and the larger economy. Focus on this topic has increased dramatically in recent decades, and our discussion will address both the primary sources and insights from cross-cultural analysis. We will highlight the duties of women in food preparation and their responsibilities in sustaining family members, along with a host of other issues. This chapter will also address the situation of widows in the social structure, including the critical question of whether they could inherit property. In this regard a pertinent issue is how much levirate marriage (i.e., marrying the brother of one's deceased husband) continued as a custom during the Second Temple period. The second half of the chapter will consider the status of children. Sons usually adopted the work of their father, in most cases assisting with farming duties as they matured. Those from more elite, literate households had greater opportunities, including the possibility of a scribal career or a priestly office if they came from the right family. With regard to daughters, this topic has received little attention in studies of the period. This chapter will argue that most daughters had to maintain a more public existence than sources such as Ben Sira and Philo allow, since the majority of households could not afford to keep their female children in seclusion. The discussion of women and children will also consider the task of "honoring" one's parents and the economic implications of this requirement. Finally we will examine inheritance questions, including the possibilities for daughters in this regard, and the experience of debt slavery for children.

Chapter 3, "Work and Financial Exchanges," will move beyond the household level to the larger marketplace. First, we will survey the most common activities, with specific attention to the responsibilities of agriculturalists in Judah. Most households engaged in farming pursuits under trying conditions, creating a somewhat predictable but challenging rhythm to their year. Other activities included animal husbandry, pottery making, and more elitist pursuits like that of the scribe, priest, or large landowner. The rest of this chapter will examine public transactions. During the Second Temple period, the use of coinage became more commonplace, even though bartering remained the predominant form of exchange. Interest charges, including the practice of vouching for the loan of another (surety), receive attention in the sources from this period, as does the practice of bribery. Here the discussion will highlight wariness about loans and becoming a guarantor, especially in the Wisdom literature. A culture of reciprocity characterized many exchanges, with persons seeking either social advancement or the maintenance of their kinship group and reputation. In our discussion of financial exchanges, we will consider the influence of the regulations in the Pentateuch on such matters as interest and bribery.

Chapter 4, "Taxation and the Role of the State," will adopt a more diachronic approach. First, the topic of taxation will be examined in light of social anthropology. Many theoretical studies have found continuities across different cultural contexts in terms of taxation, especially when methods of farming are similar. After establishing some common trends in settings like that of postexilic Judah, we will proceed with a historical analysis from the Persian period to the Roman period. Of particular importance will be the difficulty most persons faced in meeting revenue obligations to imperial rulers, local governors and officials, and the priestly establishment. Exacting requirements continued throughout the Second Temple period and not just during the reign of major figures like Darius I (550–486 BCE; reigned 522–486) or Herod the Great (73–4 BCE; reigned 37–4). This chapter will consider key passages in the biblical texts and extracanonical writings that address taxation, including the critical writings of Josephus (37–95 CE).

Finally, Chapter 5, "The Ethics of Wealth and Poverty," will study the ethics of material holdings in certain Second Temple texts, most notably the Wisdom and apocalyptic literature. Is it acceptable to become a wealthy individual in these sources? Can divine judgment reverse the effects of poverty? The sapiential texts from this period offer a variety of propositions on financial holdings, not all of them consistent. In some passages, wealth functions as a reward for virtue and blessing from God, while other sayings highlight wisdom as preferred over material possessions and the corrupting influence of money. Most sapiential books, including Proverbs, Ecclesiastes, Job, and Ben Sira, do not have an eschatological framework for adjudicating the consequences of human behavior in relation to economics. According to these texts, a righteous individual who has struggled with poverty cannot hope for heavenly reward to reverse the unfairness of earthly existence. Here our discussion will point to a profound shift on this point in some of the later sapiential and apocalyptic texts of the Second Temple period. In certain passages from the Dead Sea Scrolls, the Enochic books, and the New Testament (esp. the Gospel of Luke), the promise of a blessed afterlife allowed for an otherworldly judgment scene that could reverse the plight of the righteous poor and the unfair advantages of any rich persons who had cheated. Apocalyptic ideas created a new horizon for examining wealth and poverty and how God might evaluate human conduct in this area.

Before proceeding with this discussion, a few terminological and historical matters require clarification. First is the issue of proper terminology for the people who are the focus of this study: those who lived in Judah during the Second Temple period or considered themselves part of this entity. Such terms as "Israelite," "Judean," and especially "Jewish" often appear interchangeably in discussions of this type, and this can lead to confusion. In particular, the use of "Jewish" to refer to the inhabitants of Judah during this period is a complex matter. As Shaye J. D. Cohen and other commentators have pointed out, "Judean" is a more accurate designation.[1] The English usage of "Jewish" often indicates a practitioner of "Judaism," a contemporary religious tradition.[2] Of course the roots of this tradition stretch back well before the Babylonian exile (586–532 BCE). In sources from the Second Temple period, however, terminology in this regard usually has more of an ethnic or geographic connotation. Greek *Ioudaios* derives from Hebrew *yĕhûdî* (pl. *yĕhûdîm*), which describes an inhabitant of Judah/Judea or someone who is to be identified with that group (i.e., a "Judean"). Cohen explains that only after the Maccabean revolt (167–160 BCE) does Greek *Ioudaïsmos* (usually translated as "Jewish") appear in 2 Maccabees (first century BCE) and have a more cultural and religious connotation.[3] The extant evidence suggests that outside rulers from this period, such as the Persians and Seleucids, understood the usage of *yĕhûdî* or *Ioudaios* to indicate a specific people, alongside other ethnic-geographic entities (e.g., Egyptian). Consequently, in this volume the discussion will generally employ the term "Judean" rather than "Jewish" when referring to the inhabitants of the region under consideration, especially when discussing events before the Maccabean revolt.[4] Another defensible way of proceeding in this regard is to refer to the post-biblical literature, especially texts and ideas that arose after the death of Alexander the Great (323 BCE), as characteristic of "Early Judaism," a tactic that we also will take at several points in the discussion.[5]

Similar caution is in order when referring to the "religious" identity of Judeans and how their "religion" changed during this formative period.

1. S. J. D. Cohen, *The Beginnings of Jewishness: Boundaries, Varieties, Uncertainties* (Berkeley: University of California Press, 1999), 69–70.

2. The use of "Jewish" can also indicate an ethnic and/or cultural group, including nonobservant Jews.

3. See 2 Macc. 2:21; 8:1; 14:38. Even this point is disputed. Steve Mason, "Jews, Judaeans, Judaizing, Judaism: Problems of Categorization in Ancient History," *JSJ* 38 (2007): 457–512, argues that *Ioudaïsmos* in 2 Maccabees is still more of an ethnic designation.

4. This designation becomes more complex when discussing those in Diaspora, but Cohen and other scholars retain "Judean" as an ethnic label rather than a religious one even when referring to persons in other areas (e.g., Elephantine). See Cohen, *Beginnings of Jewishness*, 75–76.

5. John J. Collins, "Early Judaism in Modern Scholarship," in *The Eerdmans Dictionary of Early Judaism* (hereafter *DEJ*), ed. John J. Collins and Daniel C. Harlow (Grand Rapids: Eerdmans, 2010), 1–2, distinguishes between the preexilic practices of ancient Israel and the "Early Judaism" that emerged after the exile, especially after the reign of Alexander the Great. The Early Judaism designation functions as a welcome corrective to an earlier scholarly tendency to refer to this period as "Late Judaism" (*Spätjudentum*), implying a decline from the more pristine traditions of the Prophets.

Studies of this type often proceed as if "religious" dynamics can be distilled from political, social, and economic factors. The distinction between "secular" and "religious" that often occurs in contemporary discourse does not generally work when describing events in antiquity. As Brent Nongbri explains in an important new book, those living in the ancient world did not understand their "religion" as a separate sphere of human existence. The idea of ancient Mesopotamian, Egyptian, Greek, or Judean "religion" largely developed after the European Enlightenment. These ancient civilizations had intricate, fascinating portraits of the divine, but we risk projecting our own modern taxonomies onto the ancient world by seeking to separate the religious from the ethnic, cultural, or economic. Nongbri urges the need for restraint on this point: "Religion is a modern category; it may be able to shed light on some aspects of the ancient world when applied in certain strategic ways, but we have to be honest about the category's origins and not pretend that it somehow organically and magically arises from our sources."[6] Such a cautionary note does not mitigate the rich theological perspectives in the many texts that date from the Second Temple period. The fact that the sources do not reflect a gulf between "religion" and other forms of human experience actually highlights the profound nature of faith perspectives in these ancient texts. One of the aims of this study is to demonstrate that economics, politics, and complex beliefs in a higher power interact frequently in the biblical sources and other works, and one should not attempt to separate these strands too neatly.

Another pertinent issue is the treatment of sources prior to or beyond the period under consideration. Although one can define the Second Temple period with major historical bookends (the return from exile around 532 BCE and the destruction of Jerusalem by the Romans in 70 CE), it will be necessary to probe earlier and later evidence in order to assess social and economic life. For example, one cannot understand the perspective on economics in the book of Nehemiah without considering the import of antecedent legislation in the Pentateuch. Nor do the woe oracles in the Epistle of Enoch (*1 En.* 92–105) make sense unless one recognizes the employment of this literary form in eighth-century-BCE prophets like Amos. Along similar lines, the rabbinic texts often shed light on sources from the Second Temple period. The references in the Mishnah and the Talmud help us to contextualize the understanding of marriage in such documents as the contracts from Elephantine or

6. Brent Nongbri, *Before Religion: A History of a Modern Concept* (New Haven, CT: Yale University Press, 2013), 153. One can and should make generic distinctions in examining literature from this period, and in certain sources cultic activities receive far greater attention (e.g., the priestly laws of Leviticus). Yet Nongbri's caution is a welcome reminder that even generic categories like Wisdom literature were not seen as "secular" in the ancient world.

the book of Tobit.[7] Similarly, many of the New Testament books postdate the destruction of the temple in 70 CE, and yet these sources are helpful for understanding economic life in Judea under the Romans.

Along similar lines, we will analyze texts where the date of composition remains uncertain. Disagreement over the exact period for certain sections in the Pentateuch is one example (e.g., the Holiness Code in Lev. 17–26), as are the dates for the books of Proverbs and Ruth. With regard to the Wisdom literature, there is widespread agreement that the sayings in Proverbs came together before and after the exile. Scribal sages worked under Israelite kings (e.g., Prov. 25:1, "proverbs of Solomon that the officials of King Hezekiah of Judah copied"), but the collection continued to take shape after the exile, especially during the Persian period (the same is true for the Pentateuch).[8] The period for the book of Ruth is also uncertain, although recent studies have forcefully argued for a postexilic date.[9] Our discussion will point to the creative manner in which Ruth wrestles with pentateuchal legislation as a counter to the more rigid perspectives in books like Ezra and Nehemiah, suggesting the Persian period as the most likely composition date.

In assessing all of this material, we will point to persistent stratification in Judah, with most households engaging in farming pursuits under challenging conditions. Persons of privilege, especially those who curried favor with local officials and foreign rulers, stood to benefit from their connections, while most of the population lacked access to such possibilities. Lopsided lending arrangements and taxation demands exacerbated the challenges of living in the region, and many sources from this period reflect considerable tensions between rich and poor. In the midst of this challenging economic climate, we will highlight the relationship between economics and the social visions of the Hebrew Bible and New Testament (and other important texts). Those who placed their faith in the God of Israel understood economic issues through the lens of fidelity to the commandments. Second Temple sources indicate an ongoing debate over how to live in the world, with all of its hierarchies and financial challenges, and remain faithful to the call for benevolence that the tradition demanded.

---

7. Most commentators put the editing of the Mishnah around 200 CE.

8. Richard J. Clifford, *Proverbs*, OTL (Louisville, KY: Westminster John Knox Press, 1999), 6.

9. P. H. W. Lau, *Identity and Ethics in the Book of Ruth: A Social Identity Approach*, BZAW 416 (Berlin: de Gruyter, 2011), surveys the content of Ruth and how it relates to the dynamics of both the preexilic and postexilic landscape; he argues convincingly that the Persian period is the most likely date of composition.

1

Family Life and Marriage

The family stood at the center of life in Judah, before and after the exile. A long-standing kinship system played a fundamental role in determining settlement patterns, social hierarchies, and the distribution of wealth. The various literary genres in the Hebrew Bible, along with the New Testament and extracanonical evidence, reflect the centrality of the family in the social structure and its significance for a person's well-being. The importance of household structures persisted, even through exile and when foreign powers took control of Judah. The possibility of healthy offspring, financial stability, a good reputation, and in some cases survival remained much higher if an individual had a place in an established household with a living patriarch.[1] Those who found themselves on the periphery, such as widows and orphans, faced many disadvantages, which often led to desperate circumstances.

Family life is both a critical and elusive topic in the study of the Second Temple period. Those living in Judah had to adapt to a succession of colonial powers and such developments as an increase in coinage and trade. When examining this period, it is necessary to consider the relationship between households and external dynamics, including the challenge of adjusting to imperial rule, changing social institutions, urbanization, and an array of taxation demands. Yet the specifics of household life, especially in relation to economics, are largely unknown to the modern interpreter. The Persians and their successors did not always maintain careful archives, and little

---

1. Many households required a living male as head of a hierarchical grouping in order to remain as socially and economically viable as possible. Such a figure could perpetuate the family trade and facilitate marriage arrangements for his offspring. See below for further discussion.

inscriptional evidence from Judah dates to these centuries.[2] The rabbinic literature provides a more thorough picture of financial dynamics in this regard, but one cannot simply apply these writings to an earlier era without analysis of the Second Temple sources and other evidence. Biblical books and extracanonical sources, such as the contracts from Elephantine and the Zeno papyri, shed light on the socioeconomic landscape during this period, but from the outset we recognize the guesswork in exploring this topic, particularly in relation to the subsistence farmers who made up the majority of the population.

The present chapter will address the economics of family life during the Second Temple period, with special attention to basic demographics and the financial aspects of marriage.[3] Key factors, such as the permanent loss of national sovereignty, the revenue needs of colonial powers and local officials/priests, and challenging farming conditions had an impact on families during this period, and these topics will receive attention throughout our study. Archaeological and inscriptional evidence will be helpful for this inquiry, including documents that did not originate in Judah (e.g., family concerns in the contracts from Elephantine). Throughout our discussion, we will consult the biblical texts from this period for clues about economics and family life. One should not sweep aside as irrelevant the books with fictional details (e.g., Ruth), advice that transcends a particular era (e.g., Proverbs and Ben Sira), or content with a clearly historiographic intent (e.g., Chronicles). The careful reader often finds incidental information and implicit commentary on financial matters in these and other sources. Many passages, such as the prohibition against intermarriage in Ezra 9–10, offer important hints about the pecuniary aspects of family life. Much of this chapter will take up the topic of marriage, and we will demonstrate that one cannot detach the economic aspects of betrothal and marriage customs from other dynamics at work, including theological issues.

Before proceeding, it is worth noting that the terms "family" and "household" are not exactly synonymous. A "family" can be defined as a "group of kin-related people . . . who may or may not reside together and whose primary function is to reproduce members biologically."[4] The "household," on the

---

2. Pierre Briant, *From Cyrus to Alexander: A History of the Persian Empire*, trans. P. T. Daniels (Winona Lake, IN: Eisenbrauns, 2002), 5–9, describes the particular difficulties of examining the Persian period with little inscriptional evidence. Archives from later rules, such as the Ptolemies, reveal more information (see below).

3. Chapter 2 (below) will then focus on the status of women and children.

4. Nesta Anderson, "Finding the Space between Spatial Boundaries and Social Dynamics: The Archaeology of Nested Households," in *Household Chores and Household Choices: Theorizing the Domestic Sphere in Historical Archaeology*, ed. Kerri Saige Barile and Jamie C. Brandon (Tuscaloosa: University of Alabama Press, 2004), 111.

other hand, is a residential arrangement of persons "who live together in one or more structures, who carry out daily activities necessary for the maintenance and social reproduction of the group living within a specific space associated with the residence, and who interact with other households."[5] In this context "household" means not just biological relatives; it could also include slaves, concubines, and other retainers who assist with productivity. There can be overlap between the categories (i.e., an entire "family" can be situated in one locale as a "household"), but failure to notice this distinction often leads to confusion.

BASIC HOUSEHOLD STRUCTURES

Our first task is to consider household structures in the Second Temple period, including the import of residential patterns for economic life. Throughout the ancient Near East, a network of interdependent kinship groups and tribal associations connected most households, and these ties usually mattered more than any national loyalties. In a major study on this topic, J. David Schloen presents a "patrimonial household model" to explain the organizing principle of societies. According to his analysis, "the social order consists of a hierarchy of subhouseholds linked by personal ties at each level between individual 'masters' and 'slaves' or 'fathers' and 'sons.'"[6] Within this system, a person's identity and success hinged on participation in a functioning household, with its hierarchical network of relationships and larger kinship group.

Terminology in the Hebrew Bible and beyond illustrates the significance of this "patrimonial household model," including the many references to the "house of the father" (Heb. *bêt 'āb*) as the basic structure for family life.[7] This "house of the father" term indicates a family unit with various kinship ties and a patriarch at the head of a hierarchical grouping. This system was patrilocal in the sense that young females who married became members of their husband's household and also patrilineal since family identity and inheritance

5. Anderson, "Finding the Space," 111. In many cases, the citation of family members is not historically accurate in the biblical texts, such that commentators speak of "fictive" kin.

6. J. David Schloen, *The House of the Father as Fact and Symbol: Patrimonialism in Ugarit and the Ancient Near East*, SAHL 2 (Winona Lake, IN: Eisenbrauns, 2001), 51, relies on the seminal work of Max Weber in this area.

7. Shunya Bendor, *The Social Structure of Ancient Israel: The Institution of the Family* (Beit 'Ab) *from the Settlement to the End of the Monarchy*, JBS 7 (Jerusalem: Simor, 1996), provides a comprehensive treatment of the "house of the father" terminology and its occurrences in the biblical texts.

usually passed from the father to his son(s). The "house of the father" structure frequently included siblings, as evidenced by the important fraternal relationships throughout the Bible.[8] In addition, tiers of organization existed beyond the baseline "house of the father," including the "extended family" or "clan" (Heb. *mišpāḥâ*) and then the "tribe" (Heb. *šēbet*) level. The many genealogies in the Hebrew Bible and New Testament underscore the significance of this terminology for individual families and the society at large. For example, when the Lord commands Abram in Genesis, "Go from your country and your kindred and your *father's house* to the land that I will show you" (Gen. 12:1, emphasis added), this verse emphasizes Abram's ties to his father Terah's house and the risk he takes in leaving. Later references highlight the significance of Abram's departure and the importance of living securely within a "house of the father" structure (e.g., Gen. 20:13; 24:7).

For the current discussion, one pressing question is the amount of change that occurred within household structures after the exile, especially in relation to land distribution and the long-standing "house of the father" system. Those living in Judah under the Persians and subsequent rulers faced numerous challenges, including foreign interest in their land and its resources, tensions between returnees from exile and those who stayed in the region, urbanization (esp. later in the Second Temple period), and the need to rebuild the temple. Within this context, Jon Berquist cites the significance of foreign rulers and how they put into place a class of "nonagricultural elites" who could work at the local level to maximize food output, tax revenues, and the production of indigenous goods.[9] As families encountered the shifting landscape during this period, we should consider to what extent household patterns changed, especially as larger estates became more prominent and many kinship groups lost their land.

According to an influential but ultimately questionable thesis from Joel Weinberg, the inhabitants of Judah developed greater solidarity and therefore a more communal identity after the exile. Weinberg proposed that a large network of households in and around Jerusalem formed a solidarity group, a "citizen-temple community." There are many references in the biblical lists from Ezra–Nehemiah and Chronicles to the "house of the *fathers*" (Heb. *bêt 'ābôt*),

---

8. The Hebrew Bible contains numerous examples of both "segmented" genealogies, which show the relationship among current family members (e.g., Gen. 35:22–26 and the brothers who are the offspring of Jacob) and "linear" genealogies, which highlight a family's ancestral line across generations (e.g., Gen. 5 and the descendants of Adam).

9. Jon L. Berquist, *Judaism in Persia's Shadow: A Social and Historical Approach* (Minneapolis: Fortress Press, 1995), 141.

as opposed to "house of the *father*."[10] Weinberg argued that local authorities in Judah divided the land into parcels for individual families, but all of the estates ultimately functioned as the common property of the "citizen-temple community" and the God it worshiped.[11] This shift toward a more collective mentality represented a response to exile and permanent colonization as the community sought to remain cohesive. Weinberg's idea of common ownership is intriguing, and he is undoubtedly correct that certain factions competed for land and favor with the authorities during the Persian period, leading to a more collectivist mentality. The tension between those returning from exile and those who stayed in the land is the clearest example of this trend, and this type of factionalism paved the way for the sects of later eras (i.e., Pharisees, Sadducees, and Essenes).[12] Yet there is no real textual or archaeological evidence for the "citizen-temple community" that Weinberg proposes. It is more likely that the "house of the fathers" replaced the larger "clan" (*mišpāḥâ*) terminology that existed before the exile.[13] In certain cases, references to the "house of the fathers" seem to represent the efforts of postexilic families to link their ancestry to the long-standing "clans" (800–1,000 males) of preexilic Israel, sometimes as a means of authenticating land possession. For example, after the exile members of the Benjaminite tribe occupied the town of Geba (just north of Jerusalem), and the language concerning the "house of the fathers" in 1 Chronicles 8 enlarges the borders of Benjaminite territory by connecting earlier ancestors to the surrounding towns in this area.[14] Yet in such passages or in extracanonical texts from this period, one strains to find clues of collective ownership on the scale that Weinberg suggests.[15] Those in charge of the temple treasury and other officials had to placate the royal authorities who allowed them to serve and the local elites who supported them rather than a large guild of Judean families holding property in common.

---

10. Joel Weinberg, *The Citizen-Temple Community*, trans. Daniel L. Smith-Christopher, JSOTSup 151 (Sheffield: JSOT Press, 1992). The *bêt 'ābôt* terminology occurs 65 times in Ezra–Nehemiah and Chronicles but only six times in the Deuteronomistic History. NRSV translates *bêt 'ābôt* as "ancestral houses."

11. Ibid., 28–29, 57.

12. Joseph Blenkinsopp, *Judaism, the First Phase: The Place of Ezra and Nehemiah in the Origins of Judaism* (Grand Rapids: Eerdmans, 2009), 189–227.

13. John J. Collins, "Marriage, Divorce, and Family in Second Temple Judaism," in *Families in Ancient Israel*, ed. L. G. Perdue et al. (Louisville, KY: Westminster John Knox Press, 1997), 105.

14. Ralph W. Klein, *1 Chronicles*, Hermeneia (Minneapolis: Fortress Press, 2006), 246–52.

15. Joseph Blenkinsopp, "Temple and Society in Achaemenid Judah," in *Second Temple Studies*, vol. 1, *Persian Period*, ed. Philip R. Davies, JSOTSup 117 (Sheffield: JSOT Press, 1991), 44–53, critiques Weinberg's thesis.

If it is inaccurate to speak of widespread collective ownership, to what extent did residential patterns during the Second Temple period approximate the "house of the father" system of earlier eras? Living circumstances for households varied: some resided on isolated farms while others inhabited villages with interconnected units.[16] Many agriculturalists lived in smaller villages after the exile, often sharing a courtyard with other family members and/or strangers.[17] If working on a large estate, a common occurrence after the exile, a person might reside only with his nuclear family, along with other workers at that particular site. Both foreign rulers and local elites became proficient in usurping land for themselves, such that long-standing agrarian households (whether a nuclear family or larger kinship group) often lost the territory and stability that went with one location over many generations. Under the Ptolemaic and Seleucid regimes in particular (fourth–second centuries BCE), intricate tax measures and land seizures became commonplace, and this forced many households into becoming landless peasants, perhaps serving as tenant farmers on estates where they had no property claim (see chap. 4). Such dynamics meant the splintering of kinship groups, especially if indebtedness required the parceling out of members to serve in disparate areas, sometimes in order to work off a loan to a creditor. Some archaeologists have pointed to smaller tombs in the Second Temple period, suggesting that the extended family ceased to have the same level of cohesiveness.[18] In light of these factors, perhaps the "house of the father" has somewhat less relevance for this period as a descriptive term.

Yet Judean society continued to rely on long-standing household structures and kinship patterns as organizing principles. Even if certain developments disrupted the system that permitted continuity on one plot of land for a household, the importance of kinship ties persisted all the way into the Roman period. The Greek word *oikonomia*, referring to the structure and maintenance of the household and its property (*oikos* means "house," and *nomos* means "law/rule"), is the noun from which the English word "economy" derives. Certain texts from the Second Temple period refer to the kinship group and its importance as an *economic* mode of production (e.g., "the

---

16. David A. Fiensy, *The Social History of Palestine in the Herodian Period: The Land Is Mine*, Studies in the Bible and Early Christianity 20 (Lewiston, NY: Edwin Mellen, 1991), 119–46.

17. Ibid., 123–26, shows that the four-roomed house that characterized preexilic Israel often gave way to more of a courtyard structure.

18. Rachel Hachlili and Ann E. Killibrew, "Jewish Funerary Customs during the Second Temple Period, in Light of the Excavations at the Jericho Necropolis," *PEQ* 115 (1983): 109–39; Rachel Hachlili, *Jewish Funerary Customs, Practices, and Rites in the Second Temple Period*, JSJSup 94 (Leiden: E. J. Brill, 2005).

families of the guild of linen workers at Beth-ashbea" in 1 Chr. 4:21). In the book of Ruth, which most likely dates after the Babylonian exile, the significance of the household as a mode of production is apparent in the opening chapter as the widows become unmoored from their "house of the father" and enter desperate economic straits. Among the important themes in Ruth, the security of the "house of the father" structure and the danger of living outside of it are very prominent topics. Later references in the New Testament to the families of Simon and Andrew as sharing the same house in Capernaum (Mark 1:29) and earning their living together (1:16) underscore the significance of kinship ties for understanding social structures and economic production.[19] Along similar lines, some archaeologists have claimed that extended family members often shared a common courtyard at many sites, thereby perpetuating the patrimonial household model.[20] A passage in the Mishnah refers to a pattern where "brothers ate at their father's table but slept in their own houses" (m. 'Erub. 6:7).[21] In many cases, household efficiency determined the well-being of members: kinship groups networked together in order to pool resources, divide labor efficiently, and perform daily tasks.[22] The failure of a household to maintain its effectiveness could lead to drastic losses, including property, personal autonomy through a tenant-farming situation, and even selling children to debt slavery (e.g., Neh. 5). Finally, the endorsement of insider marriages in books like *Jubilees* and Tobit serves as an indicator of ongoing allegiance to earlier kinship patterns and a more insular understanding of desirable acquaintances (see below).

This type of solidarity extended into the Diaspora. In many instances, Judeans in such locations as Alexandria cultivated an existence that allowed them to retain their cultural identity and the unity of their household. As both Philo and Josephus attest, those in a Diaspora context frequently congregated in specific neighborhoods.[23] At Elephantine, offspring frequently lived close to their parents, allowing for greater household stability. As families interacted with outsiders during this period, especially in Diaspora settings, practices such as circumcision, dietary protocols (i.e., the laws of kashruth), and Sabbath observance allowed communities to maintain their distinct identity and

19. Fiensy, *Social History of Palestine*, 132.

20. Shim'on Dar, *Landscape and Pattern: An Archaeological Survey of Samaria, 800 B.C.E.–636 C.E.*, British Archaeological Reports Series 308 (Oxford: BAR, 1986). See also Fiensy, *Social History of Palestine*, 128–29.

21. Translation from Herbert Danby, *The Mishnah: Translation from the Hebrew with Introduction and Brief Explanatory Notes* (Oxford: Oxford University Press, 1933).

22. See Douglas A. Knight, *Law, Power, and Justice in Ancient Israel*, LAI (Louisville, KY: Westminster John Knox Press, 2011), 131.

23. Josephus (*J.W.* 2.488) and Philo (*Flacc.* 8.55) both confirm such separation from the general population as common practice.

preserve family unity. Even households that were separated from extended family members could appreciate the solidarity that certain practices engendered among their immediate members and the community at large, both inside and outside of Judah.

HOUSEHOLD SIZE AND LARGER POPULATION ESTIMATES

All of these dynamics raise the question of household size. This figure depended on a host of factors, including the extent of landholdings, genetic tendencies, and the decisions of individual families. Households frequently had extended family members in their lot, including siblings, cousins, and nephews/nieces. In addition, nonrelatives such as slaves and "resident aliens" (Heb. *gērîm*) could be incorporated into the household to facilitate emergent needs. Yet even with such variables, many if not most households were fairly small because of difficult living conditions and high mortality rates. The average life span is impossible to quantify based on extant sources, but an abundance of three-generation households is unlikely. In the preexilic period, the biblical chronologies suggest that many kings in the "house of David" did not live past their forties, and those working in more menial conditions faced greater health challenges. In addition, women had to deal with the considerable risks of childbirth: the frequent mortality rate during pregnancy remained a tragic aspect of life, as did the high occurrence of infant mortality.[24] Utilizing a variety of statistical measures, Schloen calculates the average joint family size during Iron Age Israel (1200–586 BCE) at ten, including servants and more distant kin.[25] Households could pool their resources, especially in a village setting, and archaeologists have found communal storage sites in Judah that reflect more common efforts across a larger kinship group, or "clan."[26]

There is little reason to suppose larger households after the exile, especially if one considers the dispersal of Judeans throughout the Mediterranean region and the careful studies done on family size during the period of the Roman Empire. Based on archaeological and literary evidence, Richard

24. P. J. King and L. E. Stager, *Life in Biblical Israel*, LAI (Louisville, KY: Westminster John Knox Press, 2001), 37.

25. Schloen, *House of the Father*, 122–27.

26. Avraham Faust, "Household Economies in the Kingdoms of Israel and Judah," in *Household Archaeology in Ancient Israel and Beyond*, ed. Assaf Yasur-Landau, Jennie R. Ebeling, and Laura B. Mazow, CHANE 50 (Leiden: E. J. Brill, 2011), 265, highlights the emphasis on communal storage in many sites from Iron Age II.

Saller has done a statistical analysis of mortality rates for the larger Mediterranean region under the Romans. He claims that the health risks for women
in childbirth, the average age of marriage for males and females, and other
factors such as sterility meant that most households did not have three generations living together for a lengthy period, if at all.[27] Based on Saller's analysis, Schloen argues that for most of the Mediterranean families before and
after the Babylonian exile, the size of the household living together in one
residence typically remained small.[28] Even if one counts slaves and extended
family members, the average size probably did not exceed ten persons, especially since most households could not afford servants. Schloen argues that
even this estimate is probably too large when we consider the specific context of Judah, and Fiensy suggests that in the Roman period most nuclear
families took one room of a courtyard house and usually had small numbers.[29]
With life expectancy so low for both genders in this preindustrial society, the
households that continued the long-standing patrilocal pattern continued to
be small in most cases. Even if certain households had more members, the
high rate of early death for women and children made it challenging for living
sons and their wives to perpetuate the family line.

Overall population levels are also relevant for our examination of economic
life among Second Temple households. Scholarly estimates differ widely on
this question, and the biblical texts from this period, such as Ezra–Nehemiah
and Chronicles, are not an accurate source.[30] In seeking to define the extent
of any changes resulting from the Babylonian exile in the sixth century BCE,
some archaeologists have expressed skepticism that this event entailed a universal retreat from Judah, followed by a mass return.[31] Certain studies have
highlighted the continuing presence of rural settlements during this period,
arguing that life for many kinship groups continued in much the same way as

27. Richard Saller, *Patriarchy, Property, and Death in the Roman Family*, Cambridge
Studies in Population, Economy, and Society in Past Time 25 (Cambridge: Cambridge University Press, 1994), 51–57; see chap. 2 of the current study for the question
of age at betrothal.
28. Schloen, *House of the Father*, 126.
29. Fiensy, *Social History of Palestine*, 119.
30. Charles E. Carter, "The Province of Yehud in the Post-Exilic Period: Soundings in Site Distribution and Demography," in *Second Temple Studies*, vol. 2, *Temple
and Community in the Persian Period*, ed. Tamara C. Eskenazi and Kent H. Richards,
JSOTSup 175 (Sheffield: JSOT Press, 1994), 120, argues that the number of returnees
cited in Ezra 7 and Neh. 2 (50,000 persons) is much larger than the likely total.
31. Hans M. Barstad, *The Myth of the Empty Land: A Study in the History and Archaeology of Judah during the "Exilic" Period*, SOFS 28 (Oslo: Scandinavian University Press,
1996).

it did before 586 BCE.[32] Yet the exile clearly marked a watershed event: many individuals experienced the upheaval of forced migration, loss of property, and in certain instances the disintegration of their kinship group. Based on certain archaeological assessments of dwellings, far fewer people lived in the region when the Persians first took control, and only under later powers did settlement patterns begin to approximate earlier levels prior to the exile.[33] These studies have also reported the lack of evidence for significant urban growth right after the exile, including in Jerusalem.[34] One study estimates the population of Judah or Yehud (the Persian province that included Jerusalem) to be 13,350 persons during the early period of Persian rule (539–450 BCE), with as many as 4,000 of these being returnees from exile; other proposals are considerably higher.[35]

Consequently, the process of postexilic growth was intermittent and somewhat dependent on the decisions of colonial powers to provide funding and infrastructure changes (e.g., the missions of Ezra and Nehemiah in the fifth century).[36] The Persians built up settlements and sent envoys along the coast

32. See Oded Lipschits, "Achaemenid Imperial Policy, Settlement Processes in Palestine, and the Status of Jerusalem in the Middle of the Fifth Century B.C.E.," in *Judah and the Judeans in the Persian Period*, ed. Oded Lipschits and Manfred Oeming (Winona Lake, IN: Eisenbrauns, 2006), 19–52; idem, "Shedding New Light on the Dark Years of the 'Exilic Period': New Studies, Further Elucidation, and Some Questions regarding the Archaeology of Judah as an 'Empty Land,'" in *Interpreting Exile: Displacement and Deportation in Biblical and Modern Contexts*, ed. Brad E. Kelle, Frank R. Ames, and Jacob L. Wright, AIL 10 (Atlanta: Society of Biblical Literature, 2011), 57–90, cites continuity at multiple rural sites in Judah; cf. Charles E. Carter, *The Emergence of Yehud in the Persian Period: A Social and Demographic Study*, JSOTSup 294 (Sheffield: JSOT Press, 1999), 137–66; Bob Becking, "'We All Returned as One!': Critical Notes on the Myth of the Mass Return," in Lipschits and Oeming, *Judah and the Judeans*, 8–10.

33. Avraham Faust, "Settlement Dynamics and Demographic Fluctuations in Judah from the Late Iron Age to the Hellenistic Period and the Archaeology of Persian-Period Yehud," in *A Time of Change: Judah and Its Neighbours in the Persian and Early Hellenistic Periods*, ed. Yigal Levin, LSTS 65 (London: T&T Clark, 2006), 23–51, analyzes demographic and settlement patterns, claiming that the number of people in the region remained considerably lower during the Persian period than during the Iron Age or the era of Hellenistic rule.

34. Lipschits, "Achaemenid Imperial Policy," 29–30.

35. Carter, *Emergence of Yehud*, 201. For other estimates, see Jack Pastor, *Land and Economy in Ancient Palestine* (London: Routledge, 1997), 6–8.

36. The chronological order and exact dates for the missions of Ezra and Nehemiah are exceedingly complex topics, have received significant attention elsewhere, and are beyond the scope of the present discussion. For the placement of Ezra's mission in 458 BCE and Nehemiah's in 445 BCE (the dates assumed in the present work), see Joseph Blenkinsopp, *Ezra–Nehemiah*, OTL (Philadelphia: Westminster Press, 1988), 60–69; for a cogent summary of alternative proposals, see H. G. M. Williamson, *Ezra and Nehemiah*, OTG (Sheffield: JSOT Press, 1987), 55–69.

to foster maritime trade, while the numbers in the interior regions remained small and largely devoted to agrarian activities.[37] This demographic evidence has implications for our study since a small population had to subsist in a region that was of little importance to a succession of imperial governments, other than as a minor source of revenue and a buffer between larger powers (e.g., Egypt and the territories in the Mesopotamian region). During the period of Ptolemaic and Seleucid rule, development along the Mediterranean continued to occur, and those living in the interior regions experienced more financial opportunities and greater population density than they had under the Persians.[38] Greek-speaking towns sprang up throughout Judea and in the Galilee region. Settlement growth continued to rise, and commercial activities created new opportunities, especially for those who had favorable connections within the local administrative systems of the foreign power. The consequences of this growth will receive attention throughout our study; in general, the process was gradual and somewhat dependent on shifting politics and the decision of imperial rulers to intervene in the region, thereby creating an environment for enhanced commercial activity and population increases.

LIFE IN THE HOUSEHOLD

With regard to actual conditions at the household level, most persons before and after the exile had to structure their lives and dwellings in order to maintain a sufficient supply of food. Daily efforts revolved around this goal of food/meal production, with little opportunity for other pursuits. Domiciles usually included living space, working areas (often the same as living space), storage rooms for household goods and food, sleeping quarters for domestic animals, and in some cases a larger storeroom(s) for other bulk needs, such as seed reserves, agricultural tools, and olive oil jars. As previously mentioned, many houses had an exterior courtyard, which might have included an oven for outdoor baking. The living/sleeping area might be on the second floor of a two-story dwelling, and many of these houses had a retractable roof, especially in tightly fortified villages.[39] In their efforts at identifying various layouts, archaeologists have noted a large number of joint-family compounds

---

37. Lipschits, "Achaemenid Imperial Policy," 29–40.
38. See the chart in Faust, "Settlement Dynamics," 27.
39. John S. Holladay, "'Home Economics 1407' and the Israelite Family and Their Neighbors: An Anthropological/Archaeological Exploration," in *The Family in Life and in Death: The Family in Ancient Israel, Sociological and Anthropological Perspectives*, ed. Patricia Dutcher-Walls, LHB/OTS 504 (New York: T&T Clark, 2009), 65–71, provides a number of one-story and two-story plans for typical houses.

in the region.[40] Kinship ties often played a role in how larger households constructed their compounds, and it is clear that larger pools of labor made farming and animal husbandry easier (albeit with more persons to feed). The Hebrew Bible demonstrates the popularity of these housing arrangements: such passages as the laws against sexual intercourse with various relatives (e.g., Lev. 18:6–18) indicate the need to regulate life in close quarters, with many persons living together.

Many households operated at the subsistence level, and there is also evidence for a small but powerful class of wealthy citizens. With regard to the former category, many farmers tended areas that could barely support those residing on their small plot, in some cases only a few acres.[41] Under such circumstances, those with small holdings (10–80 iugera, or 6–50 acres) had to make difficult decisions about how much produce to devote to internal consumption and what to grow and trade (as cash crops) for other essential items.[42] In terms of output, these households usually generated staples of the region, including grains, olives, and grapes, with a small number of animals.[43] In contrast, medium-sized estates had greater capacity for output, including more animals, and the owners of such properties generally had more leverage in the society, since they had wealth and in many cases an array of laborers/servants facilitating their efforts. These households frequently possessed significant amounts of arable property. One estimate places the average size of medium estates at 80–500 iugera (50–315 acres), with very wealthy landholders having even larger properties to manage (over 500 iugera, or more than 315 acres).[44] There is evidence of differentiation between poor and wealthy farmers at several sites that date to the Second Temple period, including Tell en-Naṣbeh, En-Gedi, and even more clearly at coastal cities such as Acco.[45] Wealthy households often clustered in the coastal regions along the Mediterranean, where trade occurred with greater frequency. Yet many persons did not own land at all. As the sources attest, tenant farming remained a common phenomenon during

40. Lawrence E. Stager, "The Archaeology of the Family in Ancient Israel," *BASOR* 260 (1985): 18–19. Many of these houses had common walls, but each had a separate entrance, often in a shared courtyard.

41. The Mishnah cites the minimum plot of land to be nine *kabs* (*m. B. Bat.* 1:6), which is equivalent to almost a *dunam* (one thousand square meters), or approximately four acres. See Pastor, *Land and Economy*, 9.

42. Pastor, *Land and Economy*, 10. An *iugera* is equivalent to .65 acres.

43. See chap. 3 below for more detailed discussion of farming life and its challenges in the region.

44. Fiensy, *Social History of Palestine*, 23–24.

45. Carter, *Emergence of Yehud*, 130; Ephraim Stern, *Archaeology of the Land of the Bible*, vol. 2, *The Assyrian, Babylonian, and Persian Periods (732–332 B.C.E.)*, ABRL 2 (New York: Doubleday, 2001), 382–83.

this period: individuals and their families worked land, including royal territories, to which they had no property claim. All of these issues related to farming will receive more detailed treatment in chapter 3 of this study.

Biblical texts confirm financial inequality among households, including the book of Nehemiah (fifth century BCE). When Nehemiah as governor prepares to defend the province against hostile forces from Samaria, he arranges the population in a hierarchical manner, addressing "the nobles and officials and the rest of the people" (Neh. 4:14 [8]).[46] Here the terminology points to distinctions based on money and social status, with the implication that wealthy families and provincial administrators have greater power. Moreover, the biblical author refers to classism when he condemns the "nobles" and "officials" for seizing fellow Judeans' persons and property that had been pledged against debt (Neh. 5:7).[47] Evidence from later periods indicates that such inequalities not only continued into the Hellenistic age, but also increased amid the growing number of commercial interests in the region. The wisdom author Ben Sira (ca. 190 BCE) highlights the entrepreneurial ethos of his age and the impact of economic disparities on individual households. He repeatedly mentions the tension between rich and poor: "A rich person will exploit you if you can be of use to him, but if you are in need he will abandon you. . . . He will embarrass you with his delicacies, until he has drained you two or three times" (Sir. 13:4, 7). Such sayings reflect the wisdom tradition's common discourse on money, but it is clear from Ben Sira's incisive commentary that he has in mind actual abuses and financial inequalities. The expansion of trade during this period, which benefited a minority of households, highlighted the gap between rich and poor. Ben Sira confirms this situation as he points to the possibility for rapid advancement and loss (e.g., Sir. 18:25–26).

The fluid economic climate and income disparities among households are apparent in other sources, including the archives of the Ptolemies.[48] The Zeno papyri, which date from the middle of the third century BCE, emphasize the financial opportunities available to elite individuals and their families within the Ptolemaic system. Zeno, a subordinate to the Ptolemaic finance minister

---

46. References to the "nobles" and "officials" appear in Neh. 2:16; 4:14, 19 [8, 13]; 5:7; 7:5. These two broad categories seem to include "noble" families by virtue of their hereditary status (cf. Jer. 27:20) but also provincial administrators (the "officials") and other individuals of means.

47. See Blenkinsopp, *Ezra–Nehemiah*, 259. This important passage from the Nehemiah Memoir will receive attention throughout our discussion.

48. For background on the Ptolemies, their imperial organization, and their impact on the Palestinian region, see Günther Hölbl, *A History of the Ptolemaic Empire*, trans. Tina Saavedra (New York: Routledge, 2001).

Apollonius, toured the Palestinian region during 260–258 BCE and fulfilled various duties. This official's correspondence with his superior Apollonius reveals the Ptolemaic policy of granting, or leasing, land to wealthy families and military settlers, who would then reciprocate with revenue streams to the ruler and his administration. The Zeno archives demonstrate an intricate system of districts, many of them run by local aristocracy.[49] Those households with connections to the imperial administration and status in the society could thrive under this hierarchical system, but they represented a small minority. The book of Ecclesiastes, which also dates from this period, notes that the voice of the poor man does not receive much attention when such stratification occurs (Eccl. 9:14–16).

Along with the Zeno papyri, Josephus's colorful tale of the Tobiads (*Ant.* 12.154–236, often known as the Tobiad Romance) indicates the possibility of rapid wealth for persons who built alliances with local and imperial authorities. One Joseph son of Tobiah (who also appears in the Zeno correspondence) gains power and prestige by entertaining an Egyptian envoy and staving off a diplomatic crisis. This Joseph, the nephew of the high priest Onias, promises to pay the necessary government tribute that his uncle threatened to withhold. Through forced taxation and brutal suppression of dissent, Joseph achieves great success in gathering the necessary funds. Such examples from Josephus and the Zeno correspondence suggest that wealthier families had the potential to thrive under foreign rule while most individuals continued under difficult farming conditions and oppressive tax structures set by colonial powers and local officials. The majority of households struggled at the subsistence level.

We will return to these texts and the issue of forced adaptation to colonial rule throughout our study, especially in chapter 4 with our discussion of taxation; yet from the outset we notice the effects of stratification on the majority of households. Avoiding the intrinsic pitfalls of subsistence farming—such as drought, famine, and burdensome loans—required careful planning and oversight along with adequate resources. Exile and colonization led to a more uncertain and fluid network of property holdings in the region, and potential loss of land posed a constant threat. Within this system, the continuation of the family line represented an essential way for a household to maintain its livelihood and possessions. The extant texts of the Second Temple period underscore the importance of this goal, which was reached through the institution of marriage. In order to understand economic life

49. See ibid., 58–61; Victor Tcherikover, *Hellenistic Civilization and the Jews* (Philadelphia: Jewish Publication Society, 1959; repr., Peabody, MA: Hendrickson Publishers, 1999), 67–72.

for postexilic families, a careful assessment of what the sources tell us about marriage and its financial implications is essential. This line of investigation will allow us to consider more fully the status of women and children in the next chapter.

MARRIAGE

When taking up this topic, it is necessary to consider the relationship between the economic and sacred aspects of marriage/divorce in the ancient sources. Regarding the sacred elements, multiple works affirm the importance of finding an appropriate partner, viewing marriage as a basic rite of passage. For example, the book of Proverbs cites the significance of the marital union for an individual's relationship with the Deity: "He who finds a wife finds a good thing, and obtains favor from the LORD" (Prov. 18:22). Echoing the creation accounts in Genesis, Ben Sira offers a similar pronouncement: "He who acquires a wife gets his best possession, a helper fit for him and a pillar of support" (Sir. 36:29; cf. Gen. 2:20). With regard to divorce, certain voices from this period criticize the dissolution of marriages from a theological perspective. The prophet Malachi (2:10–16) offers a passionate speech that reflects the contentious nature of divorce and the use of earlier traditions to justify one's position.

Yet at the same time, many sources from this period highlight the economic aspects of marriage. The process of "acquiring" a spouse presented challenges, especially in relation to the task of finding a marriage partner at the betrothal stage. The dispersal of Judeans across the larger region and frequent interaction with outsiders raised major disagreements over who could marry whom. Key texts from the Second Temple period, including Ezra–Nehemiah, Proverbs, Ben Sira, and the Elephantine papyri, point to the financial aspects of marriage. Many of these sources reflect a contractual understanding of the custom, with decisions based on a variety of strategic factors. Through the process of betrothal and marriage, families could secure a future for their offspring, maintain or augment their inheritance, and receive gifts from other kinship groups. Practical concerns were often paramount: the contracts from Elephantine, for example, involve a system of checks and balances at the start of a union. This section will examine such sources, with special attention to the exchange of funds as marriage gifts (i.e., bridewealth and dowry), ongoing financial expectations between the two families, and the material consequences of divorce. We will demonstrate that the contractual features of the marital union played a major role throughout the Second Temple period, especially with regard to marriage gifts and divorce.

Finding a Partner

If marriage with outsiders generated controversy during this period, then what constituted desirable unions, especially from a financial perspective? Many who have studied this issue point to endogamy, which is the requirement to marry within a specific group.[50] For example, Ezra's reform (chaps. 9–10) demarcates the returning exiles as the only possible option for the author's community, thus consolidating wealth, resources, and social identity into one identifiable subset of persons (see below). In many other biblical narratives, marriage within a specified kinship group seems to be acceptable and in some cases obligatory. One of the more common unions in this regard is marriage among cousins. The patriarchal stories in Genesis demonstrate an affinity for this practice: Rebekah seems to be Isaac's first or second-cousin, and Jacob clearly marries two cousins in Leah and Rachel, the daughters of his mother's brother (Gen. 28:2; 29:10). Cross-cultural work has confirmed the popularity of this union: Claude Lévi-Strauss and other anthropologists have cited the frequency of cousin marriage in diverse contexts, especially when endogamy is a central concern in the culture.[51]

When considering the rationale for such unions, economic motivations are a central factor. If such a marriage occurs, the patriarch in the "house of the father" structure does not have to extend property rights beyond his kinship group, and the process of inheritance can unfold in a more straightforward matter. For the father of a daughter, the dowry stays within his extended family when cousin marriage or similar arrangements occur among members of the kinship group. Philo specifically cites the favorability of these unions in relation to dowry (*Spec.* 2.126). Such concerns did not just reflect cultural preferences, but also consequential decisions for the maintenance of a household and larger kinship group under difficult conditions. Property ownership is often a very tenuous matter in small village cultures like that of ancient Judah. Endogamous societies do not necessarily maintain their insular practices as preferable custom but rather encourage marriage within the kinship group in order to survive.[52]

---

50. The classic formulation is that of Claude Lévi-Strauss, *The Elementary Structures of Kinship*, rev. ed. (Boston: Beacon Press, 1969), 45, where he defines endogamy as "the obligation to marry within an objectively defined group."

51. For a useful application of Lévi-Strauss and other anthropologists in studying the biblical narratives, see Robert A. Oden, "Jacob as Father, Husband, and Nephew: Kinship Studies and the Patriarchal Narratives," *JBL* 102 (1983): 197–98.

52. Knight, *Law, Power, and Justice*, 131.

Second Temple texts such as the book of Tobit indicate that this type of endogamous union was still popular after the exile.[53] Tobit's son Tobias and Raguel's daughter Sarah come together in an elaborate narrative that upholds the practice of endogamous marriage. The familial tie between the couple signifies a union "according to the decree of the book of Moses" (Tob. 6:13; cf. 7:11). For the author of this text, the close relation of these two individuals is a decisive factor in their betrothal: the angel Raphael tells Tobias that he has "a hereditary claim" on Sarah (6:12), and while their precise relationship is not clear, their union is an endogamous one. Evidence for cousin marriage also appears in *Jubilees*, which dates from the second century BCE and contains a reworking of many Genesis stories within a priestly framework. *Jubilees* rewrites the genealogies from Genesis with the following formula: "N took for himself a wife, and her name was N., the daughter of his father's brother" (e.g., 4:15).[54] Similarly, the book of Judith (second century BCE) speaks of the heroine's husband, Manasseh, "who belonged to her tribe and family" (8:2).

In postexilic sources the lively treatment of intermarriage with outsiders, or exogamy, (e.g., Ezra–Nehemiah, Ruth, and Malachi) also demonstrates the cultural preference for endogamy and the lack of clarity in antecedent texts. On the one hand, certain sections of the Pentateuch prohibited Israelites from intermarrying with the seven Canaanite nations that God promised to eradicate on their behalf (Exod. 34:16; Deut. 7:3–4). Yet Deuteronomy 23 presents a somewhat different understanding: the Ammonite and Moabite cannot enter "the assembly of the LORD," but since the Israelites resided as aliens in the land of the Edomites and Egyptians, "the children of the third generation that are born to them may be admitted to the assembly of the LORD" (23:8). There is confusion over whether this statement refers just to sanctuary admittance or "entry" into the community through intermarriage. Since the previous chapter (Deut. 22) addresses numerous marital issues, this stipulation in 23:8 would seem to allow for both levels of interpretation.[55] Such passages relay an ambiguous message, however, such that no universal ban on intermarriage appears in the Pentateuch. The fact that the biblical

---

53. Tobit most likely dates from the late third or early second century BCE. For a summary of scholarly positions on this date and provenance, see C. A. Moore, *Tobit*, AB 40A (New York: Doubleday, 1991), 40–44. The author of the book assumes a corpus of prophetic works (Tob. 14:4) and seems unaware of the turbulent dynamics of the Maccabean period. References to "the law of Moses" (6:12; 7:13) also point to a postexilic dating.

54. See Léonie J. Archer, *Her Price Is beyond Rubies: The Jewish Woman in Greco-Roman Palestine*, JSOTSup 60 (Sheffield: JSOT Press, 1990), 146–47.

55. Christine E. Hayes, *Gentile Impurities and Jewish Identities: Intermarriage and Conversion from the Bible to the Talmud* (Oxford: Oxford University Press, 2002), 24–26.

writers single out some groups such as the Moabites implies that others could intermarry with insiders.

Intermarriage became acutely important during the transitional period after the exile, and the authors of Ezra–Nehemiah attempted to resolve the issue by eliminating any loopholes. In the famous language of Ezra 9–10, the protagonist instills an absolute ban on the practice after being informed that men are taking foreign wives: "Thus the holy seed has mixed itself with the peoples of the lands, and in this faithlessness the officials and leaders have led the way" (9:2). A conflation of earlier traditions is at work in "Ezra's reform": the biblical author brings together prohibitions in Deuteronomy 7 and 23, along with language from Leviticus 18:24–30, in an effort to proscribe *all* forms of intermarriage.[56] Ezra understands every nonreturnee to be profane, and therefore both marriage partners should come from a household of returning exiles. According to this creative reading of earlier legislation, since the nation and its people represent God's holy creation (Ezra 9:8; cf. Deut. 7:6), any form of exogamy signifies a profanation of this sacred entity or "seed." As Hayes argues, a desire to create an absolute binary opposition between the holy community and profane outsiders is fundamental to Ezra 9–10: "It is difficult to imagine a more restrictive and impermeable boundary than that constructed by Ezra."[57]

In accounting for Ezra's exclusivism, commentators have offered a variety of explanations. The ambiguity of earlier laws forced the author to provide an early midrash on intermarriage. The conflation of sources in Ezra 9–10 represents a justification based on an innovative reading of the Torah. The standard Deuteronomic diatribe against the corrupting influence of foreign wives is another part of the rationale in this passage (e.g., Ezra 9:11).[58] The demographics of Judah are also a factor: the presence of different ethnic groups and the common occurrence of intermarriage led to reevaluation, as Judeans sought to identify the true devotees of their tradition during an uncertain transitional period. Within this setting, one possible reason is the need to

---

56. Michael Fishbane, *Biblical Interpretation in Ancient Israel* (Oxford: Oxford University Press, 1985), 116–21.

57. C. Hayes, *Gentile Impurities*, 33. This type of "holy seed" language can also be found in the Pentateuch in relation to priests and intermarriage (e.g., Lev. 21:14–15). For a detailed analysis, see ibid., 27–34. Saul M. Olyan, *Rites and Rank: Hierarchy in Biblical Representations of Cult* (Princeton: Princeton University Press, 2000), 89–90, also notes the dyadic framework in this passage and the use of "separation" (Heb. *bdl*) language borrowed from the Holiness School (e.g., Lev. 20:24–26).

58. From the perspective of the Deuteronomist, the basic problem with marriage to a foreign woman is that it leads to apostate worship. One of the paradigmatic examples is Ahab's marriage to Jezebel and its consequences (1 Kgs. 16:31–33). Ezra clearly falls in line with this thinking.

cultivate clear boundaries when a community is struggling with its identity
and very existence. Daniel Smith-Christopher (then Smith) argues that we
should read the drastic measures in Ezra as a defensible effort to instill "group
solidarity" in the fluid climate after the exile. Ezra's reform efforts "add up to
a self-conscious community that is occupied with self-preservation."[59]

Smith-Christopher is undoubtedly correct that the prohibition reflects a
concern with purity and communal identity, but his argument underestimates
the economic issues at stake. The explicit theological basis for this stance, that
the "holy seed" has been corrupted by intermarriage, should not lead one to
minimize underlying financial incentives for prohibiting intermarriage. Ezra's
reading of the legal sources seems to reflect an exclusivist party, and one of
the motivations for their rigid viewpoint is tight control of ancestral property
rights. The language of Ezra–Nehemiah frequently alludes to the conflict
between "the exiles" and "the peoples of the land" such that the returnees
represent the true "Israel" (e.g., Ezra 9:1, 4; Neh. 10:30–31 [31–32]; etc.).
Ezra does not want intermarriage to thwart the goal of authority and financial
control for his group of returnees.

While this is not the only factor in the intermarriage ban, certain clues in
the text point to the value of a more economic reading of Ezra 9–10. First is
the statement that the "officials and leaders have led the way" (Ezra 9:2) in
intermarrying with unacceptable partners. This detail highlights the example
set by powerful households and their complicity in allowing others to follow
suit. The decision by such persons to intermarry would have meant potential forfeiture of property to outsiders, especially those who did not go into
exile.[60] Many of these "officials and leaders" had significant wealth, and Ezra's
exclusivist party does not want to risk mingling their holdings with families
that are not part of the faithful remnant. In support of an economic motivation behind these verses, the Hebrew root 'rb appears in the phrase from Ezra
9:2: "Thus the holy seed has mixed itself [Heb. wĕhitʿārĕbû] with the people of
the lands." This root often has an economic connotation ("to stand surety" or
"vouch for the loan" of someone), and therefore the notion of "corrupting"
the holy seed probably included the idea of "mixing" property with undesirable persons. Because of this terminology, we cannot assume that the statement here is merely one of social separation, especially since the text cites

59. Daniel L. Smith, "The Politics of Ezra: Sociological Indicators of Postexilic
Judean Society," in Davies, *Persian Period*, 97.

60. As many commentators have noted, the precise ethnicity of the women in
Ezra 9:1–2 is unclear, but the content of Deuteronomy and Ezra's strong preference
for returning exiles point to intermarriage on both levels, with "foreigners" like the
Moabites and with Judeans who never left the region during the exile. Ezra clearly
regards anyone who is not part of his community of returnees to be "foreign."

additional economic factors. For those who do not attend the great assembly in which foreign spouses are to be sent away, confiscation of landholdings and expulsion from the congregation are the requisite punishments (e.g., Ezra 10:8). This verse indicates that Ezra's rigid opposition to intermarriage represents the best means for the exilic community to maintain property for themselves. Even if this great assembly is a propagandistic literary device and the "reform" of ending intermarriage never occurred on a large scale, the biblical writer concerns himself with how the community of returning exiles can assert control in an uncertain environment. Intermarriage with nonreturnee families (i.e., the "peoples of the land") would have created a Gordian knot of inheritance claims, and Ezra 9–10 seeks to avoid such a predicament.

There is evidence that foreign wives could threaten the landholding rights of returning male exiles. Certain legal passages grant inheritance rights to women in exceptional circumstances (e.g., Num. 27:1–11 and the daughters of Zelophehad), and property claims within the context of marriage are a major concern in the patriarchal stories of Genesis 12–50 and in the book of Ruth.[61] Moreover, the Elephantine documents from Egypt indicate that women could not only initiate divorce proceedings, but also buy, sell, and manage property (see below). We find no explicit indicators of this in Ezra–Nehemiah, but as Tamara Eskenazi argues, Ezra's desire to maintain rigid boundaries and the mention of women in the lists of returnees point to concerns about female inheritance as a factor in the prohibition.[62]

Kenneth Hoglund has suggested that Persian authorities actually supported Ezra and Nehemiah in their goal of banning all forms of intermarriage. According to this argument, Athenian participation in an Egyptian revolt (464–454 BCE) signified an ongoing threat to Persian hegemony within the larger region, and imperial officials attempted to solidify their power through fortifications and tightly controlled ethnic/religious groups. By asserting greater control over agricultural production and the construction of fortresses, the Persians sought to turn back this uprising in Egypt and raise additional revenue in the process. According to the theory, the "assembly" (qāhāl)

---

61. Blenkinsopp, Ezra–Nehemiah, 176. If Ruth dates from the Persian period, as seems likely, this would serve as another indicator of the close relationship between marriage and property issues, especially when inheritance claims are part of the equation. We will take up the issue of inheritance in the next chapter.

62. Tamara C. Eskenazi, "Out from the Shadows: Biblical Women in the Postexilic Era," JSOT 54 (1992): 25–43. For an example of females in the lists, Eskenazi notes the reference to the Barzillai clan in Ezra 2:61. It is also possible that the matrilineal principle of later Jewish tradition is already in effect during this period. Perhaps Ezra and his followers believe that the offspring of female outsiders do not carry the same status and that the mother had a greater impact on the sacred practices of the children and their identity in this regard.

mentioned in Ezra–Nehemiah functioned as "an administrative collective," and colonial authorities had a vested interest in maintaining the integrity of this group and similar factions in neighboring provinces.[63] Hoglund claims that intermarriage threatened the goal of tight control over the collective, and therefore the polemic in Ezra–Nehemiah actually represents imperial policy. Such a creative proposal is very difficult to prove, but we can assume that Persian officials appreciated the efforts of their envoys to consolidate power and property, especially if these missions might counter revolt in a neighboring region. Stability in the provinces meant reliable revenue streams and more stable agricultural output, which are priorities for colonial powers. For those pushing the reforms in Ezra–Nehemiah, intermarriage restrictions signified a major means of consolidation, and it is possible that this polemic against intermarriage occurred with at least tacit support from imperial officials.

These arguments raise the question of the socioeconomic status among the returnees and those who remained in the region. Much discussion in recent years has focused on whether the families coming back from exile had the more advantageous position, and if union with the "peoples of the land" signified a reckless decision to "marry down." Smith-Christopher has argued that the exilic community actually had the weaker position. Since they had experienced "signs of disintegration and trauma," the returnees tried to better their station through intermarriage.[64] According to this argument, the passage in Nehemiah 13, which also addresses intermarriage, relates to improving one's lot. In this unit, the circumstances are slightly different than in Ezra 9–10: the author repeats the standard prohibition against the Ammonite and Moabite (Neh. 13:23) and includes concerns about language differences with neighboring peoples and its implications for communal identity (v. 24). The primary confrontation in Nehemiah 13 is with Eliashib the priest (v. 4), whose grandson is the son-in-law of Sanballat, a Samaritan (v. 28). Nehemiah chases him and other like-minded offenders away, because they have "defiled the priesthood" through intermarriage (v. 29). This passage bemoans the corruption of the priestly aristocracy and, by extension, the sanctity of the temple. Yet Nehemiah's caution also suggests that Eliashib and his family had something to lose by marrying outsiders. The argument that Judean males attempted to better their station through marriage with foreign women is possible in certain cases, but this book does not give any explicit indication of this dynamic.

---

63. Kenneth G. Hoglund, *Achaemenid Imperial Administration in Syria-Palestine and the Missions of Ezra–Nehemiah*, SBLDS 125 (Atlanta: Scholars Press, 1992), 239.

64. D. Smith-Christopher, "The Mixed Marriage Crisis in Ezra 9–10 and Nehemiah 13: A Study of the Sociology of Post-Exilic Judaean Community," in Eskenazi and Richards, *Temple and Community*, 260–61. For a similar argument, see Williamson, *Ezra and Nehemiah*, 90.

It is far more likely that the group with the official backing of the imperial administration (i.e., Ezra and Nehemiah's) had the more advantageous position, and this party sought to limit its ranks, maintain the inheritance claims of its families, and keep good relations with benefactors.[65] Intermarriage with outsiders would have jeopardized their status in this regard.

The most disturbing aspect of these accounts in Ezra–Nehemiah is the proposal to send away the offspring from these marriages. In the midst of the crisis, Shecaniah suggests to Ezra, "So now let us make a covenant with our God to send away all these wives and their children, according to the counsel of my lord and of those who tremble at the commandment of our God" (Ezra 10:3).[66] Few commentators note that the very last line of the book of Ezra recounts the wives being exiled "with their children" (10:44). Such final emphasis seems to be intentional: in a biblical book full of genealogies, the children from these marriages are not to be remembered. As with other elements of "Ezra's reform," this drastic measure seems to have an economic component. If enacted, such a course of action would separate both mother and child from their household unit, and then the man could remarry and retain all of his property rights without future claimants from the offspring of his first wife. This provision offers total annulment of the first marriage, and inheritance concerns are part of the motivation for this startling feature. Like Ishmael in the Abraham story (Gen. 16), each child is to be forcibly detached from his family and become persona non grata.

With this review, it becomes apparent that intermarriage, perspectives on endogamy, and the overall process of selecting a partner have economic as well as sacred components. The treatment of the topic in Second Temple texts reflects a contractual understanding of marriage, with both family reputations and financial livelihoods at stake. While the sources present the union of husband and wife as a sacred act, marriage also brings with it an array of concomitant financial obligations on the part of both households. Since the sources reflect the economic importance of marriage and the significance of this institution for the identity and stability of families during the Second Temple period, a study of financial exchanges during the betrothal process is also in order.

Marriage Gifts and Dowry Arrangements

The exchange of funds/possessions has a critical function during the betrothal process in many cultural contexts, including ancient Judah. Marriage gifts

---

65. Blenkinsopp, *Ezra–Nehemiah*, 176–77.
66. As many commentators have noted, "those who tremble" (*ḥărēdîm*) may represent an appellation for Ezra's party of "God-fearing" returnees.

can provide compensation to a household for the loss of a functioning member, secure future resources for one party if the other decides to divorce, and advance the social status of one or more kinship groups. The mention of marriage gifts in the Hebrew Bible and outside of it highlights their significance: the society set up financial incentives for individuals and their kinship group to go through with a marriage and preserve it. Marriage gifts played a significant role in the social structure and economy of the Second Temple period.

Various studies, including the recent examination of Tracy Lemos, have shown that before the exile, the most common marriage gift came in the form of "bridewealth" (Heb. *mōhar*), or "marriage present" (NRSV), which is payment from the bridegroom to the bride's family.[67] Several sources from this earlier period point to bridewealth and its significance in ancient Israel. One example is Genesis 34, the disturbing account of Dinah's rape by the Hivite, Shechem.[68] Shechem's plea for the hand of Dinah in marriage contains an important example of marriage-gift terminology: "Shechem also said to her father and to her brothers, 'Let me find favor with you, and whatever you say to me I will give. Put the marriage present and gift [Heb. *mattān*] as high as you like, and I will give whatever you ask me; only give me the girl to be my wife'" (Gen. 34:11–12). In this statement, Shechem promises payment to the family of the bride, rather than to the bride herself. Other preexilic texts, both legal and narrative, contain references to the bridewealth payment, with the understanding that the bridegroom will compensate the bride's household for the transfer of a female family member to another "house of the father." In these examples, the bridegroom pays the father of the prospective bride rather than the young woman.[69]

---

67. Tracy M. Lemos, *Marriage Gifts and Social Change in Ancient Palestine, 1200 BCE to 200 CE* (Cambridge: Cambridge University Press, 2010). Many scholars now recognize that the translation "marriage price" or "marriage present" is inaccurate, since *mōhar* does not imply that the prospective bride is a purchasable commodity in any of these passages.

68. Most commentators assign this passage to the preexilic period, regardless of the commentator's perspective on the existence and date for the J (Yahwist) source.

69. All of these passages address special circumstances. The Covenant Code describes the necessity of the bridewealth payment when a man rapes a virgin to whom he is not betrothed (Exod. 22:15–16 [16–17]). In the corollary passage from Deuteronomy, coercion in this regard requires payment to the father of the bride, rather than to the young woman herself (Deut. 22:28–29, which does not have the *mhr* root). The colorful account of Michal's betrothal to David also contains marriage-gift terminology. When the young hero seeks Saul's daughter, the king declares to David that he "'desires no marriage present [*mōhar*] except a hundred foreskins of the Philistines'" (1 Sam. 18:25). This fantastic request does not shed much light on common requirements, but it does point to the preexilic practice of giving money or gifts directly to the bride's father. Finally, Jacob's service to Laban (Gen. 29) in order to marry Leah and

During the Second Temple period, extracanonical texts reveal a major shift from bridewealth to dowry as the more common practice among Judean families. While Ezra–Nehemiah, Chronicles, and Esther do not mention payments, references occur in other sources, including the nine Elephantine marriage contracts that date from the fifth century BCE.[70] Some have questioned the relevance of an Egyptian settlement for understanding the socio-economic landscape of Jerusalem and its environs, but such a rigid position is dismissive of vital evidence for family life during this period. Those living at Elephantine used Yahwistic names, maintained regular correspondence (in Aramaic) with persons in Judah, and followed many aspects of the tradition (e.g., Passover). This community's understanding of marriage has to relate, at least in part, to their identity as Judeans and not just to the influence of Egyptian legal customs. They left complex records that indicate their contractual understanding of marriage, unvarnished by the layer of theological assertion one finds in a book like Ezra.

The marriage documents from Elephantine (nine have been found) follow a formulaic pattern, and all of them mention payments to the groom and his family that we can accurately call dowry. One complete contract (*TAD* B2.6) provides the course of events for a woman named Miptaḥiah and her husband, Eshor, and the sequence is largely the same in the other documents from the settlement.[71] First, the groom requests the bride's hand in marriage from her caretaker and promises to support her: "She is my wife, and I am her husband from this day forever and ever" (lines 4–5). Along with this pledge, the groom guarantees five shekels of silver as payment (lines 4–5, which include an Aramaic form of *mōhar*). The evidence suggests that this amount was actually added to the dowry total.[72] In the next section, the contract lists a variety of gifts from the bride's family, including a woolen garment, bronze objects, and other items, with a total value of 65.5 shekels (lines 13–15). This type of payment constitutes dowry, money and goods from the bride's family for her new household. The amount here is substantially more than anything offered by the groom or his family. Finally, there is lengthy provision for one spouse to inherit all the wealth if the other one dies (line 16) and for dissolution of the marriage (lines 17–36). With such details, this

Rachel also reflects payment from the bridegroom (in the form of labor) in exchange for betrothal. For further examination, see Lemos, *Marriage Gifts*, 41–61, who also discusses possible examples of dowry payments (e.g., 1 Kgs. 9:16–17).

70. B. Porten and A. Yardeni, *Textbook of Aramaic Documents from Ancient Egypt*, vol. 2, *Contracts* (Winona Lake, IN: Eisenbrauns 1989).

71. Ibid., 30–33.

72. Lemos, *Marriage Gifts*, 63–65, argues that the five shekels actually constitute part of the total amount for the dowry.

contract provides a great deal of financial specificity for marriage gifts and a
clear emphasis on dowry.

Literary sources from the Second Temple period also mention marriage
gifts, and dowry is once again the common practice in these texts. The most
famous reference is from Tobit, which contains the colorful account of a
betrothal process for Sarah and Tobias. In the midst of the wedding feast,
Sarah's father, Raguel, makes the following statement to his new son-in-law,
Tobias: "Take at once half of what I own and return in safety to your father;
the other half will be yours when my wife and I die" (Tob. 8:21). The father of
the bride is clearly elated that his near kinsman has come to marry Sarah and
rewards the family of Tobias in very generous fashion. Yet it is uncertain if
Raguel's bestowal of land and goods reflects actual practice. Since the author
of Tobit is a master of literary flair and Raguel has considerable resources in
the story, we cannot consider such largess to be the norm for most families.
This passage does suggest a sense of obligation on the part of the bride's family and the possibility of very generous bestowals for households with close
connections and significant resources.[73] In the midst of the festive celebration
and prayers, Raguel's actions seem to indicate established custom: "Then he
called her mother and told her to bring writing material; and he wrote out
a copy of a marriage contract, to the effect that he gave her to him as wife
according to the decree of the law of Moses" (Tob. 7:13). The brief references
to these practices in Tobit imply the audience's familiarity with this type of
gift and a contractual understanding of marriage.

Additional examples point to dowry exchange during this period, including wisdom texts. Ben Sira cautions his addressees, "Do not be ensnared by
a woman's beauty, and do not desire a woman for her possessions. There is
wrath and impudence and great disgrace when a wife supports her husband"
(Sir. 25:21–22). While no term for dowry appears here, the sage warns against
choosing a spouse because of the wealth she brings into the marriage, and this
seems to be a veiled reference to dowry. In Pseudo-Phocylides, a sapiential
text from the turn of the era, the addressee receives similar advice: "Do not
bring as a wife into your home a wicked, very wealthy woman; you will be a
slave to (your) spouse on account of the baneful dowry" (lines 199–200).[74]
These two examples point to the allure of plentiful dowries among eligible
men in the wealthier classes. Josephus and Philo also mention the giving of
dowry, and even if the references in their writings do not shed much light
on exchanges among nonelite Judeans, they indicate the prominence of the

73. It is significant that Raguel has no sons with whom to leave his possessions.
74. See Pieter Willem van der Horst, *The Sentences of Pseudo-Phocylides* (Leiden:
E. J. Brill, 1978). This collection of sayings probably originated in Egypt.

custom during the Hellenistic and Roman periods.[75] Significantly, these literary sources do not refer to bridewealth payments, and this raises the question of whether the practice of giving money to the bride's family ceased altogether or simply became less common in favor of a dowry system.[76]

Lemos argues that the preference for dowry in later texts coincided with the transition to greater economic class stratification during the Second Temple period. In her cross-cultural work on marriage gifts, she demonstrates a preference for bridewealth in contexts when there is not as much income disparity among households. Employing the work of such anthropologists as Jack Goody, Lemos argues that economic distinctions certainly existed among pastoralists and farmers in early, premonarchic Israel (Iron Age I: 1200–1000 BCE), but the society was more homogeneous before greater centralization and economic development. The social dynamics of this earlier period created a more suitable backdrop for payments from the bridegroom to the bride's family: "corporate kinship, and especially corporate kinship of the patrilineal variety, little or no stratification, subsistence agriculture, and widespread pastoralism all 'fit' with the giving of bridewealth."[77]

This situation gradually changed, however, with the advent of the monarchy during Iron Age II (1000–586 BCE) as Israel developed a centralized bureaucracy, powerful ruling authorities, and a larger class of elite citizens. As wealthy families solidified their status, fathers turned increasingly to dowry as an acceptable means of securing a future for their daughters and furthering their own standing. This shift coincided with greater inequality in the society. The many references to financial stratification in Second Temple sources and the preference for dowry over bridewealth payments work in favor of this proposed development. If Judean society during the Hellenistic and Roman periods led to an increasingly clear distinction between the wealthy classes and the rest of the population, dowry became an important mechanism for

75. For Josephus, see *C. Ap.* 2.200; *Ant.* 12.154; 13.82; 16.228; 17.11; *J.W.* 1.483, 553. The Greek term for "dowry" (*proix*) appears in many of these passages, and the award is often substantial (more than 100 talents). Yet these references relate to political marriages among leaders (Ptolemies and Seleucids) and do not have direct relevance for contractual agreements among Judeans. See Lemos, *Marriage Gifts*, 82n85.

76. Philo, in his commentary on 1 Sam. 18, actually translates *mōhar* with *proix* (dowry), underscoring the preference for dowry during this later period. According to Michael L. Satlow, *Jewish Marriage in Antiquity* (Princeton: Princeton University Press, 2001), 200, the evidence suggests that Greek-speaking Jews stopped the custom of bridewealth payments from the groom to the bride's family.

77. Lemos, *Marriage Gifts*, 233. See also Jack Goody, *The Oriental, the Ancient, and the Primitive: Systems of Marriage and the Family in the Pre-industrial Societies of Eurasia*, Studies in Literacy, Family, Culture and the State (Cambridge: Cambridge University Press, 1990).

wealthier households to secure their daughter's future. The fact that the same dynamic has occurred in other contexts, including ancient Babylon, preindustrial Europe, and India, points to the importance of dowry in such a context. This shift from bridewealth to dowry also highlights the necessary adaptation of families to difficult circumstances, as they lived in an environment where the marriage gift represented an opportunity for alliance building but also a custom that could lead to catastrophe. Marriage decisions and the amount of any financial exchanges became consequential for rich and poor families alike.[78]

The Economics of Divorce

It is difficult to know the extent and acceptability of divorce during the Second Temple period and earlier. Divorce receives attention in a section of Deuteronomy (24:1–4), but the passage here only describes the husband's initiation of the process and does not present a full accounting of how the custom worked.[79] If a man's wife "does not please him because he finds something objectionable [Heb. 'erwat dābār] about her," then the first husband can write "a certificate of divorce" and send his spouse away (Deut. 24:1).[80] The exact connotation of "something objectionable" ('erwat dābār) is unclear, but the language seems to give the husband latitude in finding fault. This passage from Deuteronomy 24 also allows the second husband to draw up a certificate of divorce against this same woman, because he "hates her" (Heb. šĕnē'āh, v. 3). The meaning of "hate" in 24:3 is legal, representing a technical term for divorce. We find similar language in the marriage allegory between God and Israel in Hosea: "Plead with your mother, plead—for she is not my wife, and I am not her husband" (Hos. 2:2 [4]). Geller cites the same divorce terminology in the Elephantine marriage documents, and he claims that the connection points to the use of divorce contracts in Israel as early as the eighth century.[81] Even if this argument is uncertain, the references from Deuteronomy and other prophetic texts (e.g., Jer. 3:8) demonstrate the ability of a husband to obtain a divorce. None of these earlier passages stipulate the wife's ability to

78. The next chapter will take up inheritance customs, including the possibility of women inheriting property upon the death of their husbands.

79. This particular law warns against remarriage between a twice-divorced wife and her first husband.

80. The Hebrew literally means "nakedness of a thing." This vague wording would lead to diverse interpretations in rabbinic texts (see below). For similar references to a "certificate of divorce," see Isa. 50:1 and Jer. 3:8.

81. Markham J. Geller, "The Elephantine Papyri and Hosea 2, 3: Evidence for the Form of the Early Jewish Divorce Writ," *JSJ* 8 (1977): 139–48. The same formula appears in Old Babylonian and Middle Assyrian contracts; see Edward Lipiński, "Marriage and Divorce in the Judaism of the Persian Period," *Transeu* 4 (1991): 66n6.

initiate the process, however. Yet definitive conclusions on this point in either direction are impossible since we have so little evidence.

With regard to the Second Temple period, one of the more complex passages is from Malachi (2:10–16), an early postexilic text that stands against the endorsement of divorce in Ezra 9–10.[82] The pivotal statement on divorce in Malachi 2:16 is quite difficult to interpret. The NRSV renders the phrase as follows: "For I hate divorce, says the LORD, the God of Israel, and covering one's garment with violence." Yet there is no first-person form in the Hebrew text, and the more accurate translation of the perfect verb would be an impersonal third-person subject, referring to the husband: "He has hated/divorced, sent away, . . . and covered his garment with violence."[83] Either way the verse is translated, this is a clear condemnation of divorce by the prophet. As we seek to clarify the meaning of this statement in Malachi, important clues are Judah's multiple offenses against Yahweh, which are cited in Malachi 2:11: "Judah has profaned the sanctuary of the LORD, which he loves, and has married the daughter of a foreign god." This last statement does not seem to indicate goddess worship, as some scholars have argued, but instead refers to the type of intermarriage with foreign women (i.e., "daughter") that the books of Ezra–Nehemiah criticize so harshly. Although he does not condone the practice of intermarriage in verse 11, the prophet also declares that a person should not "be faithless to the wife of his youth" (2:15).[84] Even if someone makes an unwise decision to intermarry an outsider, he should not later decide to divorce the woman in order to separate from a nonbeliever. Malachi does not reveal the motivation for his passionate criticism of divorce, but he might be targeting those who wanted to ban all forms of intermarriage during the Persian period. He supports the growth of families as encouraged in the Genesis creation stories, and divorce does not mesh with such a goal.[85]

The existence of specific rules and extracanonical evidence from this period, primarily in the form of contracts, indicates the acceptability of divorce in

82. On the chronological possibilities for Malachi, Ezra, and Nehemiah, see Gordon P. Hugenberger, *Marriage as a Covenant: A Study of Biblical Law and Ethics Governing Marriage, Developed from the Perspective of Malachi* (Leiden: E. J. Brill, 1994), 14–17. A Persian period date for Malachi is not in dispute.

83. The first verb (śn') is the same technical term that occurs in Deut. 24:3 and in the contracts from Elephantine. The verb is pointed śānē' in the MT, and this probably should be read as a third-person perfect form with an indefinite subject (i.e., "if one hates"). See Hugenberger, *Marriage as a Covenant*, 70; J. Collins, "Marriage, Divorce, and Family," 125. If this is the case, šallaḥ can logically be repointed as a Piel perfect (šillaḥ), which is reflected in the translation above.

84. Andres E. Hill, *Malachi*, AB 25D (New York: Doubleday, 1998), 241.

85. J. Collins, "Marriage, Divorce, and Family," 126–27, cites a possible allusion to Gen. 2:24 in the difficult Hebrew of Mal. 2:15.

the society and the perception of marriage as in many respects a contractual arrangement. Such texts indicate more developed divorce customs than in previous eras, with greater specificity concerning financial issues and agency for the wife in certain cases. The number of Judeans living in foreign settlements and their exposure to Babylonian and Egyptian legal traditions contributed to a more explicit set of norms concerning divorce. Returning to the Elephantine papyri, several marriage contracts allow either spouse to seek a divorce. In the same document involving Miptaḥiah that we just examined (*TAD* B2.6), there is provision for this woman to file a public complaint in "the assembly" and declare "I hate [šnʾ] my husband."[86] She has to pay divorce money ("silver of hatred"), and then she may "go wherever she desires without suit or process" (lines 22–26), implying a sense of freedom for the woman from her marriage.[87] This section also states that Miptaḥiah is able to keep the dowry payments that she brought to the marriage. Her husband can also petition for divorce, but he must return without delay ("on one day on one stroke") all of the currency and goods that comprised the original dowry to the bride and her family (lines 27–28). This requirement would have provided a natural check against hasty divorces, especially for husbands with limited resources who were seeking to benefit from a generous dowry by absconding with the contribution of the bride's household. Such specific details reflect commonsense knowledge of typical disputes and tactics during a divorce, including the need to specify from the outset any financial exchanges in the event of separation.

Turning to much later examples, certain contracts from the Dead Sea region depict a framework for marriage/divorce that also grants agency to the woman and includes specific details on financial exchanges.[88] One Greek document from Naḥal Ḥever (128 CE) allows a woman, Shelamzion, to obtain a divorce from her husband, Judah Cimber, and seek compensation "whenever she may demand it of him, in silver secured in due form, at his own expense, interposing no objection" (5/6 Ḥev 18).[89] This is a text from the so-called Babatha archive, and this woman Shelamzion is the stepdaughter of Babatha through her husband, Judah Cimber. As with the Elephantine papyri, the husband's failure to pay the sum quickly is unacceptable,

86. This Miptaḥiah had already divorced an Egyptian husband, which points to the allowance of intermarriage in this colony.
87. The contract does not address specific circumstances that might warrant such a step, but other contracts mention adultery as grounds for divorce.
88. There were also two Aramaic contracts found at Murabbaʿat in which the husband promises to support his wife with an earlier *mōhar* payment.
89. For the primary text, see Naphtali Lewis, Ranon Katzoff, Jonas C. Greenfield, "Papyrus Yadin 18," *IEJ* 37 (1987): 229–50.

and negligence in this regard will lead to financial obligations. The contract indicates that Judah Cimber will owe three hundred denarii if the couple ultimately gets a divorce—this was the amount Shelamzion brought to the marriage as dowry—but the penalty will double if he delays.[90] The wife therefore has noteworthy rights in this document, including the ability to exit the marriage with the financial resources she brought into it and the latitude to initiate the process herself. We do not know how widespread such freedoms were, but this text suggests that divorce customs continued to evolve late into the Roman period. In certain instances, women had more agency than in earlier eras, including the ability to end a marriage and retain some measure of financial security.

Another fragment from this period is less certain (P.Ḥever/Ṣe'elim 13). In this text, the wife (also named Shelamzion) appears to return items to one Eleazer, "who was formerly her husband and who received a bill of divorce from her."[91] Yet the Aramaic can also be translated the other way around ("who received a bill of divorce from him"), such that the husband actually sends the writ to his wife.[92] When examining such evidence from the Roman period, commentators often point to the Gospel of Mark (10:11–12), which seems to acknowledge a woman's ability to seek a divorce (v. 12: "if she divorces her husband and marries another"). The fact that Jesus condemns this practice suggests its occurrence among certain sectors of the population, but it is difficult to determine the larger relevance of this statement for understanding widespread customs in the first century CE.

Rabbinic texts on divorce and its economic implications contain more specific details than anything we have examined in this chapter. Yet caution is in order because these texts date from a later period, and it is difficult to assess which rabbinic writings might reflect actual practices in the late Second Temple period.[93] The Mishnah contains some views that are more restrictive than some of the contracts we have examined with regard

90. Lipiński, "Marriage and Divorce," 70, cites the same penalty in Egyptian documents from this period.

91. See Klaus Beyer, *Die aramäischen Texte vom Toten Meer*, Ergänzungsband (Göttingen: Vandenhoeck & Ruprecht, 1994); Tal Ilan, "On a Newly Published Divorce Bill from the Judaean Desert," *HTR* 89 (1996): 195–202.

92. Tal Ilan, *Integrating Women into Second Temple History* (Peabody, MA: Hendrickson Publishers, 2001), 253–63, provides a detailed analysis of the text and the scholarly debate, maintaining that this is clearly a bill of divorce from the woman to the man. For other possibilities, including the argument that this is not even a divorce document, see David W. Chapman, "Marriage and Family in Second Temple Judaism," in *Marriage and the Family in the Biblical World*, ed. Ken M. Campbell (Downers Grove, IL: InterVarsity Press, 2003), 230–31n321.

93. See Archer, *Her Price Is beyond Rubies*, 123–206.

to latitude for obtaining a divorce. On the one hand, a husband can divorce his wife "irrespective of her will" (*m. Yebam.* 14:1). In another passage, a woman can seek a divorce if she goes through the courts (*m. Ketub.* 7:5–10). This literature includes references to the *ketubbah,* a financial custom that is a descendant of the earlier bridewealth amount paid to the father of the bride. An enactment attributed to Simeon ben Shetach (a prominent Pharisee during the first century BCE) describes a series of stages in the evolution of marriage presents and their relationship to divorce: (1) in its earlier form, bridewealth was given directly to the father of the bride, and this had the effect of discouraging marriage proposals from insincere young suitors; (2) for the next stage, the bridegroom did not have to pay in currency, but a specific amount was converted into jewelry/utensils and added to the dowry (as in the Elephantine contracts); (3) Simeon ben Shetach's reform released the groom from any financial obligation during the betrothal stage, but he had to promise payment at a future date if he tried to dissolve the marriage (*b. Ketub.* 82b). This final step relates to the institution of the *ketubbah.* By the time of the first century BCE, direct bridewealth payments to the father of the bride had long fallen out of favor, and they became a penalty assessed to the groom in the event of divorce.

The *ketubbah* therefore functioned as a promissory note such that the woman only received the amount upon the death of her husband or in the event of divorce.[94] Since the husband knew that divorce would necessitate this payment, the *ketubbah* worked as a deterrent to breaking up the marriage. If historically accurate, Simeon's reform might have signified an effort to curb divorce in the society. Perhaps such measures became necessary if some of the contracts we have examined are any indication of what was actually taking place.[95] Efforts to sidestep the *ketubbah* appear in the Mishnah, which includes a debate over when the husband can be released from this obligation. One rabbinic school (Shammai) sought to limit defensible reasons for seeking a divorce (e.g., adultery) and avoiding any payment, while the other (Hillel) attempted to broaden the husband's discretion to separate from his wife for any number of reasons (e.g., poor housekeeping skills: see *m. Git.* 9:10).[96]

When considering this topic and such evidence, some caveats are in order. Our discussion of divorce in the Second Temple period has dealt with documents that either did not originate in Judah (e.g., Elephantine) or date from

94. See David W. Chapman, "Family," *DEJ* 631.
95. J. Collins, "Marriage, Divorce, and Family," 115.
96. See Archer, *Her Price Is beyond Rubies,* 219. The different positions on this topic include an argument over how loosely to interpret "something objectionable" in Deut. 24:1.

a later period (e.g., the Mishnah) than the focus of this study. Perhaps we should attribute the right of a woman to seek a divorce at Elephantine and the specification of the dowry amount entirely to the influence of Egyptian customs. This would explain why we do not find widespread mention of similar practices in texts that originated in Judah. In fact, some scholars have categorized the Elephantine contracts as a deviation from what most believers thought permissible in divorce proceedings.[97] Yet those persons living in the Palestinian region could easily have followed similar practices. The scattered evidence in literary sources (e.g., Deuteronomy, Jeremiah, and Tobit) indicates a contractual understanding of marriage and divorce that took the financial aspect quite seriously. Even if the Elephantine documents reflect foreign legal customs, those living in Judah had their own comparable practices, and it is probable that in some cases women could and did divorce at their own initiative, retaining their dowry in the process.[98] Since later biblical passages allude to controversies over divorce, we can assume diverse interpretations regarding this practice and the common occurrence of divorce both in and outside of Judah.

The discussion in this chapter has demonstrated that one cannot separate the sacred and mundane aspects of marriage/divorce, nor should we seek to do so, since the ancients would not have made this distinction. The texts we have examined thus far, such as Ezra 9–10, combine practical, economic considerations with passionate theological statements. When the subject at hand is marriage and divorce, one usually finds complex reasons for a particular outlook. For example, the drastic measures taken by Ruth and Naomi and the strong acceptance of intermarriage in this colorful story demonstrate the intensity of disputes over endogamy/exogamy and the impossibility of untangling the sacred aspects of betrothal customs from the more pragmatic ones. The evidence from books like Tobit and the contracts from Elephantine and the Dead Sea indicates that betrothal and divorce always have financial repercussions. As Judeans developed their customs after the exile, they tried to delineate the economic consequences relating to marriage in much greater detail. Certain sources from the Second Temple period reflect the seriousness of divorce and set up checks to protect both parties from financial ruin, and in some cases these safeguards include noteworthy rights for women living in a patriarchal society.

97. For summaries of this debate and the issues at stake, see Bernadette J. Brooten, "Zur Debatte über das Scheidungsrecht der jüdischen Frau," *EvTh* 43 (1983): 466–78.
98. See J. Collins, "Marriage, Divorce, and Family," 120–21, for a discussion of the references to divorce in Josephus (e.g., the divorce sought by Herod's sister, in *Ant.* 15.259).

SUMMARY

This chapter has highlighted the significance of the household structure and the difficulties many families faced. We have suggested that the long-standing "house of the father" structure persisted into the Second Temple period, especially at the village and rural level. Colonial demands and exploitation by wealthy landowners exacerbated difficult conditions for lower economic classes as demanding levies continued throughout the region (see chap. 4). We have also pointed to the contractual understanding of marriage, including intermarriage and its economic aspects, the evolution of marriage gifts during this period, and the financial aspects of divorce. What we have not yet considered in detail is the status of women and children in the household structure, the manner in which they contributed to the economic viability of their kinship group, and the opportunities available to them. These are major issues in the study of this period that are often neglected. Woman and children will be the focus of the next chapter.

2

The Status of Women and Children

Despite the ancient sources' relative inattention to their contributions, women and children played a consequential role in their households and the society as a whole, both before and after the exile. Women frequently managed essential aspects of daily life, such as food preparation, family worship, and the nurture of offspring. Many children also took on important duties at an early age. For many families, the skills of women and children allowed a household to ply a trade other than farming (e.g., weaving) and attain a living standard not otherwise possible, in some cases selling their surplus at a profit. Women also formed networks to foster their productivity and solidarity. Nevertheless, biblical texts and extracanonical sources often reflect the androcentric orientation of the culture, focusing on the collective destiny of the people from a male, urban perspective.[1] Second Temple sources frequently ignore the rhythms of daily existence for women and children, whose diligent efforts made their household and society function properly. While this lack of attention makes it impossible to gain a complete picture of the situation for women and children during this period, clues in the extant material shed light on the topic.

For most of the twentieth century, textual critics and archaeologists largely pursued other questions and ignored women and children's significant contributions to social and economic life. Yet this tendency has changed in recent decades. More studies have acknowledged this gap in our knowledge and

1. For example, in *Jubilees* and Josephus's descriptions in *Jewish Antiquities*, the authors minimize the role of women in their explication of stories from Genesis and Exodus. See Eileen Schuller, "Women of the Exodus in Biblical Retellings of the Second Temple Period," in *Gender and Difference in Ancient Israel*, ed. Peggy L. Day (Minneapolis: Fortress Press, 1989), 178–94.

directed considerable focus to the status of women and children. The interest in modern methods, such as feminist and social-scientific criticism, has played a role in this development, along with innovative avenues for archaeological research (e.g., gender archaeology). As experts have mined both written sources and the fields of the Palestinian region for clues, greater insights are possible, although many details and patterns remain unknown or obscure.[2]

The current chapter will consider the status of women and children during the Second Temple period, particularly in relation to economics. The circumstances for widows will receive attention in this context, with specific focus on the situation of a childless woman whose husband died. We will also examine the situation of children, including some discussion of the precarious circumstances for daughters. This latter topic has received relatively little attention in studies of this period, and we must explore the roles that offspring played in contributing to their kinship group and the larger economy. While the financial success of a household depended on a variety of factors, such as occupation, wealth, and social reputation, the efforts of unheralded voices contributed a great deal to the functionality of the family and the larger society. Despite a hierarchical framework in which women and children faced many challenges and often found themselves on the margins, the evidence suggests that many of them made important contributions to the economy and had more public lives than some of the sources suggest, and social class usually mattered more than gender or age in terms of stability and financial success. The current chapter will consider these questions even as we acknowledge the difficulties of such an inquiry with limited source material.

ROLES AND RESPONSIBILITIES OF WOMEN

Our discussion begins with the status and roles for women during this period. There is no certainty about the distribution of daily responsibilities according to gender: material remains do not reveal this information, and therefore it is very difficult to ascertain the division of duties between husband, wife, children, and any servants. Practices undoubtedly differed from community to community, and women in upper-class settings did not have to engage in the type of menial work that the majority of the population undertook on a regular basis. Nevertheless, we can draw some tentative conclusions about the

2. Carol L. Meyers has led the way in this effort. Her influential work, *Discovering Eve: Ancient Israelite Women in Context* (New York: Oxford University Press, 1988), and many articles have addressed neglected questions in this area. She has recently offered a reworking of this important study: *Rediscovering Eve: Ancient Israelite Women in Context* (Oxford: Oxford University Press, 2013).

roles and responsibilities of women in the economy, including their activities. Such information appears in scattered references, along with what we can glean through sociological and ethnographic inquiry.

Most women had to devote significant attention to food preparation. The earliest sources supply important clues about female leadership in this area.[3] The previous chapter highlighted the reality that most households had to structure their lives to facilitate constant food needs. As anthropologists have noted and anyone who has lived in challenging conditions can attest, requirements in this area are both exacting and time consuming, with important decisions on a daily basis. In many instances, women had to determine the regimen for everyone in the household, how much to ration when resources became scarce, and in some cases dietary protocols for cultic observances.[4] Carol Meyers and other scholars have demonstrated the importance of food preparation in a subsistence economy, where famine and starvation are recurrent threats, and the critical role of women in guaranteeing their household's survival. These studies have challenged the tendency of earlier interpreters to regard such duties to be merely "domestic" and therefore of secondary importance. Gender archaeologists have referred to the "maintenance activities" of women that attend to the well-being and in some cases survival of a social group such as a household. Such terminology enables the interpreter to "valorize" rather than "marginalize" the vital contributions of women in this regard.[5]

Grain was the most important source of daily sustenance (*leḥem* means both "food" and "bread" in Biblical Hebrew); for their households women regularly prepared wheat and barley products, along with other foods.[6] The production of bread items required threshing, winnowing, and milling.[7]

---

3. See Carol L. Meyers, "From Field Crops to Food: Attributing Gender and Meaning to Bread Production in Iron Age Israel," in *The Archaeology of Difference: Gender, Ethnicity, Class, and the 'Other' in Antiquity; Studies in Honor of Eric M. Meyers*, ed. Douglas R. Edwards and C. Thomas McCollough (Boston: American Schools of Oriental Research, 2007), 68–71.

4. The biblical texts indicate that women often had responsibility for food preparation (e.g., Tamar in 2 Sam. 13:8) and other daily tasks such as drawing water (e.g., Gen. 24:11 and the reference to "the time when women go out to draw water").

5. C. Meyers, *Rediscovering Eve*, 126.

6. According to many sources, men often took the primary role in meat preparation, especially for festival observances or to welcome a guest (e.g., 1 Sam. 9:22–24 and Saul's dinner with Samuel). Yet many families did not eat meat on a regular basis: Pastor, *Land and Economy*, 5, estimates that more than half of the diet during this period consisted of grain items. For a larger survey of what was grown during this period and the challenges of farming, see the discussion in chap. 3 below.

7. For more on the specific types of wheat and barley products, see Nathan MacDonald, *What Did the Ancient Israelites Eat?* (Grand Rapids: Eerdmans, 2008), 19–23. For many types of bread, the process of preparation could take three hours a day or more.

Grindstones made of limestone or basalt became the mechanism for preparing grain (e.g., Prov. 27:22), and this work frequently became a communal enterprise. Adjacent households might develop into small villages through such efforts, and their collective productivity determined the health of the community. In the Second Temple period, small living spaces with a common courtyard became more frequent, and the public area in these domiciles frequently included an oven.[8]

Textual evidence points to the prominent role of women in these efforts and the communal nature of the work. An early wisdom text, the Egyptian Instruction of Ptahhotep (ca. 1800 BCE), contains an incidental reference to such work: "Good advice is rarer than emeralds, and yet it may be found among women at the grindstones" (5.10).[9] With regard to the postexilic context, Second Isaiah (sixth century BCE) describes the descent of the "virgin daughter Babylon" into lowly status: "Take the millstones and grind meal, remove your veil, strip off your robe, uncover your legs, pass through the rivers" (Isa. 47:2; cf. Exod. 11:5). Despite the fact that the prophet depicts grinding as lowly work, one cannot deny its vital importance for daily living. It is noteworthy that both of these passages mention women grinding. In addition, Qoheleth (third century BCE) has a final poem on death that envisions a point when "the women who grind cease working because they are few" (Eccl. 12:3).[10] The only two biblical texts depicting male involvement in this area assume gender reversal: Samson's emasculation in Judges 16:21 and Lamentations 5:13, which describes a topsy-turvy situation where "young men are compelled to grind." In addition, the Mishnah mentions "grinding, sifting, kneading, baking" as the tasks of women and servants (m. Šabb. 12:2).[11] Finally, various ethnographic studies of Middle Eastern practices indicate the primary role of females in producing foods from wheat and barley. From Iranian villages to the Palestinian communities of recent centuries, women have continued to take the lead in this area.[12]

The implications of female leadership in food preparation are significant. The ability to network while engaging in this task allowed women to stay abreast of local events (e.g., marital possibilities for their children, important

8. Fiensy, *Social History of Palestine*, 127.

9. For the Egyptian text, see William Kelly Simpson, *The Literature of Ancient Egypt*, 3rd ed. (New Haven: Yale University Press, 2003).

10. Even if this verse actually refers to tooth loss in old age (i.e., the "grinding" of molars), the biblical author assumes familiarity with grain milling by females. See Choon Leong Seow, *Ecclesiastes*, AB 18C (New York: Doubleday, 1997), 355.

11. Translation is from Danby, *The Mishnah*.

12. C. Meyers, "From Field Crops to Food," 72–73, surveys the ethnographic evidence to demonstrate the role of women in preparing grain products throughout the history of ancient Israel and up to the present day in many communities.

developments within their vicinity). The interactive nature of the work (i.e., women grinding grain together) also gave them the opportunity to build important relationships with other households and influence public opinion. The end of Ruth is an instructive example in this regard, since the "women of the neighborhood" actually give Obed his name (4:17). Because of their interconnectedness, the cabal of women in this story represents a powerful force in the community.[13] Moreover, by controlling the final preparation of food, females had a pivotal role in the health of their households. Women had to prepare many items, such as legumes, fruits, and other foods, including fish products if these were available.[14] For most persons living in Judah, survival depended directly on the amount of food they produced. Proper caloric intake in a subsistence economy can be difficult to manage, especially if a family member contracts an illness or resources become scarce. Under such circumstances, children are especially vulnerable. A passage from the covenant curses at the end of Leviticus reflects the power of women in this regard. If Israel remains unfaithful, "When I [the LORD your God] break your staff of bread, ten women shall bake your bread in a single oven, and they shall dole out your bread by weight; and though you eat, you shall not be satisfied" (Lev. 26:26). Though the topic here is divine judgment, the incidental reference to baking and food distribution by a collective of women is noteworthy.

Finally, this study has highlighted the demands of local and imperial authorities after the exile. Many households in the Second Temple period did not have discretionary resources, and therefore any decisions about how to ration food under the threat of unfair lending practices and oppressive taxation remained consequential, in some cases a matter of life and death.[15] The scenario in Nehemiah 5 is instructive, since it concerns households struggling with their ability to obtain grain and survive (v. 2). The pitfalls of destitution include debt slavery for their children and loss of land (vv. 4–6). The demands of imperial taxation play a key role in this passage, since these poor families have to pay both local officials (v. 7) and Persian authorities (v. 4). Maintaining a sufficient supply of food can be very difficult under such circumstances so that the failure of households to allocate resources and distribute food items properly had severe consequences.

13. See Carol Meyers, "'Women of the Neighborhood' (Ruth 4:17): Informal Female Networks in Ancient Israel," in *A Feminist Companion to Ruth*, ed. Athalya Brenner (Sheffield: Sheffield Academic Press, 1999), 110–27.
14. N. MacDonald, *What Did the Ancient Israelites Eat?*, 25–38, sketches the probable diet, based on extant sources and archaeological remains.
15. The balance between food for internal consumption and for selling (as cash crops) continued to be a challenge for many households during this period.

With regard to other farming tasks and the contributions of women, anthropological insight is helpful for this inquiry. Jack Goody, Ester Boserup, and others have studied the distribution of labor in different agricultural economies and found some noteworthy patterns. A woman's level of involvement often coincided with the income of her household, whether she lived in a rural or urban area, and a number of other variables, including household size, gender distribution within the kinship group, and level of wealth. According to Boserup's cross-cultural analysis, many women in agrarian contexts did not engage in regular fieldwork, while others expended a great deal of effort in this area. Boserup has shown that in societies where the means of farming are more primitive, with reliance on hoe cultivation and less population density (and a higher incidence of polygamy), women tend to do more of the daily farming. When population levels are higher and the plow becomes commonplace, males generally dominate the field duties.[16] The advanced agrarian economy of Second Temple Judea seems to fit more the latter model such that men usually performed more of the farming tasks (e.g., Sir. 38:25; *m. Šabb.* 7:2) and women had less autonomy and a greater number of non-agrarian duties. Significantly, there are no references in the Hebrew Bible or in other Second Temple sources to women working the plow. Yet we must be careful about any definitive conclusions on this point. Both Boserup and Goody acknowledge the participation of both genders in agricultural pursuits when property holdings are small and the household must direct all efforts toward survival.[17] Such a challenging scenario applied to many households after the exile, as they struggled on small parcels with high levels of taxation and the chronic threat of losing their land. Even on larger plots, the system of tenant farming forced many individuals into a life of indentured servitude, leading to regular responsibilities for men and women.[18]

If men dominated certain agricultural duties, this did not exempt women from an array of demanding tasks. During this period females had diverse responsibilities, especially if they lacked the resources of the urban elite, and these duties might have included grape farming and wine making (viticulture). Households committing to this enterprise frequently had to enlist all members, especially for pruning and harvesting. One biblical text, Proverbs

16. Ester Boserup, *Women's Role in Economic Development* (New York: St. Martin's Press, 1970), 50–51. Cf. Jack Goody, *Production and Reproduction: A Comparative Study of the Domestic Domain*, Cambridge Studies in Social Anthropology 17 (Cambridge: Cambridge University Press, 1976), 32–33.

17. Goody, *Production and Reproduction*, 32; Boserup, *Women's Role*, 35.

18. Pastor, *Land and Economy*, 14, argues that the returnees from exile, by virtue of their wealth and ties to the colonial authorities, reclaimed much of the land and forced many residents into a tenant-farmer situation.

31:10–31, mentions the initiative of a wealthy woman in wine production. This is the praise of the "capable wife," and the vocabulary and content point to the postexilic period as the most likely setting.[19] This woman's industry receives special commendation: "She considers a field and buys it; with the fruit of her hands she plants a vineyard" (31:16). The "fruit of her hands" refers to her financial resources (i.e., she purchases the vineyard), and this "capable wife" (31:10) has male and female servants to assist with the manufacture of wine.[20] Women also parlayed their expertise into other profitable ventures, such as beer production. The evidence is overwhelming that women took the lead in beer making, both in Judah and throughout the region.[21] In terms of trading such goods, archaeological efforts have uncovered Persian period storage jars for exporting wine and other items, especially along the coastal areas.[22] The exacting requirements of producing wine and beer, especially for trading, demanded the participation of women throughout the process.[23]

Other women performed more intricate work, particularly in the areas of ceramics and weaving. With regard to the former, archaeologists have used pottery remains to establish chronologies at the various sites and to ascertain

19. Christine R. Yoder, *Wisdom as a Woman of Substance: A Socioeconomic Reading of Proverbs 1–9 and 31:10–31*, BZAW 304 (Berlin: de Gruyter, 2001), 73–110, locates Prov. 31:10–31 during the Persian period, based on Hebrew vocabulary and subject matter. She compares this passage with a wealth of primary evidence from Achaemenid sources. Michael V. Fox, *Proverbs 10–31*, AYB 18B (New Haven: Yale University Press, 2009), 901, questions whether we can date this passage so confidently and leaves open the possibility of a Hellenistic setting.

20. Yoder, *Wisdom as a Woman of Substance*, 87. Another reference to wine making occurs in Neh. 13:15, where people are "treading wine presses on the sabbath." This accusation reflects commercial production in Jerusalem and the frequent conflict between cultic observance and business pursuits. There is also an earlier passage in Judges where the young women dance in the vineyards (Judg. 21:2–23).

21. The ingredients of ancient beer provided far more sustenance than the modern beverage, and women took the lead in brewing. Jennie R. Ebeling and Michael M. Homan, "Baking and Brewing Beer in the Israelite Household: A Study of Women's Cooking Technology," in *The World of Women in the Ancient and Classical Near East*, ed. Beth A. Nakhai (Newcastle: Cambridge Scholars Publishing, 2008), 45–62, examine beer production in the ancient Near East. In both Egypt and Mesopotamia, iconographic representations indicate the predominant role of women in this effort. Cf. Carol L. Meyers, "Having Their Space and Eating There Too: Bread Production and Female Power in Ancient Israelite Households," *Nashim: A Journal of Jewish Women's Studies and Gender Issues* 5 (2002): 14–44.

22. See Ephraim Stern, *Material Culture of the Land of the Bible in the Persian Period, 538–322 B.C.* (Warminster, UK: Aris & Phillips; Jerusalem: Israel Exploration Society, 1982), 109–27, for an overview of jars and bottles from this period.

23. Another reference to viticulture occurs in the Song of Songs, where the young maiden mentions a vineyard she owns, but her brothers force her to work on their vineyards (1:6).

the purposes of different vessels. As with all archaeological remains, it is impossible to know whether a man or woman made a particular piece based on physical inspection. In searching the biblical record, 1 Chronicles 4:22–23 mentions a family of male potters, and in Jeremiah 18:1–12 the prophet compares divine control over Israel with the authority of a male artisan over his spinning potter's wheel.[24] There are no references in the Hebrew Bible to women making pottery. Nevertheless, we can posit a role for them in this essential task. Most clay vessels had a utilitarian purpose at the household level, and the needs of the populace made it necessary to produce pottery quickly and effectively.[25] Ethnographic evidence indicates that throughout the centuries women in the Middle East have worked on ceramics in order to equip their households with necessary domestic wares or produce items for commercial purposes.[26] Like most household jobs, more experienced men and women would have taken the lead in these efforts, teaching the younger ones how to shape and fire clay objects.[27]

If the distribution of labor for ceramics is somewhat unclear, there can be no doubt that many women took primary responsibility for making garments and other cloth items. Ancient Near Eastern sources describe women as engaging in textile production. Mesopotamian and Egyptian texts mention individual weavers and female guilds, and the Hebrew Bible also reflects this tradition.[28] In speaking of the "capable wife," Proverbs 31:10–31 focuses on textiles. This ideal woman "seeks wool and flax, and works with willing hands" (v. 13). In addition, "She puts her hand to the distaff, and her hands hold the spindle" (v. 19). Not only does the "capable wife" produce "fine linen and purple" (v. 22), but also "she makes linen garments and sells them; she supplies the merchant with sashes" (v. 24).[29] Similarly, Anna, the wife

24. The image of God as potter also appears throughout the Hebrew Bible, most famously in Genesis and Isaiah (e.g., Gen. 2:7; Isa. 29:16; 45:9; cf. Sir. 33:13).

25. Oded Borowski, *Daily Life in Biblical Times*, ABS 5 (Atlanta: Society of Biblical Literature, 2003), 30–31.

26. C. Meyers, *Rediscovering Eve*, 134, cites the presence of female village potters in the Palestinian region, along with Turkey and Cyprus, in recent centuries and the communal nature of the work.

27. Jennie R. Ebeling, *Women's Lives in Biblical Times* (London: T&T Clark, 2010), 54–55.

28. Hennie J. Marsman, *Women in Ugarit and Israel: Their Social and Religious Position in the Context of the Ancient Near East* (Leiden: E. J. Brill, 2003), 407–8, surveys the evidence (seal impressions, administrative lists from Nuzi and Mari, letters, Egyptian titles) that shows the prominence of women in textile work.

29. The Hebrew word for "merchants" in Prov. 31:24 is actually "Canaanite," referring to the Phoenician traders who worked along the Mediterranean (cf. Neh. 13:16 and the mention of Tyrians). During the Persian period, "Canaanite" came to be synonymous with "trader" (Yoder, *Wisdom as a Woman of Substance*, 79).

of Tobit, weaves garments for sale during the period when her husband is blind (Tob. 2:11–12). The book of Tobit even refers to Anna's efforts as "women's work" (2:11). From the New Testament, we have Roman period attestation of similar efforts: Dorcas makes tunics (Acts 9:39), and Lydia is a "dealer in purple cloth" (Acts 16:14). The latter reference implies commercial pursuits. Such descriptions point to the involvement of women in textile work, including the possibility for resourceful individuals to prosper by selling their wares. For women with more limited resources, we can also assume a strong knowledge of essential skills. The process of spinning and weaving demanded repetitive efforts, and daughters had to learn under the tutelage of their mothers and other capable elders.[30] Using the primary ingredients of wool and flax, they worked both upright and horizontal looms. As with baking, women sometimes gathered in groups to facilitate production, and this type of networking created a space for both solidarity and commercial opportunity (i.e., merchants might hear about the quality of product stemming from a particular group).

Women also had influence at the household level and beyond in the area of cultic activities. The androcentric perspectives of many priests and prophets that dominate the Hebrew Bible do not fully represent the scope of devotional activity, especially in the domestic sphere and within local communities. The fact that women played a major role in baking and textile production gave them significant input into such matters within their household. For example, bread items appear as common offerings in the biblical texts (e.g., Lev. 24:5–9).[31] The description of the cult of the "queen of heaven" (probably Astarte) in Jeremiah 7:18 (sixth century BCE) indicates a family affair: "The children gather wood, the fathers kindle fire, and the women knead dough, to make cakes for the queen of heaven."[32] The prophet condemns what he regards as syncretistic worship of this "queen of heaven" (Jer. 44:19), yet the role of women in household worship is both logical and significant, especially since many women associated Astarte with fertility and childbirth. The contributions of women to household worship are not the focus of this study, but their leadership in food preparation coincided with cultic rites and tutelage of

30. "Spinning" is the process of drawing out and placing fibers into a ball of yarn, often through the use of a spindle and a pulley (whorl) at the bottom of it. "Weaving" refers to the interlacing of two separate rolls of thread (the warp and the weft) at a right angle to each other (Ebeling, *Women's Lives*, 57–58).

31. Ibid., 75–76.

32. For background on this reference, see Susan Ackerman, "'And the Women Knead Dough': The Worship of the Queen of Heaven," in *Gender and Difference in Ancient Israel*, ed. Peggy L. Day (Minneapolis: Fortress Press, 1989), 109–24. The "Queen of Heaven" seems to represent an amalgam of the east Semitic goddess Ištar and the west Semitic Astarte.

children. The respect due to both parents in the legal and sapiential traditions is a consequence of the significant influence of women in household affairs.

These various responsibilities for women contributed to the rhythms of daily life during this period. Interpreters often focus on the careers of such figures as Ezra, Nehemiah, and the succession of high priests recorded in Josephus, asking how much we can know about them historically and the dynamics of their careers. Such an approach is both understandable and necessary as we ascertain political and cultural developments during the Second Temple period. Yet the heroic tenacity of women had as much to do with the welfare of the people of Judah through resettlement and colonization as any political event. The androcentric focus of many sources should not obscure the contributions of women, both to their households and the larger society. We have already seen that the Elephantine archives and sections of the wisdom books acknowledge the involvement of women in different activities, from food preparation to property management.[33] Returning once again to the conclusion of Proverbs, this final poem praises the "capable wife" for her extraordinary efforts: "She rises while it is still night and provides food for her household" (Prov. 31:15). Women like the "capable wife" functioned as essential facilitators, and they added to the society well beyond the confines of their domicile. In the final verse of this poem (and the book), the initiative of the "capable wife" speaks for itself: "Let her works praise her in the city gates" (31:31).

This acrostic poem from Proverbs suggests the rarity of such a person: "A capable wife who can find? She is far more precious than jewels" (31:10). In his praise of the woman, the sapiential writer repeats some of the exceptional qualities of Lady Wisdom in Proverbs 1–9 (cf. 3:15; 8:11).[34] Does this literary connection make the "capable wife" an idealized or even supernatural portrait, as some commentators have argued? Probably not: the preceding analysis suggests that many women did actually embody the characteristics of this "capable wife," rising early and completing a myriad of tasks to keep their households safe and healthy.[35] Therefore, the rendering of Hebrew ḥayil as "capable" in the NRSV is appropriate: this poem describes the woman's daily strength and

33. For example, the Elephantine archives attest to the resourcefulness of women in acquiring and selling such goods as salt, barley, and cucumber seed. Women also bought and sold property. See Yoder, *Wisdom as a Woman of Substance*, 84.

34. Fox, *Proverbs*, 1:908–9. While there are common features in descriptions of the "capable wife" and Lady Wisdom, they are not identical. The figure of Prov. 31:10–31 embodies the qualities of Wisdom, especially in Prov. 1–9, but this depiction addresses real-life scenarios and actual characteristics.

35. Christine R. Yoder, *Proverbs* (Abingdon; Nashville: Abingdon Press, 2003), 299, also notes the problematic aspects of this portrait. The woman is domesticated and desirable for the material goods she brings to her husband, reflecting a culture that is "patriarchal in structure and androcentric in bias."

resourcefulness.[36] Even if her extraordinary wealth fell outside the norm of usual experience, the details of Proverbs 31:10–31 applied to countless women in the Second Temple period, especially those working in as difficult a context as farming in this region.[37] Their diligence in a variety of tasks, from textiles to raising children (e.g., Prov. 31:28), and even helping with the rebuilding of the Jerusalem wall (i.e., the daughters of Shallum in Neh. 3:12), can hardly be called a rarity.[38] Most women performed their jobs without much acclaim, and in the final analysis we cannot depict any "average" experience for women during the Second Temple period. The sources do not devote enough attention to their daily lives, and in many cases class mattered far more than gender in terms of how women struggled. Yet it is clear that they made indispensable contributions during this formative period in the history of Judah.

THE STATUS OF WIDOWS

Many women faced more adverse circumstances, and widowhood (Heb. 'almānâ) was a frequent and often tragic development. With the average lifespan so short, women often lacked a partner at an early age. This situation created numerous difficulties, from mere survival to the prickly issue of inheritance rights, particularly if the woman did not have surviving male sons and could not inherit property.[39] The vulnerability of widows continued to be an issue after the exile: questions of property ownership and communal identity (i.e., who was accepted as having full rights and privileges in the society) remained in a state of uncertainty.

36. Fox, *Proverbs*, 1:891, explains that ḥayil in this passage denotes resilience, competency, and material wealth. According to this understanding, "even her practical competencies are not simply technical skills but manifestations of her focus, selflessness, and determination."

37. John J. Collins, *Jewish Wisdom in the Hellenistic Age*, OTL (Louisville, KY: Westminster John Knox Press, 1997), 70, argues that Ben Sira is a contrast on this point, since he counsels the "good wife" to remain in the background: "A silent wife is a gift from the Lord, and nothing is so precious as her self-discipline" (Sir. 26:14). This advice indicates the urban perspective of a more elite sage, and it probably reflects the influence of Greek ideals for female modesty. On the other hand, Prov. 31 values an industrious woman in more of a village/agrarian setting.

38. Since the author of Nehemiah does not comment on the involvement of the daughters in this effort, it is reasonable to assume that other women also contributed in the same manner. See Marsman, *Women in Ugarit and Israel*, 427, and the discussion below.

39. See below for a discussion of whether women could inherit property. In the Babylonian context, a woman only became a "widow" (almattu) if she had no surviving male sons.

The ancient sources pay close attention to the situation of widows and for good reason: these women lacked the security of the "house of the father" structure. In many cases, a widow could return to her father's house, but the patrilocal nature of the society often worked against this option. Once the woman married into her husband's family, she became a member of and dependent on his "house of the father" for her security such that his household had to care for her well-being and perhaps provide a suitable replacement if her husband died (i.e., the custom of levirate marriage).[40] In many cases, however, ongoing assistance went against the wishes of the dead husband's family. If they rejected her, the widow could become unmoored from her social standing, losing the essential benefits of the marital union. The Pentateuchal laws acknowledge this scenario by seeking to protect and assist widows, including the allocation of food for them. Both the Covenant Code (Exod. 22:21–23 [22–24]) and Deuteronomy (24:17–18) address the tenuous status of widows in the social structure. There is provision for their food (Deut. 24:19–21), including shares from a triennial tithe (Deut. 14:27–29) and festival observances (Deut. 16:11–15). The Hebrew Bible frequently depicts God as the advocate for and even the "father of orphans and protector of widows" (Ps. 68:5). Later sources also show concern for women in this category (e.g., Mal. 3:5). A passage from Ben Sira depicts the plaintive cry of a widow to her oppressor: "Do not the tears of the widow run down her cheek as she cries out against the one who causes them to fall?" (Sir. 35:18–19). Many Second Temple texts defend the right of widows to at least subsistence living (e.g., Sir. 35:17; Tob. 1:8).

Unless they could rely on property holdings or some other measure of security, widows faced the prospect of poor social standing, destitution, and possibly death. Upon the passing of their husbands, these women frequently lost the land and possessions that had sustained them, especially if they had no living sons. Land ownership provided the best means of security, and some Judean women could and did own property during the Second Temple period. The Elephantine contracts include provisions for wives to retain their dowry in the event of their husband's death or in case of divorce (e.g., the marriage of Miptahiah and Eshor in *TAD* B2.6), and the book of Judith mentions the maintenance of land by the heroine (8:7). Yet other sources, including the biblical laws on widowhood, suggest that many women did not have the same legal rights as Miptahiah at Elephantine or the fictional character of Judith. Unless they had living sons or the ongoing support of their deceased

40. For an overview of laws pertaining to widows in the ancient Near East, see Paula S. Hiebert, "'Whence Shall Help Come to Me?': The Biblical Widow," in *Gender and Difference in Ancient Israel*, ed. Peggy L. Day (Minneapolis: Fortress Press, 1989), 125–41.

husband's relatives, they became an 'almānâ, a designation that placed them in a desperate social position. The loss of membership in her husband's family and the resulting vulnerability moved a woman into this unfavorable category of widowhood, rather than just the death of her husband. Like the "resident alien," many widows had no ties to a patriarch or his assets and lived in a liminal state, leaving them susceptible to abject poverty.[41] The fact that the Hebrew Bible often groups widows with orphans and resident aliens (e.g., Deut 14:29) demonstrates the power of the patrilineal system and the need to be part of a functioning household with property holdings. Many widows found themselves on the periphery of society if they did not retain anything from their husband's assets or the earlier exchange of marriage gifts.

Along with food allocation, the practice of levirate marriage receives attention in the sources. In response to the precarious situation of widows, the society put mechanisms in place to protect them. A case law in the Torah, Deuteronomy 25:5–10, acknowledges their situation and seeks to preserve ties with surviving in-laws. This custom, common in patrilineal and endogamous societies, required the male sibling of a deceased man (Lat. levir, "husband's brother") to marry his sister-in-law in order to keep the woman within his brother's larger family, maintain family control over the estate of the deceased, and possibly produce a male heir. For an agrarian context in which one household often controlled a parcel of land for many generations, such a custom has logic to it, as does marriage among cousins and a variety of related practices.[42] Levirate marriage preserved the memory of the dead husband, as evidenced by Deuteronomy 25:6, "so that his name may not be blotted out of Israel." Perhaps more important, the practice kept the husband's possessions within his kinship group and provided security to the vulnerable woman. Widows did not automatically marry their husband's brother, however. The potential levir (brother of the deceased) often did not want to meet this obligation. There is provision for a shaming ceremony in the Deuteronomic legislation, where the widow could publicly spit in the face of the brother, take off his sandal, and declare, "'This is what is done to the man who does not build up his brother's house'" (25:9–10).

Financial concerns often prompted the brothers of a dead man to shun this custom, if the stories of Tamar (Gen. 38) and the book of Ruth are any indication. By submitting to the practice and producing male heirs with his sister-in-law, the relative might lose the opportunity to obtain his brother's land and possessions for himself. In fulfilling this requirement, the levir also risked his

41. Ibid., 130.
42. Dvora E. Weisberg, *Levirate Marriage and the Family in Ancient Judaism* (Waltham, MA: Brandeis University Press, 2009), 34.

own landholdings and other possessions, especially if additional male heirs became part of his "new" family. In Genesis 38, Tamar's brothers-in-law do not want to perform the duty and take great efforts to avoid it (e.g., 38:8–10 and Onan's fateful decision with Tamar: "He spilled his semen on the ground whenever he went in to his brother's wife"). The extreme behavior of Onan appears to stem from his reluctance to provide Tamar with an heir, thereby jeopardizing his own inheritance (v. 9) and the possibility of obtaining his brother's holdings. Onan does not reckon any future offspring he might produce with Tamar as being his own descendant and heir.

Similarly, economic motivations seem to drive the behavior of the "next-of-kin" (Heb. *gō'ēl*) in Ruth 4, a text that most likely dates after the exile, during the Persian period. After his encounter with Ruth on the threshing floor, Boaz acknowledges that there is a closer relative than him (this unnamed next-of-kin) who has the right to the estate of Naomi's husband, Elimelech (who had no surviving sons). What follows in Ruth 4:1–11 is a legal procedure to determine the ultimate fate of Ruth but also the rights of this next-of-kin and Boaz to the property of Elimelech. When Boaz announces to the next-of-kin that whoever exercises that right to purchase Elimelech's hereditary land will also "acquire" Ruth (4:5), this unnamed fellow declines: "'I cannot redeem it for myself *without damaging my own inheritance*. Take my right of redemption yourself, for I cannot redeem it'" (v. 6, emphasis added). The Hebrew verb for "damaging" the inheritance (*šḥt*) is the same one used to describe Onan as "spilling" his semen on the ground to avoid the levirate duty (Gen. 38:9). We cannot avoid the conclusion that inheritance concerns lie at the heart of both refusals. This cautious next-of-kin might have to forfeit some of his current holdings to any future male heirs with Ruth, and he seems to want all of Elimelech's land for himself. Therefore, this unnamed fellow recuses himself from the situation. His sudden decision raises the question of why the next-of-kin initially accepts Boaz's request to take Naomi's (and by extension Elimelech's) land (vv. 3–4) if he correctly understands the custom of levirate marriage. The most plausible answer is that he assumes he has to marry not Ruth, but *Naomi*, who is past childbearing age.[43] Such a union

43. See Eryl W. Davies, "Ruth IV 5 and the Duties of the *gō'ēl*," *VT* 33 (1983): 233; Peter H. W. Lau, *Identity and Ethics in the Book of Ruth: A Social Identity Approach*, BZAW 416 (Berlin: de Gruyter, 2011), 74–80. This is the most likely interpretation since Boaz tells the unnamed fellow that Naomi is selling the parcel of land that belonged to her husband, and he does not mention Ruth (Ruth 4:2–4). The "next-of-kin" only hears about Ruth *after* he expresses initial interest in the transaction. It is also an open question whether he is married with children. If he already has offspring, a second wife would complicate his inheritance plans even further (and possibly jeopardize his current holdings if he were to have children with Ruth), even if polygyny is an acceptable practice in this scenario.

would allow the next-of-kin to claim the land without jeopardizing any of his property holdings with future heirs. When read from the perspective of economics, both of these stories (Gen. 38 and Ruth) demonstrate the complexity of inheritance issues when a man dies without male heirs and show the vulnerability of widows within that system.

These stories from Genesis and Ruth also indicate flexibility in terms of who could fulfill the responsibilities of a levir, as the husband's family seeks to preserve the "name" (= property) of the deceased. The fact that Tamar conceives with her father-in-law suggests a broader understanding of who might constitute an acceptable "kinsman." Various details in the book of Ruth indicate that Boaz and the unnamed next-of-kin represent suitable candidates for this duty, and therefore we can call this a creative application of the levirate marriage custom.[44] The discussion of the elders at the gate in Ruth 4 occurs in the precise context stipulated by Deuteronomy 25:5–10: there is exchange of a sandal to mark the significance of the event (Ruth 4:7; cf. Deut. 25:9), and the parties seek to preserve the "name" of the deceased in Israel (Ruth 4:5, 10; Deut. 25:6–7).[45] Here the use of "name" probably does not indicate the reputation of Elimelech but instead represents a technical term for the dead man's actual estate. Consequently, concern for the "name" of the deceased is about property maintenance within the same family.[46] The larger family of Boaz and the next-of-kin wants to keep the property of Elimelech, which Naomi was about to sell, and according to the customs in Ruth, relatives other than brothers could be candidates for marriage.

For purposes of this study, we must consider the extent of this practice later in the Second Temple period. Even if the book of Ruth dates from the Persian period, as the current study maintains, this is a colorful story and probably does not represent the most common experience for widows. It is impossible to know the frequency of levirate marriage in earlier times. Yet as Judeans developed their customs after the exile, as urbanization occurred for many families and Greco-Roman cultural norms spread, the occurrence and importance of the custom are even less clear. Josephus refers to levirate marriage as advantageous for families and widows, since it preserves property

44. The fact that Boaz and the "next-of-kin" can opt out of the requirement so easily might stem from the fact that they are not Elimelech's brothers.

45. The use of the sandal in the shaming ceremony of Deut. 25 is slightly different, but the mention of the custom in both scenes is too similar to be mere coincidence. Whether we call it a literal case of "levirate marriage" or a creative application of the custom is less important than the fact that the book of Ruth seems to assume the case law of Deuteronomy.

46. Raymond Westbrook, *Property and the Family in Biblical Law*, JSOTSup 113 (Sheffield: Sheffield Academic Press, 1991), 75.

within a family and benefits a vulnerable widow (*Ant.* 4.254–56). The custom also receives brief attention in the *Testaments of the Twelve Patriarchs*.[47] In the New Testament, Jesus alludes to levirate marriage in a larger discussion about resurrection (Mark 12:19–25; Matt. 22:24–30; Luke 20:28–36), making a clear acknowledgment of the legal stipulations in Deuteronomy on this topic.[48] All of these passages reflect an awareness of the levirate marriage law in the Torah, but at the same time we do not know the frequency of the practice based on a few scattered references. Widows clearly remained vulnerable within the social and economic structure of Second Temple Judea, and the statute in Deuteronomy became a reference point for determining how to proceed.

The rabbinic literature mentions the practice, and the relevant passages indicate a preference for the rights of the living relatives more than the deceased husband. Urbanization and the changing dynamics of later periods prompted many families to live in disparate regions, with sons not necessarily residing in the same joint family compounds as their father. The landholdings of kinship groups were threatened by colonial taxation and the usurpation of estates, not to mention the expansion of tenant-farming arrangements. Without stability on a single plot and a tight-knit kinship group to supervise the management of the land, levirate marriage perhaps lost some of its relevance in the later sources. Yet the Tannaitic sources still mention it as a way of securing a future for the widow and the levir. Rather than perpetuating the line of the dead brother, any offspring from this type of union were considered to be the descendants of the levir (contra Deuteronomy, Ruth, and Gen. 38), who also inherited his brother's estate. In addition, the levir could choose not to marry his recently widowed sister-in-law, and the Mishnah devotes an entire tractate to this process, known as *halitzah* (Heb. ḥălîṣâ). If he decides to marry her, "she is like his wife in every way" (*m. Yebam.* 4:4), and his marriage to the widow occurs with a variety of safeguards for both parties. Many details in this tractate (*Yebamot*) of the Mishnah address the rights of the widow, including her ability to maintain her husband's estate and also control her sexual partners if she does not go through with levirate marriage.[49] With all of these stipulations, the rabbinic literature shifts focus to the widow and any

---

47. See *T. Jud.* 10:1–6; *T. Zeb.* 3:4–5; Weisberg, *Levirate Marriage*, 38–39.

48. The question concerns whose husband a wife will be in an afterlife context after marrying seven brothers in sequence. Jesus explains that the question is moot: after death, people "neither marry nor are given in marriage, but are like angels in heaven" (Mark 12:25).

49. If the woman chooses to retain the status of "widow," she has the right to a marriage settlement from the estate of her deceased husband. See Weisberg, *Levirate Marriage*, 40–42, who also points to the restrictiveness of the rabbinic laws in the sense that only brothers of the husband can fulfill the duty of levir (contra Gen. 38 and Ruth).

surviving brothers-in-law, and thus away from the deceased husband. This discussion also acknowledges the difficult circumstances of childless widows and seeks to expand their rights and choices.

All of these sources underscore the significance of property rights, the dynamics of the outsider-insider relationship (e.g., Moabites as acceptable marriage partners), *and* the resourcefulness of widows. For example, the brave and mutually supportive actions of Ruth and Naomi (e.g., Ruth 1:16–17), along with their trickery (e.g., Ruth 3), highlight the difficult circumstances facing widows and their need to adapt. Naomi's declaration to Ruth prior to the threshing-floor scene with Boaz encapsulates both the core message of this biblical book and the fundamental difficulties facing widows: "'My daughter, *I need to seek some security for you, so that it may be well with you*'" (Ruth 3:1, emphasis added). Like Tamar's clever disguise in Genesis 38, the plans of Naomi and Ruth to surprise Boaz (3:1–4) reflect necessary ingenuity under a challenging social structure. Both Ruth and Tamar resort to trickery, and while their exploits do not necessarily represent common responses, these stories suggest that widows had to utilize creative means as they faced the twin perils of a dead spouse and possible destitution.[50]

Other sources from the Second Temple period also commend resourcefulness in widows, including the apocryphal book of Judith. This tale dates from the Hellenistic period (second century BCE), and the heroine receives praise for following the customs of widowhood, such as wearing appropriate garments, fasting the requisite amount, and maintaining "fear of God" (Jdt. 8:4–8).[51] She inherits money and property from her husband and has permission to maintain the land (8:7). Even though the story of Judith is fictional, such details could point to actual practices. Like Ruth and Naomi, Judith is extremely resourceful. When the Assyrian commander Holofernes prepares to attack the town of Bethulia, she stealthily leaves her town (after praying for the gift of "deceitful words": 9:13) and enters the opposing camp. She provides false information about the Jews in the town, tricks Holofernes into a drunken sleep, and then cuts off his head (Jdt. 10–12). The story contains more graphic images than the rural tale of Ruth, but both narratives prize courage and deceptive tactics, including sexual trickery in the service of a larger goal. In the book of Judith the economic issues are not specifically for a widow; instead, Judith's people face grave physical and economic threats, and the resourcefulness of this widow drives the narrative. We can assume that the hyperbolic stories of Ruth, Judith, and Esther provided their postexilic

---

50. Lau, *Identity and Ethics*, 74–80.

51. For background on Judith, including the date, see Carey A. Moore, *Judith*, AB 40 (Garden City, NY: Doubleday, 1985).

audiences not just with colorful tales, but also with social commentary on oppressive social structures and the bravery needed to live in them and in some cases circumvent traditional customs. The preservation of these works proves that while the androcentric perspective in passages like Ezra 9–10 represents a powerful stream of thought, the ancient record contains other voices that address more directly and sympathetically the situation of widows in the social structure and their ability to survive.

Not all widows had the same level of success as the figures in these stories, and many of them fell into a liminal state. They lost ties to their deceased husband's house, perhaps because of rejection, and they did not have surviving or welcoming relatives within their family of origin. Extant sources contain many references to the desperate circumstances of widows, and the content of these passages is often informative. For example, the offering of the widow in Luke (21:1–4) indicates the piety of this woman in giving "out of her poverty" (v. 4). Similarly, there is a passing reference in Acts to widows being shortchanged in the "daily distribution of food" (6:1). Other texts urge kindness to widows, including financial contributions, as an obligatory aspect of faithful practice (e.g., Tob. 1:8), and it seems clear that the vulnerability of widows (and orphans) in the social structure persisted into the period of Roman rule. Many widows faced a daily struggle for survival, and their lack of attachment to a secure household stands as the primary reason for such a plight.

CHILDREN

Now we turn to the status and roles for children in the Second Temple period. When considering this topic, we must admit that modern, Western assumptions do not necessarily cohere with ancient perspectives. The sources indicate that parents valued their offspring and believed in attentive child rearing, but they lived many centuries before the era of Benjamin Spock's *Baby and Child Care*, "helicopter parenting," and "free play."[52] Some historians even suggest that the identification and celebration of a distinct period known as "childhood" is a modern phenomenon. For example, Philippe Ariès has claimed that before the Enlightenment, most families viewed the period between infancy and fully productive adulthood years

---

52. Benjamin M. Spock, *The Common Sense Book of Baby and Child Care* (New York: E. P. Dutton, 1946), utilized psychoanalytic theory in his highly influential work, encouraging parents to become more attuned to their child's needs and less disciplinarian in their approach. The colloquial phrase "helicopter parent" describes the phenomenon of intense involvement such that the child's development, status, and future become the predominant preoccupation in the family.

as a transitional phase, when individuals functioned as "small-scale adults" to the best of their ability.[53] According to the proposal, families promoted physical and cognitive development in children, but only as a means of making them more suitable for work and marriage. When we apply the thesis to ancient Judah, there is a measure of support for it. The biblical texts frequently refer to children as unmarried dependents who lack necessary skills and require tutelage. Yet at the same time, we cannot oversimplify the diverse experiences of children in the ancient world, particularly with such limited evidence. Certain biblical passages recognize the pivotal importance and special nature of childhood, before the weight of experience changes youthful perspectives. The patriarchal stories in Genesis and the book of Ecclesiastes are both explicit in this regard. The scene of Ishmael "playing" (mĕṣaḥēq) with Isaac (Gen. 21:9) acknowledges the joys of a youthful spirit.[54] In addition, the book of Ecclesiastes refers to youth as a celebratory period in the life cycle (11:9–12:1).

The question of a carefree childhood is largely moot in any case: the demands of subsistence farming prohibited many offspring from leisurely pursuits. Parents needed the contributions of their children to make the household function and had considerable expectations for productiveness after the period of infancy and before adulthood.[55] Since the average life span remained so low, activities during the early years represented a significant portion of each person's lifetime. Therefore it is necessary to consider the expectations for children in agrarian households and then across the socioeconomic spectrum. Responsibilities naturally varied depending on whether the child's family engaged in farming or another trade, lived in an urban or rural setting, and/or had significant material assets. For most children, it is safe to assume that work began at an early age (see below) and that parents regarded offspring as desirable and necessary. The demands of the agrarian lifestyle and the high infant mortality rate perpetuated the desire for progeny. The famous language of Genesis 1:28, "Be fruitful and multiply, and fill the earth and subdue it," became an important mandate after the exile as the reconstituted community sought to establish a network of

53. Philippe Ariès, *Centuries of Childhood: A Social History of Family Life*, trans. Robert Baldick (New York: Alfred A. Knopf, 1962), 132–33, focused his study on the transitions from medieval Europe to the Enlightenment.

54. The name "Isaac" (yiṣḥāq) derives from the same root as the Hebrew verb for "playing" (ṣḥq). Joseph Blenkinsopp, "The Family in First Temple Israel," in Perdue et al., *Families in Ancient Israel*, 66, also points to the many depictions of children in Egyptian and Greek funerary art.

55. It is unclear when "adulthood" began for males and females during this period. For many children, heavy responsibilities and rites of passage such as marriage occurred at a very young age. See below for further discussion.

viable households with enough members to accomplish daily farming tasks, continue family lines, and stake out Judean identity in a larger imperial context. This command in Genesis related far more to survival than dominion over the earth.

The Hebrew terms for children are relevant for this type of inquiry, but they are not systematic. As with other cultural contexts, the first months marked a period of obligation for the mother and initial development for the "nursing child" (yōnēq). If the mother managed to guide her infant through the weaning process successfully, and statistics indicate a tragically high mortality rate during the early years for both mother and child, the individual would become a yeled or na'ar. The yeled designation is more of a generic term for "child," or "one who has been born." In certain postexilic texts, yeled can indicate a collective group of nonadults (Ezra 10:1; Neh. 12:43; Job 21:11). The word na'ar (feminine na'ărâ) has a variety of meanings in Biblical Hebrew. It can refer to a young person living in the house of his father, an unmarried "lad" who is dependent upon his family of origin.[56] This term can also indicate an assistant of some authority, or a junior military person.[57] There appears to be no specific age limitation on who could be a na'ar, and therefore we cannot extrapolate definitive stages of childhood from the use of this term. A similar designation, baḥûrîm, represents a collective category for "young men," and this term often appears with bĕtûlôt, one of the words for "virgins" or "young women" (e.g., Ps. 78:63). Like the other vocabulary we have mentioned, baḥûrîm and bĕtûlôt do not seem to delineate a precise age, but they do reflect a belief in youth as a phase of life. All these terms demonstrate an awareness of childhood and its distinctive features, such as greater health risks, lack of autonomy, and the need for instruction in specific skills. Yet these designations do not really indicate specific phases of development in the same manner that modern societies mark the stages of childhood. In order to pursue this question of the nature and contributions of children more fully, we should consider the range of responsibilities and possibilities.

56. Benjamin is repeatedly called a "boy" (na'ar) in the Joseph cycle (e.g., Gen. 43:8). The form na'ărâ usually designates a "girl" of marriageable age (e.g., Esth. 2:12). The na'ar term can also describe a baby (e.g., Moses in Exod. 2:6), but this is rare.

57. John MacDonald, "The Status and Role of the Na'ar in Israelite Society," JNES 35 (1976): 147–70, shows that the na'ar could be a servant in charge of other servants. In the book of Ruth "the servant [na'ar] who was in charge of the reapers" (2:5–6) has a leadership role, although the text never discusses his age. Similarly, it can function as a military term for a younger soldier (e.g., David is a na'ar when he comes on the scene in 1 Sam. 16:11; 17:33, 42, 55, 58).

Roles and Responsibilities of Male Offspring

Our inquiry into the status of children can proceed more effectively by separating them according to gender. With regard to male children, difficult conditions demanded the early attention of boys to household duties and in most cases learning their father's trade. In the agrarian context of ancient Judah, many young boys had to contribute as early as six years old and then did more demanding tasks as they entered later years.[58] Daily chores would have included crop maintenance, tending to animals, and overseeing any servants, especially if the patriarch was old or occupied with other matters.[59] Many scenarios could lead to higher expectations for early involvement: the illness or death of a parent, the father's travels in order to sell and barter for supplies, the temporary absence of the father on behalf of the state/cultus (e.g., construction of the wall in Jerusalem: Neh. 3:1–38), or his need to find suitable marriage partners for his children (a source of considerable distraction). Since olive and grape production were central to the culture, all available male offspring with the requisite physical skills would have helped with these essential tasks.[60] The vast majority of sons learned their father's work and joined in the effort to keep the household functional. Endeavors such as the manufacture of linen required intricate skills and a family effort (e.g., "the families of the guild of linen workers at Beth-ashbea" in 1 Chr. 4:21), including the regular contributions of both male and female children.[61]

The demands of the agrarian lifestyle and high infant mortality rate perpetuated the desire for male children. Parents needed multiple sons to ensure candidates for their inheritance and to have an adequate labor pool (most households could not afford outside servants). The postexilic society remained both patrilineal, with descendants traced through the father's line,

58. Carol L. Meyers, "The Family in Early Israel" in Perdue et al., *Families in Ancient Israel*, 27, describes some of these early duties for both genders: helping with food preparation, watching after smaller children, and gathering fuel.

59. Borowski, *Daily Life*, 109–26, outlines a typical day for an ancient Israelite family where the sons engage in multiple tasks, including supervisory roles. King and Stager, *Life in Biblical Israel*, 87–93, explain the demands of the agricultural year and the tools used to facilitate the work. The heavy labor demands for grain cultivation required early contributions from children.

60. King and Stager, *Life in Biblical Israel*, 95–101, discuss the many workers required for olive oil and wine production.

61. The genealogies of 1 Chr. 1–9 and the lists in Ezra–Nehemiah describe other family occupations, from pasturing to the more prestigious cultic responsibilities of certain sons. A different set of circumstances would have applied to young male slaves, since these individuals were often treated as a commodity to be utilized for their labor potential.

and patrilocal, such that women usually left their household to join the kin-ship group of their new husband. With daughters vacating the family dwelling and the ongoing need for offspring, parents had logical reasons for wanting sons to "fill the earth, and subdue it."

The extent of the preference for male children is uncertain and probably varied among families. Many of the sources reflect a much greater interest in male offspring, including the lengthy genealogies in Ezra–Nehemiah and Chronicles. In these sources, family lines continue to run through the patriarch, and the meticulous attention to sons and brothers underscores the preference for male children. Some of the later sources are also emphatic about sons. Writing in the late third/early second century BCE, Ben Sira stands out as the most passionate voice: "It is a disgrace to be the father of an undisciplined son, and the birth of a daughter is a loss" (Sir. 22:3). This author's sexism seems to represent an extreme viewpoint.[62] Other voices offer a balanced treatment. We have indicated the tangible benefits women provided to their families, and many parents undoubtedly considered female offspring to be a great blessing. For example, the favorable status of Sarah in the book of Tobit (7:16) stands in opposition to Ben Sira's negative outlook, and the women in Ruth have considerable agency. Yet we cannot deny the androcentric orientation of both Persian and Greco-Roman society and many of the extant sources. Infanticide stands out as the most tragic consequence of this androcentrism, and the practice clearly occurred in the larger Greco-Roman culture (Jewish sources forbid it). While we cannot know the frequency of this act, it is certain that male infants would have been less frequent victims than female ones.[63]

If families during this period favored male offspring, many sources insist on discipline as a necessary aspect of raising sons. Both Proverbs and Ben Sira emphasize the dangers of youthful transgressions. In the depiction of the "strange woman" in Proverbs 1–9, the married temptress (NRSV: "loose woman") preys on the immaturity of a vulnerable lad by seducing him: "For at the window of my house I looked out through my lattice, I saw among the simple ones, I observed among the youths, a young man [Heb. naʿar] without

62. See Warren C. Trenchard, *Ben Sira's View of Women: A Literary Analysis*, BJS 38 (Chico, CA: Scholar's Press, 1982); Claudia V. Camp, "Understanding a Patriarchy: Women in Second-Century Jerusalem through the Eyes of Ben Sira," in *"Women like This": New Perspectives on Jewish Women in the Greco-Roman World*, ed. Amy-Jill Levine (Atlanta: Scholars Press, 1991), 1–39.

63. Tacitus, a Roman historian, reports the Jewish opposition to infanticide (*Hist.* 5.3). In response to that practice in the Greco-Roman period, Josephus declares, "The law orders that all offspring be brought up" (*C. Ap.* 2.202). This statement is based on Exod. 21:22–23, which addresses unintentional injury to a pregnant woman. See J. Collins, "Marriage, Divorce, and Family," 140, who includes a discussion of abortion.

sense" (Prov. 7:6–7). When the strange woman beckons this callow fellow, he is no match for her "seductive speech" (7:21). The implication is that young men are susceptible to temptation, and parents/teachers must instill proper reverence before God ("fear of the LORD") and righteous behavior in the public sphere. The prologue to Proverbs states this fundamental goal quite clearly: "to teach shrewdness to the simple, knowledge and prudence to the young [na'ar]" (1:4). To accomplish the task, the sages endorse strict discipline, including the use of corporal punishment as a necessary check against waywardness (e.g., Prov. 23:13–14; cf. Sir. 22:3–6; 30:1–13).[64]

When considering the rationale for such concrete advice on character formation, productivity is a major reason. In their lengthy teachings on discipline and "fear of the LORD," the sapiential authors address financial matters, especially the need for a proper work ethic. The book of Proverbs seeks to foster good work habits among young people: "A child [Heb. bēn] who gathers in summer is prudent, but a child who sleeps in harvest brings shame" (Prov. 10:5). This saying encourages resourceful sons; it also emphasizes the need for industriousness, in whatever trade the young man might undertake. Ben Sira echoes this advice, urging his charges to develop independence: "My child, do not lead the life of a beggar; it is better to die than to beg" (Sir. 40:28). We will take up sayings on marketplace ethics in following chapters; here we notice the wisdom tradition's encouragement of resourcefulness among children, for their own development yet also for the sustainability of their household.

Most male children had to struggle under difficult conditions, while others experienced more favorable circumstances. Social status usually determined potential occupations, and sons of privilege had better opportunities, particularly the offspring of priests, scribes, and households with sizeable landholdings.[65] For families not toiling as subsistence farmers, their sons could attempt less taxing vocations, such as scribal positions or managing estates. These pursuits required social connections and sufficient collateral to acquire the requisite training. More favorable paths only became possible for a young apprentice if his parents had the resources to support him without needing his physical labor.

With regard to aspiring priests, young males born into priestly families enjoyed many advantages, including higher social status and economic security. The larger role of the priesthood in the Second Temple economy will

64. Many Second Temple sources endorse corporal punishment as a helpful measure that shapes character and prevents children from going astray (e.g., *Ahiqar* 81–82).

65. With regard to this last category, Nehemiah (as in 2:16) often refers to a class of "nobles" (ḥōrîm) who seem to have greater leverage in the society. Ben Sira also highlights the significant advantages of the wealthy (Sir. 8:2; 13:3–4).

receive attention in later chapters, but here we recognize the necessary training and benefits for priests. Many texts from this period mention a demanding process of education for inclusion into the priestly guild, including *Jubilees* (where the "sons" of Levi have a special status: 30:18) and the Dead Sea Scrolls (*Testament of Levi*).[66] Later authors (Philo, Josephus, New Testament writers) point to the synagogue as a primary locus for instruction and activity. In all of these texts, both literacy and pedigree (i.e., membership in a priestly family) are usually prerequisites for young males in this category, and this type of training required a lofty social standing. Once they completed training, priests had a great deal of influence in Second Temple society (see chaps. 3–4 below).

Extant sources also valued the contributions of scribes: male children with the resources for this type of pursuit could prosper. The Chronicler mentions scribal clans by referring to "the families also of the scribes that lived at Jabez" (1 Chr. 2:55); there is also a passage that describes King Jehoshaphat's officials as teaching in the cities of Judah (2 Chr. 17:7–9). Both references probably represent postexilic educational practices. In addition, Ben Sira beckons his young charges to come to his "house of instruction" (Heb. *bêt midraš*), presumably to receive training in literacy, the wisdom tradition, and other administrative tasks (Sir. 51:23). Whether this reference indicates official "schools" is a difficult question and depends on what one takes "house of instruction" to mean. At a minimum, certain young men could receive literacy training and exposure to various bureaucratic tasks from teachers like Ben Sira, and this probably qualifies as a school.[67] Some of these young males studied at the local level in order to develop more limited administrative competency (e.g., village copyists, contract writers), while others trained for more prestigious work, serving wealthier families and the national bureaucracy.[68] Many scribes had to learn both Hebrew and Aramaic, the lingua franca of the Persian period, and in later periods Greek became a necessary language for literate persons in Judea. Such study required time and financial resources. As Ben Sira explains, the scribal life "depends on the opportunity of leisure" (Sir. 38:24).

66. David M. Carr, *Writing on the Tablet of the Heart: Origins of Scripture and Literature* (Oxford: Oxford University Press, 2005), 204–5.

67. For similar passages with a teacher-student framework, see Isa. 50:4; Prov. 5:12–14. On the larger question of schools, see ibid., 114–73, 206–14.

68. Karel van der Toorn, *Scribal Culture and the Making of the Hebrew Bible* (Cambridge, MA: Harvard University Press, 2007), 81–96, distinguishes between village scribes/copyists who worked at the local level and those with more scholarly abilities, such as Ezra. Within this latter category, the Levitical scribes merit special attention. According to sources from this period, the Levites have cultic responsibilities and also interpret the law and teach the tradition. The Chronicler's genealogies suggest that membership in this select group is usually determined by hereditary status.

These diverse possibilities for male children reflect social stratification during the Second Temple period. In his commentary on the trades, Ben Sira asks "How can one become wise who handles the plow?" (Sir. 38:25). This is not merely the recitation of an age-old maxim: the sage's question points to inequality and classism among the more elite sectors.[69] When discussing the disparities in wealth among families in ancient Israel, Blenkinsopp observes that the heavy-handed maxims in Proverbs and Sirach are indicative of a small segment of the population. According to his reading, advice about disciplining children, treating one's slave (e.g., Sir. 33:25–27), and learning the wisdom tradition comes from a "particular social class with a very limited and sclerotic view of human relations."[70] We must qualify Blenkinsopp's assertion since many sources from this period, including Ben Sira, address a range of economic situations and speak out on behalf of the poor. Yet the larger point is valid: the biblical texts and extracanonical evidence from this period often reveal a scribal or priestly bias, removed from the daily situations of families who lacked the literacy skills and financial resources to codify their perspectives. Even when the complexities of Greek thought began to influence the elite classes, this development had little influence on the majority of boys living in Judea. The experience of most sons involved difficult labor at an early age, with the threats of disease, hunger, and the early death of their parents constantly looming over them. Their stories do not receive much attention in the various sources from this period. Most sons learned their father's trade, which usually involved arduous farming tasks with little acclaim or chance for social advancement. While their voices do not receive full representation in the extant sources from this period, these male children faced challenging experiences. They remained vulnerable to a host of dangers, including the likelihood that their perspective would not be heard or appreciated in the more powerful circles of the society (e.g., Eccl. 9:15–16).

Roles and Responsibilities of Daughters

Although the rhythms of daily life for daughters are elusive during this period, it is possible to draw tentative conclusions based on what we can find in the sources and from cross-cultural analysis. Since most families in Judah maintained an agrarian lifestyle, parents would have given their daughters certain responsibilities while at the same time placing them under constraints. During their early years, regular tasks would have resembled those of male

---

69. Most commentators note the thematic connection between Sir. 38:24–34 and the Satire on the Trades (Instruction of Duauf), a much earlier Egyptian text.

70. Blenkinsopp, "Family in First Temple Israel," 84.

siblings: helping with food preparation, other domestic chores, and the needs of smaller siblings, particularly when their parents had other pressing matters. As daughters matured, duties naturally increased, with an emphasis on domestic responsibilities.[71] Since older women in charge of meals had considerable agency in the life of the household, young females also gained expertise in such work, especially when they needed to conserve rations (e.g., during a drought or famine). Nehemiah 5:5 mentions "sons *and daughters*" being sold into debt slavery at great loss, indicating the productivity of both genders and the fact that young women engaged in work to make households function.

At the same time, daughters faced limited options, and they did not have opportunities to train for loftier professions as scribes or priests. The educational paths available to certain males in Second Temple society did not apply to females, even those young women in more elite circles. Ben Sira declares, "He who teaches his son will make his enemies envious, and will glory in him among his friends" (Sir. 30:3; cf. 2 *Bar.* 84:9; *Jub.* 7:38–39), but the sage does not mention similar training for daughters. Of the available texts from this period that emphasize father-son tutelage, none mention the teaching of girls in the same manner.[72]

During the Roman period (beginning in the first century BCE) and beyond, there is inscriptional evidence for female leadership in synagogues, and the New Testament contains references to women with prominent roles in house churches.[73] Despite the patriarchal nature of the society, such passages point to opportunities for at least some young women, including the ability to have a leadership role in cultic life. These roles would have necessitated training of some sort, though how this occurred is unclear. None of the sources advocate formal training for girls, even after Judeans adopted more elaborate patterns of education in the Hellenistic and Roman periods. Daughters undoubtedly learned sacred traditions, at the household level and in their locality. They

71. Rabbinic sources spell out specific stages of life beyond the period of nursing, with age twelve representing a milestone (e.g., *m. Nid.* 5:7). While Second Temple texts do not establish explicit timelines of this sort, it is likely that daughters had greater responsibility with age, and the point at which they left their family of origin to join their new husband's house was decisive. See Archer, *Her Price Is beyond Rubies*, 43–45.

72. The New Testament and rabbinic sources are also exclusive in that they do not mention formal training for women (Archer, *Her Price Is beyond Rubies*, 89–101), and some texts actively suppress women (e.g., 1 Tim. 2:11–14).

73. On the sparse inscriptional evidence for women having leadership roles in synagogues, dating from the first century BCE to the sixth century CE, see Bernadette J. Brooten, *Women Leaders in the Ancient Synagogue*, BJS 36 (Chico, CA: Scholars Press, 1982). In the New Testament is mention of Junia as an apostle (Rom. 16:7); Prisca, a missionary and "tentmaker" (Acts 18; Rom. 16:3–4; 1 Cor. 16:19; 2 Tim. 4:19); Phoebe, "a deacon of the church at Cenchreae" (Rom. 16:1).

would have gained exposure to their family's work and to the Torah from both parents.

Certain families might have kept their daughters in seclusion in order to protect their virginity while they developed and reached a marriageable age. The focus of the sources suggests that Hellenistic ideas about honor and shame had an influence on this practice. Some Second Temple texts point to the value of a chaste daughter, with separation from wider society as a necessary safety measure. Ben Sira provides the most anxious commentary on this topic: he urges fathers to remain vigilant with a "headstrong daughter," so that she does not make the father into a "laughingstock" among his enemies and bring shame upon the family (Sir. 42:11). His concrete advice for avoiding such a development is seclusion: "See that there is no lattice in her room, no spot that overlooks the approaches to her house" (v. 11). According to Ben Sira, such action is essential because public activity could lead to interaction not just with men, but also with married women who might influence the impressionable girl (vv. 12–13). His recommendation on this point reflects a concern with chastity within the structures of elite Judean society during the Hellenistic period.[74] Similar sentiments about protecting virgins appear in other sources from the Hellenistic period, including Tobit.[75] Philo also mentions the importance of seclusion, declaring the marketplace to be the purview of men. A woman "should not be a busybody, meddling with matters outside her household concerns, but should seek a life of seclusion" (*Spec.* 3.169). In this same passage, he speaks of an "inner door" in houses that further insulates virgins. These passages offer further validation that honor and shame played a major role in the perceived need to seclude daughters.[76]

While some modern interpreters have taken such recommendations to be indicative of widespread practice, we cannot assume that the seclusion of daughters was the norm during this period since most families could not afford that. Only a small minority of households with sufficient wealth could separate their daughters in the ways that Ben Sira, Philo, and other sources envision. Most parents did not have the resources to construct domiciles that insulated their daughter(s) in this manner, nor could they allow any offspring

74. See Halvor Moxnes, "Honor and Shame," *BTB* 23 (1993): 167–76; Satlow, *Jewish Marriage*, 102–3.

75. See, e.g., Tob. 3:14–15, where Raguel's daughter Sarah declares: "I am innocent of any defilement with a man; . . . I have not disgraced my name or the name of my father in the land of my exile." The close connection between the misdeeds by the daughter and the stain on her father's reputation is noteworthy.

76. Similar advice appears in Pseudo-Phocylides (215–16). See Archer, *Her Price Is beyond Rubies*, 111–22, who cites a variety of texts, including rabbinic literature, that address the seclusion of female offspring.

to stay idle.[77] Regulations in the Pentateuch affirm the reality of frequent interaction: the laws against various forms of incest in Leviticus 18 suggest regular association between the sexes and the need to specify appropriate boundaries during the average workday. Moreover, the close living quarters, including joint-family compounds with a common courtyard and the many households living in urban areas, work against taking Ben Sira's restrictiveness as normative for most households. The type of seclusion endorsed by more elite voices undoubtedly occurred, but this does not necessarily represent the common experience for agrarian families with limited resources, a group that made up the majority of the population.

Additional clues point to more public experiences for girls and also for young, unmarried women. Most children, especially the ones whose families worked as farmers, had to contribute their share of labor. We have discussed the anthropological studies of Goody and Boserup, who document the tendency for all household members to put in extra hours when food supplies become scarce. Survival trumps any preference for seclusion, and during the Second Temple period, many families had to spread their labor pool to work in tenant-farming situations at the behest of large estate owners. Debt slavery for sons and daughters became an unfortunate reality for many families within the stratified society (e.g., Neh. 5:5). In addition, the list of workers on the Jerusalem wall documents two daughters as helping with the reconstruction: "Next to him Shallum son of Hallohesh, ruler of half the district of Jerusalem, made repairs, he and his daughters" (Neh. 3:12). If this Shallum had no sons (or even if he did), it is noteworthy that his daughters assist with this rebuilding effort. Finally, *4QInstruction*, from the Dead Sea Scrolls corpus, includes advice aimed directly at women and does not indicate the same level of anxiety about daughters appearing in public (e.g., 4Q415 frg. 2 2.1–9). Such examples and the economic realities for many households point to the participation of most daughters in public life, despite the protestations of more elite sources like Ben Sira.[78]

---

77. It must be allowed that seclusion did not necessarily prevent daughters from working in some capacity.

78. In many biblical passages, however, daughters appear in public settings, especially in Genesis. Karla G. Shargent, "Living on the Edge: The Liminality of Daughters in Genesis to 2 Samuel," in *A Feminist Companion to Samuel and Kings*, ed. Athalya Brenner, FCB 5 (Sheffield: Sheffield Academic Press, 1994), 36, argues that most of the significant and positive occurrences for women in Scripture are in the public sphere. For example, Rebekah at the well (Gen. 24:14–28); Rachel in the same setting (29:2–12); the daughters of Midian (Exod. 2:15–17); the appearance of the daughters of Zelophedad at the "tent of meeting" (Num. 27:2). Conversely, the home is not necessarily a safe haven (e.g., the violation of David's daughter Tamar by her half-brother Amnon in 2 Sam. 13:8–22).

Nevertheless, more protective voices identify the real pitfalls of such public activity. For daughters and their families, negotiating the years prior to marriage involved significant risks, including social and economic repercussions if a reputation became tarnished. In the birth story of Jesus in Matthew, Joseph finds out about Mary's conception (without yet knowing the miraculous nature of the event) and plans to "dismiss her quietly" (Matt. 1:19). Such a detail suggests that many women and their families endured public disgrace because of questions about their chastity. Many daughters had to work, but they faced tremendous vulnerability in their daily interactions, both within and outside of their kinship groups. If a girl found herself in an illicit situation, even if the cause was forcible assault, financial hardship usually coincided with personal trauma and damage to the family reputation. Economic consequences surely do not compare with the physical and emotional toll of rape or other acts of violence, but the sources repeatedly mention financial loss as part of the reason for protecting young girls. Several legal sections of the Pentateuch lay out the financial responsibilities that accompany illicit sex, whether consensual intercourse or rape. The Covenant Code includes the phrase "bride-price [or "bridewealth"] for virgins" (Exod. 22:16–17 [15–16]); this law addresses the case of a man who engages in sexual relations with a "virgin who is not engaged to be married" (22:16 [15]). The legislation in Deuteronomy 22 expands on this issue to address a variety of scenarios, many of which involve sexual relations with an unmarried girl/virgin and the financial obligations for a man who has intercourse with her. The most basic case is Deuteronomy 22:28–29: "If a man meets a virgin who is not engaged, and seizes her and lies with her, and they are caught in the act, the man who lay with her shall give fifty shekels of silver to the young woman's father, and she shall become his wife."[79]

Such legislation suggests that public discovery of an illicit encounter, whether voluntary or involuntary, could also mean higher dowry payments or the possibility of the girl not being able to marry at all. The previous chapter (above) highlighted the decreasing importance of bridewealth payment in favor of dowry exchanges during the Second Temple. For wealthier families, a daughter's public humiliation could mean the loss of social reputation, perhaps with attendant economic consequences. Many households had few discretionary resources in the first place, and therefore a sudden spike in

79. The financial aspects of the biblical legislation on this topic are noteworthy. On the question of whether "seizes her" in this context indicates rape or consensual premarital sex, see Hugenberger, *Marriage as a Covenant*, 255–60. Another example describes restitution due to the father of the daughter, if the bridegroom in question has "slandered a virgin of Israel" by falsely questioning her chastity in order to get out of his marital commitment (Deut. 22:19).

the dowry would have presented considerable problems. If the groom or his family balked at the potential marriage because of scandal, this refusal might prevent the girl's father from building a favorable alliance with another kinship group. Ben Sira also uses heated language to describe such situations for families: "A daughter is a secret anxiety to her father, and worry over her robs him of sleep; when she is young, for fear she may not marry, or if married, for fear she may be disliked" (Sir. 42:9). Similarly, Philo addresses the issue of "virginity suits" and damaging accusations about unmarried daughters in the public square (*Spec.* 3.81–82).

Yet even if many daughters experienced lives of quiet desperation, certain voices from this period highlight solidarity and initiative among young women as they went about their public work. The book of Ruth contains the language of camaraderie among unmarried females as they perform tasks in the public arena. When first encountering Ruth, Boaz urges her to remain with the young women working in the field: "Do not go to glean in another field or leave this one, but keep close to my young women [Heb. *na'ărōtāy*]. Keep your eyes on the field that is being reaped, and follow behind them. I have ordered the young men not to bother you" (Ruth 2:8–9). Not only do these young women glean together in an open field, but a set of preestablished rules limits interaction with males. The potential risks to them are significant, as human experience and the laws in the Pentateuch suggest. Boaz's order that the men are "not to bother you" (Heb. *nog'ēk*) conveys more than lewd comments or mildly offensive behavior, but physical contact with the intent to harm or violate (cf. the wife-sister stories: Gen. 20:6; 26:11). The Greek translators of this passage read it in such a way by using the verb *haptō*, which can mean "grasp" or "take hold of." The image is therefore more violent than the NRSV translation suggests (NJPS translates with "not to molest you"). The kind of check put in place by Boaz suggests that many unmarried women had to work in the fields and could not afford a life of seclusion. In this story, they form solidarity groups, working alongside each other to avoid a compromising situation. Indeed, the entire book of Ruth celebrates female solidarity and initiative, with no absolute separation according to gender and women engaging in agrarian activities alongside men.

The Song of Songs, which follows Ruth in the Jewish canon and probably dates after the exile, also points to initiative on the part of the young female protagonist and her peers.[80] The poem serves as an affirmation of physical

---

80. On the probable postexilic date for the Song, see Roland E. Murphy, *The Song of Songs*, Hermeneia (Minneapolis: Fortress Press, 1990), 3–4. The text contains Persian loanwords, including *'appiryôn* (palanquin) in 3:9 and *pardēs* (orchard) in 4:13.

love among two unmarried persons, and the female speaker articulates passionate feelings about her "beloved" to the "daughters of Zion" and "daughters of Jerusalem," her fellow "maidens" (e.g., Song 1:3).[81] References to "the Shulammite" (e.g., 6:13 [7:1]) could imply that her skin has been affected by working as "keeper of the vineyards," a task her brothers have assigned to the young woman (1:5–6). She describes bringing the young man "into the house of my mother" (3:4; 8:2). Such references underscore the prominent role of females in the Song. The vivid celebration of romantic love represents a departure from and even a response to the prevailing androcentrism in the larger society, which one finds in books like Ezra or Ben Sira. As with most patriarchal contexts, daughters had limited mobility and opportunity during this period.[82] Yet the witnesses of Ruth and the Song, even if idealized, provide alternative voices describing what young women experienced. These sources celebrate the perseverance, expressiveness, and contributions, both social and economic, of young unmarried daughters.

Finally, when exploring the roles and responsibilities for daughters and this question of seclusion, their age at betrothal is a major consideration. Betrothal usually marked the occasion for dowry payments and the daughter's transfer to a new household, and in most cases it represented the most significant rite of passage up to this point in her life. In fact, most ancient sources pay scant attention to daughters until they reach the point of sexual maturity and marriageable age. Second Temple texts offer little information about a standard age in this regard, and we can assume variation based on local custom and the tendencies of individual households. In many instances, betrothal probably occurred at a very young age: the evidence points to fathers often arranging marriage before their daughters fully developed.[83] For example, the Talmud indicates a variety of challenges for young girls who have not yet reached full puberty when it comes to betrothal (b. Yebam. 12b, 100b; b. Ned. 35b; b. Nid. 45a).[84] Along similar lines, Josephus restricts cohabitation until a girl has menstruated three times (J.W. 2.161). Such prohibitions assume that the groom and his very young bride often lived under one roof. The

81. Murphy, Song of Songs, 84, suggests that the woman may be a country girl with a darker complexion (1:5–6). These young women are not her wedding attendants but are her onstage chorus, perhaps comprised of city dwellers.

82. The Song acknowledges this reality, as the male "sentinels" threaten the girl's ability to find her beloved (3:3). These male guards represent the power structure in the society, and the Song describes their brutality toward the girl: "Making their rounds in the city the sentinels found me; they beat me, they wounded me, they took away my mantle, those sentinels of the walls" (5:7).

83. Satlow, Jewish Marriage, 107.

84. Ibid., 309n52.

betrothal of Joseph and Mary in the New Testament is another case in point. In Matthew's version of the story, the two are engaged but living apart, and Joseph fears public reprisals against Mary when her pregnancy is discovered (Matt. 1:18–19).[85]

Practical concerns stand out as some of the more important motivations for early betrothal and marriage, primarily for the benefit of the bride's father and her new husband.[86] Early betrothal increased the number of years that a wife could contribute healthy labor to her new household, and perhaps more important, it provided a longer window for childbirth. With the high infant mortality rate and desire for male progeny, marriage at a young age often reflected this primary concern of procreation. Such a phenomenon is quite common in similar cultural contexts, as anthropological analysis has attested. In addition, fathers had to facilitate a match quickly if they wanted to ensure their daughter's security, establish a favorable kinship alliance, and attend the wedding ceremony. The prevalence of disease, difficult working conditions, and shorter life spans for both men and women necessitated early action. In many cases, the groom was older at the time of betrothal, with more developed vocational skills and life experience, but this also varied.[87]

RESPONSIBILITIES TOWARD PARENTS

While parents provided for and taught their offspring, children had to respond with obedience toward both their father *and* mother. Filial piety was a core requirement: children across the socioeconomic spectrum had to respect their parents. A saying from the end of Proverbs employs powerful imagery to make the case: "The eye that mocks a father and scorns to obey a mother will be pecked out by the ravens of the valley and eaten by the vultures" (30:17). A text from the Dead Sea Scrolls, *4QInstruction*, takes the advice even further. Speaking to a struggling audience in the second century BCE, this passage compares both parents to the Deity: "Honor your father in your poverty and your mother in your steps. For like God is to a human being, so is his father, and as the Lord is to a person, so his mother. For they are the crucible [i.e.,

85. Luke's account does not clarify whether the two of them were living together at the time. When the census occurs, the text simply states, "He went to be registered with Mary, to whom he was engaged and who was expecting a child" (Luke 2:5).

86. Negotiations usually occurred between the prospective groom and the bride's father (or another of her family members) rather than with the girl herself. See Tob. 7:9b; *Jub.* 30:3.

87. Satlow, *Jewish Marriage*, 106–9.

womb] of your origin" (4Q416 frg. 2 3.15–16; cf. Prov. 23:25).[88] One of the distinguishing features of wisdom texts from this period is that they foster respect for both parents and not just the father. Such advice is clearly in the tradition of the fifth commandment: "Honor your father and your mother, so that your days may be long in the land that the LORD your God is giving you" (Exod. 20:12; cf. Deut. 5:16). The motive clause ("so that your days may be long") demonstrates a desire to tilt youthful priorities in the right direction, to convey that the best chance for success lies in valuing one's parents and kinship group.

This command to "honor" (Heb. *kabbēd*) parents did not mean sentimental attachment, but rather concrete action for the reputation and health of one's family. Subsequent responses to the Decalogue often took the advice in this manner, as many sources point to the practical aspects of "honoring" parents. For example, children had to care for them at the end of their lives. Ben Sira offers pointed advice in this regard: "My child, help your father in his old age, and do not grieve him as long as he lives; even if his mind fails, be patient with him; because you have all your faculties do not despise him" (Sir. 3:12–13). Other sources cite the necessity of end-of-life care, including Philo, who offers an extended section on this requirement (*Decal.* 107–17). In addition to this type of support, offspring had to facilitate a proper and expeditious burial when a parent died. Archaeologists have uncovered family tombs from ancient Israel, and many biblical passages indicate the importance of a proper burial.[89] These tombs in the Second Temple period often consisted of several chambers, with bodies in long burial niches (Lat. *loculi*).[90] Quick and proper burial continued to be a major requirement down to the Roman period, and this responsibility included upkeep of the grave and certain mourning rites.[91] Such an undertaking required rapid efforts on the part of survivors.

88. On the difficult textual issues and best translation for this passage, see John Strugnell, Daniel J. Harrington, and Torleif Elvgin, *Qumran Cave 4*, vol. 24, *Sapiential Texts*, part 2, *4QInstruction (Mûsār lĕ Mēvîn): 4Q415ff.; With a Re-edition of 1Q26*, DJD 34 (Oxford: Clarendon Press, 1999), 120–21 (hereafter DJD 34).

89. The burial sites of the patriarchs and their wives in Genesis are of great importance to the biblical writers (e.g., Gen. 23:1–20 and Abraham's purchase).

90. King and Stager, *Life in Biblical Israel*, 363–72, survey the various types of burial in ancient Israel. The use of ossuaries to store bones became very common after the exile.

91. Suzanne Dixon, *The Roman Family* (Baltimore: Johns Hopkins University Press, 1992), 109, cites the importance of grown children arranging their parents' proper burial during the Roman period. Some studies have suggested that in the context of Judean culture, this type of maintenance on the part of surviving children included a belief in the afterlife. See Herbert C. Brichto, "Kin, Cult, Land, and Afterlife—A Biblical Complex," *HUCA* 44 (1973): 1–54; Elizabeth Bloch-Smith, *Judahite Burial Practices and Beliefs about the Dead*, JSOTSup 123 (Sheffield: Sheffield Academic Press, 1992).

INHERITANCE

If children had to honor their parents in concrete ways, they also inherited family landholdings and possessions through an established system. Within the kinship structure, inheritance customs served to perpetuate the family line, preserve the land of the deceased, and allow offspring the opportunity to gain collateral and a degree of stability. We have discussed the patrilineal and patrilocal nature of the society: families traced descendants through the father, and a daughter usually left her household of origin to join a new family. Legislation in the Hebrew Bible reflects such practices, as do narrative texts.

In some of the relevant passages, sons in general and the firstborn son (Heb. *běkōr*) in particular had greater claims to the property and possessions of their father. A system of *primogeniture* guided many inheritance decisions, such that the firstborn son received a larger share or even all of the inheritance. For example, the account of Abraham's marriage to Keturah in Genesis 25:1–6 and the ranking of Isaac over the patriarch's other sons (v. 5) reflect the priority claim for the firstborn.[92] Legislation in Deuteronomy 21:15–17 orders a man with two wives to give a "double portion" to "the firstborn son of the one who is disliked; . . . the right of the firstborn is his" (v. 17). This prohibition does not allow the husband to favor the offspring of the preferred wife, since he must give a larger share to his firstborn son. Yet the applicability of this case to other scenarios is far from clear: no law in the Hebrew Bible stipulates a larger, double inheritance for the firstborn son as standard procedure.[93]

As many sources attest, the composition of households varied, and the circumstances of transfer could be unclear and messy. In most cases, fathers passed their inheritance to surviving sons according to patrilineal principles (e.g., Ezek. 46:16; 2 Chr. 21:1–3). Yet extant sources do not always recount transitions of this type: we have discussed levirate marriage and the fact that widows could inherit in certain instances. Moreover, with more than one surviving son, conflict might ensue over who would inherit the property and possessions. The story of Jacob, Esau, and the birthright deals with the complex situation of parental favoritism and inheritance; the account of

92. The emphasis on God's claim to firstborn animals and human beings (e.g., Exod. 13:2) demonstrates the importance of this system in the society. See King and Stager, *Life in Biblical Israel*, 47.

93. Richard H. Hiers, "Transfer of Property by Inheritance and Bequest in Biblical Law and Tradition," *Journal of Law and Religion* 10 (1993–94): 121–55, notes that the stipulations of Num. 27 are silent on special entitlements for the firstborn. The situation of Deut. 21:15–17 treats the specific circumstances of a man with two wives who dislikes the mother of his firstborn son. This unique case does not necessarily represent normal procedure for inheritance laws, especially since the meaning of "double portion" (Heb. *pî šěnayim*) in v. 17 is unclear.

the Prodigal Son in Luke takes up the same theme (Gen. 27:1–40; cf. Luke 15:12). Uncertainty often surrounded the bestowal of land and goods, especially when the survivors did not include sons or the offspring came from a union besides patriarch and matriarch (e.g., the father coupling with a maidservant or prostitute).[94] The account of the daughters of Zelophehad (Num. 27:1–11) takes up the common situation of no male heirs. The biblical author uses the direct speech of Moses to show that such daughters have a right to their father's property (v. 7), and this passage in fact prioritizes the daughters' claims over the father's brothers or any other relatives (vv. 8–11).

With regard to specific inheritance customs in the Second Temple period, the available evidence suggests that males usually inherited the property, but not in every case. In the story of Tobit, Sarah does not receive the property of her parents when they die; her husband Tobias receives the land from his in-laws (Tob. 14:12–13), and this detail points to male inheritance. Yet alternative understandings are also at work in postexilic texts. Widows could inherit property and goods, as we find in Judith (8:7) and the Elephantine contracts, and there is an intriguing passage from Job that points to the possibility of female inheritance even when there are living sons. When Job starts a new family after his lengthy ordeal, he has seven sons and three daughters (Job 42:13). In describing the three females, the epilogist makes a startling statement: "In all the land there were no women so beautiful as Job's daughters; and their father gave them an inheritance [Heb. *naḥălâ*] along with their brothers" (42:15). The sons are still alive and able to divide Job's many possessions among themselves, but the text specifically allocates a share for the three female offspring. The narrative seems to imply that these "beautiful" daughters from a wealthy family would have no difficulties finding a spouse within a favorable kinship group, but their father gives them a portion of his holdings anyway.

There are many open questions regarding Job 42:13–15 (in all likelihood a postexilic text) and this issue of female inheritance. First of all, we cannot be sure about the identity of the mother who gives birth to these children. It is unclear whether the mother of Job's children at the end of the book is the same individual who, earlier in the narrative, encourages Job to "curse God, and die" (2:9). Job's age is another factor: if he lived 140 years (42:16), then does the statement about inheritance entail transference only upon his death? This interpretation is unlikely, because it assumes that the offspring will outlive

---

94. There are numerous cases of this phenomenon in the Hebrew Bible, beginning with Abraham, Hagar, and Ishmael (Gen. 16:1–16). Rachel and Leah give their maids to Jacob as surrogates (Gen. 30). Through this practice, the wife of the patriarch can "obtain children" of her own (16:2; 30:3). In the story of Jephthah, the legitimate sons of Gilead try to drive him away, and this suggests that he had a rightful claim to the inheritance (Judg. 11:1–2).

his very lengthy years. Or perhaps Job shares some of his holdings with them in the present, keeping only what he needs. The final possibility is that he bestows all of his holdings to them at this point in the narrative. Of these three options, the second one is most likely: the practice of a father sharing a portion of his possessions while still alive has parallels in Ezekiel 40–48 (e.g., 46:16) and in the New Testament story of the Prodigal Son (Luke 15:12).[95]

The relationship between this section of Job and actual inheritance practices during the Second Temple period is the most relevant question for the current study. Peter Machinist suggests that this narrative detail represents a deliberate effort to expand the law concerning the daughters of Zelophehad (Num. 27:1–11) and the situation of having no male offspring. If the author of Job 42:15 is seeking to convey an ideological position through this detail in the epilogue, the message is that daughters with living brothers can now inherit in the same manner as their male siblings.[96]

Later interpreters did not necessarily agree with the possibility of female inheritance, including the author of the *Testament of Job*, an apocryphal work from the first century BCE or first century CE. In reworking certain aspects from the biblical version of the epilogue, the final section of the *Testament of Job* (chaps. 46–50) highlights the three daughters. The work alters the thrust of the biblical text by pointing to the *spiritual* nature of the daughters' "inheritance."[97] Rather than bestowing earthly gifts, Job promises his

95. See Ezek. 46:16: "Thus says the Lord GOD: If the prince makes a gift to any of his sons out of his inheritance, it shall belong to his sons, it is their holding by inheritance." Hiers, "Transfer of Property," 149–50, cites the connection between the second possibility (division while Job is still alive) and the story of the Prodigal Son in Luke (15:11–32). In Ben Sira, the sage explicitly opposes any distribution before a person dies (Sir. 33:20–24). If these are merely gifts during Job's lifetime, then perhaps the bestowal does not qualify as an "inheritance" in the manner of Num. 27:1–11. See Jacob Milgrom, *Numbers*, JPS 4 (Philadelphia: Jewish Publication Society, 1990), 483. Yet the standard "inheritance" term (*naḥălâ*) does appear in Job 42:15.

96. Peter Machinist, "Job's Daughters and Their Inheritance in the *Testament of Job* and Its Biblical Congeners," in *The Echoes of Many Texts: Reflections on Jewish and Christian Traditions in Honor of Lou H. Silberman*, ed. William G. Dever and J. Edward Wright, BJS 313 (Atlanta: Scholars Press, 1997), 73. Male inheritance is still the norm in this passage, since the Hebrew phrase literally reads "in the midst of their brothers" and not "along with." In addition, the terminological similarities between Job 45:15 and Num. 27:7 are compelling (cf. Prov. 17:2). Machinist allows that there are other interpretations, such as the daughters' beauty, as a reason for their inheritance.

97. Michael C. Legaspi, "Job's Wives in the *Testament of Job*: A Note on the Synthesis of Two Traditions," *JBL* 127 (2008): 71–79, discusses the combination of narrative traditions to explain the background for Job's wife. The *Testament of Job* identifies the mother of the children in Job 42:15 with Dinah in Gen. 34. Instead of earthly property or goods, in this text the daughters inherit cords that allow them to engage in angelic singing (chaps. 46–53).

daughters an "inheritance better than that of your seven brothers" (46:5).[98] They receive "three multicolored cords that are not from earth, but from heaven" (46:8). In this way, the *Testament of Job* offers a significant reinterpretation of the epilogue to Job and certain details elsewhere in the original book (e.g., Job 38:3; 40:7). One of the primary reasons for this shift is an effort to minimize the bestowal of material possessions to Job's daughters.[99] The original epilogue makes no mention of spiritual inheritance, and we can only conclude that the author of the *Testament of Job* wanted to affirm a preference for male inheritance while not ignoring this narrative detail in the book of Job. This final section opposes female inheritance of a material nature.

While definitive conclusions on this question are impossible, the content of Numbers 27:1–11, the epilogue to Job, the *Testament of Job*, and extracanonical sources suggests that female inheritance did occur in certain cases and that it stirred controversy. Divorce or widowhood represented the most common avenues for female inheritance; the Elephantine contracts stipulate that a woman in the midst of divorce proceedings may go out of the marriage with what she brought in (e.g., Miptaḥiah in *TAD* B2.6), the dowry amount. Yet this brief reference in Job 42:15 proves that we do not know the full extent of inheritance customs or the rights of women in the Second Temple period. In a society where sons and living male relatives usually received the property and possessions of the patriarch, perhaps in certain cases female offspring had a chance at part of the total, even when they had living brothers. Such a scenario becomes even more plausible if a family had the means to divide resources more comfortably among the various offspring.

DEBT SLAVERY

Other sons and daughters had more drastic issues to face than inheritance matters: they struggled to stay with their household and avoid debt slavery. It is important to distinguish here between *chattel* slavery involving foreigners/outsiders and *debt* slavery, which entails servitude within a particular group or nationality. Several ancient laws mention the latter practice as a periodic necessity, especially among orphans and dependents of poor farmers. Earlier

---

98. Translation is from James C. Charlesworth, ed., *The Old Testament Pseudepigrapha*, 2 vols., ABRL (Doubleday: New York, 1983–85).

99. Machinist, "Job's Daughters," 75–77, shows how the *Testament of Job* is innovating the story from certain passages in the biblical book, working from the LXX of Job. The *Testament of Job* understands God's command to Job in 38:3 ("Gird up your loins like a man") to represent the moment at which Job "girded" on the cords that figure prominently in his bestowal of inheritance upon the daughters.

legal traditions in Mesopotamia allowed for the voluntary sale of one's dependents, whether offspring or a spouse, to creditors in order to buy grain.[100] Biblical legislation makes provision for Israelites to serve local masters, presumably to settle a loan, and then obtain freedom after a set period (Exod. 21:2–11; Deut. 15:12–18). Both of these laws seem to address a situation where a landholder has to force his dependents into servitude on account of insolvency.[101] In addition, one narrative text from the Elisha cycle, 2 Kings 4:1–7, describes a widow needing to sell her two boys into slavery in order to meet a loan obligation (v. 1). Elisha has to perform a miracle to alleviate the situation (vv. 2–7). This reference implies the use of debt slavery by households to escape destitution and the favorable position of the creditor. The tenuous circumstances of farming in the ancient Near East often led to a crisis: contingencies like drought, higher taxation, and widowhood forced many individuals to take desperate measures. Perhaps in certain cases a finite period of servitude for one's children made for a more pragmatic choice than permanent sale of the family plot, even with the many attendant risks.[102]

During the Second Temple period, an elaborate system of tenant farming left older sons and daughters vulnerable to debt slavery, especially if their father lost his land and owed sizeable amounts to lenders and/or the ruling power. In periods of crisis, farmers sometimes had to borrow against the yield of the next harvest, and this almost always worked to the advantage of the creditor. The details of Nehemiah 5 highlight just such a scenario: "We are having to put up our sons and daughters as surety in order to buy grain and live" (Neh. 5:2, my trans.).[103] This leads to divisions between the majority of the populace and more elite members of the Judean community: "Now our flesh is the same as that of our kindred; our children are the same as their children; and yet we are forcing our sons and daughters to be slaves, and

100. For example, there are provisions in the Code of Hammurabi for selling one's wife or children into slavery for three years in order to satisfy a debt (117–19). See Gregory C. Chirichigno, *Debt-Slavery in Israel and the Ancient Near East* (JSOTSup 141; Sheffield: JSOT Press, 1993), 61–72. The struggling Judeans in Neh. 5 face this exact same scenario (see below).

101. See ibid., 277–82. The inclusion of a "Hebrew woman" in this stipulation probably refers to debt slavery and work by either gender of a nonsexual nature. A third legal text, Lev. 25, addresses a more desperate situation, including the loss of patrimonial inheritance and the patriarch's eventual servitude. We will treat this passage from the Holiness Code and the larger question of the Jubilee Year in the next chapter.

102. Blenkinsopp, *Ezra–Nehemiah*, 256–57.

103. As many commentators have noted, Neh. 5:2 almost certainly refers to providing "surety" rather than a "multitude" of sons and daughters. This requires a slight emendation of the consonantal text, from *rbym* to *'rbym*.

some of our daughters have been ravished; we are powerless, and our fields and vineyards now belong to others" (v. 5).[104] Nehemiah's solution is total manumission and restoration of property (v. 11), a practice that reflects in certain respects the Jubilee legislation of Leviticus 25. While the precise circumstances and even the historicity of Nehemiah's benevolent act are highly uncertain, this unit from the Nehemiah Memoir accurately reflects income inequality during the Persian period, the usurpation of land and goods by imperial forces and local elites, and the apparent loss of both sons and daughters to debt slavery.

Slavery involving children continued into later periods throughout the Mediterranean, as multiple sources attest.[105] Judean involvement at the local level, especially enslavement among fellow Judeans, is more difficult to determine.[106] Yet papyrological evidence suggests that those in Judea and beyond participated in the larger economy at all levels, and poorer families in dire straits remained susceptible to debt slavery, along with orphans who did not have guardians to protect them. The Zeno archives indicate slaveholding during Ptolemaic rule of Judea (third century BCE). This material preserves correspondence regarding young slaves whom this official Zeno had bought, but they escaped to their former masters.[107] The letters indicate acceptance of slavery in the economic system of the Ptolemies and the involvement of government officials in perpetuating its effectiveness. This correspondence also shows that much younger slaves became a regular part of the system, and in some cases these youth were exported from Judea to Egypt and forced into prostitution.[108] Tragic circumstances for many children persisted into the Roman period, and there is ongoing evidence for slavery.[109] For example, the apostle Paul's Letter to Philemon discusses the fate of a slave named

104. It is unclear how the two categories "peoples of the land" and the "returned exiles" relate to the crisis of Neh. 5. The text identifies the struggling group simply as "Jewish kin" (yĕhûdîm) in Neh. 5:1, and "the nobles and the officials" are oppressing them (5:7).

105. See James A. Harrill, *The Manumission of Slaves in Early Christianity* (Tübingen: Mohr, 1995), 11–67.

106. For a list of scholars who deny enslavement among fellow Judeans during this period, see Pastor, *Land and Economy*, 242n56.

107. Tcherikover, *Hellenistic Civilization and the Jews*, 62.

108. Ibid., 69.

109. Dale B. Martin, "Slavery and the Jewish Family," in *The Jewish Family in Antiquity*, ed. Shaye J. D. Cohen, BJS 289 (Atlanta: Scholars Press, 1993), 113–29, shows that women and children continued to serve as slaves during the Hellenistic and Roman periods. Drawing from epitaphs, he observes the difficulty of adjudicating between slaves and free persons. In some cases, inscriptions from the Roman period mention the circumcision of these young slaves, which probably points to their Jewish identity.

Onesimus, and the Letter to the Ephesians advises slaves on their proper roles (chap. 5). In another New Testament example, the parable of the Unforgiving Servant, the master is able to sell his servant's wife and children in order to meet a loan obligation (Matt. 18:24–25). This story suggests that debt slavery among children continued, though the frequency of the practice is not clear. Such references demonstrate that many children faced precarious and uncertain paths to adulthood. Not just orphans but also those belonging to a struggling household often reached a point where inheritance subsided as a possibility and survival became the sole concern. As with many other cultural contexts, harsh circumstances could lead to disastrous outcomes for the most vulnerable members of a society, especially children.

SUMMARY

The preceding discussion has highlighted the vital contributions of women and children under trying conditions at the household level and beyond it. While living in a context that limited their freedom and did not usually give voice to their concerns, women and children had to exercise resourcefulness, especially those who found themselves in precarious situations (e.g., widows, orphans, those consigned to debt slavery). The hierarchical nature of the society allowed people of certain elite categories to prosper: sons training as priests or scribes and those who came from households with significant land-holdings had opportunities for prestige and economic advancement during the Second Temple period. Yet for the vast majority of women and children, daily living challenged their resolve as they sought to meet the requirements of food production and other external demands, such as taxation by the ruling power. Although the sources are largely silent on the contributions of women and children in this and other respects, by examining incidental references in sources from this period (e.g., the daughters of Shallum in Neh. 3:12), the economic aspects of works like Ruth and Tobit, extracanonical evidence such as the Elephantine contracts, and anthropological insights into agrarian economies, it becomes possible to sketch pivotal roles for women and children in daily life. For most of these individuals, daily living was difficult and monotonous. The record also suggests that women and children (esp. daughters) were quite vulnerable within the social structure, and loss of status, destitution, and even death loomed as tragic possibilities, especially among persons who lacked a secure place in a household. While the sources do not always herald their accomplishments and the roles they played in facilitating economic life, certain evidence points to their indispensable contributions at the household level and beyond.

Up to this point in our study, the bulk of the discussion has focused on the various aspects of social and economic life at the household level. While certain topics have necessitated a probe into the larger socioeconomic context, the nature of the marketplace has been a peripheral matter in the discussion. It is to this topic we now turn, with special attention to different professions and the manner in which the nascent tradition, from the laws in the Torah to the sayings of the sages, had begun to frame social and economic life. We now turn to the larger marketplace, including the topics of borrowing, lending, and bribery.

3

Work and Financial Exchanges

The current chapter will consider the range of occupations and financial exchanges. We have examined the status of women, sons, and daughters, but further attention to the larger economic landscape of the Second Temple period is necessary, insofar as one can assess this topic with limited evidence. Our inquiry will continue to highlight the agrarian context of Judah and the challenges of daily life. Many individuals had difficulty maintaining their land and livelihood, especially the poor farmers who comprised the majority of the population. Other persons, such as those connected to the imperial bureaucracy, including wealthy landholders and priests, experienced more favorable circumstances. Complex lending arrangements contributed to the tenuous nature of daily life, and this requires careful attention. We will examine the nature of transactions, including the matter of currency, interest levies, surety (i.e., vouching for the loan of another), and bribery. Both the biblical texts and extracanonical sources present a complex portrait on the acceptability of usury. In some cases, the dynamics of the system provided opportunities for the accumulation of great wealth. Our discussion will underscore the possibility for advancement through resourcefulness, a favorable position in the social structure, and in some cases fraud. Yet most individuals faced a challenging existence, particularly those with small landholdings or no property at all.

OCCUPATIONS

The Challenges of Farming

During the Second Temple period, the majority of the population continued to engage in agricultural pursuits. The available evidence does not reveal percentages in this regard, but most individuals farmed the land in some form or another. Agrarian life was not so much a choice as a way to survive, maintain family plots, and provide for one's household. In many cases, farmers worked for landlords in order to settle debts or to subsist on fields they did not own. The evidence points to an advanced agrarian economy, which involved metal tools for farming (e.g., iron plow points), the efficient harnessing of animal power, and a powerful ruling state, which in the case of Judah consisted of a succession of colonial powers.[1] All of these factors correlate with the Second Temple period, even though the arid conditions made farming a perennial challenge for those with small property holdings.

With regard to the terrain these farmers negotiated, there are three basic categories of land in the Palestinian region: rough and mountainous areas; terraced slopes that have limestone, sandstone, and clay deposits (good for olive and vineyard cultivation); and alluvial plains that provide the most fertile areas for vegetative growth.[2] Average rainfall is sparse and occurs predominantly during certain months. Much if not all of the rainfall happens from October through March (esp. December to February), and the patterns during these months can be variable.[3] There is a reference in Deuteronomy 11:14 to God giving the "early rain" [Heb. *yôreh*], presumably in October–November, and the "later rain [Heb. *malqôš*]," usually in March–April. The same basic cycle exists today. Deviations from this pattern have a huge impact on sustainability: both modern and ancient farmers have dealt with erratic rainfall in the Middle East for centuries, from exceedingly dry seasons to sudden, torrential storms that wash away recently planted seed.

The annual cycle revolved around planting and harvesting cereals, with careful attention to rainfall patterns. By studying ancient inscriptional evidence, along with recent trends, it is possible to determine the rhythm of the farming year with relative precision. The process generally began with sowing for two months (October to December), followed by a colder period. The grounds generally softened during these months, and farmers would loosen the soil with a plow and spread seed, followed by a scuffling pass (perhaps by dragging

1. This is the terminology of Gerhard E. Lenski, *Power and Privilege: A Theory of Social Stratification* (New York: McGraw-Hill, 1966; repr., Chapel Hill: University of North Carolina Press, 1984), who demonstrates common features of an advanced agrarian economy across different cultural contexts.

2. See Gildas H. Hamel, *Poverty and Charity in Roman Palestine, First Three Centuries C.E.*, University of California Near Eastern Studies 23 (Berkeley: University of California Press, 1990), 101. C. Meyers, *Rediscovering Eve*, 46, discusses the painstaking effort of maintaining terraces for farming in this region.

3. Hamel, *Poverty and Charity*, 102–3, cites studies that have charted the average rainfall over a thirty-year period in Israel.

branches) to cover the grain.[4] For a "winter" period from mid-February to mid-April, the sowing of barley (harvested in April–early May; Ruth 1:22) and legumes occurred. Flax was cut in March–April (Josh. 2:6). Such efforts provided a greater variety of food choices and insurance against poor grain yields. Wheat was harvested from May to mid-June (1 Sam. 12:17). Farmers would cut stalks of grain with sickles (Deut. 16:9), tie them into sheaves (Gen. 37:7), and bring the stalks to threshing floors. To thresh the grain, workers beat it with a flail (Judg. 6:11), let animals trample it (Deut. 25:4), or had them pull weighted wooden sledges with embedded sharp stones or metal across it (Isa. 28:27–28). Then workers winnowed the remains by tossing it into the air, letting the wind blow stalks and chaff aside as the grain dropped onto a pile (Ps. 1:4; Matt. 3:12). They put the grain into silos, barns, granaries, barrels, or large jars. The last chapter suggested that the entire household often joined in these labor-intensive efforts, including children. After the grain harvest, the summer (mid-June to mid-August) provided a time for gathering other items, and then came the harvest of olives, figs, grapes, and pomegranates at the end of the agricultural year, from mid-August to October.[5] This basic cycle existed through many centuries: earlier inscriptions had mentioned a similar rhythm for agricultural life, including the famous Gezer Calendar (tenth century BCE). The division of the agricultural year into one-month and two-month increments in the Gezer Calendar mirrors descriptions in some of the rabbinic texts and in more recent studies of the process in Israel.[6]

Farmers varied their plantings in order to prepare for contingencies such as drought, maintain acceptable levels of food intake for their household, and possibly create a surplus.[7] In terms of specific items, barley proved more durable than wheat, and beans and other vegetables could supplement a household's diet and compensate for a weak harvest in cereals. Irrigation was important during the summer months in order to produce vegetables, and this is a major reason so many households built cisterns for their gardens. Olive trees show resilience in the hilly arid climate, and many farmers cultivated them for oil production. In the ancient world, oil provided fuel for lamps, and it was often the key ingredient for perfumes, medicines, and many aspects of cultic life. Local trade and export in olive-related products occurred throughout this period, and there is archival evidence for buying and selling in contracts from

---

4. King and Stager, *Life in Biblical Israel*, 86–89.

5. Hamel, *Poverty and Charity*, 109–10, finds interesting correlations between the Mishnaic references to the agricultural cycle and the farmlands around the modern city of Kufr al-Ma', Jordan.

6. See William F. Albright, "The Gezer Calendar," *BASOR* 92 (1943): 16–26. Even if this is a schoolboy exercise, it sheds light on the rhythms of agricultural life.

7. Josephus mentions the devastating consequences of drought, such as disease and loss of morale among farmers (*Ant.* 15.300–10).

the Second Temple period.[8] The harvest season for olives usually fell between late August and late October, several months after the wheat harvest, and this staggered schedule allowed many farmers to cultivate both grains and olive trees. Some planters also devoted their efforts to grapes, though this took longer, usually several seasons for successful development of a vineyard. This process, whether on the ground or through the use of poles, required considerable effort and careful planning. The gathering of grapes happened in August and September; the discovery of winepresses throughout the region attests to the importance of vineyards for local consumption and the regional economy.[9]

With all of these different crops, it is appropriate to consider the restrictions in the Torah on mixing diverse seeds (e.g., Lev. 19:19: "You shall not sow your field with two kinds of seed"). Those adhering to this stipulation had to be cautious about overlap between different crops in the field, but the rabbinic sources suggest that creative planting and liberal interpretations of the law provided latitude as farmers diversified their efforts.[10]

Because of the difficult terrain and climate, problems such as drought and locust infestation occurred regularly, and agriculturalists had to grow as much as possible in order to remain solvent and avoid a myriad of problems. The majority tried to use every inch of arable soil for planting. Some farmers had an advantage due to their strategic location on more fertile soil with access to better irrigation.[11] In certain localities, the hilly terrain provided

8. King and Stager, *Life in Biblical Israel*, 95–98, document the production process. There are also fourth-century-BCE contracts that reflect local trade in oil, along with barley, wheat, and fruit products. Scribes recorded the quantities in registries, and the repetition of cereal and oil purchases demonstrates the importance of these items. See Bezalel Porten and Ada Yardeni, "Social, Economic, and Onomastic Issues in the Aramaic Ostraca of the Fourth Century B.C.E.," in *Judah and the Judeans in the Persian Period*, ed. Oded Lipschits, Manfred Oeming (Winona Lake, IN: Eisenbrauns, 2006), 457–88, esp. the account ledgers on 468–70, 476–78.

9. King and Stager, *Life in Biblical Israel*, 101, cite the use of wooden beam presses in the Hellenistic period and probably earlier, such that one end of the press was attached to a wall and the other weighted with rocks.

10. Hamel, *Poverty and Charity*, 115, discusses the rabbinic tractate on "Mixed Kinds" (*Kil'ayim*) and the leniency in allowing creative cultivation, such as vines trailing close to cereals. It is difficult to determine how closely this regulation on mixing crops was followed during the Second Temple period.

11. Ibid., 114–15, cites the more favorable soil of the coastal plain areas such as the Shephelah, where farmers could try to engage in intercultivation (e.g., the growing of fruit trees with cereals). In Galilee and elsewhere, terraced farming required significant labor by households, with the need to channel sufficient water from springs and wells. Poorer families often inhabited plots above valleys, where soil erosion occurred with greater frequency and terracing was more difficult. Other farmers made use of more-difficult, rocky terrain in areas like the Negev, planting olive trees and other crops in much harsher conditions.

an opportunity for "runoff farming," which involved collecting rainwater through channels and dams and funneling it into cisterns for drinking, watering animals, and irrigation.[12] Despite these safeguards, challenges could arise beyond their control (e.g., unpredictable rainfall, taxation demands), and weak yields had significant repercussions. The threat of sudden disaster left many farmers vulnerable, particularly those who lacked sufficient reserves to subsist for a lengthy period. Shortfalls, especially from drought, could lead to family strife and major financial difficulties, from starvation to the need for stopgap loans with high interest rates. Many farmers eventually had to work as tenants on land they previously owned when they encountered difficult straits. Banditry became a huge problem during crisis periods, and thieves often targeted granaries. For example, Josephus and others repeatedly cite the lawlessness that can ensue under drought conditions and other challenging circumstances.[13] Such threats point to the need for a variety of crops, especially when grain yields did not meet expectations.

As they worked through the cycles of the agricultural year, one recurrent task facing farmers was the efficient harnessing of animal power and its impact on successful cultivation. In a context where survival depended on crop yields, animals had to be durable. Some of the ancient sources reflect this need. For example, Proverbs 14:4: "Where there are no oxen, there is no grain; abundant crops come by the strength of the ox." Well-fed oxen, cows, and donkeys could work for longer periods. Yet many animals did not receive sufficient nourishment due to lack of food supplies or concerns about excessive feeding. Some Second Temple sources indicate a belief that robust animals are more difficult to handle. For example, Philo cites the possibility of stubborn livestock as a reason to avoid overfeeding (*Plant.* 32). If animals fell below their potential size and strength, this meant inefficient plowing and further repercussions.[14] Their manure provided fertilization for fields, and malnourished animals could not drop necessary nutrients in large amounts. Consequently, crop yield (and size) became smaller.

Favorable yield, including a surplus, remained the fundamental goal. Even so, it is very difficult to determine average annual produce for farmers, or even their aims. The most common statistic in the ancient sources is the ratio of crop yield to seed planting. The Mishnah and Talmud give some figures in this area, but there is variation in the citations, and in most instances the

12. Oded Borowski, *Agriculture in Iron Age Israel* (Boston: American Schools of Oriental Research, 2002), 18–19.

13. Richard A. Horsley, "Josephus and the Bandits," *JSJ* 19 (1979): 37–63; Richard A. Horsley and John S. Hanson, *Bandits, Prophets, and Messiahs: Popular Movements at the Time of Jesus* (Harrisburg, PA: Trinity Press International, 1999), 48–87.

14. Hamel, *Poverty and Charity*, 122.

statistics seem to be exaggerated.[15] Detailed figures in this regard would help us understand more clearly what constituted a productive harvest and what put a farmer in peril of major shortfall and possibly losing his land. Based on his comprehensive study of the evidence, Hamel proposes a 5:1 average ratio in terms of wheat harvested to seed that was sown during the Roman period. This estimate is much lower than many of the ancient sources indicate as the norm, but it is consistent with our knowledge of the Judean farmer's difficulty in dealing with both natural and political issues. Higher yields, especially on larger plots, enabled the farmer to sell produce; there is ample evidence of exchange and purchase of food products during this period. Aramaic ostraca from the fourth century BCE document regular exchanges of wheat, barley, and other products for consumption.[16] Yet even if some farmers had higher yields because of favorable weather or a more advantageous estate, the challenging conditions point to uncertainty and rigorous work for the majority of the population, with heavy tax burdens and quite possibly debts to a landlord (see chap. 4).

One of the primary challenges in answering such questions as crop yield is the tendency of the sources to view agricultural productivity through a theological lens. The obstacles facing farmers, including drought, weeds, famine, pests such as locusts (e.g., Joel 2), birds or other animals (Song 2:15; Mark 4:4), and political or military developments led to a close association between divine favor and a successful harvest. In response to the difficult conditions, a variety of prayers and festival observances coincided with the rhythms of the agricultural year (e.g., the Feast of Weeks/Shavuot). Many ancient Near Eastern sources note the power of deities to determine fertility (e.g., Baal as a storm god; Israel's Deity as "him who rides upon the clouds" in Ps. 68:4), and this belief continued into later periods. If something went wrong, believers often concluded that a household member(s) had sinned, thereby jeopardizing the favorable status of the entire family. Tannaitic sources contain prayers for predictable and plentiful rain cycles, and there is acknowledgment that lack of rain indicates human culpability. According to the theology, right relations with the One "who causes the wind to blow and rain to fall" (*m. Ta'an.* 1:1–2) bring nourishment for this arid climate, and the Mishnah mentions fasting as a response to the lack of rain (*m. Ta'an.* 3:1–3).[17] Another example of

15. Ibid., 125–37, demonstrates the numerous references to yield per seed in the various rabbinic passages and the inflated nature of the figures. According to his analysis, one passage in the Talmud seems to give a more realistic assessment (*b. B. Meṣi'a* 105b).

16. Porten and Yardeni, "Aramaic Ostraca," 459–61, demonstrate the volume of transactions in these records, which seem to comprise a "dossier" of purchases, with specific names in the ledger sheets, from 362–350 BCE.

17. Hamel, *Poverty and Charity*, 108.

this theological perspective is the Parable of the Sower in the New Testament (Mark 4:1–20; Matt. 13:1–23; Luke 8:4–15). Jesus declares that rocky ground, weeds, and parched conditions are facts of life for farmers, and the parable accurately captures the challenges of producing a surplus in this region. All versions of this story draw a clear connection between divine blessing and productive fields. Such references and the difficult conditions suggest that even farmers who worked diligently and prepared carefully for contingencies found major obstacles to a successful harvest, and many of them looked to God for the viability of their crops and their very survival.

The law of Sabbatical Year of "release" (Heb. šĕmîṭâ), which requires all land to lie fallow during the seventh year, also demonstrates the perceived relationship between faithfulness to God and fertile soil. Descriptions of the practice appear in the Pentateuch (Exod. 23:10–11; Lev. 25:20–22; Deut. 15:1–6) with the promise that the Deity will provide enough surplus in the sixth year to supply adequate food for three years (e.g., Deut. 15:4: "There will, however, be no one in need among you, because the LORD is sure to bless you in the land that the LORD your God is giving you"). This law clearly made an impression on early interpreters: references to the Sabbatical Year appear in various postexilic texts, including Nehemiah 10. In this passage, those who submit to "the law of God" agree that "we will forego the crops of the seventh year and the exaction of every debt" (10:31).[18] A parallel statement occurs in 1 Maccabees 6:49, which dates to the era of the Hasmoneans (first century BCE). In this account, the people of the town of Beth-Zur flee from the invading Seleucid king, Antiochus IV, "because they had no provisions there to withstand a siege, since it was a sabbatical year for the land" (cf. v. 53). Similarly, Josephus mentions the fallow year in his recounting of events, and he claims that various foreign rulers gave Judeans leniency with regard to tributes because of the break in productivity.[19] These accounts respect the authority of this tradition, but the widespread observance of the practice is unclear. There is no inscriptional evidence for it in archival sources in the manner described by Josephus and 1 Maccabees. If farmers had to set aside reserves for an entire year, such a step would have compounded their already-demanding situation of producing sufficient yield for their households. Later

18. This statement combines the restrictions on the fallow year with laws about debt slaves in Deut. 15:1–8 (cf. Exod. 21:2–6). The Sabbatical Year does not appear in the context of Neh. 5.

19. Josephus mentions lack of necessities during Antiochus's military campaigns against Jerusalem (*Ant.* 12.378). He also states that Alexander the Great and Julius Caesar did not require tributes during the Sabbatical Year (*Ant.* 11.342–43; 14.202–3). For further consideration, see Jeffrey A. Fager, *Land Tenure and the Biblical Jubilee*, JSOTSup 155 (Sheffield: JSOT Press, 1993), 35, and the discussion in the next chapter.

interpretations, from the rabbinic literature up to the present day, have also struggled with this requirement since it poses such a threat to the small farmer. Some authorities have endorsed the temporary farming of the land by non-Jews during the Sabbatical Year as an acceptable means of adhering to the original statute.[20] Jews could then consume the produce from these efforts since they had not farmed the land themselves (the law did not apply to those living in the Diaspora). Even if this restriction had more symbolic than literal importance for many farmers, the law demonstrates a close connection between sacred beliefs and a successful harvest, including an abiding understanding of the land as a gift from the creator God (see below for a discussion of the Jubilee Year legislation).

All of this background on farming indicates the tenuous nature of agrarian life. Farmers had to set aside a certain amount of crop for the next year's seed (as much as a third), use one-fourth or more to pay various taxes and tithes, and then have as little as a third of their yield for subsistence. If they lacked the necessary amounts to meet these demands, great misfortune could ensue, including land seizures by creditors or the state (e.g., Neh. 5). Land tenure arrangements became more complex as a result of the taxation requirements and the ability of wealthy, powerful interests to gain extra territory, along with the fact that colonial powers obtained a great deal of land for their own usage. For example, the Ptolemies, who ruled Judea from their Egyptian stronghold during the third century BCE, took more direct control than their predecessors, the Persians, had done. Estates and entire regions came under royal ownership as imperial authorities worked with the local aristocracy to squeeze the territories for goods and taxes.[21] Similar policies persisted under later powers (Seleucids, Romans), and these had a significant impact. Local officials and priests also expected payments and tithes, including provisions for the upkeep of the temple. As we consider the import of these requirements, especially in the next chapter, we recognize that farmers had to meet their tax and tithe obligations in a setting where mere subsistence posed a regular challenge. Our examination of agrarian life has shown that they had little margin for error, especially those living in more challenging settings like the arid land of the Negev. Farmers regularly faced the prospect of land seizures, and this is one of the primary reasons we find so many stories in the

20. The debate continues to the present day over whether the land must lie fallow or if it is permissible for non-Jews to "purchase" farming sites temporarily. See Steven Erlanger, "Israel's Top Court Backs Loophole in Farming Law," *The New York Times*, October 25, 2007.

21. See the landmark study of Martin Hengel, *Judaism and Hellenism: Studies in Their Encounter in Palestine during the Early Hellenistic Period*, trans. John Bowden (Minneapolis: Fortress Press, 1974), 1:18–23.

New Testament and other sources about lenders, debtors, and tenant farmers working on large estates.

Animal Husbandry

Pastoral activities played a complementary role in the economy, and in many cases shepherding and farming pursuits occurred within the same household. There is widespread archaeological evidence for animal husbandry and farming at the same domestic locations. Such efforts brought stability to many households and localities, and it is accurate to speak of an agropastoral economy in reference to this region.[22] A sedentary structure meant that the animals often lived close to the settlement, even sleeping on the ground floor of domiciles.[23] The hilly terrain provided opportunities for such an arrangement, and shepherds could work undeveloped areas or even cultivated fields if they had access to the property of others. The benefits of planting and herding made for a more efficient operation.

If the shepherd and farmer did not come from the same kinship group (or even if they did), the differences between these pursuits could lead to discord, as in other cultural contexts. The enmity between Cain and Abel in the Primeval History (Gen. 4:1–16) represents a vivid portrait of this mistrust, as indicated by the hostility of Cain, "a tiller of the ground," to his brother Abel, "a keeper of sheep" (v. 2). In the other direction, many of the later sources depict the shepherd as an aggressive cheat who does not respect the farmer or his land, allowing animals to graze on restricted land. In some of the rabbinic sources on this topic, shepherds have a reputation for being bandits who steal from farming households and fail to pay their taxes.[24] Their animals could also pose a threat, especially in more urban areas, where they might steal food from neighbors' homes or otherwise disrupt the daily flow of events. The accuracy of the negative characterization is difficult to assess, and we do not know the extent of tensions in the Second Temple period. Several texts point to the all-consuming nature of animal husbandry and the possibility of shepherds withdrawing from the larger society. The threat of predatory

---

22. King and Stager, *Life in Biblical Israel*, 112.

23. Schloen, *House of the Father*, 138, notes the number of dwellings where the archaeological remains indicate both agricultural and pastoral pursuits at the same location. Oded Borowski, *Every Living Thing: Daily Use of Animals in Ancient Israel* (Walnut Creek, CA: Altamira Press, 1998), 40, contrasts the sedentary arrangement with transhumant (seasonal movement but also a home base) patterns and also a completely nomadic lifestyle. There is evidence for all three lifestyles in the Palestinian region during the Second Temple period.

24. See Hamel, *Poverty and Charity*, 120.

animals required constant vigilance (e.g., 1 Sam. 17:34–35; Luke 2:8), especially if someone had a larger flock, and this made it harder for shepherds to participate fully in cultic activities (e.g., Sabbath observance, temple tithes).

With regard to the specific benefits of various animals, goats provided milk and cheese, and their hair was useful for clothing, making tents, the exterior of various containers (e.g., for liquids), and parchment. In many instances, small cattle offered essential quantities of milk for households.[25] Sheep provided wool for garments of all types (the shearing process usually occurred once a year) and also for meat. If any of these types produced more than sufficient quantities of a particular item, then the owner could sell or barter the surplus. Killing animals for food meant an end to their production, and therefore meat eating did not occur on a regular basis among many households, at least until the beast had lost its usefulness in other areas.[26] There is clear evidence for horses in the region, but these larger animals were more expensive to maintain and often fulfilled military roles, as suggested by references to chariotry in the Hebrew Bible and elsewhere (e.g., Job 39:19–25). Oxen often pulled the plows, frequently in teams of two, and farmers made great use of their endurance (e.g., Deut. 22:4). Their power proved to be an indispensable asset on most farms. With regard to transportation, caravans had long existed in the region as a means of carrying spices and other essential goods across great distances. Such efforts regularly involved donkeys, mules, and camels, enabling more efficient distribution of goods by merchants.[27] All of these animals have continued to play a vital role in Middle Eastern economies to the present day.

Other Occupations

With regard to other pursuits, the archaeological record and literary texts point to pottery making as an essential and demanding task. Some persons clearly specialized in this work, as evidenced by the discovery of local pieces throughout the region and the references in extant sources. For example, 1 Chronicles 4:22–23 mentions a family of male potters, and we have argued that women frequently played a role in this process, especially if a larger kinship group engaged in such work. In his satire on the trades, Ben Sira points to the tedious nature of the process and the need to produce items in bulk: "So it

25. Borowski, *Every Living Thing*, 55–56, catalogs the various dairy products used by the ancient Israelites, including yogurt, butter, and cheese items.

26. Pastor, *Land and Economy*, 5, argues that grain made up at least 50 percent of the diet during this period.

27. King and Stager, *Life in Biblical Israel*, 118–19, discuss the significance of these caravans.

is with the potter sitting at his work and turning the wheel with his feet; he is always deeply concerned over his products, and he produces them in quantity" (Sir. 38:29). This passage is instructive in two respects: it demonstrates the patronizing perspective of a scribal voice and the fact that potters had to work diligently and effectively in order to meet the needs of the populace. Part of the constant demand stemmed from purity laws, since priestly tradition held that impure vessels had to be broken (e.g., Lev. 11:33).[28] According to many archaeologists, one of the reasons so many stone (and dung) vessels date from the Second Temple period is because many Judeans believed that clay-fired objects were impure.[29] Some of the vessels from the Roman period have a neat hole in them, and this could indicate an intentional puncture to identify an impure item and render it unusable.[30] The rapid discarding of such pieces would have intensified the demand upon potters; in any case many clay items were easily breakable. In addition, the existence of joint family compounds and the proliferation of sectarian groups during this period also necessitated an array of pieces, and there is clear evidence of common dining within adjacent houses, including sects that lived together in one locale (e.g., the pottery at Qumran). All of these factors point to the importance of the potter's work in Second Temple culture, especially as the population expanded. Potters had to produce a variety of items and conduct their work quickly.[31]

Most clay items had a utilitarian purpose, and there are a number of common features among each of the various types. Archaeologists have discovered containers, including bowls of all sizes, cooking pots, hole-mouth jars, flasks, jugs, and other items, including vessels for sacred observances.[32] Potters also constructed lamps of closed and open types, and by the first century BCE, wheel-made lamps had become popular in the region. The number of similar lamps reflects a goal of uniformity, though archaeologists often disagree over whether production occurred within the region or outside of it. Some items originated in locations like Phoenicia and Cyprus, but the construction

28. Later interpreters took this regulation to break impure vessels quite seriously, as we find references to it in the *Temple Scroll* (11QTemple 50.17–19) and in the Mishnah (*m. Kelim* 2:1). See Jodi Magness, *Stone and Dung, Oil and Spit: Jewish Daily Life in the Time of Jesus* (Grand Rapids: Eerdmans, 2011), 58–61, who argues that many Judeans tightened their observance of purity laws during the Roman period with regard to acceptable vessels.

29. The number of baths (Heb. *miqvāʾôt*) that date from this period, for purifying various items and for ritual immersion by individuals, also attests to the increasing emphasis on purity.

30. Magness, *Stone and Dung*, 58–59; Meir Ben-Dov, *In the Shadow of the Temple: The Discovery of Ancient Jerusalem* (New York: Harper & Row, 1985), 156–57.

31. Borowski, *Daily Life*, 30–31.

32. For an overview, see Stern, *Material Culture*; cf. Magness, *Stone and Dung*, 54–76.

of many basic pieces occurred at the local level. Local potters often modeled their efforts on foreign types, such as Phoenician jugs and Greek bowls and flasks.[33] These efforts did not necessarily match the prototype in terms of quality and decoration, and many potters had to produce items quickly, without much regard for aesthetics. For most pieces, decorative touches and elaborate aspects mattered less than the rapidity of production.

Yet certain items catered to the small minority that comprised the elite classes. Elaborate wares, especially from the Greek and Roman periods, belonged to wealthier households. Some of these items have intricate paintings on the sides and probably functioned as "fine china" for the wealthy. Certain jars, bowls, and sacred vessels have more ornamentation than the majority of items.[34] Traders brought these pieces into the region in order to make a profit, though some production of luxury items happened in Jerusalem and other locations. Moreover, amphorae (large jars for transporting wine and other goods) that date from the third and second centuries BCE are another example of more affluent Judeans obtaining items that did not necessarily reach the rest of the population.[35] The overall findings, including the presence of Roman mural paintings, bathhouses, and other elements of the larger Mediterranean culture, point to an influential wealthy class with disposable income and a willingness to adopt foreign cultural practices. The presence of fine pottery at a particular site is one way of verifying the elite status of a household and the disparities in wealth across the larger population.[36]

To facilitate the transport of these and other goods, traders and merchants became important figures in the social landscape, despite the smaller, agropastoral economy. When considering the importance of this profession and the volume of activity, Josephus states that trade did not occur on a grand scale, due to the location of many Judean cities far from the coast and the focus on internal production (*C. Ap.* 1.60). With so few internal trading centers, the flow of goods remained minimal, according to Josephus, who characterizes the merchants controlling the sea lanes, such as the Phoenicians, with a degree of condescension.[37] He lauds the insularity of Judeans and their

33. Stern, *Material Culture*, 232.

34. Magness, *Stone and Dung*, 56.

35. Ibid., 55, describes amphorae found near Jerusalem and in greater number from the Upper Galilee region. These items often have stamps that reflect an origin in Rhodes. Archaeologists have discovered fine wares elsewhere in the region (e.g., Sepphoris).

36. Eric M. Meyers and Mark A. Chancey, *Alexander to Constantine: Archaeology of the Land of the Bible*, AYBRL 3 (New Haven: Yale University Press, 2012), 4–7.

37. Judeans did not always control the nearby Mediterranean sea lanes. Roman dominance of key cities such as Joppa and the buildup of Caesarea (Josephus, *Ant.* 15.333–34) led to greater opportunities for the colonial power but more restrictive possibilities for local traders.

interest in educating themselves according to a separate legal code and way of life. This statement on trade seems to convey a degree of accuracy, especially when one considers the geography of the region. Yet the existence of pottery from other areas and the interests of a succession of colonial powers in utilizing the resources of their territories suggest that commerce occurred with greater frequency than Josephus allows.[38] We mentioned the presence of foreign pottery at certain sites, especially in the dwellings of wealthier households. Traders also imported linen (e.g., Ezek. 27:7) and other items, such as spices for the temple cult. In addition, without the natural resources and capability to produce metals other than copper, officials also had to garner items for military, agricultural, and construction needs. Material for large structures like the temple, elaborate private dwellings, and other building projects (e.g., the wall around Jerusalem) created the need for nonagricultural specialists (stone masons, carpenters). These workers often used metals and goods not intrinsic to the region.

With regard to exports, there is evidence of balsam, date, oil, and wine shipments to other localities, in addition to the movement of these goods along local trading networks.[39] The plentiful supply of olive trees in the region and the discovery of oil presses for the manufacture of various items point to both regional and international trade, especially when one considers the significance of oil-based products in the diet and culture. Similarly, the discovery of winepresses at multiple sites and the references to cultivation of grapes imply commercial activity. If individuals wished to obtain necessary goods, staples of the region such as oil and wine offered the best mechanism for achieving this goal. Within this context, Judean merchants had to work with foreigners as intermediaries, as evidenced by the references in Nehemiah 13:16 to Tyrian traders and the prophet Ezekiel's lengthy oracle against Tyre in chapter 27. This latter unit reflects a familiarity with trading lanes and highlights a variety of middlemen who facilitated the exporting of the few natural resources that merchants and officials could ship in exchange for other goods. Caravans continued into the Second Temple period, as did maritime trade along the Mediterranean. The sea routes and the north-south axis leading into Mesopotamia also persisted, and those involved in transporting and selling commodities stood to make a profit.

38. See Fabian E. Udoh, "Economics in Palestine," *DEJ* 559, who casts doubt on the veracity of Josephus's statement.

39. Among the Roman sources for references to balsam, see Pliny the Elder (*Nat.* 12.11) and Tacitus (*Hist.* 5.6). See Udoh, "Economics in Palestine," 560; cf. Peter Garnsey, Keith Hopkins, and Charles R. Whittaker, eds., *Trade in the Ancient Economy* (Berkeley: University of California Press, 1983).

Unfortunately, a full portrait of merchants and traders and the volume they facilitated is not available. Although commerce occurred with regularity during this period, especially as colonial powers sought to maintain reliable networks and caravans, specific archival records to document exchanges are for the most part lacking. There is no quantitative data for imports and exports that would illuminate larger patterns and beliefs about trade. Information at individual sites is also frequently lacking. To take a specific example, the coastal city of Caesarea functioned as a commercial center (the Ptolemaic official Zeno visited in 259 BCE), but we do not know the level of local involvement in trading activities at this location, before or after the rebuilding of the city by Herod the Great in the first century BCE. The use of literary and archaeological evidence, along with theoretical models, is necessary for this line of inquiry, but it is impossible to gain a thorough understanding of trading patterns based on extant records.

It is probable that the localized, agrarian focus of most households meant a real limit to trading possibilities. Some scholars have even argued that during the relative stability of Roman rule, commerce on a massive scale did not occur: the economy remained underdeveloped, and local agriculture, animal husbandry, and pottery production met most of the needs.[40] In addition, economic historians and theorists have cautioned against assuming an ambitious mind-set in premarket societies like Second Temple Judea. Most individuals did not function within a capitalist framework of profit-seeking, but rather the majority of exchanges worked to retain existing hierarchies and foster solidarity among groups conducting a transaction (see below). While many merchants undoubtedly sought to transport and sell goods as quickly and efficiently as possible, the demand for a diverse set of products remained quite low during this period, aside from the purchasing power of a small cadre of elite property owners and officials. Even within this category, many of these individuals had vast tracts of land and wanted to maintain the status quo. They depended on humans and animals for their well-being, as opposed to the flow of commerce.[41] Such factors should not lead one to discount the impact of trade in the Second Temple period, but the lack of evidence and the agropastoral economy suggest caution when it comes to sweeping conclusions or the assumption of a dynamic marketplace on an industrial scale.

When considering trading activity, it is instructive to consult the available sources on the status of the profession. The portrait is ambivalent on

40. See the influential study of Peter Garnsey and Richard C. Saller, *The Roman Empire: Economy, Society, and Culture* (Berkeley: University of California Press, 1987), 43–63.

41. Ibid., 52.

this point. Some of the biblical texts indicate concern about a trader's ability to maintain faithfulness both to the commandments and his demanding profession. Two postexilic texts use the designation "Canaanite" as the term for "tradesperson/merchant" (Prov. 31:24; Zech. 11:7, 11 LXX; 14:21). This usage reflects a long-standing association of the Phoenicians with maritime commerce, especially those in the city of Tyre, but it can also have a derogatory connotation for persons engaging in this work. In similar fashion, Nehemiah describes the activities of these coastal traders: "Tyrians also, who lived in the city, brought in fish and all kinds of merchandise and sold them on the sabbath to the people of Judah, and in Jerusalem" (Neh. 13:16). Such a blatant violation of Sabbath rules is unacceptable and a bad influence. This statement in Nehemiah distinguishes devout believers from traders.[42] Similarly, Ben Sira views the exchange of goods with a highly suspicious eye: "A merchant can hardly keep from wrongdoing, nor is a tradesman innocent of sin. Many have committed sin for gain, and those who seek to get rich will avert their eyes. . . . As a stake is driven firmly into a fissure between stones, so sin is wedged in between selling and buying" (Sir. 26:29–27:2). With such references, perceptions about commercial activity and the threat it poses to pious living ("fear of the LORD") become more apparent, and Ben Sira's statements indicate both his allegiance to the Torah and his witnessing of dishonest exchanges in the marketplace.

If the tasks of a merchant receive mixed reviews in Second Temple sources, the vocation of the scribe has a much more favorable status. As previously discussed, male children with the resources for training in this area could prosper.[43] Different levels of opportunity existed within this vocation: some aspiring scribes studied at the local level to develop administrative competency (e.g., village copyists). When scribes became proficient in administrative tasks, their chance for success increased greatly. Since most of the population could not read, the ability of the local scribe to broker deals gave him power in the social structure and an indispensable role in the economy. Some persons in this category trained for more prestigious work: serving the national bureaucracy, working with and for wealthy individuals, and cataloguing important works.[44] During the Persian period, Levites and other scribes

---

42. The cleansing of the temple in the Gospels (Mark 11:11, 15–19; Matt. 21:12–17; Luke 19:45–48; John 2:13–17) reflects this same tension between adherence to the Torah and commercial transactions.

43. Ben Sira mentions acquisition of silver and gold as a benefit of scribal training (Sir. 51:28).

44. Van der Toorn, *Scribal Culture*, 81–96, distinguishes between "scribes" (Heb. *sōpĕrîm*) and "sages" (Heb. *ḥăkāmîm*) or "scholars." The Talmud regularly uses the "scribe" designation to indicate copyists and those who taught basic subjects. "Sages,"

played a pivotal role in identifying a corpus of sacred texts and preserving it through careful reproduction. It is significant that Ezra refers to himself as a "scribe skilled in the law of Moses" (7:6). This station indicates his education, desirable social location, and his allegiance to an authoritative tradition that he calls the "law of Moses." The task of preserving (and in many instances shaping) these sacred sources fell in large measure to the scribes.[45] They could unlock the mysteries of the tradition (e.g., Dan. 9:2) and foster "the reading of the Law and the Prophets and the other books of our ancestors" (Sirach prologue). Part of this favorable portrait stems from the scribe's ability to laud his own profession, but it also relates to their advantageous place in the social structure and their essential role in cataloging authoritative traditions.

Possibilities for the scribal class expanded during the Hellenistic period as persons of privilege gained further exposure to Greek culture. Such education occurred most frequently in Diaspora settings like Alexandria but also within Judea. Ben Sira offers his charges favorable opportunities: unlike other occupations, the scribe has the potential to "attain eminence in the public assembly" and "expound discipline or judgment" (Sir. 38:33).[46] For Ben Sira and other scribal sages of the Hellenistic period, instruction usually involved a conflation of Torah teaching (Sir. 24:23), exposure to Greek philosophy (39:1–3), and the ability to facilitate more mundane matters like contracts. The increasing reliance on papyri for record keeping necessitated cohorts of scribes throughout the region.[47] Young males with the time and resources to pursue this vocation developed a better sense of their larger cultural context, including the economic landscape, and this benefited them both politically and financially.

For those who reached an even higher level of exposure to rhetoric and other aspects of Hellenistic culture, including athletics, membership in an elite gymnasium became a possibility. According to 2 Maccabees 4:7–17, the

---

however, are "scholars of Scripture." The distinction is not so neat in Second Temple nomenclature: a "scribe" can have a variety of administrative responsibilities but also more lofty tasks. There is also the category of Levites, a group that becomes responsible for the transmission of much tradition and administrative matters in cultic life.

45. Ibid., 106.

46. Contrary to certain arguments about Ben Sira, this instruction is not the work of a priest. While he clearly has great reverence for the priesthood (Sir. 7:29–31) and the office of high priest (e.g., the praise of Simon in 50:1–24), this text correlates with the long-standing milieu of the ancient Near Eastern wisdom tradition. See Samuel L. Adams, *Wisdom in Transition: Act and Consequence in Second Temple Instructions*, JSJSup 125 (Leiden: E. J. Brill, 2008), 161–62.

47. Carr, *Writing on the Tablet of the Heart*, 187, cites the importance of literacy during the Ptolemaic period. Those who could not read simple contracts or other documents were vulnerable to fraud.

high priest Jason introduced dramatic changes after purchasing his office, such as establishing an *ephēbeia* (training institute for adolescent males) and a gymnasium in Jerusalem (ca. 175 BCE; cf. 1 Macc. 1:14–15).[48] These *gymnasia* served as centers for athletic training plus political and cultural education; they also functioned as status markers in cities like Alexandria and then later in Jerusalem. Those who chose to assimilate to Greek culture through their involvement in this most Hellenistic of institutions often made connections and became more familiar with influential customs and powerful benefactors. Their affiliation with a gymnasium provided an important arena for social advancement, even a chance to attain citizenship in the Greek *polis* of Antioch (the Seleucid capital). Greek cultural norms challenged longstanding customs, with practices (e.g., a lack of clothing during sporting events) that did not cohere with ideas concerning Israel's God (2 Macc. 4:12–14).[49] Many Jews did not support the assimilation of young men into this cultural world, and such matters became a source of great controversy between those who developed an affinity for the larger culture and those who felt that the new ideas represented a betrayal of laws and principles in the Torah (Jason is called "ungodly and no true high priest" in 2 Macc. 4:13). Young men with connections *and* the willingness to test the limits of their tradition participated. Persons who assimilated stood to gain both social and economic benefits from benefactors even as they pressed beyond certain long-standing norms of their Jewish tradition.

With no monarchy after the exile, the priesthood also achieved even greater prominence during the Second Temple period. Those who belonged to this profession generally enjoyed a respectable social status and leadership roles within the postexilic political structure. The lists of priestly families in Ezra–Nehemiah demonstrate the hereditary nature of the profession and the elite position of those who filled cultic offices. Both of these texts mention prominent priestly and Levitical families among the thousands coming back to Judah (Ezra 2:36–40; Neh. 7:39–43). Even if the authors embellish the numbers here, the multitude of priestly genealogies in Second Temple texts highlights the importance of these descendants for the postexilic community. The Levites in particular gained in status: the books of 1 and 2 Chronicles give special prominence to this group (e.g., 1 Chr. 23:3–5), though the Levites are subservient to the Aaronide priests, the cultic officials thought to be

---

48. The *ephēbeia* represented an educational effort to train young men roughly between the ages of 18 to 20 in a variety of disciplines that were Hellenistic in orientation.

49. J. Collins, *Jewish Wisdom*, 148–53. For a summary of Jason's hellenizing reforms, see the recent study by Anathea E. Portier-Young, *Apocalypse against Empire: Theologies of Resistance in Early Judaism* (Grand Rapids: Eerdmans, 2011), 93–103.

descendants of Aaron (e.g., Neh. 10:38; 12:47). Those who held the priestly office interpreted the law and oversaw official sacrifices (e.g., Sir. 50:12–16). The high priest also became a major figure, particularly as the postexilic community developed a hierarchical temple bureaucracy with obligatory donations to cultic officials (e.g., Mal. 3:8–10; Sir. 7:29–31).[50] With an array of powers, the priestly office had a major impact on economic life. The role of the priesthood in terms of larger economic and social dynamics will receive significant attention in the next chapter.

This survey of occupations has highlighted the agrarian economy and the difficult conditions for the majority of the population. Most farmers could only hope for moderate yields above the subsistence level, and this created an anxious cycle, especially for those who owned plots or worked fields in challenging areas. We have also pointed to the more literate vocations, such as the scribe and the priest, where the potential for a stable career among the elite sectors of society became possible. In addition, many merchants made a favorable living during this period; but the assumption of Judah as a hub of trading activity does not square with its more likely status as a minor province and a source of few natural resources. Yet in order to understand more about exchanges, it is necessary to consider the financial system and the nature of transactions during this period. Such an inquiry will underscore the vast disparities in wealth and the rapidity with which a person and his household could fall into desperate straits, with loss of land and total destitution as real possibilities.

FINANCIAL EXCHANGES

When discussing financial exchanges, we must first acknowledge that most individuals did not engage in complex purchasing. They knew only the insular world of their household and its immediate surroundings. The patrilocal system meant limited interactions and in many instances self-sufficiency, with no real possibility or need for a more complex market. In fact, we should be careful about assuming a capitalist mentality as the operative dynamic in exchanges, with persons always seeking to maximize profit. The economic historian Karl Polanyi has noted that for many communities in precapitalist societies, including those in the ancient Near East, stability within the kinship group and/or village mattered more than the acquisition of material goods or

50. On the significance of the high priesthood and the potential for wealthy families to profit, especially in the Hellenistic period, see James C. VanderKam, *From Joshua to Caiaphas: High Priests after the Exile* (Minneapolis: Fortress Press, 2004).

money.[51] A person might render a service or send goods to another as a means of preserving his social status and retaining existing hierarchies, and such a transaction could happen without expectation of monetary payment. Polanyi calls such acts examples of "reciprocity." Along similar lines and referring to this period, Seth Schwartz argues that "societies are bound together by densely overlapping networks of relationships of personal dependency constituted and sustained by reciprocal exchange."[52] Rather than assuming that profit seeking is always the motivating factor for transactions, one can look to other reasons, especially the maintenance of existing family relationships and control over one's property.[53] Consequently, caution is in order when using terms like "market exchange" in reference to the ancient Near East. Many individuals had no framework for profit gains, since they produced what they needed for survival and the maintenance of their household and its network. Polanyi's discussion provides some helpful insight, though he understates some of the economic forces at work in the ancient world, and these will receive attention in the rest of this chapter.[54]

We have discussed the storage capacity of dwellings in the region and the ability of many households/communities to maintain self-sufficiency. Most households had to structure their lives with the goal of survival.[55] Within such a challenging context, bartering offered the most practical means of acquiring essential goods. For example, when someone required tools in preparation for the next wave of planting or harvesting, he could trade supplies or offer present (or future) yield in exchange for certain items. The oracle against Tyre in Ezekiel 27 describes numerous exchanges between groups, including precious

51. Karl Polanyi, *The Great Transformation: The Political and Economic Origins of Our Time* (Boston: Beacon Press, 1944; repr., 2001), 46.

52. Seth Schwartz, *Were the Jews a Mediterranean Society? Reciprocity and Solidarity in Ancient Judaism* (Princeton: Princeton University Press, 2010), 14–15, contrasts reciprocity with "corporate solidarity," where there is a greater value on "shared ideals (piety, wisdom) or myths (for example, about common descent)." The Torah reflects the latter framework.

53. Polanyi maintained that students of ancient economies should not immediately adapt the perspective of Adam Smith, who had argued that self-interest dictates individual decisions in the marketplace, in *An Inquiry into the Nature and Causes of the Wealth of Nations* (London: Strahan and Cadell, 1776; repr., Oxford: Clarendon Press, 1976), 1.2. According to Polanyi, individuals sought to preserve relationship norms (father and son, master and slave, etc.), and this stability mattered more than profit.

54. Polanyi's suggestions have generated both praise and critical response. Formalist responses have criticized his underestimation of the innate human desire to maximize all facets of one life and his tendency to overlook or understate the market forces at work in the ancient Near East. For a review, see Roger S. Nam, *Portrayals of Economic Exchange in the Book of Kings* (Leiden: E. J. Brill, 2012).

55. King and Stager, *Life in Biblical Israel*, 192.

metals for various luxury goods. The prophet catalogs familiar trade routes and mechanisms for bartering through the network of Mediterranean ports. More mundane examples occurred at the local level as households and communities acquired various items through simple exchange in order to conduct a transaction. The remains at Qumran are a helpful example. Due to the limited number of coins found at the site and the paucity of contractual evidence to indicate larger transactions, we can assume frequent bartering for those who lived at Qumran and traveled the route south of Jericho. The remains at the site reflect an emphasis on self-sufficiency rather than profit seeking.[56]

Yet the desire for monetary gain and social advancement also played a role in the society, and a system of weights and measures provided uniformity for financial exchanges. Even if many exchanges involved bartering, metal weights created a standard for other transactions. The Hebrew word for "silver" is the same term for "money," and there are many references in the Hebrew Bible to the weighing of "silver" and other metals in order to settle a deal. Archaeological discoveries in the Palestinian region attest to the importance of such measurements. Weight balances (Heb. *mō'zĕnāyim*) have been found, and these determined the amount present for a transaction according to a relatively uniform system. Ingots (metal bars) effectively served as currency, and the metal cast of these pieces made them useful for storage and shipping. Additional metal items, such as jewelry and other ornaments, could function as tender, along with limestone or flint pieces with markings.[57] Among the various weight measurements were the talent (Heb. *kikkār*: Exod. 25:39), the mina (*maneh*: Ezek. 45:12), the shekel (also becomes a coin), the *beqa'* (Gen. 24:22), the *pîm* (1 Sam. 13:21), and the *gērâ* (Ezek. 45:12). The smaller measures were valued against the larger ones (e.g., a *gērâ* is equal to one-twentieth of a shekel).[58] The biblical texts and inscriptional evidence indicate that transactions often occurred in a specific section(s) of town, with references to "the gate" as a center of exchange.[59] Corruption posed a threat within this system, and the Wisdom literature protests the manipulation of weights in the pursuit of dishonest gain (e.g., Prov. 20:23: "Differing weights are an abomination to

56. See Catherine M. Murphy, *Wealth in the Dead Sea Scrolls and in the Qumran Community*, STDJ 40 (Leiden: E. J. Brill, 2002), 359. Facilities for pottery production, grain and date storage silos, and other basic amenities at the Qumran site point to *relative* self-sufficiency.

57. See King and Stager, *Life in Biblical Israel*, 195–97, for Babylonian and Egyptian systems as well as evidence of weight balances in Israelite cities like Ashkelon.

58. The influence of the Egyptian system is apparent with these weights, since many of them contain hieratic markings.

59. The gate functioned as a place for business transactions, in some cases unfair ones: "Do not rob the poor because they are poor, or crush the afflicted at the gate" (Prov. 22:22). Larger urban areas had more than one business center (e.g., Jer. 37:21).

the LORD, and false scales are not good"). Adherence to weight measures persisted into the Persian period, and there is evidence for a relatively uniform
system that stretched from Egypt to Babylon.[60]

This system of weights led to the usage of coinage as tender, often with
the depictions of decorative emblems or rulers on the surface. The use of
such coins increased in Judah after the exile, coinciding with the growth of
the economy and the expansion of trade and financial exchanges by imperial authorities and local officials/entrepreneurs.[61] A silver-based currency
became increasingly important as merchants established themselves along
trade routes. The evidence from the Persian period is slender, but there is
clear attestation of silver-based exchanges and coinage.[62] Greek (including
Cypriot), Egyptian, and Phoenician coins circulated in the region, attesting
to commercial interchange and the use of coins to make purchases. The con-
centration of coins along the coast is not surprising, since shipments occurred
with greater regularity in this area. With regard to indigenous coins, some
have a "YHD" stamp on them (in paleo-Hebrew or Aramaic), perhaps to indicate the Yehud province or the capital of Jerusalem ("city of Judah").[63] Most
archaeologists agree that minting occurred in Jerusalem, along with other
cities (Gaza, Ashdod, Ashkelon), probably with the endorsement of Persian
authorities. While comprehensive details are not available, currency models
existed according to Persian, Phoenician, Greek (Athenian), and Roman systems. All of these had a base silver (or gold) standard in grams, and smaller
currencies (drachms, shekels, etc.) derived from the weight standard.[64]

The use of coins became more frequent as the economy developed, especially under the Ptolemaic, Seleucid, and Hasmonean rulers. Hasmonean
coins (second–first century BCE) have depictions of various emblems and

60. Stern, *Assyrian, Babylonian, and Persian Periods*, 572–75, explains the system: 1
karash = 10 *sheqels*; 1 *sheqel* = 4 r (thus 1 r [rb'] is one-fourth of a *sheqel*); 1 r = 10 *hallurin*.
Yet there are also references to the mina (*maneh*) in inscriptions.

61. E. Meyers and Chancey, *Alexander to Constantine*, 3–50.

62. A papyrus from the Wadi Daliyeh mentions a slave transaction in exchange
for silver, and reference to weighted silver appears in one of the Arad ostraca (41).
Archaeologists also uncovered a collection of coins in Samaria. See Stern, *Material
Culture*, 215; idem, *Assyrian, Babylonian, and Persian Periods*, 426–27. For a comprehensive treatment, see Ya'akov Meshorer, *Ancient Jewish Coinage*, vol. 1, *Persian Period
through Hasmonaeans* (Dix Hills, NY: Amphora Books, 1982). There is ample attestation of the use of coins and metal ingots (for storage and/or shipping) in the Elephantine documents.

63. See Haim Gitler, "Coins," *DEJ* 480.

64. For example, the daric (8.4 grams) became the baseline (gold) standard for the
Persian system. This could be divided into twenty shekels of silver, each weighing 5.6
grams. Ezra 2:69 describes the contribution from families of "sixty-one thousand dar-
ics of gold" for building the temple.

fertility motifs, including the lily and the pomegranate. The rulers from this family often included lengthy inscriptions, and there are numerous examples of their coins. Herodian kings also minted imperial currency as they consolidated economic power in locations such as Caesarea. The silver-based or copper-based denarius became a common form of tender (e.g., Matt. 18:28), with smaller denominations (e.g., the sestercius) appearing in bronze form. The increase in coinage coincided with their efforts to enhance the infrastructure of Judea and obtain the ongoing favor of their Roman overlords. In the New Testament, passing references to coinage include the story of the widow's offering (Mark 12:41–44; Luke 21:1–4) and the question of paying royal taxes with a denarius (Matt. 22:15–22; Mark 12:13–17; Luke 20:20–26). Financial exchanges with coins also occurred in more remote locations. Numismatic evidence appears in such locations as the Qumran site, pointing to the use of currency even by sectarians in nonelite quarters. While the number of coins found at the site is relatively small, the community clearly had currency to purchase essential goods.[65]

When considering these and other finds, the implications for the increase in currency during the Second Temple period are considerable. Even if many exchanges continued to occur through bartering, reliance on weights and coins led to more complex and detailed financial arrangements. The writing of contracts, involvement of third parties, and ability to quantify the cost of items and services with greater precision led to a more complex financial system. Profit seekers could benefit from detailed transactions because it allowed them to hold purchasers and borrowers to the terms of an agreement. More precise transactions could also lead to the seizure of property and possessions by the more powerful party. In many cases these transactions involved loans, often with exorbitant interest rates. It is to the topic of usury that we now turn.

BORROWING AND LENDING

Within the advanced agrarian economy of the Second Temple period, a system of borrowing and lending presented opportunities for certain individuals but considerable risks for many others. In certain quarters, lending was encouraged as a means of helping those in a difficult situation and adhering

---

65. Magness, *Stone and Dung*, 97–101, discusses the frequent argument that the sectarians at Qumran pooled their resources upon entry into the community, as stipulated in 1QS 1.11–12. Whether the lack of coins in the caves points to such a phenomenon is an interesting question that lies beyond the scope of the present discussion.

to the principles of the Torah (e.g., Sir. 29:1–7). Yet these loans often carried pitfalls. With contracts and silver currency, it became much harder to alter or mitigate the terms of a specific agreement, especially since lenders often kept the contract in their possession as insurance against someone defaulting on a loan. Consequently borrowers often faced greater accountability measures, including written documents that might force them to pay extra sums. For those negotiating the demands of difficult farming conditions, the exacting nature of the currency system, and a burdensome tax structure, solvency became a perennial challenge. Long-standing kinship structures provided a safeguard for many individuals, but as the biblical and extracanonical evidence attests, difficult circumstances often prevented a person from functioning in the society without borrowing. If adversity struck in the form of a bad harvest, drought, or another serious hurdle such as illness, individuals and their families might find themselves in need of a loan. Such transactions receive attention in texts from this period, including the practice of usury, becoming a guarantor for an associate or a stranger (i.e., surety), and the use of bribes. While these arrangements often provided a necessary stopgap, the borrower could suffer severe and permanent losses. The present section will address such practices in an effort to understand different types of financial exchange and their level of acceptability within Second Temple society. The sources are disparate on this point and do not yield a complete picture, but there is enough evidence to sketch certain features and highlight the prevalence of usury as a core aspect of the economy.

Interest

From a very early date, interest charges marked many exchanges in the ancient Near East. During earlier periods, Babylonian archives attest to a variety of credit-based transactions, including property acquisition and the advancement of currency or goods to meet a shortfall, especially for farming purposes. With many of these arrangements, lenders charged above the original amount, stipulating a fraction of the debt principal, and then that sum (i.e., the interest) accrued on a monthly basis. Babylonian contracts indicate the frequency of such interest-bearing loans, which usually involved a witness.[66] Law codes like those of Eshnunna and Hammurabi often mandated a 20 percent interest rate per year for money and 33.3 percent (or higher) for

---

66. For a detailed study of the Babylonian material, see Michael C. Hudson and Marc van de Mieroop, eds., *Debt and Economic Renewal in the Ancient Near East*, International Scholars Conference on Ancient Near Eastern Economies 3 (Bethesda: CDL Press, 2002).

grain.[67] The rate of 20 percent, accumulating over a calendar year, continued into the neo-Babylonian and early Persian periods (sixth and early fifth centuries BCE) for many transactions.[68]

Along with these exorbitant rates, the creditor could change the terms of these loans and place additional burdens on the borrower. This practice, known as antichresis (*antichrēsis*), usually occurred when a debtor lacked the resources to adhere to the original agreement so that the lender claimed the produce from the borrower's land or the land itself. A more demanding arrangement might ensue because of difficult circumstances for the borrower, such as drought.[69] If a debtor had to pledge his assets and still could not adapt to the new terms of the loan (i.e., higher interest on the principal), then he might find himself serving as a tenant-farmer on land he used to own. The unpredictability of the agricultural cycle left many persons vulnerable to such antichretic loan arrangements and the loss of land, possessions, and possibly their personal autonomy. This model for lending would have a lasting impact on later practices (e.g., the significant number of lender-debtor relations in the New Testament).

The Hebrew Bible indicates similar scenarios for borrowing, but the emphasis on mutual solidarity and concern for the poor (i.e., social justice) led to greater restrictions. The focus on justice stems from a striking theological framework, as in Psalm 99: "Mighty King, lover of justice, you have established equity; you have executed justice and righteousness in Jacob" (v. 4).[70] Because Israel's God establishes "justice and righteousness" in the earthly sphere (vertical relationship), humanity has to follow their Creator's lead by seeking fairness in their horizontal relations with each other. This "theology of obligation" included restrictions on usury among Israelites, particularly those with unequal holdings.[71] The prophet Ezekiel illustrates the more restrictive framework: "If a man is righteous and does what is lawful and right—. . . does not take advance or accrued interest, withholds his hand from iniquity, executes true justice between contending parties . . .—such a one is righteous; he shall surely live, says the Lord GOD" (18:5–9). The justice requirement here and in other passages leads to specific laws on fairness. The concrete

67. Reuven Yaron, *The Laws of Eshnunna*, 2nd rev. ed. (Jerusalem: Magnes Press, 1988), 235–46.

68. Cornelia Wunsch, "Debt, Interest, Pledge, and Forfeiture in the Neo-Babylonian and Early Achaemenid Period: The Evidence from Private Archives," in Hudson and Meiroop, *Debt and Economic Renewal*, 234–38.

69. Ibid., 228–29, 240.

70. On the economic significance of "justice and righteousness" in relation to the Deity, see Moshe Weinfeld, *Social Justice in Ancient Israel and the Ancient Near East* (Minneapolis: Fortress Press, 1995).

71. On the "theology of obligation," see J. David Pleins, *The Social Visions of the Hebrew Bible* (Louisville, KY: Westminster John Knox Press, 2001).

stipulations in Ezekiel underscore the theology of obligation: the motivation for righteous behavior is favorable judgment from God. Yet the question of whether this type of theological framework translated into widespread practice requires closer examination of the actual laws pertaining to interest.

In the Torah, legislation regulates interest, and a brief examination of this material provides necessary context for Second Temple practices. The earliest case law, from the Covenant Code in Exodus, acknowledges the power imbalance in many lending arrangements: "If you lend money to my people, to the poor among you, you shall not deal with them as a creditor [Heb. *kĕnōšeh*]; you shall not exact interest [Heb. *nešek*] from them. If you take your neighbor's cloak in pawn, you shall restore it before the sun goes down; for it may be your neighbor's only clothing to use as cover; in what else shall that person sleep?" (Exod. 22:25–27 [24–26]). As many commentators have noted, the root word for "interest" (*nšk*) can also describe the "bite" of a serpent, clearly a negative image. The entire regulation reflects the tendency for the wealthy to manipulate the vulnerable classes through usury, especially when the social structure allows for such behavior. The early, preexilic context for the Covenant Code fits this type of scenario.[72] Without other forms of collateral, lending arrangements with superiors could deprive persons of basic necessities. This law recognizes the possibility of creditors claiming even the most personal resources from poor borrowers, including clothing items. This passage does not forbid usury in all circumstances (e.g., interest-bearing loans seem to be acceptable among two people of equal standing or with a foreign merchant). Yet one should avoid such unfair loans with vulnerable persons because these arrangements run contrary to the compassionate nature of God. Such a theological framework would have great resonance for the interpreters of these laws in the Second Temple period (see below).

A more detailed regulation on interest appears in the Holiness Code (Lev. 17–26), quite possibly a postexilic source and therefore highly relevant for our study.[73] A lengthy section of Leviticus (25:1–26:2) details the Jubilee Year and

---

72. The date for the Covenant Code (Exod. 20:19–23:33) is beyond the scope of this discussion, but the society in these laws reflects a preexilic setting, and the dependence of the Deuteronomic legal reforms on this corpus indicates an earlier period. See David P. Wright, *Inventing God's Law: How the Covenant Code of the Bible Used and Revised the Laws of Hammurabi* (Oxford: Oxford University Press, 2009).

73. The date for the Holiness Code (Lev. 17–26) and its relationship to the rest of the Priestly material in Leviticus are highly controversial topics in biblical studies. It is quite possible that H is a later source, dating from the exilic or postexilic period. See Israel Knohl, *The Sanctuary of Silence: The Priestly Torah and the Holiness School* (Minneapolis: Fortress Press, 1995). Regardless of the exact date, this law clearly draws on earlier traditions, like the Covenant Code, to call for benevolent lending practices among fellow believers.

the requirement to forgive all loan balances, including outstanding interest, every fifty years. While addressing a more complex scenario than the passage in Exodus, Leviticus 25:35–38 contains a similar message about interest, especially with a fellow member of the Israelite community. When an Israelite landowner ("your brother") experiences dire straits, there is an obligation to assist this person without charging interest: "Do not take interest [nešek] in advance or otherwise make a profit [wĕtarbît] from them [the debtors], but fear your God; let them live with you. You shall not lend them your money at interest taken in advance, or provide them food at a profit [bĕmarbît]" (25:36–37).[74] The entire chapter in Leviticus 25 depicts the difficult circumstances many Israelites faced (e.g., 25:25: "If anyone of your kin falls into difficulty and sells a piece of property . . .") and the possibility of high interest rates, loss of property, and eventual debt slavery.[75] There are different levels of difficulty here, each one more serious than the previous stage: (1) partial sale of land to cover a debt (vv. 25–34); (2) tenant farming, with no interest as part of the loan arrangement (vv. 35–38); (3) service to creditors *not as slaves* but as someone "like hired or bound laborers [Heb. kĕśākîr kĕtôšāb]" (v. 40), such that the debtor no longer has usufruct from the lost land (vv. 39–55); (4) forgiveness of all debts at the Jubilee Year.[76] Milgrom calls the regulations in Leviticus 25 "a total reversal of the antichretic loan arrangement" found in the Mesopotamian context, since the Israelite debtor can amortize the principal by working his own fields and living in his house. During this period of working off the loan, the borrower pays no interest and labors until the creditor has received everything he is due.[77] In principle, these safeguards

74. The different words for interest here, nešek and tarbît/marbît (cf. Prov. 28:8; Ezek. 18:8, 13, 17; 22:12), have generated much discussion. They are not necessarily synonymous: nešek refers to interest on money, while tarbît seems to indicate interest on food or other provisions (as the NRSV translation suggests). See Samuel E. Lowenstamm, "nešek and tarbît/m," *JBL* 88 (1969): 78–80; D. L. Baker, *Tight Fists or Open Hands? Wealth and Poverty in Old Testament Law* (Grand Rapids: Eerdmans, 2009), 260.

75. This explains the need to treat a debtor "as a resident alien" in Lev. 25:35 (i.e., the creditor should allow his neighbor to live with him and not charge interest as he normally would with an outsider). See Jacob Milgrom, *Leviticus 23–27*, AB 3B (New York: Doubleday, 2001), 2207–8.

76. Ibid., 2221, reads kĕśākîr kĕtôšāb in Lev. 25:40 as a hendiadys: "as a resident hireling." During this third stage, the debtor effectively becomes a member of the creditor's household until payment of the principal, but he can return home to his family each evening. This "resident hireling" has certain contractual rights, including a set number of hours each day to work and the completion only of specified tasks (i.e., he is not a slave). See also Chirichigno, *Debt-Slavery in Israel*, 332–34.

77. Milgrom, *Leviticus 23–27*, 2207–9, claims that the creditor cannot seize the land of the debtor if there is a delay in repayment, something he could do if the borrower were a resident alien.

prohibited the permanent seizure of land and unending debt slavery among fellow Israelites. They also reflect the generous spirit of the God of "justice and righteousness," who provides the template for the people to follow (e.g., Gen. 18:19).

The question then becomes whether this Jubilee legislation ever became common practice, particularly with regard to interest charges. Israelite society placed a premium on family property holdings, even after the establishment of the monarchy (e.g., the Naboth story in 1 Kgs. 21:1–19). Perhaps the regulations in Leviticus 25 provided a check against predatory land seizures, such that persons in trouble could hope for "redemption" from debt (vv. 25–26), avoidance of antichretic loan arrangements, and ultimate restoration of their land. Yet caution is in order when assuming these regulations to be normative, before or after the exile. The clearest example of massive debt problems in the Hebrew Bible occurs in Nehemiah 5, where the charging of interest and imposition of debt slavery have reached crisis proportions. In this passage, the Jubilee legislation does not appear as a specific remedy (contrast the reference to the Sabbath Year in Neh. 10:31–32). In fact, there is no concrete evidence that this Jubilee law became a reality.[78] The prohibition against interest in this section (Lev. 25:35–37) probably reflects more utopian vision than actual practice.

A similar law in Deuteronomy forbids usury among all community members, regardless of circumstances: "You shall not charge interest on loans to another Israelite, interest on money, interest on provisions, interest on anything that is lent. On loans to a foreigner you may charge interest, but on loans to another Israelite you may not charge interest" (23:19–20). If the law in Exodus leaves open the possibility of interest among insiders of certain means, this expanded statute from Deuteronomy allows interest-bearing loans only to a "foreigner." Such a restrictive law again raises the question of whether an absolute ban on interest became common practice. Some commentators have argued that the legal traditions of the Hebrew Bible categorically prohibit usury among members of the covenant community since the "children of Israel" regard each other as brothers and sisters.[79] Following this line of thought, the prohibition in Deuteronomy embodies the goal of mutual solidarity. One must be careful, however, about reading the sweep-

---

78. Westbrook, *Property and Family*, 48–49. Babylonian edicts that provided for periodic cancellation of debts by the king did not occur with the same regularity as this legislation in the Holiness Code.

79. Baker, *Tight Fists or Open Hands?*, 260; cf. Edward Neufeld, "The Prohibitions against Loans at Interest in Ancient Hebrew Laws," *HUCA* 26 (1955): 401–2, who locates this prohibition during the period of Ezra–Nehemiah (fifth century BCE), when the *qāhāl* represented a sacred (theocratic) community.

ing reforms of Deuteronomy as indicative of actual dynamics on the ground. Why would prophets like Ezekiel (e.g., 18:5–17) and the sages responsible for Proverbs (e.g., 28:8) condemn the charging of interest if such practices were not occurring? Another relevant passage is Psalm 109:11, where the speaker's enemy suggests total destitution as a possibility: "May the creditor seize all that he has." Even if symbolic, the psalmist's scenario points to antichretic loan arrangements and established structures for the seizure of assets. This analogy would have no force if interest charges did not occur on a regular basis. In assessing these examples and the evidence from later sources, it is more likely that the Deuteronomic legislation indicated an ideal for which reformers strived, much like the prohibition of bribes among officials (Deut. 16:18–20) and the tight regulations concerning the behavior of the monarch (17:14–20).

We should mention again the Sabbatical Year or Sabbath Year legislation, a call in Deuteronomy for loan forgiveness every seven years: "Every seventh year you shall grant a remission [or '"release"'] of debts. And this is the manner of the remission: every creditor shall remit the claim that is held against a neighbor, not exacting it of a neighbor who is a member of the community, because the LORD's remission has been proclaimed" (Deut. 15:1–2). As with Deuteronomy 23:19–20, this provision stipulates that one does not have to offer remission when dealing with a foreigner, but a debtor who is a member of the covenant community should receive this benevolent gesture. Not only should creditors provide debtors with this "release," but additional legislation stipulates that the land must lie fallow during this seventh year (Lev. 25:1–7, 20–22). Later interpreters addressed this requirement directly, and there is evidence that the Sabbatical Year release from debts occurred in certain circles during the Second Temple period and that officials took steps to circumvent the Sabbatical Year through a deliberative body that allowed creditors to receive the entire loan amount plus interest (see below).

Interest charges continued into the Second Temple period as the multi-layered economy and increasing reliance on silver currency contributed to its staying power. For example, the entire scene in Nehemiah 5 involves complex lending arrangements among members of the postexilic community. The fact that the governor directly accuses Judeans of charging interest from each other (5:7–11), contrary to what the legal tradition allows, points to the common occurrence of the practice and the familiarity of his audience with Torah stipulations:

> After thinking it over, I brought charges against the nobles and the officials; I said to them, "You are all taking interest from your own people." And I called a great assembly to deal with them, and said to them, "As far as we were able, we have bought back our Jewish

kindred who had been sold to other nations; but now you are selling your own kin, who must then be bought back by us!" They were
silent, and could not find a word to say. So I said, "The thing that you
are doing is not good. Should you not walk in the fear of our God,
to prevent the taunts of the nations our enemies? Moreover I and
my brothers and my servants are lending them money and grain. Let
us stop this taking of interest. Restore to them, this very day, their
fields, their vineyards, their olive orchards, and their houses, and the
interest on money, grain, wine, and oil that you have been exacting
from them." (5:7–11)

While the precise circumstances of this crisis elude us, usury presents a
problem for social cohesion. The dynamics in Nehemiah 5 suggest that individuals from wealthy families (identified in 5:1 as "Jewish kin" [Heb. *yĕhûdîm*])
have capitalized on the vulnerability of poorer citizens.[80] Even if the great
assembly in verses 8–19 represents a literary device rather than an actual historical gathering, the initial accusation to the creditors is forceful: "You are
all taking interest [Heb. *maśśā'*] from your own people" (5:7). This indictment
might indicate a recurrent feature of the Persian period rather than a onetime
event. Other Second Temple sources demonstrate the repetitive nature of difficult conditions, especially in relation to farming (cf. Mal. 3:9–12; Joel 1–2).[81]
Nehemiah 5 suggests that a class of creditors worked with farmers, who had
to speculate on the next year's produce in order to buy seed and other necessary supplies. The creditors' practice of charging interest and then heighten-
ing their demands (i.e., antichresis) included the possibility of debt slavery.
All of these details point to a developed system for usury. Perhaps the pledge
of these nobles to cease such practices (Neh. 5:11–13) reflects knowledge of
legislation like Deuteronomy 23:19–20. Even if this is the case, the practice
of borrowing at interest to meet financial obligations, especially among agriculturalists whose situation remained tenuous, is clearly a factor in this unit.[82]

With regard to contractual evidence from this period, there are examples
of charging interest among fellow Judeans in the community at Elephantine
in Egypt. In the so-called Ananiah Archive, there is a silver loan agreement
from 456 BCE (3.69) that involves a woman named Jehohen borrowing four
shekels from a lender, Meshullam, at a 5 percent monthly rate. According to
the stipulations in this contract, if she does not pay back the sum, Meshullam

80. The *yĕhûdîm* reference in this verse designates certain families of means, including some who had returned from exile. It can also refer to "Jews/Judeans" living abroad
(e.g., Neh. 5:8). See Blenkinsopp, *Judaism, the First Phase*, 112–13.
81. Blenkinsopp, *Ezra–Nehemiah*, 258.
82. Along with interest payments, taxation demands (Neh. 5:4) contributed to
their precarious situation, a topic we will take up in the next chapter.

can seize any of her assets as security (including imperishable items like gold and perishable ones like food: lines 7–11), and he keeps the contract in his possession as insurance against future protests. The precise terms imply a familiar custom among all parties in the loan agreement. In addition, the possession of the contract by Meshullam makes it much more difficult for the borrower to renege on the agreement. Additional evidence from this corpus points to interest as a common element in lending arrangements from this period. Other contractual documents from this colony in Egypt involve interest rates as high as 60 to 75 percent, and this highlights the ability of creditors to turn a large profit.[83] When considering the importance of this evidence, it is too simplistic to categorize these documents as removed from the more "compassionate" system at work in Judah. The evidence of Nehemiah 5 and later voices, including Ben Sira (e.g., Sir. 29:14–20), work against such an interpretation. Usury played a major role in exchanges in both Judah and Egypt.

Moving to later periods, texts from the Dead Sea Scrolls corpus also mention interest and its dangers. One of the manuscripts of the *Damascus Document* (first century BCE) prohibits certain financial practices among members of the sectarian community. Although this Hebrew text from Cave 4 is fragmentary, the context clearly relates to usury and standing surety for someone: "Let him not giv[e as su]rety (b[']rwbwt), and his money for usury (bns[k]), and his [fo]od for increase (btrbyt)" (4Q267 frg. 4 lines 9–10).[84] This regulation contains the same two terms for interest that appear in Leviticus 25:36–37, nešek and tarbît, implying a familiarity with the Torah regulations on this topic. The *Damascus Document* sketches a relatively open framework for the recipients of these rules (e.g., individuals can live in camps and marry), but this particular manuscript prohibits usury in the interest of preserving group solidarity, and it does so by utilizing vocabulary from Leviticus.[85] In addition, this fragment lumps surety,

83. Bezalel Porten, *Archives from Elephantine: The Life of an Ancient Jewish Military Colony* (Berkeley: University of California Press, 1968), 78–79.

84. There is some debate about the reference to surety (Heb. 'rb), but the content of the passage and the actual manuscript suggest reading the missing letter as an 'ayin. For the interpretation and best translation of these lines, see C. Murphy, *Wealth in the Dead Sea Scrolls*, 45–47. For the primary text, see Joseph M. Baumgarten, *Qumran Cave 4.XIII: The Damascus Document (4Q266–273)*, DJD 18 (Oxford: Clarendon Press, 1996), plate XX.

85. The fragmentary manuscript (4Q267) mentions "in the covenant" in line 8, suggesting an internal prohibition against usury among members of this sect. On the open, yet restrictive, context for the *Damascus Document*, see John J. Collins, *Beyond the Qumran Community: The Sectarian Movement of the Dead Sea Scrolls* (Grand Rapids: Eerdmans, 2010), 14–19, 24–31. The recipients of this advice seem to have certain freedoms, but there are also prohibitions that derive from the Torah, including the regulations on usury.

the act of vouching for the loan of another, into the same undesirable list as usury, a move that the biblical laws do not make (see below).[86] Although the *Damascus Document* does not advocate total withdrawal from society, the wariness about interest and surety indicates a degree of corporate solidarity and otherness among those receiving this advice. This sectarian group defines itself against the acquisitive spirit of the larger marketplace. The prohibition also shows that complex loan arrangements were occurring, or the author would not prohibit such practices among his tight-knit audience.

Philo and Josephus also oppose usury based on their reading of the interest laws in the Torah. In his work *On the Virtues*, Philo draws upon the various laws highlighted above (Exod. 22:25 [24]; Lev. 25:36–37; Deut. 23:19–20) to formulate a clear prohibition against charging interest. The reliance on Deuteronomy 23 is clear: according to Philo, God "forbids anyone to lend money on interest to a brother, meaning by this name not merely a child of the same parents, but anyone of the same citizenship or nation" (*Virt.* 82). In addition to interpreting Deuteronomy, Philo explains that benevolence leads to joy for lenders. When wealthier persons refrain from charging interest and extend help to those who need it most, they are able to bask in the gratitude of such persons as their reward. Such virtuous behavior stands in contrast to "money-grubbing usurers," who "may seem to be kings with purses full of gold, but they never even in their dreams have had a glimpse of the wealth that has eyes to see" (*Virt.* 85). As with the *Damascus Document*, this vivid language seems to denounce practices as Philo witnesses them, based on his reading of the biblical laws (cf. *Spec.* 2.74–78). Similarly, Josephus utilizes Deuteronomy 23:19–20 to oppose usury among fellow believers. He also emphasizes the gratitude of the borrower as sufficient reward for the lender (*Ant.* 4.266).

Along with these examples, the New Testament contains several references to interest and to the situation of being a debtor. In the parable of the Talents, the master condemns the servant who does not invest money so that interest might accrue (Matt. 25:27). In the version of the Lord's Prayer that appears in Matthew, the appeal to benevolence includes commercial terminology: "And forgive us our debts [Gk. *opheilēmata*], as we also have forgiven our debtors" (6:12). Although the Lukan version of the prayer has "sins" instead of "debts" (11:4), the economic vocabulary in Matthew is significant. The prayer implies that human indebtedness to God requires a plea for divine forgiveness, and this appeal to the Deity should at the same time lead to generosity toward others and to debt forgiveness of every sort. The philanthropic spirit of the

---

86. Murphy, *Wealth in the Dead Sea Scrolls*, 46, notes that later rabbinic texts allow a person to become a guarantor but not to charge interest (*b. B. Meṣiʿa* 71a). Consequently, the double prohibition in the *Damascus Document* is somewhat unique.

prayer parallels the perspective in Philo, Josephus, and earlier traditions, and the reference to debts among humans includes the possibility of usurious situations. The parable of the Unforgiving Servant (Matt. 18:23–35) reflects the same logic, especially since the servant who escapes slavery over his massive debt of ten thousand talents will not forgive the one who owes him a hundred denarii (vv. 24, 28). A call for forbearance is at the heart of this parable and in the Lord's Prayer; in both cases the Matthean writer employs a legal/commercial context to illustrate a larger point.[87] These passages assume an established system of borrowing and lending, with the possibility of heavy interest payments and eventual debt slavery. The message is consistent not only with Jesus' larger ethic in the Gospels, but also with much earlier legal traditions concerning interest and debt forgiveness.

Finally, the institution of the *prosbul* during the Roman period merits attention. In his description of the First Jewish Revolt beginning in 66 CE, Josephus highlights the charging of interest among the population and the efforts of certain debtors to erase any record of the transaction. He describes the burning of debt records at the treasury department in Jerusalem at the beginning of the war to prevent creditors from collecting payment (*J.W.* 2.427). During this period, the *prosbul* emerged as an institutional body that allowed creditors to seek repayment of debts, even during the Sabbatical Year, with the support of the judicial system.[88] This court effectively served as the collector of the debt, providing a more secure framework for lenders to allow transactions. Since the *prosbul* now handled the loan, a lender who submitted records to judicial authorities would not be guilty of violating Deuteronomy 15:3, and the borrower would be held to the original terms of the loan. Efforts to sidestep the law from Deuteronomy 15 demonstrate the tension between the philanthropic spirit of earlier legislation and the desire of creditors to reclaim their loans. The militants (the Sicarii) who burned the debt records wanted to follow the Mosaic tradition more closely and also persuade debtors of their upright cause.[89] Yet this description also indicates stratification in the society and the fact that usury continued to play a major role in economic life into the era of Roman rule.

87. Hans D. Betz, *The Sermon on the Mount: A Commentary on the Sermon on the Mount, including the Sermon on the Plain (Matthew 5:3–7:27 and Luke 6:20–49)*, ed. Adela Yarbro Collins, Hermeneia (Minneapolis: Fortress Press, 1995), 400–4.

88. Rabbi Hillel is attributed with the institution of the *prosbul* around the turn of the era.

89. This group, the Sicarii, eventually fled to Masada and had a protracted standoff with the Romans. For background on these developments and their relationship to larger events, see Martin Goodman, "The First Jewish Revolt: Social Conflict and the Problem of Debt," *JJS* 33 (1982): 417–27.

While the evidence for interest varies, the import of these passages remains significant. We do not have a complete picture of how usury worked or its necessity among many sectors of the population, but it is clear that the agricultural cycle and the vulnerability of many individuals/households to financial ruin created opportunities for some and pitfalls for others. The evidence from disparate sources like Nehemiah, the Dead Sea Scrolls, and the New Testament shows that interest played a significant role in trade and other daily transactions, especially when one considers the numerous references to surety in texts from this period. Authors from this period knew the negative appraisal of usury in the Torah, although it is hard to determine the effect of this legislation on everyday financial exchanges. We cannot state with confidence that the legislation in Deuteronomy and Leviticus successfully restricted usury in most transactions. Vouching for the loan of another (surety) became an integral part of lending arrangements during this period, and it is to this topic that we now turn.

The Practice of Surety

In many cases, a potential borrower needed a guarantor to assist him with securing a loan. This usually happened because the borrower lacked the collateral to pay back the funds and/or goods. The fact that persons stood surety for neighbors or strangers highlights the important role of lending in the Second Temple economy and the difficulty many persons had in obtaining a loan without such an arrangement. The references to surety also suggest that many creditors demanded security of some sort in case the debtor became insolvent. This practice provided a mechanism for reassuring the lender and possibly an opportunity for the guarantor to make a profit, but it also placed the one standing surety in a vulnerable position.

Extracanonical and biblical sources confirm the occurrence of this practice from the earliest of times, in some cases through the promise of labor should a borrower default on his obligation. References to surety appear in Babylonian contracts and in documents from Ugarit.[90] The Hebrew Bible also contains the verb 'ārab, which denotes vouching for the obligation of another individual

---

90. Edward Lipiński, "'ārab, 'ǎrubbâ, 'ērābôn, 'ārēb, ta'ǎrûbâ," *TDOT* 11:327, explains that most cases involved the antichretic type, which meant that the person pledging surety had to offer his labor to the creditor if all else failed. In addition to Babylonian texts, documents from Ugarit contain the verbal root 'rb, "to stand surety for someone" (*KTU* 3.3, 2; 3.7, 1; 3.8, 6). For contracts from the Second Temple period containing this root, see Murphy, *Wealth in the Dead Sea Scrolls*, 46. Standard formulas include a promise by the guarantor to put up his property or a portion of it in order to cover a loan.

through money or labor. In the Joseph story, Judah volunteers himself as a substitute for his brother Benjamin. Judah declares to a disguised Joseph, "I myself *will be surety* for him; you can hold me accountable for him" (Gen. 43:9; cf. 44:32). The implication here is that Judah makes a courageous gesture, and the incidental reference to surety points to a familiar practice. Another figurative example is Psalm 119:122, where the supplicant asks the Lord to stand surety for him: "Guarantee [Heb. *'ārab*] your servant's well-being; do not let the godless oppress me" (cf. Isa. 38:14; Job 17:3). Such phrases point to a familiar custom, and none of these passages refer to surety in a negative light.

In the various sections of Proverbs, however, the sages view the practice with suspicion and a highly critical eye. Two of the sayings (Prov. 11:15; 20:16) begin with an implied accuser, perhaps in an arbitration setting of some sort.[91] In a statement that seems to reflect an ongoing dispute, Proverbs 11:15 contrasts the unfortunate fate of the one who stands surety with a more cautious fellow who has the good sense to refrain: "He will suffer grievous harm, since he has stood surety for a stranger [Heb. *zār*], but the one who hates making agreements [lit., "clasping" hands] will be confident" (my trans.).[92] In this proverb, the "stranger" (*zār*) is not necessarily a foreigner, but someone who is unfamiliar to the other parties, not part of their known group of associates. Proverbs 20:16 involves a similar accusation within a courtroom setting: "Take his garment, since he has stood surety for a stranger, and seize it, because on behalf of outsiders [or "foreigners"] [he has pledged himself]" (my trans.; cf. Prov. 27:13). Such declarations assume that vouching for someone else's loan is foolish, especially on behalf of a stranger. The garment reference is significant, since there are laws in Exodus (22:25–27 [24–26]) and Deuteronomy (24:12–13) against extracting interest and possessions from lowly borrowers, including their basic clothing items.[93] Yet these laws *do not apply* to a guarantor. Unlike the poor debtor who gets his clothing back at night, *every* asset of the person who becomes a guarantor is subject to seizure, right down to his cloak.[94] The uncertainties of such a lending arrangement run contrary to the pragmatism of Proverbs.

The same advice appears elsewhere in Proverbs, and in two cases there is no mention of a "stranger." In Proverbs 22:26–27, the warning is general:

---

91. Fox, *Proverbs*, 2:536.

92. This translation of Prov. 11:15 reads the first word as *rōa'*, an infinitive absolute that adds emphasis to the verb (*grievous* harm), rather than *ra'* (evil one). The connotation of *bôṭēaḥ* in this verse is not "to trust" (*pace* NRSV), but "to feel confident" or "bold" (cf. Prov. 28:1). See ibid., 2:536–37.

93. Exod. 22:26 (25): "If you take your neighbor's cloak in pawn, you shall restore it before the sun goes down."

94. Fox, *Proverbs*, 2:670.

"Do not be one of those who give pledges, who become surety for debts [Heb. *maśśā'ôt*]. If you have nothing with which to pay, why should your bed be taken from under you?"[95] Debts are a common reason for needing a guarantor, and the saying here warns of destitution for the one who foolishly pledges his own financial holdings when another individual owes a great deal of money. In similar fashion, Proverbs 17:18 calls it "senseless" to stand surety for one's neighbor. The term *zār* (stranger) does not appear in either of these sayings, so it is conceivable that all three parties (lender, borrower, and guarantor) know each other. Consequently we cannot confine the prohibition against surety in Proverbs only to a situation where the original borrower is a stranger or foreigner. Vouching for the loan of such a person is riskier: the "stranger" could prove unreliable or absent, leaving the guarantor at the mercy of the lender. Yet Proverbs 17:18 and 22:26–27 also caution against standing surety for friends and associates.

The longest discourse on surety in the Hebrew Bible occurs in Proverbs 6:1–5, through the framework of advice from a father to his son, and this is most likely a postexilic text. The tone and content of this unit resemble the other sayings we have considered, and a few features are noteworthy. First, the sapiential author describes a formal handshake to seal the arrangement: "My child, if you have given your pledge to your neighbor, if you have bound yourself (lit., "clasped hands") to another [Heb. *zār*] . . ." (v. 1). No written contract is mentioned, but after this gesture, both parties have clearly obligated themselves. The force of the advice underscores the difficulty of reneging when one becomes a guarantor.[96] Second, like Proverbs 11:15 and 20:16, this statement in 6:1 portrays someone vouching for the loan of "another" (*zār*), so that the creditor is a neighbor. The borrower in this scenario cannot be the neighbor, because Proverbs 6:3 states that the vulnerable guarantor will eventually have to "plead" with this person: "So do this, my child, and save yourself, for you have come into your neighbor's power: go, hurry, and plead with your neighbor." Such a detail only makes sense if the neighbor is the creditor.[97] The "neighbor" (Heb. *rēa'*) in verse 1 is not necessarily a close friend but simply someone whom the guarantor knows.[98] Finally, neither this section nor any of the other sayings we have considered explain why

95. Unlike many of the sayings in this selection (Prov. 22:17–24:22), this statement has no antecedent in the Egyptian Instruction of Amenemope.
96. This "clasping of hands" reference only appears in the Hebrew Bible to describe standing surety, but it is possible that the practice also occurred in relation to other contractual arrangements and friendly agreements. See Fox, *Proverbs*, 1:212–13.
97. Ibid., 1:212.
98. Bruce K. Waltke, *The Book of Proverbs: Chapters 1–15*, NICOT (Grand Rapids: Eerdmans, 2004), 331.

the one standing surety fails to meet his obligations, but the sayings assume such a result to be inevitable. These passages convey the message that if an individual is foolish enough to become a guarantor, he can expect to lose everything, including his shirt. This is a common tactic in the Wisdom literature: the discussion in Proverbs 6:1–5 warns individuals about the potential trap they will fall into should they agree to vouch for a loan.

The concern with financial ruin is not surprising in a sapiential collection that values self-sufficiency, but the forcefulness of the prohibition against surety raises the question of context. Locating sapiential advice is notoriously difficult, since the content frequently has a timeless quality, and we find similar sayings in texts from other periods. Borrowing and lending occurred throughout Israel's history. Yet this study has pointed to the Second Temple period as a time of stratification, when financial exchanges became more complex and perilous, especially for the lower classes. Some of the sayings regarding surety could easily date to the monarchial period, but it is also likely that much of the explicit advice took on added importance after the exile, when standing surety became more common due to the increase of currency and complex lending arrangements (e.g., Prov. 6:1–5).

Other postexilic texts point to the frequency of this practice. The first example is Nehemiah 5, which we just examined in relation to interest. This unit describes a crisis using similar vocabulary to some of the sayings in Proverbs. The desperate situation in this section of the Nehemiah Memoir seems to be multilayered: famine (Neh. 5:2), excessive taxation on the part of both local and imperial authorities (vv. 4, 15), and unjust lending practices among the elite (v. 7). The accusation in 5:7 points to speculative lending: "I brought charges against the nobles and the officials; I said to them, 'You are all taking interest [Heb. maššāʾ] from your own people.'" These "nobles" and "officials" are identified as rapacious creditors, taking advantage of the tenuous situation of struggling citizens, referred to in this passage simply as "people" having to negotiate difficult conditions.[99] To obtain secured loans, the "people" have to put up their land, belongings, and in some cases their precious offspring as collateral. These creditors are accused of dealing harshly with their fellow Judeans and not just with foreigners.

Nehemiah's accusation against powerful creditors for charging exorbitant interest mirrors the content of Proverbs 22:26, especially the second half of the verse: "Do not be one of those who give pledges, who become surety for debts [Heb. maššāʾôt]." The same terminology is used in Nehemiah 5:7 to

---

99. John M. Halligan, "Nehemiah 5: By Way of Response to Hoglund and Smith," in *Second Temple Studies*, vol. 1, *Persian Period*, ed. Philip R. Davies, JSOTSup 117 (Sheffield: JSOT Press, 1991), 146–53.

refer to the charging of excessive "interest" (Heb. *maššā'*). The link between surety and usury is clear, especially if lenders have the opportunity to capitalize on events like famine and/or heavy taxation, when financial burdens are most acute. There is not necessarily a direct relationship between these two passages, but the description of the crisis in Nehemiah provides a typical context for the prohibitions in Proverbs. In Nehemiah 5, the "nobles" and "officials" establish ruthless mechanisms for extracting revenue, and the passionate opposition to surety in Proverbs correlates with the uncertain situation in Nehemiah. Both texts suggest that precarious circumstances lead to an increase in borrowing and standing surety, especially when one or more of the parties see an opportunity to make a profit.

The longest reflection on surety from the Second Temple period appears in the book of Ben Sira (Sir. 29:14–20), where the author offers a more nuanced assessment than his predecessors in Proverbs.[100] Ben Sira knows the sayings from Proverbs, but he unpacks the various aspects of the practice with greater detail and precision. He also incorporates the obligation to engage in charitable acts as required by the Torah. Consequently, the most important distinction from Proverbs is that Ben Sira encourages an individual to become a guarantor if he is able: "A good person will be surety for his neighbor, but the one who has lost all sense of shame will fail him" (29:14). Such willingness should not exceed an individual's means: "Assist your neighbor to the best of your ability, but be careful not to fall yourself" (v. 20).[101] Ben Sira looks at the process from all sides, encouraging the borrower not to take for granted the kindness of his guarantor, "for he has given his life for you" (v. 15). There is a moralizing aspect here that is missing in Proverbs. Implicit in such declarations is a belief that transactions among honest parties will go smoothly. Ben Sira is not naive, however: elsewhere in his instruction he warns that anyone who enters such an agreement should expect to pay back the full amount (8:13), and he also acknowledges that this practice has brought down prosperous persons (29:18). Moreover, he cautions that the sinner destroys the one standing surety (v. 16), and he declares that those who engage in the practice for pure profit will find themselves in disputes (v. 19). It is clear that the sage is struggling with the tension between the call for benevolence in the Torah and the manner in which becoming a guarantor can ruin a person's well-being.

In contrast to Ben Sira, the sapiential text *4QInstruction*, from the corpus of the Dead Sea Scrolls, condemns the practice of providing security in a manner

---

100. Unfortunately, the Hebrew text of this passage from Ben Sira is not extant.
101. The Syriac for the beginning of this verse reads "stand surety," while the Greek has "assist."

consistent with Proverbs.[102] While the text is fragmentary, there are several warnings against becoming a guarantor. For example, "Be on guard lest you stand surety" (4Q418 frg. 88 line 3). Another fragment warns against doing this on behalf of a "stranger" (4Q418 frg. 87 line 7), a continuation of the same perspective in Proverbs (11:15; 17:18; 20:16).[103] A longer section also describes the challenges of standing surety in language that echoes Proverbs (4Q416 frg. 2 2.4–6). In this passage, the concern is that the guarantor must pay the lender back quickly, and "then you will be equal to him (again)" (4Q416 frg. 2 2.4). Using the same imagery as Ben Sira, the author of *4QInstruction* declares that guarantors have given their "whole life" to creditors (line 5). He also encourages the one standing surety to act with haste in settling the debt: "Quickly give what belongs to him, and take (back) [your] money bag," (lines 5–6).[104] These lines, while fragmentary, resemble the pragmatism of Proverbs in warning against the potentially devastating decision to become a guarantor.

Why do certain instructions provide cautious support for surety (e.g., Sirach), while other wisdom texts vehemently oppose the practice under any circumstance (e.g., Proverbs, *4QInstruction*)? These differences can be traced, at least in part, to the social context of the various texts. Ben Sira offered his advice within a more upper-class milieu, counseling future scribes and more elite members of society on how to be virtuous and earn a successful living at the same time. He did not oppose commercial pursuits if a person could combine them with pious living (i.e., "fear of the Lord"). The content of his instruction indicates that some of Ben Sira's audience had resources with which to engage in lending, and his cautious endorsement of surety reflects the social location of these listeners. In addition, Ben Sira associated the Torah with Wisdom, and this contributed to his endorsement of surety among righteous persons. In contrast, the audience for *4QInstruction* is not as fortunate. The extant fragments of this text point to difficult circumstances, from advice about borrowing to repeated declarations about a lack of material resources (e.g., 4Q417 frg. 2 1.17–18). The numerous warnings about borrowing reflect their challenging status in the society.[105] It should come as no surprise that surety is discouraged in this text.

---

102. *4QInstruction* most likely dates from the second century BCE. For a summary of scholarly positions on the date and social setting for this text, see Matthew J. Goff, *The Worldly and Heavenly Wisdom of 4QInstruction*, STDJ 50 (Leiden: E. J. Brill, 2003), 228–32. For the primary text, see Strugnell et al., DJD 34.

103. The fragmentary text literally reads ". . . surety for a stranger."

104. For the translation of these lines, see Strugnell et al., DJD 34:90; Matthew J. Goff, *Discerning Wisdom: The Sapiential Literature of the Dead Sea Scrolls*, VTSup 116 (Leiden: E. J. Brill, 2007), 58.

105. For further discussion on the social setting and economic background for *4QInstruction*, see Goff, *Worldly and Heavenly Wisdom*, 145–63, and our discussion in chap. 5 below.

The prohibitions against standing surety in Proverbs cannot be contextualized so easily. As commentators have observed, many of the sayings in this collection, even if edited and pieced together by educated scribes, circulated orally among different sectors of the society.[106] The diverse content on financial matters points to a wide array of backgrounds for the advice, with many inconsistencies. For example, in some cases wealth is cited as a reward for wisdom (e.g., Prov. 8:18), while in other sayings the superiority of virtue over riches is cited (e.g., 3:13–18; 15:16; 17:1). What is noteworthy about the discussion on surety is that the authors of Proverbs are so adamant and uniform in their opposition. We suggest that the primary explanation for this skepticism lies in the manner in which the practice was occurring, especially after the exile. Surety became quite risky, as stratification, an increase in coinage, imperial and local taxation, and heightened commercial activity became significant factors in economic life. All of these developments led to more business dealings with unknown persons (i.e., "strangers" and "foreigners") and economic challenges for individuals who worked as farmers and in other demanding occupations. When we consider the many references to usurious loans and surety in the postexilic texts, along with certain commercial documents from this period, the caution in Proverbs fits with such an economic climate. According to the advice, one should not put his possessions and family at risk simply because he sees others making a profit. A potential windfall through surety does not mitigate the many possibilities for ruin.

One of the primary dangers in this area was fraud. Proverbs, Ben Sira, and Nehemiah all indicate that deceitful activity became an element in many of these lending situations. For example, the overlapping sayings in Proverbs 20:16–17 point to corruption as a common occurrence. Right after the warning against surety in verse 16, the next proverb states, "Bread gained by deceit is sweet [Heb. 'ārēb], but afterward the mouth will be full of gravel" (v. 17). The same Hebrew root for "to stand surety" and "to be sweet" ('rb) makes for an effective pun in these sayings; the placement of these two proverbs points to a connection between deceitful activity and standing surety.[107] Per-

---

106. Michael V. Fox, "The Social Location of the Book of Proverbs," in *Texts, Temples, and Traditions: A Tribute to Menahem Haran*, ed. Michael V. Fox et al. (Winona Lake, IN: Eisenbrauns, 1996), 239, makes a convincing argument about the editorial process for the book of Proverbs: Many sayings originated in rural areas, among diverse sectors of the society. As the wisdom tradition developed, "learned clerks, at least some of them the king's men, were the membrane through which principles, sayings and coinages, folk and otherwise, were filtered. The central collections of Proverbs are their filtrate, an essentially homogeneous one."

107. Andreas Scherer, "Is the Selfish Man Wise? Considerations of Context in Proverbs 10.1–22.16 with Special Regard to Surety, Bribery, and Friendship," *JSOT* 76 (1997): 59–70.

sons need to be on guard that they do not fall prey to a "sure-thing" lending situation, because such transactions do not usually involve honest brokers.

The discouragement of surety seems to contradict the requirement to engage in charitable acts, especially on behalf of those in vulnerable circumstances. Since the Hebrew Bible demanded that one's neighbor and even the "resident alien" (Heb. *gēr*) were supposed to receive compassion, how did the authors of Proverbs and *4QInstruction* rationalize their rigid advice on surety? This question becomes even more pertinent when one looks at other passages in the Hebrew Bible where surety is encouraged, such as Judah's eagerness to stand surety for his brother in the Joseph cycle (Gen. 43:9; 44:32). Even in Proverbs, it is difficult to reconcile the admonitions against surety with a saying like 14:21: "Those who despise their neighbors are sinners, but happy are those who are kind to the poor." Or one can easily spot the inconsistency between 17:17, "A friend loves at all times, and kinsfolk are born to share adversity," and the advice in verse 18 about avoiding surety.

Two primary reasons can account for the tension between charity and opposition to surety. First, the prohibition reflects the paradox in the wisdom tradition between sensible acts of self-preservation, based on accumulated knowledge, and kindness toward those who are struggling. The second reason is simple observation of the marketplace: the purveyors of this advice in Proverbs seem to have witnessed the detrimental effects of borrowing and lending. Like the authors of Nehemiah and *4QInstruction*, their passionate concern with surety points to difficult circumstances for borrowing and lending, especially among those with fewer resources. They wanted to discourage those engaging in the practice merely for profit and also alert those who did not understand the risks. In all of these texts the discussion of surety demonstrates that the authors responded to actual dynamics on the ground in perpetuating their social ethics, and sometimes caution was the better part of wisdom.

Bribery

Along with these lending practices, bribery played a key role in economic life after the exile. The system of officials, potential for quick financial gain or loss, and the expanding mercantile economy created a favorable climate for bribes as a means of influencing a situation or fostering an important relationship. Like interest and surety, the practice existed from the earliest of times. Bribery receives attention in the legal sections of the Hebrew Bible, the Wisdom literature, and in extracanonical texts from all periods of ancient Near Eastern history. While sources differ on its acceptability to accomplish a task or obtain favor, it has been effective in all cultural contexts, including the Second Temple period.

When considering specifics, we should try to differentiate, however modestly, between a "gift" (Heb. *mattān*) and a "bribe" (Heb. *šōḥad*). Such a distinction is quite subjective since the line between what constitutes acceptable gift in contrast to unjust bribe is always a matter of judgment, both in the ancient and the modern context. Despite this uncertainty, tentative definitions are possible based on the ancient sources. A "bribe" is the bestowal of money, goods, or personal labor solely for the purpose of influencing a favorable outcome. Such an act frequently occurs in secret. The biblical laws maintain that a "bribe" (*šōḥad*) generally reflects illicit motives and corruption. A prohibition in Deuteronomy is clear on this point: "Cursed be anyone who takes a bribe [*šōḥad*] to shed innocent blood" (Deut. 27:25). Bribes can warp the judgment of the recipient, often an official of some sort, who might have otherwise maintained his good intentions. Such logic appears in Exodus 23:8: "You shall take no bribe, for a bribe blinds the officials, and subverts the cause of those who are in the right" (cf. Deut. 16:19). These passages show that the Hebrew word for bribe, *šōḥad*, can indicate the pursuit of dishonest gain, often at the expense of more vulnerable individuals, or the goal of assuaging the wrath of a powerful person.[108] With fairness to those on the margins as a core principle in the Torah, bribery undermines the "justice and righteousness" that God expects in human relations (cf. Prov. 17:23; Isa. 1:23; 5:23; Ezek. 22:12; Mic. 3:11). Because of this vehement opposition, we can assume that bribery occurred with at least some frequency, especially among powerful officials, and when silver currency became more commonplace in transactions. According to many sources, it fostered inegalitarian social structures, since those with the resources to offer bribes could solidify their status and work to retain existing hierarchies.[109] There would be no need to condemn bribery so strongly unless it played a major role in exchanges.

A "gift" (Heb. *mattān* or *minḥâ*), on the other hand, constitutes a more acceptable act in some of the sources, but not all of them.[110] While there

---

108. In most cases, the use of *šōḥad* indicates something different than a "gift," such as Prov. 21:14: "A gift [*mattān*] in secret averts anger; and a concealed bribe [*šōḥad*] in the bosom, strong wrath." Yet these terms are in synonymous parallelism, with no clear distinction between the two. In many of the examples cited above, the one who takes a bribe perverts justice (e.g., Deut. 16:19).

109. S. Schwartz, *Were the Jews a Mediterranean Society?*, 58.

110. Extracanonical texts also confirm exchange patterns that included bribery. Mesopotamian texts contain terms that can mean "bribe" or "gift," (Akkadian *ṭātu*, *šulmanu*, *kadrû*), and in more than a few cases, exchanges for social advancement are acceptable. A similar understanding is at work in Egyptian texts. In the Instruction of Ani, the addressee should make friends with local officials and provide them with food and supplies to the best of his ability (22.10–13). Inequality is also part of the social landscape, and those in power are "on the take." In the Tale of the Eloquent Peasant

is clear overlap with bribes, a gift usually represents the bestowal of something to enhance an individual's public status, preserve stability within a kinship group, or provide economic benefit for all parties.[111] For example, in 2 Chronicles 21:3 Jehoshaphat offers his sons "many gifts [Heb. *mattānôt*], of silver, gold, and valuable possessions," while promising the kingdom to his eldest son, Jehoram. The decision by King Hiram of Tyre to "give" cedar and cypress to Solomon for the building of the Temple (the Israelite monarch provides wheat and oil in exchange) in 1 Kings 5:2–12 [16–26] functions as a gift exchange even though the swap also represents commerce between two states.[112] Another example is the scene in which Jacob urges his sons to take "some of the choice fruits of the land" as a "present" (Heb. *minḥâ*) to the Egyptian vizier (Joseph) in order to bring back grain (Gen. 43:11).[113] Such exchanges point to reciprocity as a means of attaining necessary items.[114] These references underscore the importance of gifts, especially during crisis periods or when an individual wants more political power or a better social standing. Access remained limited without such gestures, as Proverbs 18:16 suggests: "A gift [*mattān*] opens doors; it gives access to the great." This saying suggests that young upstarts had to produce gifts and could expect advancement in return. All of these passages demonstrate that gift giving does not reflect altruistic motives (i.e., these are not "pure gifts"): the initial bearer expects something in return.

The Wisdom literature is clear about the efficacy of bribery, and the various maxims indicate that such an act also occurred beyond elite circles. For

---

(ca. 1800 BCE), the poor petitioner accuses the nobleman of exploiting his position. Note the explicit connection between gift giving and extortion: "You have farmland in the countryside, and a salary [or a "gift"] in the district. Officials are giving to you, and [still] you take. Are you like a robber? Do men bring [bribes] to you and your cronies at the division of farmlands?" (B1 [P.Berlin 3023] lines 300–304, my trans.).

111. In chap. 1 above, we have also discussed gift terminology in the context of marriage. This discussion is not considering sacrificial terminology, which applies the language of gift giving to divine offerings and the efforts of the priestly class to establish right relations with the Deity.

112. Although this passage does not contain *mattān*, there are several forms of the Hebrew verb "to give" (1 Kgs. 5:9–11 [23–25]) that point to this transaction as a gift exchange leading to a mutually beneficial treaty (v. 12 [26]). This is not merely a commodity exchange: the two parties (Solomon and Hiram) are also acting out of their personal relationship.

113. Joseph also rewards the brothers with a banquet, extra provisions, garments, etc. For a detailed study of this pericope as an example of reciprocity, see Gary Stansell, "The Gift in Ancient Israel," *Semeia* 87 (1999): 65–90.

114. In addition to the work of Polanyi, see the seminal study by Marcel Mauss, *The Gift: The Form and Reason for Exchange in Archaic Societies*, trans. Wilfred Douglas Halls (1925; repr., New York: Norton, 1990).

example, "A bribe is like a magic stone in the eyes of those who give it; wherever they turn they prosper" (Prov. 17:8). As with Proverbs 18:1, this saying implies that a person has to offer something in order to obtain his goals.[115] For a society in which maintaining one's honor and avoiding shame represented fundamental requirements, such advice points not only to opportunistic officials wanting favor within their elite ranks, but also to an overall culture of reciprocity. Regular hospitality and generosity with favors/gifts provided a framework for interactions and the maintenance of one's reputation. If a person could enhance strategic relationships through the bestowal of something favorable, then "greasing the palms" of wealthier and more powerful individuals remained essential. As Ben Sira explains, "Favors and gifts blind the eyes of the wise; like a muzzle on the mouth they stop reproofs" (Sir. 20:29). Whether this sage from the Hellenistic period views gift giving as morally acceptable is less relevant here than his recognition of its effectiveness (cf. Sir. 3:17).

Other sources are more skeptical, suggesting that gifts/bribes solidify the corrupt hierarchy that already exists in the society. One colorful example is the polemic against bribery in the book of Ecclesiastes. The author Qoheleth takes aim against the network of officials who seem to be profiting from their advantageous position: "If you see in a province the oppression of the poor and the violation of justice and right, do not be amazed at the matter; for the high official [or "payment taker": Heb. *gābōah*] is watched by a higher, and there are yet higher ones over them" (Eccl. 5:8 [7]). There are good reasons to translate *gābōah* in this verse as "payment taker" (rather than "high official"), thus portraying a network of corruption.[116] We can also assume that such a specific warning relates to actual abuses witnessed by the author. The "oppression of the poor and the violation of justice and right" cohere with the prohibition against bribery in the Torah and Qoheleth's own objections to the marketplace practices of his day. Many commentators place Ecclesiastes in the third century BCE, the era of Ptolemaic rule.[117] An entrenched system of officials is well documented in the Zeno archives, which also date from this exact period.[118] In these documents the correspondence indicates

115. See Victor H. Matthews, "The Unwanted Gift: Implications of Obligatory Gift Giving in Ancient Israel," *Semeia* 87 (1999): 91–104.

116. James L. Kugel, "Qohelet and Money," *CBQ* 51 (1989): 35–36, proposes a slight textual emendation that clarifies this verse as a statement on corruption, and he justifies his translation of *gābōah* as "payment taker" from Mishnaic Hebrew and Aramaic parallels.

117. See, e.g., James L. Crenshaw, *Ecclesiastes*, OTL (Philadelphia: Westminster Press, 1987).

118. For the primary texts, see Xavier Durand, *Des Grecs en Palestine au IIIe siècle avant Jésus-Christ: Le dossier syrien des archives de Zénon de Caunos (261–252)*, Cahiers de la Revue biblique 38 (Paris: Gabalda, 1997).

government ownership of vast tracts (Apollonius, the finance minister, had an estate in the Galilee region), heavy taxation, vital exports to Egypt (primarily wheat and olive oil), and the potential for local officials and middlemen to profit from their connections and supervisory positions. Within such a political and economic climate, bribes played a key role. The intricate bureaucracy in the Zeno texts correlates with the network of "payment takers" in the book of Ecclesiastes. Qoheleth does not view bribery as a necessary engine of his colonial context but rather as a perk for officials already in power. In a later chapter, the author's outright dismissal restates his basic objection: "Surely oppression makes the wise foolish, and a bribe corrupts the heart" (Eccl. 7:7).

The writings of Josephus also shed light on the fluid dynamics of the Second Temple period and the prevalence of bribery. The Tobiad Romance is again relevant for this study (*Ant.* 12.154–236). Joseph son of Tobiah (who also appears in the Zeno correspondence) rises to power by placating an Egyptian envoy and staving off a diplomatic crisis. This Joseph, the nephew of the high priest Onias, promises to pay the necessary government tribute that his uncle threatened to withhold. Through forced taxation and suppression of dissent, Joseph achieves great success in gathering the necessary funds. In his efforts at advancement, he curries favor with Egyptian officials by sending them all "gifts." Such an example, even if fictional, points to the efficacy of bribery for political advancement under foreign rule, but only for a select few. The likes of Joseph could use bribes to their strategic advantage, and the fluid situation permitted a rapid rise to favorable status.

Arguments over this question continued into later periods. The rabbinic literature suggests that a person should be careful about receiving or financing gifts, since he might attune his behavior to future rewards and social advancement. Several passages reflect the tension between participation in the larger Roman society and obedience to the Torah through charity.[119] In his astute analysis of these stories, Schwartz contrasts "the values of Torah, of the pure unreciprocated gift," with the "'Mediterranean' values of honor and reciprocity."[120] In the public sphere, one should not conduct affairs for the purpose of self-aggrandizement,

---

119. In one story from the Talmud (*t. Naz.* 54b; *t. Ber.* 11d), set during the first century BCE, a pious Jew named Simeon ben-Shetach asks the king to split the cost for a sacrificial rite among Nazirites. Through a series of legal maneuvers and ingenious reasoning based on the Torah, Simon frees half of the Nazirites of their sacrificial obligation. He also tricks the king into offering them gifts. For a full analysis, see S. Schwartz, *Were the Jews a Mediterranean Society?*, 133–35, who cites this passage as an example of the conflict between euergetism, which we can define as a benefactor supporting a project or person and then receiving public acclaim, and the more altruistic expectations in the Torah. Euergetism played a major role in late antiquity, especially through memorial inscriptions and monuments to honor benefactors.

120. S. Schwartz, *Were the Jews a Mediterranean Society?*, 133.

and the reciprocity-based culture of the late Roman period made this a difficult temptation to avoid. As Judeans dealt with a Roman society in which monuments and public inscriptions for good deeds played a major role, the lure of public acclaim posed a constant threat to their value system, and certain stories reflect the conflict between assimilation to the culture of gift giving and careful rejection of it because of allegiance to the Torah.

The array of perspectives on this topic brings us back to our original problem of drawing a distinction between tolerable, effective gifts and illicit bribes. A final judgment on this question is almost always dependent upon one's perspective, as the ancient sources indicate. For example, the Egyptian Tale of the Eloquent Peasant intentionally blurs the difference between the necessary "rewards" or "gifts" of being a nobleman and the act of pure extortion (B1 300–304). Within his Second Temple context, Ben Sira seems to believe that "good gifts" are possible, as long as one does not oppress those on the margins of the society. Resourceful and even entrepreneurial efforts can be quite useful in a hierarchical, colonial economy, although Ben Sira admits that any patronage system is likely to involve corruption.[121] The rabbinic literature also wrestles with this dilemma, especially in a context that liked to reward benefactors with monuments and public acclaim. As we explore the tension in texts that address this issue, we remember that many cultures past and present involve bribery/gifts for transactions involving everything from minor land purchases to marriage between two powerful families. The danger arises when the bribe becomes a miscarriage of justice (e.g., Prov. 17:23). Yet this is a difficult matter to determine: what is a perversion of justice for some is a savvy decision for others. The references to bribery in the Wisdom literature and in other Second Temple sources demonstrate its efficacy, although there is caution about a bribe's corrupting influence on the larger society and in the heart of an individual person. All of this literature reflects the basic difficulty of determining whether "exchanges" for social advancement indicate acceptable practice or a dangerous departure from God's commandments. The line between opportunistic participation in the financial system and the need to refrain because of allegiance to the commandments was just as complex in the Second Temple period as it is today.

SUMMARY

This chapter has considered both the range of occupations and the nature of financial exchanges in the Second Temple period. For most of the population,

---

121. Ben Sira claims that "Riches are good if they are free from sin" (Sir. 13:24). Based on his statements elsewhere (e.g., 27:1–2), he considers this to be a very remote possibility. For further discussion on this issue, see chap. 5 below.

life remained cyclical and difficult as people tried to subsist on small land plots or on estates they did not own. A small minority of persons had greater opportunities for wealth and prestige, but most individuals and their families struggled under challenging conditions. Although commerce and the use of currency increased, we should not characterize Judah as a hub of commercial activity in the manner of later, capitalist economies. Nevertheless, the complexity of financial transactions during this period attests to a system in which profit could be made, and usury played a major role. The process of borrowing became more complex; individuals frequently sought guarantors to stand surety for them in order to procure necessary funds or materials. We have seen that many of the sources, especially the Wisdom literature, understood the practice of vouching for someone else's loan to be quite dangerous. In addition, the culture of reciprocity included the regular exchange of bribes/ gifts to foster social relations and preserve existing hierarchies.

Up to this point in our study, we have worked in largely thematic fashion, examining household life, the status of women and children, vocations, and the nature of financial transactions. Although the role of bureaucratic structures, both colonial and local, has received attention, these topics have yet to be the focus of our discussion. The next chapter will examine economic life on a national and international scale, working diachronically from the Persian period to the Roman period. Our study will consider the nature of imperial rule, taxation levels, and the role of local governing bodies and officials, including the priesthood, in determining how the economy functioned.

4

Taxation and the Role of the State

Taxation played a major role in the economy of the Second Temple period. Most persons had to participate in the system in one form or another, whether paying tithes to the temple and/or taxes to foreign rulers. Local and foreign officials demanded revenue from across the population to finance infrastructure and military needs and augment their wealth. The available evidence suggests that a succession of occupying forces developed intricate taxation measures, and they fostered local allies in the process. Taxes placed a hardship on many, including tenant farmers and those with small landholdings, since they had little collateral by which to protect themselves from difficult straits.

The present chapter will work chronologically, taking up taxation practices after the exile and the policies of different ruling entities. Our discussion will address foreign and local levies and their impact on the populace. A preliminary section on some of the common patterns in agrarian societies will assist us with exploring the tactics of various officials. Cross-cultural analysis demonstrates the frequency of onerous taxation by a foreign ruler in an agrarian economy, a tendency that is consistent across different cultural contexts in the ancient world (see below). While limited evidence precludes a comprehensive portrait of this topic, our inquiry will address key aspects of taxation and its effects. When examining the available sources, it becomes apparent that authorities at all levels relied on taxes to generate revenue and maintain order. Stratification persisted during this period, and taxation contributed to income inequality and in certain cases to social unrest. Various obstacles made it challenging for households to retain their land and freedom. The current discussion will underscore the role of taxes in fostering tenuous circumstances. We will also consider the ways in which the priestly class participated in the system. With no monarchy after the exile, priests, especially the office of high priest, played key leadership roles, and the Jerusalem temple became a locus of political *and* economic power.

TAXATION IN AN ADVANCED AGRARIAN ECONOMY: ANTHROPOLOGICAL PERSPECTIVES

Cross-cultural analysis is helpful for understanding the phenomenon of forced adaptation to colonial rule and the role of taxation. In his influential work on landownership patterns in ancient economies, S. N. Eisenstadt points to the frequency of independent, small property holdings among the peasantry in colonial settings. He also identifies the "traditional fetters" of a person's kinship group and the regular obligations due to local overlords and to the state.[1] Within such a setting, the colonial power generally strikes a balance between lending a measure of autonomy to households and extracting revenue and goods from them. In his examination of several preindustrial cultures, including Sassanid Persia, the Byzantine Empire, and China's T'ang Empire, Eisenstadt finds noteworthy patterns, including high taxation demands by imperial and local officials/landlords, the "nonagricultural elites" who were natives of the region. According to Eisenstadt, taxation demands increase during crisis periods, such as famine or emergent military need. The peripheral points of an empire (i.e., smaller provinces like Judah) become much more relevant when the state requires a larger resource base from which to conduct affairs.[2] Even if small landowners receive a measure of autonomy, burdensome demands often jeopardize their stability.

Another influential model is that of Gerhard Lenski, who presents his theories of power and stratification by examining a variety of preindustrial systems.[3] Noteworthy for present purposes is Lenski's discussion of *advanced agrarian economies*. As we discussed in the previous chapter, the mechanisms of farming are developed within this setting, including sophisticated plowing techniques, metallurgy, and the efficient harnessing of animal power. In advanced agrarian economies, there is usually a ruling state, often a foreign power, with a great deal of leverage. As he considers diverse, premodern cultures from ancient Rome to feudal Japan, Lenski shows that

1. Shmuel Noah Eisenstadt, *The Political Systems of Empires*, rev. and enl. ed. (New Brunswick: Transaction Publishers, 1993), 34.
2. Kajsa Eckholm-Friedman and Jonathan Friedman, "'Capital' Imperialism and Exploitation in Ancient World Systems," in *Power and Propaganda: A Symposium on Ancient Empires*, ed. Mogens Trolle Larsen, Copenhagen Studies in Assyriology 7 (Copenhagen: Akademisk Forlag, 1979), 48.
3. Lenski, *Power and Privilege*.

the state usually exerted proprietary control over the territories it held. Even when households ostensibly "owned" their land, they became subject to demanding taxation and other tributes. According to his analysis, stratification increased as the agrarian economy grew, and the empires tended to develop more intricate measures for exploitation of subject peoples.[4] All of these features correlate with Judah under Persian, Ptolemaic, Seleucid, and then Roman control, since an organized military and network of provinces provided these foreign rulers with opportunities for the expansion of economic power. Lenski cites the disproportionate suffering of the peasantry within such a framework, particularly when the foreign power and local elites develop a system for the extraction of revenue and goods. Local tax collectors, large landowners, and merchants (i.e., middlemen) become the vehicle for exchange and control, and poor households often experience distress as a result of the economic system. All of these factors are relevant for understanding the impact of taxation on the people of Judah, especially the majority of individuals whose meager resources did not leave them much latitude to meet external demands. Such a dynamic is clearly at play under the ruling powers we will now consider.

PERSIAN PERIOD

In addressing the Second Temple period and the question of levies, we must first acknowledge that social stratification and onerous taxation existed in previous eras of Israelite and Judean history. For example, earlier voices had warned of the Israelite king's tendency to demand from households a portion of their meager provisions, especially for military needs (e.g., Samuel's antimonarchical speeches).[5] The colorful critique of eighth-century-BCE prophets like Amos and Micah demonstrates that difficult economic realities, including landgrabs by the elite, had long confronted subsistence farmers in the region. In a helpful study, D. N. Premnath points to the loss of cultivable land among farmers during the eighth century and their subsequent difficulties in supporting themselves.[6] The passionate specificity that Amos, Hosea,

4. Ibid., 204–10.
5. See 1 Sam. 8:1–22; 10:17–19; 12:1–25; cf. Deut. 17:14–20.
6. Devadasan Nithya Premnath, *Eighth Century Prophets: A Social Analysis* (St. Louis: Chalice Press, 2003), 9, analyzes the social context behind the prophetic oracles in books like Amos and Micah, where economic injustice is a major concern. He points to the process of "latifundialization," which relates to the worsening situation of the peasant class due to their lack of access to arable land and disproportionate property ownership among the elite.

Micah, and Isaiah bring to their discourse seems to indicate actual realities on the ground. In addition, the periodic influx of foreign interests before the exile—whether Egyptian, Assyrian, or Babylonian—meant that the inhabitants of Israel and Judah rarely enjoyed periods of economic and political sovereignty, especially since this region lies at the intersection of so many trade routes. As a result, most households remained poor and susceptible to manipulation by foreign officials and/or local elites, including tribute and taxation demands. Yet after the exile the stream of colonial powers meant a permanent foreign presence in the region, which led to significant financial requirements. As a succession of outside forces sought to expand their revenue base, Judeans faced challenging circumstances.[7] Within colonial economies, even with less hostile governing authorities, those in power tend to demand as much as possible from subjects, and Judah experienced this type of situation during the Second Temple period, even as it remained a small province in a succession of larger empires.

Our inquiry begins with the Persian (or Achaemenid) Empire, one of the more effective and long-lasting governing structures in the history of the ancient Near East. The period of Persian dominance (558–331 BCE) represented a major consolidation of power in an expansive region. For the first time, disparate peoples were united under a kingdom whose territory stretched from the Indus to the Aegean Sea, and this included the province of Judah/Yehud.[8] The ambitious efforts of these Persian rulers succeeded, at least in part, because of a basic strategic decision. Royal officials wisely determined that culturally informed flexibility breeds loyalty. Consequently, those in charge of the bureaucratic system accepted differences across their diverse territories, and authorities used this tolerance to their advantage. Traditions involving a particular deity or other local practices might differ sharply from one region to another, but the Persians did not see this as an obstacle to stability. Rather, they allowed different customs to flourish, including cultic practices, and they encouraged local infrastructure projects and trading.[9] In pursuing this course of strategic flexibility, the ruling authorities did not act out of compassion. While granting certain freedoms, these rulers also

7. Joseph Blenkinsopp, "A Case of Benign Imperial Neglect and Its Consequences," *BI* 8 (2000): 133, cites the huge sums required to finance the various military campaigns of Darius I (522–486 BCE) and Xerxes (486–465 BCE) as a key example.

8. Briant, *From Cyrus to Alexander*, 873. "Yehud" is the official name of the province during this period (see below).

9. The Cyrus Cylinder (538 BCE), which strikes a conciliatory tone toward the Babylonians and their deities after their conflict with the Persians, is the most famous example of this policy. The Edict of Cyrus, recorded in 2 Chr. 36:23 and Ezra 1:1–4 (cf. 6:1–12), describes much the same policy in that it allows the returning exiles to rebuild the temple under the sanction of this first Persian ruler.

Figure 1. Persian period gold daric (© David Hendin; used by permission)

expected subject peoples to meet heavy taxation and tribute demands. To generate revenue, royal officials worked with local elites to harvest indigenous resources and collect taxes. This strategy led to hardship for many and power for the few with close ties to the royal bureaucracy.

Before looking more closely at the specific context of Judah, it is productive to consider basic taxation policies within the larger empire. When surveying the record, the organizational efforts of one of the first rulers, Darius I (522–486 BCE), are notable. Taking power after the first generation of Persian leaders, Darius made great organizational strides. He divided the empire into a network of "satrapies," and each of these regions consisted of smaller provinces. The efforts of Darius led to better infrastructure across the empire: the satrapies made it easier to require tax contributions from every territory and let local leaders figure out the best methods for collecting. Darius also instituted his own coin, the daric, which persisted as tender until the time of Alexander the Great.

Darius I improved upon the system of roads, standing armies, and implemented many building projects. Yet the internal details of his expansionist reign and how authorities paid for them are for the most part unknown. The Persians did not keep meticulous records, and so we do not have a full portrait of tax policies under Darius, even if it is certain that this ruler had to generate considerable resources to finance his efforts.

Greek historians, particularly Herodotus (ca. 484–425 BCE), supplement this gap with specifics about taxation and tribute collection. The complete accuracy of his *Histories* is in question: Herodotus wrote his sweeping account well after many of the events he documents, and his descriptions often reflect

Greek literary conventions and the anti-Persian bias of a Hellenistic source.[10] Yet the specificity of many details underscores the importance of his descriptions. Herodotus cites the significant ambitions of Darius, who "set up twenty provincial governorships [Gk. *nomoi*], called satrapies, . . . and assessed [each] for taxes" (*Hist.* 3.89). He includes a list of different peoples to be taxed and some specific tribute items that different satrapies had to include (e.g., eunuchs from Babylon); the details in this account suggest that he worked from an archival record.[11] The descriptions in this section of his *Histories* and in other Greek sources indicate that the Persians demanded both silver currency and indigenous goods from subject peoples. For example, Herodotus cites regular tribute requirements from Ethiopia in gold, ebony, timber, young male slaves, and elephant tusks, all for the pleasure of the Persian ruler and his minions (*Hist.* 3.97). In a culture of reciprocity, such tributes became common at all levels of governance (e.g., local governors taking food and wine from the people in Neh. 5:15). When royal officials demanded specialty items from a region, such gifts represented an additional levy beyond other forms of taxation. Yet at the same time, Herodotus claims that Darius and other Persian rulers sought to control outrageous demands so as to minimize the possibility of insurrection within the satrapies.

When probing for additional details about the extent of tax practices and the manner of collection, a few sources are valuable. One Greek author known as Pseudo-Aristotle (ca. late fourth century BCE) outlines different types of tax during the Persian period.[12] These include levies on agricultural produce, taxes on other forms of merchandise in the rural areas, "marketplace dues" (Gk. *agoraia telē*) that regulate village commerce, a cattle or "animal produce" tax, land taxes, and a "poll tax [Gk. *epikephalaion*] or tax on artisans," which seems to be a catchall category for other items (*Oec.* 2.4). If the breakdown by Pseudo-Aristotle is reasonably accurate, such a description highlights a strategy by the Persians to extract revenue in a comprehensive manner. Some commentators have suggested that these taxes describe the late fourth-century period of this author, Pseudo-Aristotle (i.e., after the defeat of

10. Briant, *From Cyrus to Alexander*, 390–91, cites the tendency of Herodotus and other Greek sources to belittle the Persian rulers and emphasize their inferiority to Hellenistic thought and culture.

11. Ibid., 392, explains that some of the taxation and tribute data could reflect later periods, but not necessarily. The specificity of the amounts suggests that Herodotus worked from official sources.

12. Lester L. Grabbe, *A History of the Jews and Judaism in the Second Temple Period*, vol. 1, *Yehud: A History of the Persian Province of Judah* (London: T&T Clark, 2004), 127–28, cites the scholarly consensus that *Oeconomica* is the work of a late fourth-century-BCE figure writing under the name of Aristotle.

the Persian Empire by Alexander the Great), rather than the efforts of earlier rulers such as Darius I. Yet these later Seleucid officials in many cases modeled their efforts after the Persians.

Other sources, including archives from the Greek city of Persepolis, confirm that the bureaucracy expanded the administrative reach of the empire through levies. The Persepolis archives (492–458 BCE) document food storehouses and the imposition of taxes upon subject peoples. While fragmentary and often difficult to decipher, these archives include taxes on both livestock and land. Many of the available documents are in Elamite and describe food rationing to slaves and greater allotments to other members of the society (e.g., priests). The imperial apparatus, through local governors and administrators, assessed the citizenry in a variety of ways, and the network of satrapies provided a structural framework for the collection of taxes and tributes.[13] Many of these taxes corresponded with each person or region's ability to pay based on landholdings, population levels, and natural resources.[14] For example, Herodotus cites the Babylonian region, where the Persians placed corvée (unpaid forced labor) obligations on larger and more prosperous satrapies and required levies and gifts "over and above the tribute" (*Hist.* 3.90–97).[15]

Archives from Idumea (the word derives from "Edom") are also instructive for understanding Persian tax policies. As a territory, Idumea included the hill country of southern Judah and portions of the Negev desert. Because of its proximity to Judah, any evidence from Idumea could parallel similar practices to the north.[16] The book of Nehemiah states that "Geshem the Arab" commanded this region (e.g., Neh. 6:1–16), presumably in some sort of alliance with the Persians. Aramaic ostraca and coins from Idumea date to the late Persian period, and the evidence from this region sheds light on taxation. The documents cite land taxes, with assessments for wheat and barley (usually after the harvest) and levies on supplies of wine and oil.[17] As the last chapter indicated, these items were food staples of the region, and therefore it is understandable that Persian authorities wanted to tax them. There is provision to keep certain food items in storage rooms, presumably for use by local officials

13. For the primary texts, see George G. Cameron, *Persepolis Treasury Tablets* (Chicago: University of Chicago Press, 1948). For additional evidence of taxes of this sort, see Briant, *From Cyrus to Alexander*, 399.

14. Rainer Kessler, *The Social History of Ancient Israel*, trans. Linda M. Maloney (Minneapolis: Fortress Press, 2008), 140.

15. See Briant, *From Cyrus to Alexander*, 399–402.

16. Josephus refers to Judah as "upper Idumea" (*Ant.* 5.81).

17. André Lemaire, "Administration in Fourth-Century B.C.E. Judah in Light of Epigraphy and Numismatics," in *Judah and the Judeans in the Fourth Century B.C.E.*, ed. Oded Lipschits, Gary N. Knoppers, and Rainer Albertz (Winona Lake, IN: Eisenbrauns, 2007), 53–74.

or for larger distribution at the discretion of ruling powers. In addition, the archives indicate that citizens in Idumea had to pay a poll tax in shekels of silver, a practice that also appears in the Elephantine documents, the Hebrew Bible, and the New Testament.[18] These poll taxes provided regular income for the upkeep of the local temple and other public buildings. Such archival evidence demonstrates different levels of taxation (local and imperial), whether in the form of silver currency or actual provisions like grain and barley. All of this is helpful background for understanding levies in the province of Judah.

When considering the specific context of Judah during the Persian period, it is helpful to clarify territorial boundaries. Extant sources mention the province of *Yehud* (the Aramaic form of "Judah"), which stretches from Bethel in the north, Ben Zur in the south, the Jordan River in the east, and the area of Emmaus-Modiin in the west (Ezra 2; Neh. 7).[19] Yet Ezra–Nehemiah and other sources also contain references to the satrapy "Beyond the River" (Heb. *ʿĀbar-Nahărâ*, as in Ezra 4:10). This satrapy Beyond the River encompassed a large territory, including Babylon (at first, when the satrap resided in Babylon), Samaria, and Judah. Before 450 BCE this satrapy was split into (1) Babylonia and (2) Beyond the River (i.e., the Euphrates).

One pertinent question is whether Judah/Yehud constituted a distinct province for administrative and tax purposes or if it remained part of a larger province that included Samaria. The debate over this topic is complex, but the evidence suggests that Judah had its own succession of semiautonomous governors and functioned as a province of the empire, with smaller districts as administrative centers.[20] The tax plan for the province might have correlated with these respective districts in some way, but this is uncertain. The relative freedom of the governors and people of Yehud depended on the Persian ruler in power, his flexibility, and the political and military dynamics of the day. In most cases, such details are unclear. Our inability to know more about even

---

18. Ibid., 59, compares the tax in these Aramaic ostraca to similar references in the Hebrew Bible and the New Testament, including regular requirements for the upkeep of the temple (e.g., Exod. 30:13; 38:26; Neh. 10:32–33; the question posed to Peter about the "temple tax" in Matt. 17:24).

19. Joshua J. Schwartz, "Judea," *DEJ* 851.

20. The debate focuses on the earlier hypothesis of Albrecht Alt, who argued that Yehud only became a recognized province when Nehemiah took over as governor: "Die Rolle Samarias bei der Entstehung des Judentums," in *Festschrift Otto Procksch zum sechzigsten Geburtstag am 9. August 1934 überreicht*, ed. Abrecht Alt et al. (Leipzig: A. Deichert & Hinrichs, 1934), 5–28. See also Grabbe, *A History of the Jews and Judaism in the Second Temple Period*, 1:139, who also surveys the districts: Jerusalem; Keilah (southwestern district); Mizpah in the north, with an urban center at Gibeon; Beth-haccerem as the western district; Jericho as an eastern district; and Beth-Zur as the southernmost district .

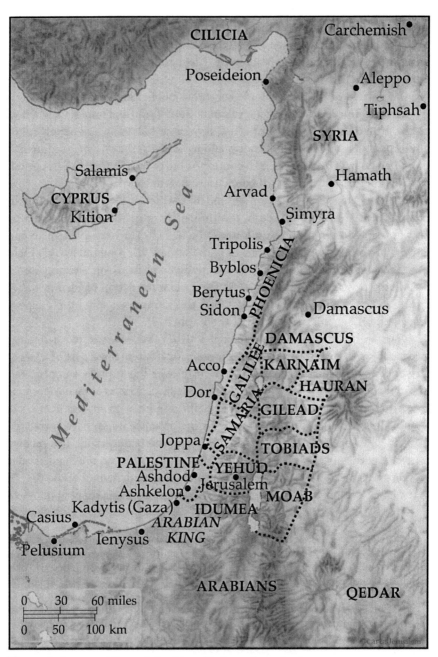

Figure 2. Satrapy of Beyond the River (© Carta, Jerusalem)

the most basic governance of Judah highlights the need for caution when making conclusions about taxes.

Despite this uncertainty, the available sources do provide indicators. For example, the book of Ezra mentions royal taxes. In the Aramaic portion, the author cites "tribute," "custom," and a "toll" (Ezra 4:13; cf. 7:24), including a reference to the actual collection of these levies (4:20). Ezra 4 is a composite text from several different sources describing political dynamics under a series of rulers. The middle section of this chapter (vv. 6–23) addresses rebellion in Judah during the reigns of Ahasuerus, or Xerxes (486–465 BCE), and Artaxerxes I (465–424 BCE). Rehum, a satrapy official from Samaria and the reported author of this correspondence, accuses certain individuals in Judah of conspiring against the empire by building up city walls and other fortifications. The consequence of these efforts, according to Rehum, is no revenue into the imperial coffers, because a certain local faction decided that construction efforts matter more than tax obligations. Despite the mention of more than one ruler in this passage and lack of certainty about its authenticity, the references to levies in Ezra suggest that the Persians expected regular streams of revenue, even from smaller provinces. This section also indicates that local leaders tried to win the favor of their Persian benefactors by guaranteeing the regular collection of taxes.

Similarly, the book of Nehemiah highlights the burdens of taxation and usury during a period of famine, as in a passage (Neh. 5) we have highlighted throughout this study. Nehemiah himself serves as governor to the province under the sanction of the Persian Empire (5:14), and his larger mission to Jerusalem (445 BCE) includes bureaucratic oversight and the rebuilding of the city wall. In his description of the crisis, the author mentions the tragic effects of famine, burdensome interest charges, debt slavery, and taxation by local and royal authorities. This leads to the following complaint:

> Now there was a great outcry of the people and of their wives against their Jewish kin. For there were those who said, "With our sons and our daughters, we are many; we must get grain, so that we may eat and stay alive." There were also those who said, "We are having to pledge our fields, our vineyards, and our houses in order to get grain during the famine." And there were those who said, "We are having to borrow money on our fields and vineyards to pay the king's tax [Heb. *middat hammelek*]. Now our flesh is the same as that of our kindred; our children are the same as their children; and yet we are forcing our sons and daughters to be slaves, and some of our daughters have been ravished; we are powerless, and our fields and vineyards now belong to others." (Neh. 5:1–5)

There seem to be three categories of people in the crisis: (1) those who have already lost their land and need to mortgage their children into debt slavery (5:2); (2) those who have retained their land or a portion of it but need to mortgage "our fields, our vineyards, and our houses in order to get grain [presumably for seed *and* food] during the famine" (v. 3); (3) those who need "to borrow money on our fields and vineyards to pay the king's tax [*middat hammelek*]" and sell children into debt slavery (vv. 4–5).[21] The specifics of this "king's tax" do not receive much attention except for the difficulty of paying it. Residents of Judah presumably have to contribute a portion of their yields, possibly in grain and/or silver, for the benefit of the larger empire.[22] Such a situation posed the greatest threat to the lower classes as they sought to provide for their households and generate enough surplus to meet taxation demands and settle any existing loans. Nehemiah 5 underscores the problem of meeting these requirements during periods of famine, especially when local elites conspire against vulnerable farmers. If repayment proved difficult, the seizure of landholdings and other possessions and even selling children into debt slavery became tragic alternatives, as the passage indicates.

This scene in the Nehemiah Memoir involves the precise set of circumstances that Lenski and Eisenstadt describe in their anthropological work: demanding imperial taxation and local overlords seeking to profit from financial inequality in the society (i.e., "nonagricultural elites" operating as harsh creditors against their neighbors). This passage supports Lenski's claim that the small landowner suffers most under such a system. Officials in Judah, estate owners, and other resourceful persons with means could operate in an advantageous intermediary role and thrive within the imperial system while most agrarian households faced adverse power structures. The description in Nehemiah 5 makes clear that the majority of the populace is in danger, and onerous taxes are contributing to the crisis.[23]

---

21. Rainer Albertz, *A History of Israelite Religion in the Old Testament Period*, vol. 2, *From the Exile to the Maccabees*, trans. John Bowden (Louisville, KY: Westminster John Knox Press, 1994), 495. To justify this threefold categorization, one has to read *rbym* (many) as *'rbym* in 5:2, as many commentators have done. Thus the correct translation of 5:2 becomes "We are having to put up our sons and daughters as surety in order to buy grain and live." See Blenkinsopp, *Ezra–Nehemiah*, 254.

22. The term for tax here, *middâ*, is a loanword from Akkadian that relates to royal collection. Hans G. Kippenberg, *Religion und Klassenbildung im antiken Judäa*, SUNT 14 (Göttingen: Vandenhoeck & Ruprecht, 1978), 49–53, has argued that the conversion to a silver-based tax system prompted the crisis among the poor farmers, but there is no clear evidence in Neh. 5 that the residents of Judah need to pay in silver. Cf. Briant, *From Cyrus to Alexander*, 406; Pastor, *Land and Economy*, 17. Hoglund, *Achaemenid Imperial Administration*, 213, maintains that many farmers could still pay with grain.

23. Philippe Guillaume, "Nehemiah 5: No Economic Crisis," *Journal of Hebrew Scriptures* 10 (2010): 4, suggests that no one is destitute in this framework because they seem to have ample credit. Yet such an assertion runs contrary to the unfair lending arrangements involving surety that we studied in the previous chapter.

In chapter 3 (above) we argued that interest charges and surety played a critical role in the economy, leading to greater stratification. According to the testimony of the people in Nehemiah 5, a class of wealthy lenders is taking advantage of the crisis for their own benefit, and they are willing to capitalize on the vulnerability of fellow Judeans by acting as manipulative creditors in the pursuit of land and child labor. Such a scenario occurred in other regions of the Persian Empire as royal authorities allied with local officials to demand tribute items and taxes.[24] Even if we cannot be certain of a singular crisis during Nehemiah's tenure, the people confront a precarious situation in this chapter, and antichretic loan arrangements by local elites have exacerbated the situation. Perhaps the demands of rebuilding the Jerusalem wall magnified this crisis by pulling farmers away from their land during critical periods, leaving them vulnerable to grain shortfalls and predatory lending. Such a scenario (i.e., work on the wall as a distraction from farming) is uncertain, however, especially since this chapter of Nehemiah might be a later insertion into the wall narrative.[25]

As a newly minted official, Nehemiah is aware of the possibilities for financial scheming among governors and other officials. Consequently, he promises, "because of the fear of God," to discontinue the burdensome practice of his predecessors, who extracted food, wine, and forty shekels of silver from households (Neh. 5:15). The fact that Nehemiah makes a special point to distinguish his policies from earlier governors indicates the difficulties many citizens experienced in paying various taxes, the potential for local officials to gain profit and power, and the devastating impact of this system on households at the subsistence level.[26] Nehemiah does not annul or cancel the imperial tax, but he does promise relief for those who are struggling.

In any case, the temporary suspension of the "king's tax" does not seem to be a possibility for the governor. Payment of this levy represents an unbending requirement, presumably because the Persians wanted regular sources of

24. There is the house of Murašu in Babylon, which charged up to a 40 percent interest rate for loans. This sum became particularly onerous in the wake of royal taxes. See Robert P. Maloney, "Usury and Restrictions on Interest-Taking in the Ancient Near East," *CBQ* 36 (1974): 1–20.

25. According to Jacob L. Wright, *Rebuilding Identity: The Nehemiah-Memoir and Its Earliest Readers*, BZAW 348 (Berlin: de Gruyter, 2004), the building narrative did not originally include Neh. 5:1–19; cf. Mark Throntveit, *Ezra–Nehemiah*, Interpretation (Louisville, KY: Westminster John Knox Press, 1992), 59.

26. The specific practices of these earlier governors are unclear since details of the Achaemenid administration during the first century of its occupation in Yehud (until the missions of Ezra–Nehemiah) remain largely uncertain. See Blenkinsopp, *Ezra–Nehemiah*, 263–64.

revenue.[27] Therefore, Nehemiah's solution is restoration of any fields that Judeans have taken from fellow members of their covenant community as well as forgiveness of all interest charges (5:10–11). The governor appeals to the benevolent spirit of what the Torah envisions (e.g., Exod. 22:25–27 and the prohibition against taking interest from poor persons), and one of the likely reasons for this move is that he cannot rescind Persian taxation requirements. While the plausibility of such a widespread remission of debts is uncertain, the statement in Nehemiah 5:14 is intriguing: "from the time that I was appointed to be their governor in the land of Judah, . . . neither I nor my brothers ate the food allowance of the governor." Nehemiah claims that previous governors had "laid heavy burdens on the people, and took food and wine from them, besides forty shekels of silver" (v. 15). The governor and other local officials have greater control over the assessment of regional levies (i.e., "the food allowance of the governor"). At his great assembly, Nehemiah as governor promises to provide relief by lifting the local tax burden. Such a decision suggests local autonomy for provincial governors, provided that they continued to pay the "king's tax." Different layers of taxation confronted the residents of Judah, and Nehemiah had the most control over revenues coming directly to him.

One question about the imposition of such levies is whether they reflected the Persian need for revenue to confront emergent political and military problems, particularly in the eastern Mediterranean. Did Achaemenid officials decide to impose higher taxes on smaller provinces such as Judah in order to finance military needs and fortify neighboring provinces?[28] According to one proposal, the threat from Egyptian and Hellenistic insurrections during the fifth century (esp. the rebellion led by Egypt's ruler Inaros from 464–454 BCE) led to greater Persian interest in extracting as much as possible

27. Guillaume, "Nehemiah 5: No Economic Crisis," 13–14, argues that the Persian authorities had the foresight to become lenient when difficulties arose in the satrapies, and they regularly considered the well-being of the small farmers who made up the majority of their tax base, just as the Romans would do. Even if the Persians considered the morale of subject peoples, both Neh. 5 and what we know of common tendencies in imperial economies suggest that royal authorities set up mechanisms to extract as much as possible from subject peoples while being careful not to trigger rebellion.

28. The message of the prophet Haggai and his endorsement of Zerubbabel are markers of such a dynamic. With the Persians needing to quell revolts in Egypt, Darius had to rely on smaller provinces like Judah to finance his military campaigns. In his concluding oracle (Hag. 2:20–23), the prophet seeks to pacify his audience about Darius's plans, lending support to official Persian policy and the authority of Zerubbabel. See Berquist, *Judaism in Persia's Shadow*, 67–68, who convincingly argues that this oracle is not about God's promise to eradicate the Persians but rather the Persians' uneventful passage through Judah in order to defeat the Egyptians.

from subject peoples.[29] The restoration of the city walls in Jerusalem and the building of military garrisons in the rural areas required financing and labor, and one motivating factor for such efforts was better infrastructure in the territories closest to Egypt. If this dynamic played a role in Persian tax policy, whether in Judah or elsewhere, such a move confirms the theoretical work of Eisenstadt, who cites the tendency of imperial powers to impose harsher levies during a crisis period such as famine or rebellion in a neighboring province. The need for steady supplies of food would have contributed to this dynamic, especially when the Persians had military personnel in a particular area and needed more provisions.[30] The fifth century BCE was a time of great revolt in Egypt, and so it is understandable that the empire's ruling power wanted regular income and supplies. While the precise motivations for the "king's tax" and the bolstering of Jerusalem and its environs are not fully clear, military needs and concerns about unrest in Egypt clearly influenced the larger policies of the Persians.

Yet we should be careful about overstating Persian concern in such a small province as Judah. Strategic interest in this region would have remained low due to the population level and scarcity of natural resources. The rebuilding of the temple, codification of legal and prophetic traditions, and the further development of "Jewish" identity were major events for the small population in Judah but not critical for the larger empire (except in terms of larger trends such as tolerance of local customs). Achaemenid authorities sent emissaries and worked with local administrators, but it is unlikely that Judah became an area of much concern to them other than as a minor source of taxation revenue/tribute and a buffer against trouble in the eastern Mediterranean. The empire's most important mechanisms for control probably came in the area of tax policy and military garrisons. The extant record shows little indication of heavy Persian involvement in the inner workings of Judah. Ruling authorities probably cared more about stability and taxes than internal political and religious dynamics.

A related question is how much favorable treatment the Persians actually bestowed on smaller provinces like Judah. When examining the laudatory

29. Hoglund, *Achaemenid Imperial Administration*, argues that the revolt of Inaros (ca. 464–454 BCE) in Egypt and its Greek supporters (the so-called Delian league) had an impact on the decision to fortify Judah and bolster its political leadership. According to the thesis, the Persians did not want unrest in the eastern Mediterranean to spread into other provinces, especially those bordering Egypt. This revolt does not correlate with the later date for Nehemiah's mission (445 BCE) assumed by the present work; yet there was periodic unrest in Egypt throughout the fifth century BCE, and therefore Hoglund's thesis is possible.

30. Diana Edelman, *The Origins of the "Second" Temple: Persian Imperial Policy and the Rebuilding of Jerusalem* (London: Equinox, 2005), 341.

language of Ezra–Nehemiah and Deutero-Isaiah about the first ruler, Cyrus (559–530 BCE), and his benevolence toward the inhabitants of the region, the impression is positive (e.g., Ezra 1; Isa. 44:28). Such praise has the tone of strategic propaganda: these authors laud the ruling authorities, and in response they apparently receive the latitude to pursue local customs, including the worship of Yahweh. A degree of flexibility provided space for the ongoing development of sacred traditions. Nevertheless, an "enlightened" despot is still a despot, and complimentary statements about Persian rulers in the Hebrew Bible should not obscure the demanding taxation system and its impact on the poor agriculturalists who made up the majority of the population. Bruce Lincoln has written persuasively on this topic, claiming that the strategy of the Persians was duplicitous, since it represented "imperial aggression as salvific action taken on behalf of divine principles, thereby recoding the empire's victims as its beneficiaries."[31] By presenting themselves as understanding deliverers, these rulers gave themselves cover to tax the population in a variety of ways and demand resources from across the empire.

Consequently, it becomes necessary to qualify the common assumption of Persian "tolerance" to diverse territories. Achaemenid officials did support many local elites, working with them to develop royal land and squeeze as much as possible from subject peoples. Most inhabitants of the region, however, came on the receiving end of demands. Those with resources and connections could advance within the imperial system, while the majority of the population could not. Much of the collected goods and revenue stayed within the local province, and such resources created stability and gave provincial governors monetary incentive to remain loyal. The imperial bureaucracy also collected tribute and taxation for the larger kingdom, and the central governing authorities benefited from such an arrangement. When analyzing this dynamic, it becomes clear that the Persians did not act from altruistic motives; instead, they sought to maintain the balance between burdensome levies and strategic flexibility.

Another primary purpose for levies had to do with supporting the temple, Levites, and priests. A variety of sources stipulate that the general population had to provide cultic personnel with monetary donations and supplies. In a putative letter from the emperor Artaxerxes I (465–424), the book of Ezra proclaims, "We also notify you that it shall not be lawful to impose tribute, custom, or toll on any of the priests, the Levites, the singers, the

---

31. Bruce Lincoln, *Religion, Empire, and Torture: The Case of Achaemenian Persia with a Postscript on Abu Ghraib* (Chicago: University of Chicago Press, 2007), 95.

doorkeepers, the temple servants, or other servants of this house of God" (Ezra 7:24).[32] Similarly, Nehemiah cites "the obligation to charge ourselves yearly one-third of a shekel for the service of the house of our God" (10:32 [33]). Following this verse is a lengthy command to bring various commodities to the temple for the priests and the Levites (10:33–39 [34–40]).[33] Several sources from the Persian period chastise anyone who shirks this requirement to support the priestly class, since it represents an insult to God (e.g., Mal. 3:8–9). The people already had to pay the "king's tax" and levies to the governor and local officials. Even if they wanted to support the temple because of their dedication to the tradition, donations for cultic personnel added another layer of obligation.

This responsibility to priests involved regular donations and tithes, with the impetus for such obligations coming from the Torah. Deuteronomy mandates tithes (one-tenth) of a farmer's agricultural produce for Jerusalem during the year (14:22) such that the donor could either consume the food offering or convert it to silver and spend the money to support the Jerusalem economy (14:23–26). Every third year the Levites and the poor should receive the tithe (14:27–29). According to Leviticus, one-tenth of produce, "whether seed from the ground or the fruit from the tree, are the LORD's" (27:30). This statement indicates a regular priestly claim to such proceeds. In the book of Numbers, the Levites receive the tithe and then distribute a tenth of that amount to the priests (18:21–32), the same procedure that appears in Nehemiah (10: 35–39 [36–40]; 13:5). With the Levites acting as collectors, this requirement functioned as a tax.[34] Later interpreters combined the legislation from Numbers and Deuteronomy in a manner that required *three* tithes per year (e.g., Tob. 1:7–8, where the speaker offers one tithe for the Levites, one for Jerusalem according to Deut. 14:23–26, and another for the poor; cf. *Jub.* 32:10–14). Pilgrimage festivals, such as Weeks and Passover, provided occasion for bringing gifts to Jerusalem, and Nehemiah also mentions storehouses

---

32. Even if the authenticity of this correspondence is uncertain, the requirement to support the priests and the temple has support from a variety of sources. See Blenkinsopp, *Ezra–Nehemiah*, 146–47.

33. The precedent for such requirements appears in the Pentateuch, where the priests, Levites, and their families have no "inheritance" or "portion" in the land and must rely on the contributions of others (Num. 18:20–21; Deut. 18:1–2). E. P. Sanders, *Judaism: Practice and Belief, 63 BCE–66 CE* (London: SCM Press, 1992), 146–47, argues that "portion" and "inheritance" indicate the ability to produce one's own food privately.

34. Blenkinsopp, *Ezra–Nehemiah*, 318–19, argues that the phrase "as it is written in the law" (Neh. 10:36 [37]), indicates an important relationship between this passage and the pentateuchal laws cited above, even if not in their final form.

for "grain, wine, and oil" (13:5). Such passages and the later references suggest that these cultic obligations in food and silver became part of communal life after the exile, compounding an already demanding tax structure and offering a measure of security to the priestly class.[35]

Within this context, the office of high priest played an important role in the socioeconomic structure. The rebuilding of the temple and its function as an administrative center gave authority to the high priest, especially with no king after the exile.[36] From the appointment of Joshua/Jeshua as high priest, the holder of this position made pivotal decisions in the community. According to Ezra and Haggai–Zechariah, Joshua oversaw the rebuilding of the temple and the reconstitution of cultic life in Jerusalem, including festival observances. He also had larger civic duties as a judge (Zech. 3:7). Though we know little of what Joshua accomplished during his tenure aside from one year of temple building (520 BCE), the significance of this figure and his successors during this period of rejuvenation and identity formation had to be considerable.[37] The references to high priests, including lengthy descriptions from Josephus, underscore their leadership role.

One open question is just how much political and, by extension, economic power the high priest wielded during the Persian period, including any power-sharing arrangements with the succession of governors in Judah. The local governor clearly had some agency under Achaemenid rule. The fact that Nehemiah can cancel "the food allowance of the governor" (Neh. 5:18) suggests that as a nonpriestly leader, he has control over certain policy decisions. The power of the high priest in financial matters is less clear. Persian-period evidence on this point is slender, but the Elephantine papyri suggest that the high priest had at least some voice in administrative policy, especially with regard to cultic decisions. In a letter that can be dated to 407 BCE, a man named Jedoniah from the "Yeb fortress" in Egypt makes an appeal for permission and quite possibly funds to rebuild the Jewish temple in that locale (*TAD* A4.7). In this correspondence Jedoniah complains to Bagohi (the governor of Yehud) that he wrote an earlier letter requesting help from both the governor and "Johanan the high priest and his colleagues, the priests who are in Jerusalem" (line 18) for the rebuilding effort, but he never received an

---

35. Kessler, *Social History of Ancient Israel*, 146, highlights the ties between the temple and the imperial system and the efforts of some households to avoid paying tithes.

36. We should be careful to distinguish between kings of the Davidic line before the exile and postexilic governors such as Zerubbabel, who had political power but not the autonomy of earlier royal figures such as Josiah.

37. VanderKam, *From Joshua to Caiaphas*, 43.

answer.[38] The fact that Jedoniah seeks the permission of the governor *and* the high priest implies that both of these officials command respect and are viewed by at least some in the Diaspora as necessary figures to consult. It is possible that the Judean community in Egypt wanted not just consent but also logistical and financial help, and the high priest could be of assistance with garnering support for the building efforts (if he in fact supported the construction of a temple outside of Judah).[39] In any case, the influx of silver and food offerings and other supplies to the temple in Jerusalem made the high priest and his administration important stewards of financial resources after the exile. As this office evolved during the Second Temple period, the power of the high priest would increase greatly (see below).

PTOLEMAIC PERIOD

The defeat of Darius III by the armies of Alexander the Great in the late fourth century BCE represented a turning point for the expansive regions the Persians ruled, including Judah/Judea.[40] Not only did this Macedonian conqueror engage in one of the most rapid and comprehensive military campaigns the world had ever seen, but his advances also meant the further spread of Hellenistic culture into diverse areas. Although his military maneuvers had little immediate effect on Judea (contra Josephus in *Ant.* 11.326–338), the policies of his successors made a permanent imprint on the political, cultural, and economic circumstances of the region.[41] Ptolemaic armies ultimately

38. Translation is that of Arthur Ernest Cowley, *Aramaic Papyri of the Fifth Century B.C.* (Oxford: Clarendon Press, 1923; repr., Osnabrück: Otto Zeller, 1967), 113. The historicity of Johanan's tenure as high priest is not in doubt. This figure appears in Neh. 12:22 and perhaps in 12:11, where the scribe incorrectly wrote Jonathan instead of Johanan. In the letter, Jedoniah also states that he has written to the sons of Sanballat, the governor of Samaria.

39. VanderKam, *From Joshua to Caiaphas*, 58. Whether the high priest failed to respond to the initial letter because he opposed the building of a temple in Egypt and away from Jerusalem is an open question.

40. We will use "Judea" rather than "Judah" for the remainder of this chapter. This designation is common in sources of the Hellenistic period, and "Judea" always includes Jerusalem and its environs. Depending on the source and the precise historical context, Judea can also refer to a much broader swath of territory. See J. Schwartz, "Judea," 850–52.

41. Regarding the direct impact of Macedonian incursions into the region, the Wadi el-Daliyeh fragments are relevant. These are a series of coins, seal impressions, and bullae from the late fourth century BCE that document slave trades, loans, and other matters relating to the Samarian community. See Douglas M. Gropp and James C. VanderKam, *Wadi Daliyeh II and Qumran Miscellanea*, part 2, *The Samaria Papyri from Wadi Daliyeh*, DJD 28, pt. 2 (Oxford: Oxford University Press, 2001).

gained control of the territories in and around Judea, and this meant that for most of the third century BCE, those in Judea had to submit to the Macedonian successors of Alexander who ruled from Egypt.

The current section will examine the impact of Ptolemaic rule, with careful attention to the role of taxation, close bureaucratic oversight, and landgrabs by officials. We will highlight the potential for profit and power among those with connections to the administration, the ongoing significance of the priestly office for cultivating Jewish identity and carrying out various financial responsibilities, the impact of Greek culture on economic life in Judea, and the challenges for households without close ties to the Ptolemies. Greek papyri from Egypt and other sources provide important insights about stratification and the tight economic control that the Ptolemies exercised over subject peoples.

After the death of Alexander the Great in 323 BCE, a period of bitter rivalry and warfare occurred among the so-called Diadochoi (Successors) of this powerful ruler. The Macedonian general Ptolemy participated in these internecine battles, which stretched on for decades. Since Alexander had no obvious heir, instability following his sudden death led to conflicts and ultimately the division of the empire into different sectors, with the Ptolemaic dynasty emerging as the predominant force in Egypt and surrounding territories.[42] Beginning with this general, who became Ptolemy (meaning "warlike") I Soter (Sōtēr, "Savior"; 305–282 BCE), or Ptolemy Lagides, a succession of rulers established a kingdom in Egypt that enabled them to work with local allies and consolidate power. Working from their vibrant capital, Alexandria, Ptolemaic rulers had to balance the preferences of their Greek compatriots with the long-standing cultural mores of Egyptian life.[43] Many Egyptians recognized the Macedonian rulers as the rightful claimants to the pharaonic succession that had existed for millennia, and the Ptolemies were able to establish dominion over most of Egypt. Judea also fell under the control of this kingdom, although the Seleucids in Syria made regular attempts to expand their reach by trying to defeat the descendants of Ptolemy, and ultimately they succeeded.

As the representative of the gods on earth, the Ptolemaic ruler had ultimate claim to the land under his control. Consequently, huge swaths of Egyptian territory belonged to the crown. Because of the land that the Persians had

---

42. Several decades of instability followed the death of Alexander the Great, and Ptolemy struggled with the Seleucids for control over a number of territories in the Palestinian region, including Judea.

43. As the capital of the Ptolemaic kingdom, Alexandria became a locus of Greek culture and a hub of trading activity. Many prominent Judeans in the Diaspora resided there.

controlled, certain territories passed to the successors of Alexander (Diado-choi), including the Ptolemaic rulers.[44] Greek records from this period indi-cate that some farmers, including certain agriculturalists in Judea, could work as half-free stewards of royal land as long as they showed regular allegiance to the king through contributions in produce and possibly silver. In these cases, the king "leased" land to local farmers, and they had to pay rent through any yields and possibly penalties for producing a bad harvest. In a related move, Ptolemaic authorities compelled farmers to bring fallow land into prof-itability for the benefit of the state.[45] This dynamic of control influenced the manner in which the royal administration treated subject peoples in foreign territories.

Yet the Ptolemaic rulers also made land concessions to key constituencies, especially the priestly class. Egyptian priests needed arable land to support cultic personnel (known in Egyptian texts as "sacred land").[46] These priests often had economic powers of their own through taxation and grain stor-age rights at local temples. The Ptolemies recognized the priests' power but made more exacting requirements than in previous eras, forcing many of the Egyptian cultic leaders to contribute to the royal administration in greater amounts. In addition, military officials claimed land tracts for use by troops across the empire, usually clustered in a colony known as a cleruchy. If a sol-dier spent time in a foreign territory, he could often obtain a plot that would support himself and perhaps his family. This type of development might hap-pen at the expense of local landowners (see below).

Such a hierarchical framework in the governing structure reduced the land available for private ownership, leaving many farmers with small plots (often called "grant land" in Egyptian texts) or working in royal fields to which they had no claim. Scholars studying this period have used the French term *diri-gisme* to describe the Ptolemaic system. Dirigisme means tight hierarchical control by the state, where the ruler(s) exercises direct oversight over territo-rial holdings and the larger economy.[47] Archival records such as the Zeno papyri document the Ptolemaic state's tendency to control the financial sys-tem through coercive and exacting measures. The Ptolemies accomplished such strict control in part through land surveys and careful census taking.[48]

44. Pastor, *Land and Economy*, 22–27, argues for continuity of royal estates in many cases.

45. A series of "land allotment receipts" documents such activity. See Hölbl, *History of the Ptolemaic Empire*, 62–63.

46. Hölbl, *History of the Ptolemaic Empire*, 25.

47. Joseph Gilbert Manning, *The Last Pharaohs: Egypt under the Ptolemies* (Princ-eton: Princeton University Press, 2009), 45–49.

48. Ibid., 34–41.

Drawing on the lofty status of the pharaoh in earlier eras, the government also issued decrees, founded new towns, and worked within the long-standing Egyptian system to consolidate its property holdings and centralize control. In particular, the founding of new Greek-speaking towns throughout the empire enabled the Ptolemies to expand their reach and give their own officials and merchants a place to conduct their affairs.[49] Such activity also meant the spread of Hellenistic ideas, even to smaller territories like Judea.

The royal administration also exercised careful oversight over the buying and selling of commodities.[50] Taxes on grain and salt proved to be very profitable for Ptolemaic authorities, but they created hardships for poor farmers in Egypt and beyond. In addition, a "yoke" tax became a common levy during this period. This requirement probably functioned as a blanket capitation tax on males, a regressive levy that did not take into account income level or resources.[51] Coinage became more widespread in Egypt and Judea during this period, and many farmers had to pay taxes in silver (see below for illustrations of silver coinage), especially when they produced goods other than grain, such as vineyards and fruit trees.[52]

One papyrus confirms this policy of strict control: it contains a provision that residents of Ptolemaic Syria must register their flocks with local officials, presumably for tax purposes.[53] Under such a demanding system, the policies of the Ptolemies tended to be more autocratic than their Persian predecessors, with watchfulness over trade as a focal point.[54] The fact that royal authorities made major decisions in the port city of Alexandria led to tight control over commerce, since the ruling party had greater awareness of trading practices. A slave trade flourished during this period, including women

49. Elias Joseph Bickerman, *The Jews in the Greek Age* (Cambridge: Harvard University Press, 1988), 70–72.

50. Tcherikover, *Hellenistic Civilization and the Jews*, 13–14, cites the large number of edibles, jewelry items, and other goods that were subject to royal taxation.

51. Brian P. Muhs, *Tax Receipts, Taxpayers, and Taxes in Early Ptolemaic Thebes*, OIP 126 (Chicago: Oriental Institute Publications, 2005), 29–35, 41–45.

52. Ibid., 23–24, outlines the different forms of currency and their value; cf. Manning, *The Last Pharaohs*, 127–38.

53. The papyrus (P.Rainer 24552) is located in Vienna and seems to corroborate the content of the Zeno archives. It also addresses questions of unlawful enslavement. See Tcherikover, *Hellenistic Civilization and the Jews*, 428n54. For an analysis, see Lester L. Grabbe, "Hyparchs, *Oikonomoi*, and Mafiosi: The Governance of Judah in the Ptolemaic Period," in *Judah between East and West: The Transition from Persian to Greek Rule (ca. 400–200 B.C.E.)*, ed. Lester L. Grabbe and Oded Lipschits, LSTS 75 (London: T&T Clark, 2011), 80.

54. See the classic study of Michael I. Rostovtzeff, *The Social and Economic History of the Hellenistic World*, 3 vols. (Oxford: Clarendon Press, 1941), where he argues that the dominant form of Ptolemaic rule was despotism.

Figure 3. Ptolemy II, AR
tetradrachm, struck at Gaza
(225/4 BCE); bust of Ptolemy
I/Eagle (© David Hendin,
used by permission)

Figure 4. Ptolemy II, AR
tetradrachm, struck at Joppa;
bust of Ptolemy I/Eagle
(© David Hendin, used by
permission)

and young girls (Gk. *paidiskai*) being sent to Egypt, in some cases for the
purpose of prostitution.

An elaborate bureaucratic structure assisted Ptolemaic rulers with enhanc-
ing their power and finances.[55] Along with royal secretaries and top military
leaders, an individual known as the *dioikētēs* served as the financial administrator of the empire, and this official had responsibility for major economic
decisions.[56] The *dioikētēs* had to maintain stability within Ptolemaic territories, and he sought to maximize revenue intake and acquire additional lands
for the ruler, and in some cases for himself. Like the Persians, Ptolemaic
rulers organized their empire into governable districts, and they utilized the
long-standing system in Egypt. A series of nomes (districts) gave structure to
the empire, and smaller subdistricts and villages provided further delineation.
Each nome had a local leader called an *oikonomos* who, along with a royal
scribe(s), managed estates and made certain that all lands were registered with
the *dioikētēs*.[57] In addition, a series of tax districts, or toparchies, gave local
administrators a helpful bureaucratic framework for collecting levies. Along

55. Muhs, *Tax Receipts, Taxpayers, and Taxes*, 13.
56. The complex demands of this position often led to a team of officials fulfilling
the duties of the *dioikētēs*.
57. Hölbl, *History of the Ptolemaic Empire*, 59. Many nomes also had a "nomarch" in
charge of larger administrative duties.

these lines, a wealth of primary texts indicate regular census taking to ascertain population levels for taxation.[58] Royal and local officials usually worked in concert, even in foreign territories, and the hierarchy of appointees led to the efficient harnessing of resources for the benefit of the Ptolemaic ruler and the upper tier of his administration. Local elites proved to be indispensable in this regard, since these individuals could enforce the tax system in accordance with the circumstances of their region. The precise manner in which the Ptolemies adapted this framework to Judea is unclear; there are no references to a civil governor during this period, and so more direct control by royal officials and cooperation with local officials, including those connected to the temple, probably remained the norm.[59]

Part of the duty of these local elites lay in the area of tax farming. Well-connected individuals could bid for the opportunity to garner revenues for a particular region, but they had to offer their assets as surety in the event that they could not provide the full amount. These individuals functioned as underwriters to guarantee the Ptolemies a steady stream of revenue from each district, and local tax collectors assisted with the process.[60] Tax farming proved to be a lucrative enterprise for many persons who engaged in it, especially since local officials had a vested interest in working toward the productivity of their territories. How much the Ptolemies used this system beyond Egypt is an open question, but there is good reason to believe that they relied on local officials to maximize tax collection on farming. The efforts of Joseph in the Tobiad Romance (*Ant.* 12.154–236) amounts to tax farming in Judea in a manner that benefited both the Ptolemies and Joseph himself (see below).

The Zeno papyri are a helpful resource for understanding Ptolemaic policies and how this controlling system played out, both in and beyond Egypt.[61] Because some of the content from these records describes events in the Syro-Palestinian region, the Zeno archives are highly significant for present purposes. The documents, which date from the middle of the third century, contain letters between Zeno, a financial officer, and Apollonius, the *dioikētēs* who served in 262–245 BCE (under Ptolemy II Philadelphus). Within Egypt, Zeno had the responsibility of overseeing an estate belonging to Apollonius in Faiyûm near Philadelphia. The specificity of the correspondence reflects

---

58. Muhs, *Tax Receipts, Taxpayers, and Taxes*, 14–17.

59. Bickerman, *Jews in the Greek Age*, 74.

60. See Rostovtzeff, *Social and Economic History*, 2:328–31; Grabbe, "Hyparchs, Oikonomoi, and Mafiosi," 71; Muhs, *Tax Receipts, Taxpayers, and Taxes*, 7.

61. For the primary texts, see Durand, *Des Grecs en Palestine*; Victor Tcherikover, *Corpus papyrorum judaicarum*, 3 vols. (Jerusalem: Magnes Press, Hebrew University; Cambridge: Harvard University Press, 1957–64).

Zeno's careful oversight, and it demonstrates the extent to which the royal administration worked the system to its own financial advantage.

Zeno also supervised territory beyond the borders of Egypt, including land in the Palestinian region. In the years 260–258 BCE, Zeno toured an estate belonging to Apollonius in the area of Bêt 'Anat (in Galilee). This sizeable property consisted of a large vineyard and cornfields, and Apollonius apparently wanted his subordinate to advise him about the land and its potential value. Zeno remained in the region for a lengthy period, presumably to make a careful assessment of the vineyard and its functionality. An upper-tier official would naturally want lucrative land, and Zeno seems to have acted as a scout for Apollonius. The Persians had also claimed valuable tracts in places like the Galilee region, and so Zeno's efforts reflected a continuation of earlier patterns.[62] Yet Egyptian policy mandated that such properties revert back to the crown upon the death of the official, following the interpretation of the pharaoh as the ultimate owner of all lands. Therefore the vineyard in Galilee and any other properties could not stay in the family of Apollonius permanently, nor could local landowners necessarily reclaim the territory once the Egyptian royal administration had taken control of it. The evidence from Zeno's archives suggests that the Ptolemaic officials took control of valuable land in Judea when it suited their expansionist ambitions.

Both for his own personal gain and for the benefit of the royal bureaucracy, Apollonius kept close watch over Ptolemaic territories and sought to expand trade routes. He tracked taxation and commerce through a network of officials in the region, particularly in the more bustling areas along the coast (Gaza, Joppa, Acco, Sidon, and Beirut).[63] Entrepreneurs established themselves along the Mediterranean in such towns as Jaffa, and they worked with local merchants in the slave trade and pursued other profitable ventures. By engaging in such endeavors, not only did the Ptolemies increase their economic control over Judea; their efforts also meant the spread of Greek culture and ideas, especially among the upper classes.

The Zeno archives also mention landowners with enough clout to maintain their possessions and conduct their business affairs, but this type of independence required financial resources and a social status that most Judeans lacked. The Ptolemies understood that cooperation with local figures could help them when they needed allies for tax collection or other emergent problems, and therefore royal officials allowed certain individuals more latitude. A few references in the extant papyri document the ability of wealthy Judeans

62. Tcherikover, *Hellenistic Civilization and the Jews*, 67.
63. Ibid., 63.

to maintain a relatively independent existence as long as they did not flaunt their status in a way that publicly damaged or questioned their Ptolemaic overlords. Such cooperation did not always occur. One papyrus (P.Cair.Zen. 59018) mentions the refusal of a wealthy landowner (Jeddous) to pay back debts he owed to Zeno. When officials came to demand payment, this Jeddous dismissed them from the village. This description highlights the discrepancy between helpful allies and insolent landowners and the fact that a local elite had enough confidence to defy Egyptian directives.[64]

This papyri collection also sheds light on the deployment of military personnel and the role of local Judeans in facilitating their living situation. Since the Ptolemies set up cleruchies for soldiers in foreign territories, they had to seize or in some cases lease property for housing, farming, and fortifications. This practice occurred in Judea, and it had significant repercussions for local farmers. Military officers could claim parcels as their own with the backing of the royal administration, especially since such transfers were occurring with frequency in Egypt. One papyrus from the collection reports a sale of property between a Greek man in Judea (identified as "one of Tobiah's people") and Zeno (P.Cair.Zen. 59003).[65] The document, which also describes the sale of a female slave, mentions a citadel as defense against Bedouin attacks from the desert, and a related papyrus refers to this area as "Tobiah's land." Such references suggest that certain landowners could work with the Ptolemies by allowing military settlers to inhabit their land, and in turn they might profit from this association. This Tobiah apparently knew how to work the system since he provided slaves to Apollonius and gifts to the king (P.Cair.Zen. 59075; 59076). The reasons for Ptolemaic flexibility in this regard are perhaps not too complex to ascertain: they wanted local allies to help them find land, maintain order, and provide assistance with tax collection.

This Tobiah figure also appears in the colorful account of the Tobiad family in the writings of Josephus (*Ant.* 12.154–236), the Tobiad Romance. This tale underscores the potential for Judean officials to gain significant wealth and power if they prove to be reliable. Tobiah came from a long-standing Judean family in the region (the Tobiads): this person is probably a descendant of Tobiah the Ammonite, one of the opponents of Nehemiah's reform efforts (e.g., Neh. 2:10). According to Josephus, the high priest Onias II (Joseph's uncle) refused to pay the required tribute to the Ptolemaic king (ca. 240 BCE), and the ruler then threatened to parcel out the land into cleruchies

64. Grabbe, "Hyparchs, *Oikonomoi*, and Mafiosi," 74.
65. Tcherikover, *Hellenistic Civilization and the Jews*, 64.

for soldiers.[66] Tobiah's son Joseph averted the crisis by entertaining the Egyptian royal envoy and offering to pay the necessary tribute with funds he had borrowed. In so doing, he also bribed his way into becoming a tax farmer/collector for the entire region (Judea, Samaria, Coele-Syria, Phoenicia), not only ingratiating himself with the royal bureaucracy, but also obtaining authority through his opportunistic showmanship. According to Josephus, this Joseph demanded taxes from different localities and quelled any dissenters through violent force.

The close ties between the local aristocracy and the Ptolemaic governing structure are apparent in the Tobiad Romance, with corruption and an oppressive tax structure as part of the system. Those who could ally themselves with royal authorities might enjoy lucrative success, but only at the expense of their struggling neighbors. The ability of Joseph to bid for the right to collect taxes indicates the manner in which the Ptolemies relied on locals and the potential for these entrepreneurs to become powerful and wealthy in the process. Yet caution is in order when assessing this account. Much of this section of *Antiquities* reads more like a folktale than actual history.[67] For example, Josephus mentions the Ptolemaic ruler inviting Joseph to sit in his chariot and be a regular guest at the palace (*Ant.* 12.172–74). This account also includes the fantastic story of how Joseph's son Hyrcanus is conceived.[68] Such details do not invalidate the usefulness of this tale for understanding economics, however. The references regarding taxation and the cozy relationship between rulers and local officials correlate with the other evidence for Ptolemaic policies, such as the Zeno papyri, and probably represent one of the more reliable features of the Tobiad Romance.

The book of Ecclesiastes (Qoheleth) also contains a passage that seems to reflect the hierarchical, corrupt system under the Ptolemies. Qoheleth's reflections most likely date from the middle of the third century BCE, when individuals like Joseph were forming alliances and exploiting their struggling neighbors.

---

66. In this section "Ptolemy" is probably Ptolemy III Euergetes (246–221 BCE), and Josephus refers to Onias as an old man at this stage in his career (*Ant.* 12.172). For further discussion on the probable context for this story and the many chronological problems, see the careful analysis of VanderKam, *From Joshua to Caiaphas*, 128–29, 174–79.

67. See Susan Niditch, "Father-Son Folktale Patterns and Tyrant Typologies in Josephus' *Ant.* 12.160–222," *JJS* 32 (1981): 47–55.

68. This is the colorful story of Joseph impregnating what he assumed to be a foreign dancer in Ptolemy's court when in reality Joseph's brother had disguised his own daughter in order to "save" the drunken Joseph from violating Jewish law. Through this union, the young woman (Joseph's niece) gives birth to Hyrcanus (*Ant.* 12.186–88).

The author notices a vast network of corruption and bribery and comments on it: "If you see in a province the oppression of the poor and the violation of justice and right, do not be amazed at the matter; for the high official [or "payment taker"] is watched by a higher, and there are yet higher ones over them" (5:8 [7]).[69] Such an observation could apply to any number of historical periods, but the commentary in Ecclesiastes highlights certain injustices within the Ptolemaic system and the complicity of local officials in allowing exploitation to occur. The hierarchical network in Qoheleth's observation correlates with the structure of Ptolemaic governance, and this verse laments the fact that the poor usually suffer the most when systemic bribery occurs.[70] A network of officials does not necessarily look out for the common person, preferring instead to augment their own power and wealth by requiring bribes and tributes. Qoheleth's incisive commentary in this verse reflects an intrinsically unfair system.

As we examine the financial situation in Judea during the Ptolemaic period, it is again necessary to consider the economic role of the succession of high priests. These priestly figures had to adapt to Ptolemaic rule and the tax system in place. We have already mentioned the story of Onias II and his refusal to offer tribute to his overlords in Egypt. Even if the Tobiad Romance contains a number of fictional elements, the responsibility of the high priest to provide twenty talents of silver on "behalf of the people" (*Ant*.12.158) is noteworthy. Perhaps these individuals had to pay such an amount in order to assume their office, and then ongoing responsibilities included such noncultic matters as some tax collection.[71] The writings of Josephus and other sources from this period contain references to the priest having the position of *prostasia*, which seems to be an office that includes the right to levy taxes.[72] Josephus never mentions a governor in Judea during this period, and the priest has obligations as a representative of the people.[73] This is not to suggest that the high

69. Kugel, "Qohelet and Money," 36–38, argues persuasively that *gābōah* in this verse should be translated as "payment taker."

70. Thomas Krüger, *Qoheleth*, Hermeneia (Minneapolis: Fortress Press, 2004), 114, cites the possible interpretation that this verse assures fairness, since the careful Ptolemaic system would act as a check against corruption. Yet the evidence from Josephus and the Zeno papyri suggest that networks of officials worked for their own mutual benefit, and this led to the frequent violation of the justice principle that lies at the heart of sapiential and legal traditions.

71. Tcherikover, *Hellenistic Civilization and the Jews*, 459n39; Grabbe, "Hyparchs, Oikonomoi, and Mafiosi," 78–80.

72. Tcherikover, *Hellenistic Civilization and the Jews*, 132; VanderKam, *From Joshua to Caiaphas*, 180–81.

73. VanderKam, *From Joshua to Caiaphas*, 181, notes that Joseph receives the priesthood and his tax-farming duties at different points in the story; therefore it would be erroneous to conclude that the high priest was the primary official in charge of tax collection.

priest functioned as the primary revenue collector, but he could have managed certain financial issues in his role as emissary to Ptolemaic officials.[74]

SELEUCID PERIOD

After many back-and-forth conflicts, Seleucid forces ultimately gained control of Judea and surrounding territories, and this meant the end of Ptolemaic control in the region. In the Fifth Syrian War, the Seleucids displaced the Ptolemies in Judea (198 BCE). According to the available sources, the Seleucid king during this period, Antiochus III (223–187 BCE), had positive relations with Judea, and Josephus claims that he respected long-standing Mosaic traditions. This ruler prohibited Gentiles and unclean animals from entering Jerusalem, and he provided materials for lawful sacrifices. His son and successor Seleucus IV Philopator (187–175 BCE) also maintained a respectful posture (*Ant.* 12.129–53). Perhaps Josephus overstates the extent of goodwill during this period, but in any case the dynamic would change radically with the reign of Antiochus IV Epiphanes (175–164 BCE) and his drastic actions against the well-being of the people (see below).

Before turning more closely to these specific events and their implications, a larger overview of economic life under the Seleucids is in order. These rulers became the most far-reaching among the Diadochoi. Like the Persians before them, their vast empire stretched from the eastern Mediterranean to the Indus River. With extensive landholdings and a base of operations in Antioch, Syria, the Seleucids imitated their Persian predecessors in allowing flexibility with local customs. They could not afford to be as restrictive as the Ptolemies since they controlled a more diverse set of territories. The royal bureaucracy sought to increase revenues, but most of the Seleucid kings also recognized the need to balance income needs with a positive reputation. In order to accommodate diversity within their empire, officials took cultural circumstances into account so as to maintain order. They established royal charters with different peoples in order to clarify tax expectations. By learning the specifics of different areas, the Seleucids developed allies and used propaganda measures to facilitate as much revenue extraction as possible.

Yet these kings and their military apparatus also presented themselves as warriors whose might should not be questioned, leading to greater acceptance

---

74. One example is the responsibility of Eleazer the high priest in the *Letter of Aristeas* (second century BCE). In his correspondence with Eleazar, the Ptolemaic king declares that he has freed a number of Jewish slaves in Egypt. Significantly, there is no mention of a civil governor in this text, and Eleazar appears to have both political and cultic roles.

of their rule. Such posturing assisted them in the area of economic control because they established a dynamic of fear and intimidation throughout the empire.[75] For example, they established a military garrison in Jerusalem (the Akra), close to the temple (1 Macc. 13:52), and this led to tighter control over subject peoples and the loss of local property and possessions to meet the needs of the soldiers.

Like their predecessors, Seleucid officials developed comprehensive measures for tax collection. In many localities they required tax payments in coin, such that even the poor farmer had to convert his meager surplus into silver.[76] Numismatic evidence from this period is more plentiful since the Seleucid kingdom preserved earlier coins from Alexander's reign, used Ptolemaic currency, and minted their own coins in different localities.

Figure 5. Demetrius I, AR tetradrachm struck at Akko-Ptolemais; head Demetrius I/Tyche on throne (© David Hendin, used by permission)

In pursuit of revenue, the Seleucids required taxes on a variety of levels, including levies on salt purchases, tolls at city gates, imports and exports, grain and fruit levies, and special taxes during periods of war. Greek authors assist us with understanding how such efforts worked. We have cited the

75. Susan Sherwin-White and Amélie Kuhrt, *From Samarkhand to Sardis: A New Approach to the Seleucid Empire* (Berkeley: University of California Press, 1993), 53–59, highlight the Seleucid military might and its intimidation tactics, as expressed in such texts as 1 Maccabees (e.g., 1:16–19).

76. Gerassimos George Aperghis, *The Seleukid Royal Economy: The Finances and Financial Administration of the Seleukid Empire* (Cambridge: Cambridge University Press, 2004), 31, argues that military needs motivated the Seleucids to enhance their minting of coins and to demand payment in silver.

writings of Pseudo-Aristotle in our discussion of the Persian period (*Oec.* 2.4). Some interpreters claim that this author's description of systematic levies (see above) applies more to the period of Seleucid dominance than to economic life under the Persians.[77]

To bolster their finances, the Seleucids placed officials in cities and towns across their empire. As with the Ptolemies, extant inscriptions mention a *dioikētēs* in charge of financial matters, but with one for each of the satrapies rather than the entire empire. Many satrapies also had a local "governor" (Gk. *stratēgos*). The *dioikētēs* had to collect taxes, supervise financial exchanges, and collaborate with local leaders. Satrapies had smaller districts within them and at least one town from which royal emissaries could conduct their affairs and implement broad taxation measures. This structural framework proved to be effective in generating revenue and a climate of subservience to the ruling power.[78]

With regard to the specific context of Judea, the reign of Antiochus III (223–187 BCE) marked a period of financial concessions and strategic alliances with key players in the Jerusalem social structure. Josephus reports a specific and generous charter between Antiochus and the inhabitants in and around Jerusalem, especially cultic leaders (*Ant.* 12.138–46).[79] Certain Judeans had assisted Seleucid forces with defeating the Ptolemies in the Fifth Syrian War, and Antiochus wanted to reward such loyalists by providing them with materials for cultic activities, including wine, spices, flour, wheat, and silver. He allowed freedom of governance for those in Judea "in accordance with their ancestral laws" (*Ant.* 12.140). Antiochus III also agreed to supply timber for temple reconstruction, since the incessant wars between the Seleucids and Ptolemies had damaged the structure. There is also a reference in this document to the *gerousia*, a Judean council of elders with decision-making authority in the community.[80] This council received a permanent exemption from taxes, along with other cultic officials (*Ant.* 12.142).[81] The generosity of this foreign ruler has parallels during the Persian period with Cyrus's decree and support for the temple, and there is little reason to doubt the basic historicity

77. See P. Schäfer, *The History of the Jews in the Greco-Roman Period* (London: Routledge, 1983; repr., 2003), 27–28.

78. Aperghis, *The Seleukid Royal Economy*, 263–95.

79. Josephus presents this as a letter to Ptolemy, the *stratēgos* of Coele-Syria.

80. Seth Schwartz, *Imperialism and Jewish Society, 200 B.C.E. to 640 C.E.* (Princeton: Princeton University Press, 2001), 62, notes the paradox between the wealth of the temple treasury in Jerusalem and the majority of the population, which was still operating at subsistence level.

81. According to the charter, the inhabitants of Jerusalem also received a three-year exemption from a variety of taxes.

of Antiochus's declaration.[82] He sought to reward those who had supported the Seleucids during their conflict with the Ptolemies and establish a favorable reputation for himself among the Judean elites. The fact that the charter places such an emphasis on taxes highlights their significance and the mutually beneficial relationship between imperial and local officials.[83]

These tax breaks for temple personnel and elite officials provided benefits for the few, but the charter shows little interest in the larger population. Those living outside of Jerusalem, including farmers, enjoyed no relief. While the influx of funds for the temple reconstruction bolstered the Judean economy, the selective exemptions reinforced the hierarchical arrangement of the society and the imperial tendency toward special dispensation for well-connected persons. In support of this understanding is a "decree" (Gk. *prostagma*) from Antiochus that prescribed zones of holiness around the temple barring foreigners, a restrictive set of dictates on what animals could wander around Jerusalem, and tight prohibitions regarding sacrifices (*Ant.* 12.145–46).[84] Such stipulations conformed to Mosaic traditions, but this development also highlighted the separation between an elect class of citizens, especially priests, and those who lacked access to the corridors of power. For persons who did not enjoy the privileges bestowed by Antiochus, the benefits for elite cultic leaders and other officials only served to marginalize the rural classes further, and taxation played a key role in this differentiation.[85]

The hierocratic character of the society is at work in the praise of the high priest Simon II (219–196 BCE) in Sirach 50. In this retrospective chapter, Ben Sira describes the rebuilding of the temple (50:1–4) and the high priest's role in facilitating the efforts.[86] This passage lauds the priestly

---

82. Elias Joseph Bickerman, "Une proclamation séleucide relative au temple de Jérusalem," *Syria* 25 (1946–48): 67–85, has written the definitive study on this question. Cf. Jörg-Dieter Gauger, *Beiträge zur jüdischen Apologetik: Untersuchungen zur Authentizität von Urkunden bei Flavius Josephus und im I. Makkabäerbuch,* BBB 49 (Cologne: Peter Hanstein, 1977).

83. For further background on his policies, see John Ma, *Antiochos III and the Cities of Western Asia Minor* (Oxford: Oxford University Press, 2000).

84. The rule concerning animals also prohibits bringing into the city the meat or skins from the banned creatures.

85. See Portier-Young, *Apocalypse against Empire,* 72–73.

86. There is some dispute as to whether this passage refers to Simon I or Simon II. Each of these high priests had a father named Onias (Sir. 50:1), and Jerusalem and the temple suffered damage during both of their careers. Consequently we cannot be absolutely certain which figure is the object of Ben Sira's praise. VanderKam, *From Joshua to Caiaphas,* 149–57, offers some valid reasons for associating this passage with Simon I, but it seems more likely that Ben Sira would praise a more recent figure he had known and the high priest whom his audience would have remembered. The fact that the temple needed restoration, as attested in the letter of Antiochus (see above),

office, underscoring the exalted status of Simon in the society. In the tradition of Aaron, Simon stands at the center of the worshiping community, "by the hearth of the altar with a garland of brothers around him" (v. 12). For present purposes, the importance of this passage lies in the fact that an establishment sage praises the temple as a locus of community and power during the reign of Antiochus III. As with the decree of Antiochus, Ben Sira sets the priestly class apart, worthy of the highest respect and adulation.

The Epistle of Enoch (*1 En.* 92–105) represents another link to this period and the inequality that existed.[87] Through the language of apocalyptic literature, the author of the epistle traces history from his own period to the *eschaton.*[88] According to this text, God's judgment will fall severely on wicked contemporaries ("sinners") who are not part of the elect group ("the righteous"). In a series of woe oracles reminiscent of Israelite prophets such as Micah and Jeremiah, the Epistle of Enoch casts this distinction in social terms and makes a stinging rebuke against the "rich." These sinners have held lavish banquets that celebrate their wealth, and the poor suffer as a result (*1 En.* 96:5–6). Conspicuous consumption, including opulent houses (94:6–7) and expensive clothing items (98:1–3), magnify the discrepancies between the two categories in this text. Yet the rich will receive their comeuppance at the last days. For example, those who "acquire gold and silver unjustly" (97:8) might feel secure in their possessions, but they fail to see that "your wealth will not remain, . . . and you will be delivered to a great curse" (97:10).[89] The idea of a promised reversal is very similar to statements in the New Testament, especially in the Gospel of Luke, and these woe statements highlight the economic stratification of the author's day and the advantages of the local aristocracy.[90] Even more than Ben Sira, this section of *1 Enoch* stands in solidarity with those who face oppression under a system marked by elitism and

---

provides a clue that the sage is referring to Simon II. See Patrick W. Skehan and Alexander A. Di Lella, *The Wisdom of Ben Sira*, AB 39 (New York: Doubleday, 1987), 12–14, 550.

87. Many commentators have noted that the Epistle of Enoch, like Ben Sira, does not indicate knowledge of the events surrounding the Maccabean revolt and therefore most likely dates to the beginning of the second century BCE.

88. George W. E. Nickelsburg, *Jewish Literature between the Bible and the Mishnah: A Historical and Literary Introduction*, 2nd ed. (Minneapolis: Fortress Press, 2005), 110.

89. Translations of *1 Enoch* are from George W. E. Nickelsburg and James C. VanderKam, *1 Enoch: A New Translation* (Minneapolis: Fortress Press, 2004).

90. See George W. E. Nickelsburg, "Revisiting the Rich and the Poor in *1 Enoch* 92–105 and the Gospel according to Luke," *SBLSP* 37 (1998): 2.579–605; original, *NTS* 25 (1978–79): 324–44.

corruption.[91] If such descriptions relate to dynamics during the early second century BCE, as seems likely, the Epistle of Enoch provides additional evidence for financial advantages among the elite.

The political and economic dynamics changed with the defeat of the Seleucids by the Romans in the battle of Magnesia (190 BCE), as the Seleucids became weaker and in greater need of revenue. Antiochus III lost much of his military strength, had to pay tribute to Rome, and ceded control of many satrapies in the Mediterranean. Such developments limited the power of Antiochus and his successors, Seleucus IV (187–175 BCE) and Antiochus IV Epiphanes (175–164 BCE). Since they had given up territories and now operated under the shadow of the Romans, the Seleucids needed to squeeze as much as possible from the populations still under their control.[92] This dynamic had a major impact on places like Judea, because such regions had to bear a larger portion of the tax and tribute burden. In pursuit of more revenue, Seleucus dispatched his assistant Heliodorus to procure significant funds from the Jerusalem temple (2 Macc. 3:4–4:1). A recently published stela confirms the historicity of this mission and its implications for understanding Seleucid policy after their military defeat.[93] The Heliodorus Stela contains a great deal of formulaic language, and it indicates that imperial officials wanted greater revenues in exchange for guaranteeing the safety of the local cult. A man named Olympiodorus was designated as the official to monitor the sanctuaries in Coele-Syria and Phoenicia, and while the stela lauds the Seleucid ruler's benevolent motivations in this regard, the mission basically represented an attempt to obtain resources.[94] The precarious military situation of the Seleucids necessitated more intentional exploitation of subject peoples.[95] The policy occurred at the directive of the Seleucid king and his

---

91. Richard A. Horsley, *Scribes, Visionaries, and the Politics of Second Temple Judea* (Louisville, KY: Westminster John Knox Press, 2007), 172, argues that the scribes responsible for this section of *1 Enoch* cast the poor as "righteous" and level an indictment against the wealthy for systematic oppression.

92. Portier-Young, *Apocalypse against Empire*, 79–80.

93. Hannah Cotton and Michael Wörrle, "Seleukos IV to Heliodoros: A New Dossier of Royal Correspondence from Israel," *ZPE* 159 (2007): 191–205. For further discussion on the political intrigue surrounding this episode and role of the official Olympiodoros in instilling order in the Coele-Syria region, see Dov Gera, "Olympiodoros, Heliodoros and the Temples of Koilê Syria and Phoinikê," *ZPE* 169 (2009): 125–55.

94. Cotton and Wörrle, "Seleukos IV to Heliodoros," 198.

95. Ibid., 203. In contrast, the author of 2 Maccabees blames the whole episode on the "impious Simon" (3:11). See Robert M. Doran, *2 Maccabees*, Hermeneia (Minneapolis: Fortress Press, 2012), 83.

royal administration as part of a larger effort to increase revenue by meddling in the affairs of local sanctuaries.[96] Yet the account in 2 Maccabees 3–4
also acknowledges the continuing efforts of local elites and officials, including
priests, to work with imperial powers for their own advantage.

This volatile climate continued with the high priest Jason, who purchased
his office from Antiochus IV Epiphanes (2 Macc. 4:7) and created an environment for widespread adoption of Greek customs. Not only did Jason
receive permission to build a gymnasium and develop training programs for
young men, but the author also claims that he led faithful Judeans away from
long-standing practices (including circumcision), such that they participated
in the "unlawful proceedings in the wrestling arena after the signal for the
discus-throwing, disdaining the honors prized by their ancestors" (4:14–15).
Jason's policy, often referred to as the Hellenistic Reform, marked a watershed event: this high priest adopted a more assimilationist policy than his
predecessors, wanting Judeans to conform more fully to the complexities of
Greek culture.

The Hellenistic Reform has received a great deal of attention in other
studies: for present purposes, what concerns us most are the economic implications of Jason's actions and his abrupt loss of power after three years.[97]
Because of the reform measures, young men training in the gymnasium could
more easily navigate beyond the confines of Judea, both socially and economically. Such plans probably included economic motivations in the sense that
these centers would integrate Hellenistic practices more fully into Judean life
and allow Greek settlers a place to make connections. In conjunction with the
gymnasium, Jason petitioned to Antiochus that Jerusalem's wealthy classes
be registered "as citizens of Antioch," the Seleucid capital (2 Macc. 4:9).[98] As
Portier-Young explains, this move had a significant impact, "drawing Jerusalem's Hellenized elite deep within the system of local and imperial patronage
and benefaction."[99] All of these steps signified an intentional effort to turn

96. The author of 2 Maccabees (often referred to as the "epitomator") wants to
blame Seleucid taxation on the cultic infidelities of the people. In 2 Maccabees, it is
Simon who alerts the Seleucids that the temple in Jerusalem "was full of untold sums
of money, so that the amount of the funds could not be reckoned, and that they did not
belong to the account of the sacrifices, but that it was possible for them to fall under
the control of the king" (3:6).

97. For background, see Klaus Bringmann, *Hellenistische Reform und Religionsverfol-
gung in Judäa: Eine Untersuchung zur jüdisch-hellenistischen Geschichte (175–163 v. Chr.)*
(Göttingen: Vandenhoeck & Ruprecht, 1983); Dov Gera, *Judaea and Mediterranean
Politics, 219–161 B.C.E.* (Leiden: E. J. Brill, 1998).

98. On the implications of this shift, see Doran, *2 Maccabees*, 99–101.

99. Portier-Young, *Apocalypse against Empire*, 102.

Jerusalem into a *polis*, a Seleucid city that could function as a more integral unit of a diminished empire. In this respect, the interests of the Seleucid king to further hellenize Judea were more practical than theological.[100]

Jason's career also proved that the high-priestly office had become a purchasable commodity, a pattern that quickly stung his own tenure. According to 2 Maccabees 4:23, Jason sent Menelaus, the brother of the Simon mentioned above, "to carry the money to the king and to complete the records of essential business" (i.e., to pay annual tribute). Instead of conveying the tribute according to Jason's instructions, Menelaus decided to buy the high priesthood for himself. Not only does this detail reveal the transactional nature of this office under the Seleucids, it demonstrates once again the high priest working as an ambassador for Judea and the role of taxes/tribute in fostering good relations with the foreign ruler. The revenue needs of the Seleucids were driving this dynamic after their defeat to the Romans at Magnesia, and they were more than willing to sell the high-priestly office to the highest bidder, even if it meant the replacement of a figure who had paid for it a few years earlier (2 Macc. 4:24).[101]

The subsequent political dynamics of this period are complex: the population splintered into various factions and entered a period of civil unrest. One faction sympathized with Menelaus and his support for the Seleucids, while others allied with Jason. Some Judeans in the region opposed both Menelaus and the policies of Jason, preferring the practices of earlier high priests and a return to a more rigorous application of the Torah.[102] Jason led a revolt against Menelaus (172 B.C.E.), and Judea remained in a state of instability (2 Macc. 5:5). Not only were long-standing cultic practices and the hereditary nature of the high priesthood under assault, but this region as a reliable source of income for the Seleucids was also now in question. In the midst of this turbulence, Antiochus IV Epiphanes decided to intervene directly into Judean affairs, probably as a response to the instability caused

---

100. Tcherikover, *Hellenistic Civilization and the Jews*, 168–69, cites further stratification between the urban elites and the rural population as a result of the hellenizing reform.

101. Antiochus also invaded Egypt during this period, presumably for the similar reason of controlling Seleucid territory and securing funds. The exact chronology of his Egyptian campaigns and Jason's rebellion is unclear. See John H. Hayes and Sara R. Mandell, *The Jewish People in Classical Antiquity: From Alexander to Bar Kochba* (Louisville, KY: Westminster John Knox Press, 1998), 58.

102. Tcherikover, *Hellenistic Civilization and the Jews*, 187–88, argues that a third party opposed Jason and eventually controlled Jerusalem. One high priest, Onias III, was murdered during this period (2 Macc. 4:30–38).

by Jason's revolt and his desire to extract more revenue. The consequences of this incursion were drastic.[103]

The actions of Antiochus IV (169–164 BCE) marked a tragic period of persecution. According to 2 Maccabees 5, Antiochus sent Apollonius the Mysarch to undertake systematic murder of the population (5:24). In this passage, the author recounts the killing of women and children and the comprehensive nature of the act (40,000 persons; 5:14). Even if 2 Maccabees uses formulaic language and embellishes the numbers, the dramatic effects of this persecution are indisputable. Not only did this Seleucid king engage in indiscriminate killing, but he enslaved others for his own benefit. He stole from the temple treasury and took "the holy vessels with his polluted hands," along with the votive offerings (5:16). Antiochus built up the Akra and tore down the city walls, establishing a cleruchy for soldiers in the heart of Jerusalem (1 Macc. 1:33–40). The presence of the Akra gave the Seleucids a permanent power base from which to collect revenues and made Judea in certain respects a military colony. Such actions by an outside imperial power led to collective trauma for the people and further diminishment of their autonomy. Antiochus humiliated the Judeans by asserting their impotence and the lack of protection from their Deity.

Believers in Yahweh had to deal with the implications of this terrible purge, especially since in 167 BCE Antiochus followed it with an edict banning certain customs. The people had to cease certain devotional practices (1 Macc. 1:41–42), Antiochus had the temple dedicated to Zeus (2 Macc. 6:1–2), and a secondary altar was built in the courtyard of this structure ("the abomination that makes desolate" in Dan. 11:31 and 1 Macc. 1:54).[104] Antiochus prohibited a variety of practices, including Sabbath observance and circumcision; he even forced the inhabitants of Jerusalem to eat pork (1 Macc. 1:41–63; 2 Macc. 6:6–11), if the accounts in the books of Maccabees are reliable. Such a comprehensive restriction of sacred traditions has no real corollary during this period and went against the more conciliatory measures of Antiochus III and many of the Persian rulers. The actions of Antiochus IV Epiphanes nullified the policy of strategic flexibility in favor of brutal suppression and

---

103. Portier-Young, *Apocalypse against Empire*, 127–29, cites the scholarly debate over whether Antiochus intervened because of a rebellion by an anti-Hellenistic third party, as Tcherikover, *Hellenistic Civilization and the Jews*, 187, had suggested. Jason's revolt had apparently ended by this time, raising the issue of what immediate political/military dynamics prompted Antiochus to invade so forcefully.

104. Elias Joseph Bickerman, *The God of the Maccabees: Studies on the Meaning and Origin of the Maccabean Revolt*, trans. Horst R. Moehring, SJLA 32 (Leiden: E. J. Brill, 1979), 73–75, shows that this deity has the characteristics of Syro-Phoenician gods.

humiliation. Whether or not these moves signified an absolute prohibition of Jewish practices is a matter of debate, but Antiochus made fundamental alterations to the culture with these acts.

Why did Antiochus take such radical steps? Historians, including those in the ancient world, have repeatedly posed this question, resulting in a great deal of controversy and no small amount of psychoanalysis. Perhaps Antiochus pursued a more evenhanded approach during the first part of his tenure, only to go insane at the time of the persecution, as some ancient sources have suggested.[105] Yet even if Antiochus was a hothead, it is speculative and essentially unprovable to claim that mental illness led him to this course. Another possibility is that he did not like certain practices such as circumcision, and he wanted to assimilate Judeans more fully into a larger Hellenistic ethos. According to 1 Maccabees 1:41–43, he set these policies across the Seleucid territories as a means of instilling uniformity (even though there is no larger evidence for such a far-reaching move).[106] Bickerman has suggested that Menelaus actually seized the opportunity to complete the Hellenistic Reform by eradicating core practices, thereby currying favor with the Seleucid ruler. Therefore the persecution originated from within Judea rather than as a policy of Antiochus.[107] These and other suggestions continue to be sources of intense scholarly debate, with no resolution about the Seleucid king's motives.

In assessing this question, financial motivations usually play at least some role in the desire to suppress a subject population. Antiochus IV Epiphanes clearly wanted to exploit Judea in a systematic manner, and several markers point to the economic features of the persecution. When Apollonius comes to Jerusalem at the direction of the king in 1 Maccabees, his title is "chief collector of tribute" (1 Macc. 1:29). This designation conveys one of the central aims of the persecution: to sap the population of resources for the benefit of Antiochus and his administration. Moreover, the Seleucids minted coins at the Akra as part of this larger effort under Antiochus. Such an undertaking coincided with restrictions on other practices, as the king established a

105. Many commentators have noted the descriptions of ancient historians such as Polybius in this regard. Rather than calling him Antiochus "[*Theos*] *Epiphanēs*" ([god] manifest), Polybius refers to him as Antiochus "*Epimanēs*" (the mad one) because of his volatility (*Hist.* 26.1). See Hayes and Mandell, *Jewish People in Classical Antiquity*, 50–51.

106. See John J. Collins, *Daniel*, Hermeneia (Minneapolis: Fortress Press, 1993), 63–64, for a list of sources. The reference in 2 Macc. 6:2 only mentions Judea and Samaria.

107. Bickerman, *The God of the Maccabees*, 88. Support for this proposal comes from Josephus (*Ant.* 12.384) and possibly Dan. 11:30.

system based on domination.[108] In addition, the mere presence of the Akra in Jerusalem led to the erosion of autonomy. The soldiers needed resources and property, and 2 Maccabees recounts a heavy force of 22,000 troops under Apollonius (5:24). The confiscation of property seems to mark the background for a statement in Daniel 11:39: "He shall deal with the strongest fortresses by the help of a foreign god. Those who acknowledge him he shall make more wealthy, and shall appoint them as rulers over many, and shall distribute the land for a price." This is a difficult verse to interpret, but the context seems to be land seizures.[109] Finally, it is important to remember that the Seleucid rulers were treading a vulnerable path in preserving their status before the rising power of the Romans. The need for greater revenues led Antiochus to tax subject peoples as much as possible, even in smaller localities like Jerusalem. The sacred aspects of this persecution had a major impact on Judeans during this period (e.g., prohibition of Sabbath observance and circumcision), but we should not overlook the goal of enhanced tribute from colonized persons during a period of weakness for the Seleucid regime.

THE HASMONEANS

A consequential rebellion followed the persecutions of Antiochus IV Epiphanes. The Seleucid king's actions, among other factors, led to the Maccabean revolt and a period of semi-independence for Judea. Operating from the town of Modein, northwest of Jerusalem, one Judas Maccabeus led an insurrection (ca. 166–65 BCE) against the forced acceptance of pagan practices under Antiochus (1 Macc. 2; 2 Macc. 5:27; 8:1–17).[110] In a series of battles, Judas, his family members (the Hasmoneans), and their loyalists won significant victories over Seleucid armies (e.g., 1 Macc. 3:38–4:23). This family also had to fight fellow Judeans who did not support them, especially the followers of Menelaus. In their military pursuits against pro-Seleucid forces, the Hasmoneans acquired territories for themselves. Following the death of Antiochus IV Epiphanes in 164 BCE, Judas eventually took control of the temple. Through a series of battles and subsequent negotiations, the Seleucid general

---

108. Dan Barag, "The Mint of Antiochus IV in Jerusalem: Numismatic Evidence on the Prelude to the Maccabean Revolt," *Israel Numismatic Journal* 14 (2002): 59–77, notes the name of the king (Antiochus) on one side of the coin and a female figure on the other. Whatever the precise significance of this figure, she seems to symbolize imperial domination. See also Portier-Young, *Apocalypse against Empire*, 190–91.

109. On the problems with this verse, see J. Collins, *Daniel*, 388.

110. The account in 1 Maccabees accentuates the role of Mattathias (Judas's father) and his sons in the revolt, while 2 Macc. 5:27 and 8:1–7 focus more exclusively on Judas.

Lysias and the new king Antiochus V made concessions that allowed Judeans to return to their ancestral laws and the more tolerant policies of Antiochus III (1 Macc. 6:59; 2 Macc. 13:23).[111]

Yet Judas and his followers did not enjoy a smooth ascendancy to power. After the murder of Antiochus V and the seizure of the Seleucid throne by Demetrius I, one Alcimus obtained the high priesthood, threatening the viability of the Hasmoneans. Despite seeking assistance and recognition from Rome, Judas had to face Alcimus and his Seleucid-backed forces, and he lost his life in 161 BCE. Then Alcimus died soon after taking his post (in 159 BCE), and no candidate emerged to fill the office of high priest. Judas's brother Jonathan became the leader of the Hasmonean forces, but he lacked real authority during this period without a high priest (159–52 BCE, often referred to as the *intersacerdotium*), effectively living in exile with a small band of followers. The Seleucid general Bacchides tried to consolidate power, but he could not subdue the Hasmonean leader, and the Seleucids worked out a peace treaty with the Hasmoneans (1 Macc. 9:70–73).

Despite internal dissent during this period, through force and shrewd political maneuvering the Hasmoneans emerged as the most powerful faction in Judea for a century.[112] The narratives in 1 and 2 Maccabees and Josephus do not offer a unified description of how this family consolidated power, but Judas, Jonathan, and their successors presented themselves as deliverer figures, offering their supporters land and in some cases financial incentives.[113] Despite questions about their hereditary right to the priestly office, Hasmonean victories enabled a succession of descendants from this family to claim the high priesthood, beginning with Jonathan. He took advantage of the conflict between Alexander Balas, who proclaimed himself the lawful successor of Antiochus IV Epiphanes, and Demetrius, as these competing figures sought Jonathan's favor. Jonathan became high priest in 152 BCE with the backing of Alexander Balas.[114] A period of Hasmonean dominance followed, with a series of figures combining cultic, military, and political roles.

111. On the irreconcilability of these two accounts, see Doran, *2 Maccabees*, 258–60.

112. For further background, see Joseph Sievers, *The Hasmoneans and Their Supporters: From Mattathias to the Death of John Hyrcanus I*, South Florida Studies in the History of Judaism 6 (Atlanta: Scholar's Press, 1990).

113. Among their allies, the Hasmoneans negotiated with the Hasideans (a transliteration of the Hebrew ḥăsîdîm, meaning "pious ones"), a group of "mighty warriors of Israel, all who offered themselves willingly for the law" (1 Macc. 2:42). Whether this group was a forerunner of the ḥăsîdîm of rabbinic literature is a matter of debate.

114. During this struggle, Demetrius appealed to other factions in Judea, promising them relief from taxation (1 Macc. 10:31), giving the high priest control of the Akra (10:32) and Judea greater control over territories in Samaria (10:38). Jonathan is not mentioned here, and it is questionable whether the proposals were sincere.

Jonathan and his successors capitalized on Seleucid instability during this period. With rapid turnover and rivalry among the Seleucid elite, the Hasmoneans seized land and established a more independent rule (e.g., 1 Macc. 11:65–66). Jonathan took control of various territories during his campaigns, and he received an estate ("Ekron and all its environs") as a reward for his service to Alexander Balas (1 Macc. 10:89). The Hasmonean success demonstrated not just the diminishing strength of the Seleucid regime, but also the military and political prowess of these local leaders. This historical background from a complex period, especially in relation to land seizures, is essential for understanding the economic situation under the Hasmoneans.

A period of expansion occurred after Jonathan's death. His brother Simon (142–134 BCE) amassed property through his military efforts, and he attained some territory from foreigners and encouraged others to convert to his Jewish tradition.[115] According to 1 Maccabees, he received the dual title "leader and high priest forever" (1 Macc. 14:41). Simon regained control of the Akra, and the Seleucids limited the amount of taxation this leader had to pay (1 Macc. 13:39). John Hyrcanus (134–104 BCE) took over as high priest and ruler after Simon's sudden death and continued the expansionist approach. After a pitched battle with the Seleucids and Antiochus VII, Hyrcanus established greater autonomy from his foreign adversaries. His efforts gave the Hasmoneans more territory, especially in Samaria, and therefore Hyrcanus had a larger base from which to extract revenue and locate landless supporters.[116] All of these rulers acquired property and redistributed it to loyalists, many of whom worked as tenants on royal estates.

With regard to the latter period of this dynasty, the sons of John Hyrcanus, Aristobulus I (104–103 BCE) and Alexander Jannaeus (103–76 BCE), sought to expand their reach even further, even as they faced sectarian divisions. The former figure had a short career, dying quickly from illness. The tenure of Jannaeus, however, marked a period of conflict and advancement, including in Galilee and Idumea, where this ruler made significant landgrabs.[117] His military ventures placed a burden on the Judean population since he needed resources and revenue to continue his efforts. Jannaeus faced

115. See Pastor, *Land and Economy*, 72–86, for a discussion of land distribution and annexation patterns during this period. For example, Simon "took Joppa for a harbor, and opened a way to the isles of the sea" (1 Macc. 14:5).

116. Shimon Applebaum, "The Hasmoneans—Logistics, Taxation and Constitution," in *Judaea in Hellenistic and Roman Times*, SJLA 40 (Leiden: E. J. Brill, 1989), 14–15, cites the significant acquisitions of Hyrcanus in Samaria and his consolidation of power in Judea.

117. See Seán Freyne, *Galilee from Alexander the Great to Hadrian, 323 B.C.E. to 135 C.E.: A Study of Second Temple Judaism* (Wilmington, DE: Glazier; Notre Dame, IN: University of Notre Dame Press, 1980).

widespread dissatisfaction during his reign, including demonstrations against him, and Josephus reports that he crucified 800 traitors, including women and children (*J.W.* 1.96–98; *Ant.* 13.379–83). Based on this passage and certain allusions in the Dead Sea Scrolls, many have understood the primary opponents of Jannaeus to be the Pharisees, who were perhaps the victims of this mass execution. The Hasmonean rulers, especially these later figures, grappled with competing factions and an emergent sectarianism (e.g., Pharisees, Sadducees, Essenes) that threatened their rule.[118] It is likely that the Pharisees emerged as leaders in the protest against the Hasmoneans. Yet caution is in order here, especially since we lack a full understanding of how developed sectarian differences were during this period.[119] Discord in the society probably involved many factors, and the incessant wars of Jannaeus led to collective fatigue and frustration. His financial demands on the people contributed to social discord.

Such an overview of the political intrigue and shifting alliances of this period is necessary in order to consider how these Hasmonean figures taxed the populace. This is a difficult question to address, especially since 1 and 2 Maccabees and Josephus's account of the Hasmoneans focus primarily on political dynamics, warfare, and cultic issues. Economic matters are usually of lesser concern in these sources, and in any case we cannot always be certain of their historical reliability. When considering this question, the resettling of property provided opportunities for some Judeans to utilize plots that foreigners had occupied. These landgrabs expanded the revenue base. In addition, the Hasmoneans had considerable support among the rural elements in the population, and it is reasonable to infer that these persons had to pay taxes, especially if they worked on royal/priestly lands. For example, Josephus reports that once he defeated the Seleucids, Hyrcanus "amassed a limitless sum of money," because he had "the leisure to exploit Judea undisturbed" (*Ant.* 13.273). Many of these Hasmonean rulers minted their own money, and some of the later figures made coins with their names in both Hebrew and Greek. As a sign of his growing might, Jannaeus made coins with the title "king," a more appropriate designation for a military governor than a priest. An increase in coinage demonstrates the more advanced nature of financial exchanges, including the probability of regular taxes for the Hasmonean coffers.

---

118. Albert I. Baumgarten, *The Flourishing of Jewish Sects in the Maccabean Era: An Interpretation* (Leiden: E. J. Brill, 1997), discusses this phenomenon as reflected in the writings of Josephus, the Dead Sea Scrolls, and other sources from this period.

119. On whether these descriptions from Josephus concerning Jannaeus correlate with the *Pesher Nahum* (4QPesher Nahum) and the reference to "the furious young lion," see VanderKam, *From Joshua to Caiaphas*, 325–32, who also considers tensions between this ruler and the Pharisees.

Figure 6. Alexander Jannaeus, AE prutah; Paleo-Hebrew/ two cornucopias (© David Hendin, used by permission)]

Figure 7. Alexander Jannaeus, AE prutah; anchor/sunwheel within diadem (© David Hendin, used by permission)

Since they combined cultic and more secular/military duties, any tributes or tithes paid to Hasmonean authorities would have gone toward both temple upkeep and administrative needs.[120] For example, Hyrcanus hired mercenaries to fight on behalf of the Hasmoneans, and he needed funds to compensate such persons (*Ant.* 12.249). The expansion of territory helped to finance such efforts, but the benefits did not necessarily carry over to the larger population. Thus it is easy to understand why resentment built up during his reign. In assessing this question of revenue and how it was distributed, Tcherikover makes the reasonable inference that the military conquests provided plunder for the Hasmonean authorities, additional territory for large landowners, and better avenues for moneylenders and merchants to ply their trade.[121] The impact of these conquests on the larger populace is far less certain, other than the requirement to contribute to the expansionist ambitions of their leaders. It is unlikely that the gulf between rich and poor narrowed under the Hasmoneans, and taxation played a role in perpetuating economic stratification.

Clues about practices under these figures also appear in the Dead Sea Scrolls, though allusions to rulers are notoriously difficult to interpret.

120. Applebaum, "The Hasmoneans—Logistics, Taxation and Constitution," 22, cites a "secular tithe" in rabbinic literature (*b. Ma'aś. š.* 33b) and plausibly argues that the Hasmoneans would have needed something on this order to develop the necessary bureaucratic and military structures.

121. Tcherikover, *Hellenistic Civilization and the Jews*, 258–65.

Many experts on this material have developed intricate hypotheses concerning the central figures mentioned in these scrolls, such as the Wicked Priest and Teacher of Righteousness. In particular, scholars have wondered which Hasmonean ruler is the reference point for the Wicked Priest designations.[122] Some have offered concrete proposals based on such texts as *Pesher Habakkuk* (*1QpHabakkuk*) and the *Damascus Document*, while other commentators exercise more caution about how much we can confidently assign references in the scrolls to specific Hasmonean rulers.[123] Even with this uncertainty, some of these texts are clearly critical of oppression and discord in the region. For example, *1QpHabakkuk* mentions "the last priests of Jerusalem, who amass wealth and profit from the plunder of the peoples" (9.4–5). Eshel argues that this refers to the point at which Pompey conquered Judea in 63 BCE, and the Hasmoneans had to cede territorial holdings and autonomy to the Romans (see below), but not before these local rulers infringed on the rights and property of the people.[124] Although debate continues on the relationship between the Dead Sea Scrolls and the Hasmonean state, most commentators agree that this sectarian group of authors distanced themselves from what they perceived to be a corrupt and greedy succession of Hasmonean rulers.

When assessing the priorities of the Hasmoneans, including their economic goals, many of these leaders acted more as regional princes than priestly figures. We mentioned the minting of coins with the "king" title on them, serving to reinforce the self-assessment of Hasmonean leaders and the public image they sought to convey. Their capture of strategic cities along the Mediterranean coast such as Joppa (1 Macc. 14:5) led to better trading opportunities and a more dynamic position for this ruling party. In his influential study of this period, Tcherikover observes that the military efforts by the Hasmoneans had economic motivations at their core rather than religious ones. By usurping strategic territories, these rulers became a more viable trading partner with other peoples and in the process gained more political power.[125] In this respect, their public persona often resembled the

---

122. For a concise treatment of the various theories, including references to the Wicked Priest in the *pesharim*, see J. Collins, *Beyond the Qumran Community*, 88–121.

123. Hanan Eshel, *The Dead Sea Scrolls and the Hasmonean State* (Grand Rapids: Eerdmans, 2008), 29–61, maintains that the Wicked Priest is Jonathan, the Hasmonean ruler. J. Collins, *Beyond the Qumran Community*, 111–21, is much more skeptical about our ability to make such firm conclusions, especially since the references in the scrolls concerning the Wicked Priest might be alluding to more than one figure.

124. Eshel, *The Dead Sea Scrolls*, 174.

125. Tcherikover, *Hellenistic Civilization and the Jews*, 244–49.

Hellenistic princes and generals of neighboring regions. Lavish banquets occurred frequently under the Hasmoneans, reflecting a lifestyle that conformed to Greek culture more than to the austerity demanded in the "justice" passages of the Torah. References to these banquets demonstrate the Greek influence on these figures (e.g., *Ant.* 13.380). Additional examples in the extant literature convey a succession of worldly rulers who demonstrated an affinity for conspicuous consumption and enjoyment of Hellenistic customs. To finance such activities, they needed taxes and tribute items from the people, and this likely fueled resentment among the poorer elements of the population.

Even as they enjoyed periods of success, the internecine warfare of the Hasmoneans could not withstand the expansion of the Roman Empire during the first century BCE. After Jannaeus died, his wife Shelamzion (Salome) Alexandra took control of the kingdom in 76–67 BCE and made her older son, Hyrcanus II, the high priest. During this period, Josephus claims that the Pharisees became the dominant party (*Ant.* 13.404–9), and the queen allied herself with them. The practice of hiring mercenaries continued, and unrest divided the society. The queen's other son, Aristobulus (II), moved to seize the kingdom, and after Shelamzion died, he took over as ruler. This development led to conflict between Aristobulus II and Hyrcanus II, with the latter ceding the crown and high priesthood to his brother. Yet Antipater, the father of King Herod the Great, incited Hyrcanus II to contest his brother's rule. Other rulers joined Hyrcanus in this effort, and he attacked Aristobulus II in Jerusalem. In the midst of this uncertainty, the Roman general Pompey captured Jerusalem in 63 BCE. Hyrcanus II gained reinstatement by Rome as high priest, but not as ruler. A new set of political dynamics emerged that would permanently alter the economic situation in Judea.

ROMAN PERIOD

The period of Roman dominance over Judea remains a source of immense fascination. Not only did Judeans have to adapt to Roman rule, but in 70 CE they also endured the destruction of the temple (extensively rebuilt by Herod the Great) and the further splintering of their number. During this period, sectarian differences continued to evolve, with the different camps foreshadowing the later schools of the rabbinic tradition. The Jesus movement came on the scene, leading to a new set of texts and another group of believers. Countless studies have focused on the specifics of these and other major developments during the Roman period. The current section will touch on some of these topics, but taxation will continue to be our focus, with attention to the demands of the Roman administration and local elites and the impact of levies on the populace.

With a vast empire and a demanding infrastructure, including a capital city that held more than a million inhabitants, the revenue and supply needs of Rome were enormous in the first century BCE and first century CE.[126] The empire imposed land taxes (Lat. *tributum soli*) on agricultural produce, and in most cases officials factored annual yields into account when determining how much landowners had to pay. A network of governors helped to guarantee the regular flow of grain and other goods for imperial use, with great variation in the provinces as to how the collection process worked. Rome continued the process of tax farming in many of the territories under its control. Guilds of Roman citizens (Lat. *publicani*) received contracts for the purpose of providing supplies to the empire in exchange for profit, and in other cases the "publicans" consisted of local officials. Taxes on other assets (Lat. *tributum capitis*, often translated as "capitation taxes") also became common, along with house taxes and levies on the exchange of other goods (e.g., salt). The question of "poll taxes," a specific amount that every member of the population (except for young children) had to pay in cash, is a matter of debate for this period (see below).[127] The regular imposition of these taxes depended on the political dynamics of each region, and practices differed across the empire.

Judeans experienced a period of transition after Pompey's invasion, including changes in their tax obligations. The inhabitants of this region had to contribute to both the larger empire and local bureaucracy, and they also lost valuable territories. Rome clearly placed a tax burden on Judea (*J.W.* 1.154): Josephus refers to a declaration from Julius Caesar that "in the second year they shall pay the tribute at Sidon, consisting of one-fourth of the produce sown" (*Ant.* 14.203), with an apparent exemption during the seventh (Sabbatical) year. This decree involved either 25 percent of a household's produce every other year (i.e., 12.5 percent per year), except for the Sabbatical Year, or a 20 percent tax per year, except for a 25 percent rate in the year after the seventh (Sabbatical) year.[128] The citation of the Sabbatical Year as a factor indicates adherence to certain laws in the Torah and their significance in

---

126. Garnsey and Saller, *The Roman Empire*, 83–84, estimate the amount of wheat and other items needed to feed the population of Rome during the first century CE.

127. Fabian E. Udoh, *To Caesar What Is Caesar's: Tribute, Taxes, and Imperial Administration in Early Roman Palestine, 63 B.C.E.–70 C.E.*, BJS 143 (Providence: Brown Judaic Studies, 2005), 220–21, provides an overview of how this tax worked.

128. Lester L. Grabbe, *Judaism from Cyrus to Hadrian*, vol. 2, *The Roman Period* (Minneapolis: Fortress Press, 1992), 335.

factoring taxation demands. This decree also cites regular payment of taxes at the seaport of Sidon, "for the city of Jerusalem" (i.e., on behalf of the people of Judea). Whether this levy signified a greater burden on the people than what they had to pay under the Hasmoneans is not entirely clear, but adding another layer of taxes (to Rome) would have compounded a household's obligations. Judeans already had to pay a regular temple tax of a half shekel and tithes to Hyrcanus and his sons (*Ant.* 14.203), and now they owed regular produce to imperial authorities.[129] During this period a related development was the wresting of many Greek cities and towns from Judean control, especially along the coast.[130] Such a move restricted the revenue base of the local administration, including the priests, and made Judea weaker in terms of resources, since the Hasmoneans and other powerful families now had fewer avenues for commerce and a smaller population base.

With regard to collection, the long-standing Hasmonean bureaucracy probably continued to collect taxes, as priestly officials under Hyrcanus II worked with Rome as a means of preserving their status. Roman *publicani* (tax gatherers) also have played a role.[131] These two means of collection are not mutually exclusive, and a passage by Cicero, the Roman philosopher and political leader of the first century BCE, seems to allude to the latter group. In a critique of Gabinius, the proconsul (governor) of Syria, Cicero describes a group of "unhappy revenue farmers [the *publicani*]; . . . he [Gabinius] handed them over as slaves to Jews and Syrians." The passage also states that Gabinius cancelled many tributes involving these revenue farmers (*Prov. cons.* 5.10). In this description, Cicero cites attempts by the *publicani* to tax persons in Syria and Judea, but it seems that Gabinius as governor preferred that Judean representatives collect the levies themselves on behalf of Rome, and therefore the ability of these "unhappy revenue farmers" to gain a profit was compromised.[132] If such a reading of events is accurate, this state of affairs left considerable authority in the hands of the Hasmonean bureaucracy and other officials to collect tribute on behalf of the empire.[133]

---

129. The half-shekel tax did not represent a large amount. The Tyrian shekel was the silver currency of this period and equivalent to four Roman denarii, or approximately two days of work for a day laborer. In many cases, the Tyrian shekel had the most favorable quantities of silver, and therefore authorities preferred this denomination for the temple tax. See Udoh, *To Caesar What Is Caesar's*, 90.

130. For a list of cities, see Grabbe, *Judaism from Cyrus to Hadrian: The Roman Period*, 321.

131. Pastor, *Land and Economy*, 88.

132. In the pursuit of bureaucratic efficiency, Gabinius organized Judea into five districts (Lat. *sanhedria*; from Gk. *synedria*). There is no evidence, however, that he permanently expelled the *publicani* (Udoh, *To Caesar What Is Caesar's*, 14–17).

133. For a review of the scholarly debate, see Pastor, *Land and Economy*, 92–93.

During this period the succession of priests and rulers and the intrigue surrounding them are of great interest and have received much attention in other studies. For present purposes, the figure of Herod the Great (73–4 BCE) warrants discussion, since his rule marked a period of expansion and infrastructure changes in Judea. Through political skill, ruthless tactics, and support from the Romans, this Idumean aristocrat ruled Judea with vigor. In the midst of infighting and bitter rivalry, including the murder of many family members, Herod became one of the most consequential figures of the Second Temple period.[134] His reign had a tremendous impact on the economic fortunes of the region, especially in terms of structural growth. Herod expanded his reach well beyond the confines of his province, including Samaria, Galilee, and areas east of the Jordan River.

Herod initiated a massive and unparalleled reconstruction of the Jerusalem temple and built fortified cities across his kingdom.[135] Such efforts not only increased his stature as a ruler but also made Jerusalem a more vibrant capital, what one Roman historian called "easily the most outstanding city in the East" (Pliny the Elder, *Nat.* 5.70). He allowed commercial activity around the temple complex, and Jerusalem became more of a pilgrimage site for those living in the Diaspora rather than just a remote town of little consequence.[136] Consequently, his efforts created jobs and revenue, and trade increased with the return of certain port cities. Herod's actions incorporated Judea more fully into Mediterranean commercial life, offering benefits to the entrepreneurs and officials with connections to the royal bureaucracy. His personal wealth assisted him with these and other pursuits, and he regularly usurped territories and resources in order to realize his ambitious programs.[137]

Yet his building schemes also required funding; even if he used personal wealth, Herod had to demand levies from subjects to realize his lavish ambitions. He relied in part on land taxes to finance his efforts (*Ant.* 15.109) just as previous rulers had counted on proceeds from farming. Such levies meant that landowners had to devote a certain amount of any surplus to the state. In this effort he might have conducted a periodic census to assess the population and the amount of tax revenue he could expect to collect. The evidence for

---

134. On the political intrigue that characterized Herod's rise to power and whether he had to pay tribute to Rome, see J. Hayes and Mandell, *Jewish People in Classical Antiquity*, 118–29; Udoh, *To Caesar What Is Caesar's*, 137–43. His problems included ongoing conflicts with the Hasmoneans (he even put his own Hasmonean wife to death) and with Cleopatra in Egypt.

135. The temple reconstruction occurred at the behest of Herod, not the high priest, a sign of the king's initiative and control over the bureaucracy. See VanderKam, *From Joshua to Caiaphas*, 408.

136. S. Schwartz, *Imperialism and Jewish Society*, 47.

137. Udoh, *To Caesar What Is Caesar's*, 190–93.

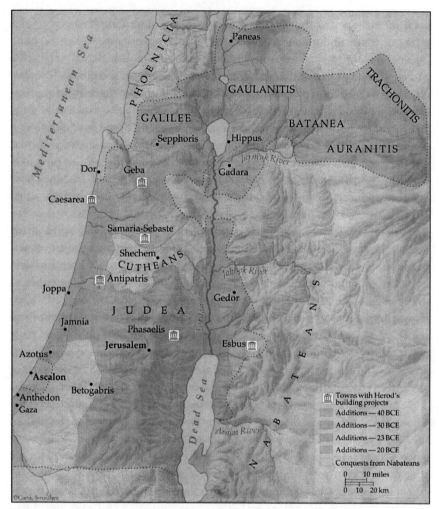

Figure 8. The growth of Herod's kingdom, 40–4 BCE (© Carta, Jerusalem)

such an effort is largely inferential, but similar processes took place in Egypt, and we have the passage in Luke 2:1–5 about a census and subsequent assessment (see below).[138] In addition, Herod built up the port city of Caesarea and Sebaste in Samaria, and customs duties from this location and other commercial sites provided him with considerable income. Semiautonomous cities also had to pay customs duties when they traded with Herod/Judea. With regard to those living in the Diaspora, Broshi argues that the king required a small

138. Abraham Schalit, *König Herodes: Der Mann und sein Werk* (Berlin: de Gruyter, 1969), 272–78.

tax from those across the larger region as a means of funding projects.[139] This influx of funds undoubtedly gave Herod significant wealth. When he faced internal dissent over his expansionist policies, he often squelched opposition and continued to demand levies from the populace. The account in Josephus describes a delegation of Jews in the court of the emperor Augustus complaining about Herod's harsh tactics, his persecution of innocent citizens, and the exorbitant spending for his projects (*Ant.* 17.300–310). Some have questioned the accuracy of this event and cited Josephus's negative assessment of Herod, but the need for resources to finance his construction efforts is indisputable. The level of tribute he had to pay to Rome is less certain since Josephus does not really address this topic, but officials would probably not have cancelled any obligations that Pompey had enacted.[140]

The impact of Herod's policies on the small farmer is a related and controversial question. Some scholars assume that Herod threatened the autonomy and in some cases the existence of the agriculturalists who made up the majority of the population, especially since subjects still had to pay taxes/tithes to the priestly establishment and their share of any tributes to Rome.[141] Josephus also refers to a sales tax under Herod, a levy "upon public purchases and sales that had been ruthlessly exacted" (*Ant.* 17.205). The scope of this tax is not fully clear, but Herod probably demanded an assessment on agricultural goods sold in the marketplace, a policy that would have affected the smaller landowners. Even if Herod derived much of his revenues from customs duties and his own personal wealth, his expansionist agenda required sacrifice among the inhabitants of Judea, and poor farmers still constituted the bulk of the king's subjects. This question of tax burden under Herod is consequential when we consider that his polices are often cited as a major determinant for Jewish discontent with Rome and the rise of early Christianity.[142]

Yet the assumption of a sudden spike in taxation under Herod is not necessarily tenable, as E. P. Sanders and others have argued. The Hasmoneans had huge expense needs, especially as they fought wars with the Seleucids and other

---

139. Magen Broshi, "The Role of the Temple in the Herodian Economy," *JJS* 38 (1987): 31–37.

140. Harold W. Hoehner, *Herod Antipas* (Cambridge: Cambridge University Press, 1972), 299n5. Yet Udoh, *To Caesar What Is Caesar's*, 148, claims that Herod's political maneuverings enabled him to operate largely free of tribute obligations to Rome.

141. Richard A. Horsley, *Galilee: History, Politics, People* (Valley Forge, PA: Trinity Press, 1995); Shimon Applebaum, "Economic Life in Palestine," in *The Jewish People in the First Century*, ed. Shmuel Safrai and Menahem Stern, CRINT 1.2 (Assen: van Gorcum, 1974), 2:661; both authors cite the oppressive nature of taxation under Herod.

142. Udoh, *To Caesar What Is Caesar's*, 180–206, underscores Herod's immense wealth and resourcefulness at facilitating his projects.

foes. Offerings to the Levites and priests would not have accomplished all of the Hasmoneans' military and infrastructure requirements.[143] This chapter has demonstrated an onerous system throughout the Second Temple period. While Judeans did not always need to fund an elaborate military apparatus during the Second Temple period (except under the Hasmoneans), they had to support the imperial power, local governors and officials, and the priestly class. The references in Josephus and the infrastructure changes under Herod all suggest that burdensome levies continued under this monarch, but Herod did not suddenly create an oppressive system. The king's requirements, especially land taxes, posed major difficulties for many households as they sought to support both the king and priesthood while also maintaining their property.[144] This type of obligation persisted throughout the period, however, and it would be overly speculative to assume a marked shift.

The impact of famine underscores the reliance on land taxes. As with previous rulers, drought and/or famine limited Herod's ability to draw upon the resources of his subjects (*Ant.* 15.299–316). Two of the biggest recorded crises of the Second Temple period involved famine and the inability of small farmers to pay taxes (the first being the events of Neh. 5 during the Persian period). With regard to the later episode, in 25 BCE, food shortages crippled the whole region and led to severe hardship and illness. According to Josephus, Herod exhibited sympathy in the midst of this crisis by using some of his own funds to buy grain from Egypt and by making temporary exceptions to tax obligations. His willingness to lower taxes acknowledged the low crop yields. Such a concession helped to limit the scope of the crisis, and it also bolstered Herod's public image. Whether or not his actions averted a major revolt is difficult to say, but this episode demonstrates a willingness to show flexibility during a crisis, a tactic that Nehemiah had also adopted (Neh. 5:14–18).

One additional issue is Herod's relationship with Judean aristocracy, especially in terms of land distribution. Like his predecessors, Herod usurped territories, including many Hasmonean properties, for his own personal use, expanding landholdings through power grabs and the elimination of rivals. He also established cleruchies for his troops (*Ant.* 15.294; 15.296; 16.285; 17.23–25). The extent of private landholdings among individuals is a matter of debate. The New Testament contains numerous examples of elite persons

143. E. Sanders, *Judaism: Practice and Belief,* 160–61, responding to the arguments of Richard A. Horsley, *Jesus and the Spiral of Violence* (San Francisco: Harper & Row, 1987), 279–84.

144. Freyne, *Galilee from Alexander the Great to Hadrian,* 190–91, notes that Herod's shrewdness led him to vary the level of taxation he demanded depending on the politics of a particular situation.

with sizeable estates (e.g., Matt. 20:1–16 and the laborers in the vineyard), suggesting that much land in Judea stayed in private hands, and many persons had to work on fields to which they had no property claim.[145] Some have stipulated that tenant farming occurred with great frequency during this period based on the archaeological record of small land plots in the vicinity of larger houses.[146] Whether this type of arrangement spiked under Herod's reign is difficult to determine, but it is probable that life for the subsistence farmer remained arduous during this period, despite the many infrastructure advancements.

In 6 CE, after Herod Archelaus (a son of Herod the Great) was deposed, the Romans annexed Judea, and it became a minor province comprised of Samaria, Idumea, and Judea (but not Galilee, which was ruled by Herod Antipas, another son of Herod the Great). For the ensuing decades, Judea fell under the direct control of imperial governors, who often had the title of "prefect." During this period, Quirinius, the legate of Syria, received orders for the people "to make an assessment of their property," a process that required a census to determine proper levels of taxation for both his region and Judea (*Ant.* 18.1–2; cf. Luke 2:1–3). The apparent goal did not involve ascertaining population levels so much as determining who owned land and how much the empire could tax households on their property. Although much later than the effort under Quirinius, the Babatha archive (127 CE) is very informative for understanding how this census might have worked. In this later text, the woman Babatha has to register her landholdings and offer a certain amount in produce from her date orchards, and she must also pay a "crown tax" based on her property size in cash (5/6 Hev 16.19–32). Roman officials supervised the payment process. Whether such a detailed census occurred under Quirinius more than a century earlier is uncertain, but the parallels between the two texts suggest an intricate pattern of taxation under the Roman governors.

The question of a poll tax under the Roman prefects is also pertinent here, especially when one considers the Gospel passages involving payment to the empire (Mark 12:13–17; Matt. 22:15–22; Luke 20:20–26). In the well-known pericope, a group of "Herodians" come to trap Jesus, asking him whether it is "lawful" to pay taxes to the emperor. After asking them to present a denarius, Jesus declares, "Give to the emperor the things that are the emperor's, and to God the things that are God's" (Mark 12:17). The distinction here is between earthly and heavenly concerns: followers of Jesus have to negotiate the taxation

---

145. Cf. Mark 12:1–9; Matt. 21:33–41; Luke 20:9–16; Varro, *Rust.* 1.17.2–3; Columella, *Rust.* 1.7; Pliny the Younger, *Ep.* 3.19; 9.37. See John E. Stambaugh and David L. Balch, *The New Testament in Its Social Environment* (Philadelphia: Westminster Press, 1986), 68.

146. See Pastor, *Land and Economy*, 104–5.

requirements of the empire while also adhering to the covenantal demands of the Torah, especially worship of Yahweh alone.[147] The answer here from Jesus is politically savvy and does not question imperial authority or mitigate the core principle of the Decalogue. With regard to the historicity of this scene, some have questioned whether this reference constitutes proof of poll taxes during Jesus' day, a levy that everyone had to pay, whether they owned land or not.[148] Perhaps Jesus produces a coin with the emperor Tiberius on it, and this story indicates a long-standing tax obligation. Yet archaeologists exploring Jerusalem, the Qumran site, and elsewhere in the region have noted the scarcity of such imperial coins during this period (Tyrian silver coins were more common), and many New Testament scholars now argue that this passage does not shed much light on imperial taxation before 70 CE.[149] The possibility still exists, even if certain details are anachronistic, that imperial authorities required regular poll taxes in small amounts of coinage from the general populace, and this created hardship for many in the region. We have little concrete information of taxation/economic policies during the period of Jesus' life, in these first decades of direct rule under the Roman prefects. The scattered references to taxation and stratification in the Gospels suggest that farmers continued to struggle under the Roman prefects, just as they had under previous imperial rulers in the Second Temple period, and the evidence for regular imposition of agricultural taxes underscores their difficulties.

With regard to collection during this period, the high priests continued to demand tithes and tributes to facilitate their efforts, and tax farming also persisted. The New Testament contains negative references to "tax collectors" (e.g., Luke 3:12–13), especially in the Galilee region, who roam the countryside in order to garner revenue on behalf of Antipas. These were probably not foreign-born *publicani*, but rather local entrepreneurs who collected tolls and took a commission from these levies.[150] Fraud apparently marked some of

147. Josephus recounts a protest against taxation (the "fourth philosophy among the Judeans"), led by the teacher Judas of Gamla and Saddok the Pharisee (*Ant.* 18.23), who claimed that a faithful Jew cannot divide allegiance between God and an earthly sovereign. Adela Yarbro Collins, *Mark: A Commentary*, ed. Harold W. Attridge, Hermeneia (Minneapolis: Fortress Press, 2007), 555, argues that the Markan author distances Jesus from the more radical, separatist agenda of the Zealots with this moderate answer on taxation.

148. Martin Rist, "Caesar or God (Mark 12:13–17)? A Study in Form-geschichte," *JR* 16 (1936): 317–31. One of the focal points of the debate is the interpretation and best translation for the phrase "to pay taxes/a census [Gk. *kēnson*]," in Mark 12:14 (cf. Matt. 17:25).

149. Udoh, *To Caesar What Is Caesar's*, 234–35, summarizes the findings of recent years, noting the preponderance of Tyrian coins over imperial denarii.

150. Freyne, *Galilee: From Alexander the Great to Hadrian*, 192.

their efforts (e.g., Luke 19:8), and this might explain why some of the sources from this period portray tax collectors with such derision. While we cannot posit widespread social unrest because of the passing references to tax farming, once again these passages point to different layers of taxation and a class of middlemen who benefited from their ability to act as a conduit between the people and imperial/local officials. Tax farming clearly played a role in the stratification of Galilee and Judea under the direct rule of Rome.

The political dynamics from Herod's death until 66 CE, the year when the First Jewish Revolt began, are complex and largely beyond the scope of this discussion, but many of the same economic factors persisted.[151] Under a series of prefects, Rome continued to rely on local officials to collect tributes and enacted other bureaucratic measures. The prefect had to maintain order by relying upon a small army and a coterie of officials from his headquarters in Caesarea, working with local elites in the process. Martin Goodman has cited the failure of the upper classes to be an effective intermediary between imperial officials and the general population, and he traces this dynamic to the fact that Herod the Great had murdered or marginalized many establishment figures, leaving a leadership void.[152] The high priests had to negotiate formidable political obstacles, and the Romans exercised tight control over the priestly office during this period, even with a series of weak governors (the brutal tactics of Pontius Pilate [26–37 CE] as prefect were an exception).

The stability of the province progressively worsened, leading to rebellion against Rome in 66–70 CE. Many have argued that stratification, unfair lending arrangements, and oppressive levies contributed to the First Jewish Revolt. Splinter groups with militant sentiments, strained relations between the priestly aristocracy and Rome, and mounting lawlessness, coupled with brutal Roman responses, precipitated the conflict, and socioeconomic factors were at play in the midst of these turbulent dynamics. Josephus's description of the revolt points to some of the financial issues at stake. Specifically, he recounts the burning of debt records in the treasury department at the beginning of the war to prevent creditors from collecting their debts. This same passage describes the burning of the high priests' houses and other elite quarters (*J.W.* 2.427). The institution of the *prosbul* had compounded tensions between lenders and debtors, since this body allowed creditors to seek repayment with the blessing of the judicial system, even after the Sabbatical Year. Such a mechanism allowed lenders to demand repayment in a manner that undermined the stringent laws against interest in the Torah, and perhaps the

151. S. Schwartz, *Imperialism and Jewish Society*, 48.
152. Martin Goodman, "The First Jewish Revolt: Social Conflict and the Problem of Debt," *JJS* 33 (1982): 417–27.

militants (the Sicarii) who burned the debt records wanted to follow the tradition more closely and also incite debtors to their cause of revolt.[153] Among the other dynamics at work in the First Jewish Revolt, banditry and debt slavery were significant factors. The impact of taxes and scarcity of available land compounded this situation.[154] Stratification in the Galilee and other regions led to tensions between wealthy (often absentee) landlords and the rest of the population.[155] Economic factors clearly played a role in the decision of some localities with commercial interests to oppose the war (e.g., Sepphoris: *J.W.* 2.574). The impact of the revolt cannot be overstated, since the sequence of events led to the decimation of Jerusalem, the looting and destruction of the temple, and the tragic displacement of many Jews. The complex political and social dynamics of this revolt, including the reliability of Josephus, are major topics in the history of this period and have been covered in great detail elsewhere.[156]

SUMMARY

This chapter has highlighted the effects of taxation in an imperial context, including the impact of levies on poor farmers who comprised the majority of the population. When societies such as ancient Judea develop and grow, revenue needs become paramount. Expansionist kings such as Darius I and Herod the Great needed funds and supplies for their ambitions to succeed, and their goals led them to tax subject peoples in a variety of ways. Under foreign powers, especially in an advanced agrarian economy, the taxation burden falls across the population, leaving the struggling agriculturalist in a precarious situation. This context forced many Judeans into a difficult tenant-farming arrangement, especially when one considers the frequency of drought, famine, and lopsided lending arrangements. Although much remains unknown about levies during the Second Temple period, the available evidence demonstrates a rather consistent burden on the people caused by demands from imperial officials and local elites, particularly when military needs or infrastructure

153. This group, the Sicarii, eventually fled to Masada and had a protracted standoff with the Romans.

154. Ibid., 419.

155. Seán Freyne, "The Revolt from a Regional Perspective,"in *The First Jewish Revolt: Archaeology, History, and Ideology*, eds. Andrea M. Berlin, J. Andrew Overman (London: Routledge, 2002), 51, highlights the economic factors at play.

156. Jonathan J. Price, *Jerusalem under Siege: The Collapse of the Jewish State 66-70 C.E.*, Brill's Series in Jewish Studies 3 (Leiden: E. J. Brill, 1992). See most recently Mladen Popović ed., *The Jewish Revolt against Rome: Interdisciplinary Perspectives*, JSJSup 154 (Leiden: E. J. Brill, 2011).

projects became factors. The priestly class also required funds, especially as the office of high priest gained in stature and the temple became a locus of political and economic power. As we assess the history of this period and the many developments that took place, taxation should continue to be a topic of great interest, since it played such a pivotal role in the stratification and social unrest that occurred.

The final chapter of this study will consider the categories of wealth and poverty from an ethical/theological perspective. How do the wisdom books explain why someone becomes wealthy or poor? How do various Second Temple sources, especially those works classified as sapiential or apocalyptic, address social stratification and the role of the Deity? To what extent does earthly conduct play a role in a person's present fortunes, and how does this change once eschatological beliefs become more commonplace in the traditions of early Judaism/Christianity? The next chapter will address such questions, with attention to the ethical basis for wealth and poverty in some of the major Second Temple sources.

5

The Ethics of Wealth and Poverty

While this study has addressed various topics in our examination of economic life in the Second Temple period, we have not fully considered the ethics of wealth and poverty in the available sources. Many of the extant texts from this period give close attention to such matters as taxation and bribery, but we also find more general reflections on the nature of money and the consequences of dishonest behavior. Such content appears most often in the Wisdom literature and the apocalyptic writings. Various sapiential texts highlight economic stratification, the tendency for the wealthy to exploit the vulnerable, and the place of the Deity in adjudicating fair results. In certain books, such as Proverbs, one finds the frequent promise that God will punish swindlers, while other works like Job and Ecclesiastes take great effort to recognize the absence of justice in this regard. Apocalyptic works address many of these issues while positing a connection between present conduct and eschatological reward or punishment.

The present chapter will survey the ethics of wealth and poverty in both sapiential and apocalyptic literature from this period, with special attention to the acceptability of financial holdings and the manner in which human initiatives and/or God intervene to create a fair system. Our analysis will indicate the diversity of perspectives on this topic, often in the same instructional text. For example, the book of Proverbs and Ben Sira cite financial rewards as a gift for the righteous, while in other sayings material holdings are a deterrent to virtuous living. Moreover, a sea change happens when eschatological proposals emerge in some of the later texts. In works like *4QInstruction* and the Gospel of Luke, a reversal of fortune can occur beyond the earthly sphere. With the benefit of apocalyptic eschatology, the virtuous poor can attain heavenly rewards, while the corrupt individual who has not received adequate punishment can no longer escape final retribution. When considering the obligation to pursue justice and righteousness and the lack of ultimate accountability for bad behavior in the wisdom tradition (i.e., no afterlife; Sheol as the universal destination for people), an eschatological framework for retribution marked a significant shift, perhaps the most important development in the Second Temple period in terms of the ethics of wealth and poverty. The following discussion will examine this shift and its implications.

ETHICS OF WEALTH AND POVERTY
IN THE WISDOM LITERATURE

A concern with social ethics in the context of economics is characteristic of many ancient Near Eastern instructions. Sapiential texts from all periods address wealth and poverty, with specific attention to the distribution of resources, the impact of greed and corruption, the causal relationship between industriousness leading to wealth and laziness leading to poverty, and God's evaluation of financial decisions. In the thought world of these texts, honesty with money functions as a test of trustworthiness, and a cheat in financial matters becomes a threat to the society and an affront to the Deity. Money remains a focal point in the instructions, whether as a reward for righteous behavior, an impediment to faithfulness, or a complicating factor in everyday existence.

Contradictions in the Book of Proverbs

One of the striking features of sapiential texts from the Second Temple period is the mixed and often contradictory presentation of economic issues, especially in works that reflect a complex editorial process. On the one hand, we find hard-nosed assessments of financial matters, such as the regular admission that the rich take advantage of the vulnerability of the poor. This type of observation is counterbalanced, however, by more hopeful assertions about the wise attaining financial rewards and the wicked struggling, because of a consistent act-consequence relationship and a just Deity.[1] Such diverse pro-

---

1. A classic formulation of the act-consequence relationship is Klaus Koch, "Is There a Doctrine of Retribution in the Old Testament?," trans. Thomas H. Trapp, in *Theodicy in the Old Testament*, ed. James L. Crenshaw, IRT 4 (Philadelphia: Fortress Press, 1983), 64; original, "Gibt es ein Vergeltungsdogma im Alten Testament?," *ZTK* 52 (1955): 1–42. According to Koch, God frequently plays the role of a "midwife" in texts such as Proverbs, setting in place a fair and self-perpetuating system in which a person's behavior determines outcomes.

nouncements are prominent in Proverbs, an anthology of sayings that date from before and after the exile. Since this is aphoristic sentence literature, gathered by scribal-sages over several centuries and then placed in a larger corpus, we should not expect absolute consistency.[2] Yet the cognitive dissonance of Proverbs is recognized. In scanning across the various subunits for a core ethical principle about economics, one instead finds several distinct theses in the sayings. This diversity holds throughout the subunits of Proverbs, in both the simple declarative statement and the admonition.

In breaking down the material in Proverbs concerning wealth and poverty, several distinct propositions are apparent. First is the promise that greed ultimately leads to failure, and those who engage in corrupt behavioral patterns can expect a reckoning, whether from God, their neighbor, or unnamed forces in the universe (the "divine passive").[3] We might call this the "character-consequence" category, since sayings in this subset promise fair outcomes that hinge on personal conduct. In this discourse, a wicked person will not retain any ill-gotten riches, nor should individuals prioritize wealth over kindness. For example, see Proverbs 11:28: "Those who trust in their riches will wither [or "fall"], but the righteous will flourish like green leaves" (cf. 18:11). The idea here is that human beings can count on fair outcomes, because God rules the universe and has set in place a just system. In this category we include the ethical dualism of the "path" or "way" motif, which appears in Proverbs 1–9 and in other biblical books (e.g., Prov. 2:9; 4:14, 18; 5:5–6; Deut. 5:33; Ps. 1:1). A useful illustration is the scenario in Proverbs 1:10–19, where young thugs invite an impressionable adolescent to join their gang. The sapiential writer declares that when persons who are greedy for material gain act with malevolence, such an impulse "takes away the life of its possessors" (v. 19). A young man should not walk "in the path" of such fellows (v. 15), because it will lead to his demise.[4] Such warnings about dishonesty and punishment are consistent with many other sayings in the book, including Proverbs 13:21: "Misfortune pursues sinners, but prosperity rewards the righteous."

This last saying promises misery for the wicked, while the righteous receive material rewards. Certain proverbs in this category offer concrete

---

2. On the gathering of these sayings in Proverbs, see Fox, "Social Location," 227–39.

3. Lennart Boström, *The God of the Sages: The Portrayal of God in the Book of Proverbs*, ConBot 29 (Stockholm: Almqvist & Wiksell International, 1990), explains that 90 percent of the statements in Proverbs contain no direct references to God. Yet even in supposedly nontheological sayings, God is often the implicit agent for determining human outcomes.

4. This is the same mentality that drives the warnings against the "loose" or "strange" woman in Prov. 1–9.

blessings for upstanding persons. Those who exhibit the "fear of the LORD," show a measured approach to life, honor their neighbor, and maintain reverence before God can expect specific blessings. For example, Proverbs 22:4: "The reward for humility and fear of the LORD is riches and honor and life." When persons engage in upright behavioral patterns, "your barns will be filled with plenty, and your vats will be bursting with wine" (3:10). When taken in isolation, these sayings posit a direct correlation between faithful living and material blessings from God. Yet this category does not exhaust the social ethics of Proverbs; the book is not a collection that endorses a "prosperity gospel."

Many of the sayings describe the pursuit of money as an unlawful distraction from virtuous behavior. Into a second category we can classify a number of proverbs that highlight the preferability of wisdom over material wealth. For example, Proverbs 16:16: "How much better to get wisdom than gold! To get understanding is to be chosen rather than silver." Such sayings have a mitigating effect on the proverbs in the first subset (i.e., financial success as a consequence of virtue), since this second category does not privilege wealth as a reward for the righteous. Instead, these sayings emphasize the superiority of faithful reflection over an acquisitive mind-set. Along these lines, one frequent trope is that the pursuit of money leads to anxiety and a departure from desirable social ethics: "Better is a dinner of vegetables where love is than a fatted ox and hatred with it" (15:17; cf. 17:1). In this grouping we can include the motif of a good name. A person should cultivate a reputation for pragmatism and kindness rather than pursuing wealth unabashedly. When virtue and common sense mark a person's behavior, a favorable reputation follows: "A good name is to be chosen rather than great riches, and favor is better than silver or gold" (22:1).

A third category contains more pragmatic observations about daily life, including honest assessments of the plight of the poor and their vulnerability in the social structure. The candor of these sayings is remarkable: "The wealth of the rich is their fortress; the poverty of the poor is their ruin" (Prov. 10:15). Another example is 13:23: "The field of the poor may yield much food, but it is swept away through injustice." This admission does not mesh with our first character-consequence category since it acknowledges the frequent unfairness demonstrated toward the poor. The maxims in this third, observational category admit stratification in a preindustrial, agrarian economy, especially when large landowners hold much power. Several sayings in this category point to the loneliness of poverty and the fact that the wealthy have many hangers-on who seek to benefit from their association with a rich person. For example, "Wealth brings many friends, but the poor are left friendless" (Prov. 19:4). "Friends" in this context has a satirical edge since the saying comments on the fawning associates who often accompany a wealthy individual. In this pragmatic category we also include the stern warnings against vouching for the loan of another person (i.e., surety) and the wariness about bribery (see chap. 3 above).

The other element in this category is divine advocacy on behalf of the poor. According to these sayings, the Lord takes up the case of underprivileged persons and defends them against aggressors. This image appears most famously in the section dependent on the Egyptian Instruction of Amenemope, where God becomes the lawyer for the poor and "pleads their cause" (Prov. 22:23). Such statements belong in the more pragmatic category because they acknowledge the situation of those who have less and their need for assistance. The function of these sayings is to generate sympathy for and solidarity with those most likely to become victims of economic oppression. This type of maxim is in line with many stipulations in the Torah that mandate kindness to the poor as a fundamental component of faithful living (e.g., Exod. 22:21–27 [20–26]).

A fourth category addresses the basis for becoming rich or poor, and the purpose is didactic. Motivational maxims in this category cite the need for diligence in order to attain material success. Conversely, loss of land and destitution result from laziness. The cluster in Proverbs 24:30–34 is a colorful example of this logic: for the "lazy person" and the "dolt," neediness will come quickly and surely. The scenario in these verses depicts the vineyard of a lazy individual: "It was all overgrown with thorns; the ground was covered with nettles, and its stone wall was broken down" (24:31). This description, along with the comparison of an industrious person to an ant (6:6–9), have the goal of cultivating a vigorous work ethic and warning against slack behavior. Implicit in such advice is the belief that meticulous work leads to concrete blessings. This is one of the clearest examples in Proverbs of emphasizing personal responsibility in relation to economics. Within this category we can also group the warnings against excessive alcohol usage and the accompanying danger of destitution: "Do not be among winebibbers, or among gluttonous eaters of meat; for the drunkard and the glutton will come to poverty, and drowsiness will clothe them with rags" (23:20–21; cf. 26:10).

These four categories—the character-consequence sayings, the discourse emphasizing the preferability of wisdom over wealth, the more candid observations of how financial dynamics actually work in a society, and the association of poverty with laziness and financial gain with industrious behavior—are somewhat similar to the divisions proposed by Timothy Sandoval in his book *The Discourse of Wealth and Poverty in the Book of Proverbs.* Sandoval cites "discourses" in Proverbs on the superiority of wisdom, social justice, and candid maxims about human behavior in the marketplace.[5] Like Sandoval and other commentators, we recognize the inconsistencies in Proverbs, as the editors conveyed their complex and often-contradictory values concerning wealth and poverty. Through sets of discourses, these sages constructed "a moral vision for its reader or hearer," but one that is not entirely consistent.[6]

So what should one make of this eclectic presentation of economics in Proverbs, especially in relation to social ethics? First, it misses the mark to divide these diverse maxims into editorial stages, with the more hard-nosed assessments about economics indicating a later redaction.[7] Such a proposal is speculative and unlikely. Nor can we in most cases make a rigid distinction between folk wisdom and the more courtly observations of the elite. Some commentators have tried to draw a clear division between the agrarian, everyday maxims and the advice reflecting elite settings, such as the royal court.[8] While a saying about agricultural pursuits could have originated at the village level, maxims about such topics as false weights and measures (e.g., Prov. 16:11; 20:10; 20:23) do not necessarily reflect a rural origin. The collecting and cataloging of sayings happened among the "learned clerks" of the scribal class; to present an accessible and colorful collection, these scribes collected material from diverse sources, including both foreign instructions and popular sayings from across the society.[9] In his discussion of the ethos, or what he calls the *Gestalt* of Proverbs, Sandoval emphasizes the unity of the collection, which represents the perspective of a "caste of intellectually elite scribes in ancient Israel and Judah."[10] Yet the contradictory nature of certain sayings in Proverbs is palpable and does not fit neatly into one model for social ethics. The four categories related to

5. Timothy J. Sandoval, *The Discourse of Wealth and Poverty in the Book of Proverbs*, BInt 77 (Leiden: E. J. Brill, 2006), 56–69, cites three discourses in Proverbs: (1) the *wisdom's virtues discourse* (impressing upon the listener to follow the path of wisdom); (2) a *"discourse of social justice"* (special concern for the poor); (3) a *"discourse of social observation,"* which simply describes realities as the sages observe them. He also high-lights the "two ways" in Proverbs, the use of wealth as a "motivational symbol," and the act-consequence (or "wisdom prosperity") nexus in the book.

6. Ibid., 205.

7. James L. Crenshaw, "Poverty and Punishment in the Book of Proverbs," QR 9 (1989): 30–43, cites a distinction between the act-consequence sayings and later, more complex portraits of outcomes. Those who make this argument often appeal to a divide between the harshness of the rural, village perspective and a more elite scribal context.

8. See Friedemann W. Golka, The *Leopard's Spots: Biblical and African Wisdom in Proverbs* (Edinburgh: T&T Clark, 1993), who locates many of the sayings at the vil-lage level.

9. Fox, "Social Location," 236: "Everything we have was channelled to the court and through it; the flow cannot be supposed to move in the other direction."

10. Sandoval, *Discourse of Wealth and Poverty*, 210.

wealth and poverty do not always cohere, making it impossible to distill a single framework.

As with many sapiential traditions, the economic sayings in Proverbs proclaim both a fair Deity and an uncertain marketplace for financial transactions. In some sayings, the swindler prospers (e.g., Prov. 22:7), while in other places he receives the requisite punishment (e.g., 11:28). Such a tension is common to many instructional documents. The contradiction between the character-consequence sayings and the ones about the efficacy of bribery would not have escaped the final editors of Proverbs, but this dichotomy reflects the complexity of the human experience in relation to money, even in a less developed economy like that of Judea. The book of Proverbs reflects the belief, or perhaps more accurately the hope, that "fear of the LORD" and virtue will ultimately win the day and that a person who is both discerning and kind will enjoy prosperous longevity. At the same time, the editors of Proverbs are willing to admit that the downtrodden suffer more and that the wealthy have obsequious "friends." The honesty in Proverbs does not match the searing commentary of Job, Qoheleth, or even Ben Sira, but these sayings do acknowledge harsh realities. The content of Proverbs does come from different sectors of the society, but it is more helpful to characterize the economic language in Proverbs as showing the ambiguous nature of money itself. In every society, commentary occurs on the distribution of resources and the nature of social and government structures. This collection seeks to cultivate virtuous individuals who by their disposition will make the right financial decisions over a sustained period.

Skepticism in the Books of Job and Ecclesiastes

Later wisdom texts are more skeptical than Proverbs about the possibility for economic fairness. While not technically an instruction, the book of Job is relevant to our examination of financial inequality and social ethics, since this is such a prominent theme in the text. No certainty exists on a precise date for Job, but most commentators place the text after the exile based on a variety of linguistic and thematic factors.[11] In the prologue, Job loses all of his possessions, family, and social status (Job 1:12–22), and then he is afflicted with physical infirmities (2:7) that leave him mournful but nevertheless faithful to God. The following dialogues between Job and his three "friends" (2:11) offer

11. For an overview of possibilities for dating Job, see John E. Hartley, *The Book of Job*, NICOT (Grand Rapids: Eerdmans, 1988), 17–20. Among the factors usually cited in favor of a postexilic date are the number of Aramaisms, the mention of the Satan figure in the prologue, and parallels between the officials in Job 3:14–15 and certain passages in Ezra (7:28; 8:25) and Esther (1:3).

extensive reflections on divine retribution, human culpability, and the reasons why people suffer for no apparent reason (2:3).

In their defense of retributive justice, the friends affirm the first category we discussed in relation to Proverbs (the character-consequence sayings), since these debate partners view destitution as a sign of disfavor with the Lord. From their perspective, Job must have done something to warrant his terrible predicament (e.g., 22:6–9). In several places, the friends explain their perspective through the lens of economics. For example, Eliphaz declares that God acts in direct response to human behavior, and he uses a financial illustration to make the case: "But he [God] saves the needy from the sword of their mouth, from the hand of the mighty. So the poor have hope, and injustice shuts its mouth" (5:15–16).[12] According to the friends' argument, divine justice extends to the area of economics, since God ensnares evildoers and rewards the virtuous with material blessings.

Yet Job maintains his innocence; through his passionate defense he undercuts the character-consequence category. Since he has not sinned, his economic misfortunes, like his other challenges, disprove the friends' assumption of a causal relationship between Job's plight and his behavior. His most memorable and lengthy speech on this point appears in chapter 24: "The wicked remove landmarks; they seize flocks and pasture them. They drive away the donkey of the orphan; they take the widow's ox for a pledge. They thrust the needy off the road; the poor of the earth all hide themselves" (vv. 2–4). Such corrosive behavior is against the requirements of Israel's legal traditions (e.g., Deut. 19:14; 27:17), reflective of a social chaos that runs counter to any assertion of a character-consequence guarantee. Job's vivid portrait captures both timeless realities and the inadequacy of the friends' position. He is specific in this speech concerning God's culpability in allowing a lawless atmosphere to fester: "From the city the dying groan, and the throat of the wounded cries for help; yet God pays no attention to their prayer" (Job 24:12). The apparent divine indifference to this moral chaos leads Job to question the friends' argument *and* the long-standing belief that the Deity sides with sufferers, especially when they are experiencing the effects of destitution.[13] In this respect, the book of Job deliberately undercuts the character-consequence category that had appeared in earlier instructions as a rhetorical strategy.

---

12. Carol A. Newsom, *The Book of Job: A Contest of Moral Imaginations* (Oxford: Oxford University Press, 2003), 103, argues that Eliphaz is less interested here in the actions that contributed to Job's plight than in a more hopeful future, "one that finds its logic in the agency of God."

13. See Samuel E. Balentine, *Job*, SHBC (Macon, GA: Smyth & Helwys, 2006), 368–69, for the disturbing theological implications of these verses.

The book of Ecclesiastes provides a similarly candid assessment of the relationship between human conduct and a person's financial situation. The author Qoheleth, writing during the era of Ptolemaic rule in the third century BCE, witnesses economic opportunity for certain elites and challenging conditions for most of the populace.[14] Among his assertions concerning wealth and poverty are the following: the rich have a number of intrinsic advantages, including status in the society and the ability to collect bribes (Eccl. 5:8 [7]; 9:13–16); yet wealth can be lost with rapidity (5:13–14 [12–13]; 10:5–7), and money creates great anxiety for the one who has it (4:7–9).[15] Qoheleth does not offer any sort of character-consequence guarantee: by his accounting, the wisdom of the poor does not lead to advancement, because their sage counsel is quickly forgotten (e.g., 9:15 and the heroic pauper who receives no acclaim). Moreover, since death strikes everyone in equal measure, it becomes a travesty to leave property and possessions to someone who did not work for them (2:21). Qoheleth's willingness to provide an honest perspective on financial dynamics makes him one of the more incisive sapiential voices of the Second Temple period.

This author's counsel on how to respond to financial uncertainty is to work hard, enjoy the fruit of one's labor, especially during the early years, and share one's wealth. The sage declares, "There is nothing better for mortals than to eat and drink, and find enjoyment in their toil. This also, I saw, is from the hand of God" (Eccl. 2:24; cf. 5:17–18; 9:7–10). Although God can thwart human delight (6:1–3), Qoheleth encourages a carpe-diem mentality, so that a person should seek pleasure in one's "portion" or "means" (Heb. ḥēleq), in life and the company of friends.[16] The book of Ecclesiastes also urges a spirit of benevolence: "Send out your bread upon the waters, for after many days you will get it back" (11:1). Commentators disagree on the best interpretation for this verse: it might refer to investing one's resources abroad and expecting a gain (cf. Prov. 31:14). Or perhaps the sage encourages diversification of one's holdings in order to minimize financial losses.[17] Yet finding the same piece of bread does not offer a return on the original investment, and so profit seeking is probably not the sense of 11:1. The following verse provides the best clue for interpretation: "Divide your means [ḥēleq] seven ways, or even eight, for you do not know what disaster may happen on earth" (11:2). Qoheleth advises

---

14. On a Ptolemaic date for the book of Ecclesiastes, see Hengel, *Judaism and Hellenism*, 1:115. See chap. 4 for more background on the Ptolemaic era in Judea.

15. See Kugel, "Qohelet and Money," 32–49.

16. Elias Joseph Bickerman, *Four Strange Books of the Bible* (New York: Schocken Books, 1967), 165, argues that "Koheleth is a sage who in an age of investment teaches not dissipation but the enjoyment of wealth."

17. Emmanuel Podechard, *L'Ecclésiaste*, *Études bibliques* (Paris: Gabalda, 1912).

that one should practice spontaneous kindness to others out of strategic self-interest rather than altruism, because life is short, and friends might return the favor when adversity strikes at a later date (cf. Eccl. 4:7–12). The same logic appears in Sirach (e.g., 3:31: "Those who repay favors give thought to the future; when they fall they will find support") and in the Egyptian Instruction of Ankhsheshonqy (ca. fourth century BCE): "Do a good deed and throw it in the water; when it dries you will find it" (19.1).[18]

Ben Sira and Social Ethics

Another sapiential voice from this period that devotes significant attention to social ethics and economics is Ben Sira, and his conclusions are in many respects similar to Qoheleth's. Like his predecessor, Ben Sira cites the inherent advantages of the wealthy (Sir. 13:3–22), the potential for rapid gain/loss (18:25–26), and the inevitable anxiety that accompanies financial holdings (31:1–17). His commentary on money and class is also reminiscent of Ecclesiastes: "The rich person speaks and all are silent; they extol to the clouds what he says. The poor person speaks and they say, 'Who is this fellow?' And should he stumble, they even push him down" (Sir. 13:23). Ben Sira is more direct than Qoheleth about the Torah as the source for wisdom (e.g., 1:26; 19:20). Moreover, he tries to sustain the wisdom-over-wealth category from Proverbs: "The poor are honored for their knowledge, while the rich are honored for their wealth" (10:30). Yet even with these factors, Ben Sira's discourses more closely resemble the book of Ecclesiastes in their blunt commentary on economics.

This candor surfaces most clearly in Ben Sira's withering critique of financial exchanges. He is descriptive about the vagaries of the marketplace and the greedy impulse that often marks commerce, declaring: "One who loves gold will not be justified; one who pursues money will be led astray by it" (Sir. 31:5–6). His most vivid description of exchanges appears in 26:29–27:2, where he lashes out against the dangers of mercantile activities:

> A merchant can hardly keep from wrongdoing,
>   nor is a tradesman innocent of sin.
> Many have committed sin for gain,
>   and those who seek to get rich will avert their eyes.
> As a stake is driven firmly into a fissure between stones,
>   so sin is wedged in between selling and buying.

---

18. For the latter text, Miriam Lichtheim, *Ancient Egyptian Literature*, vol. 3, *The Late Period* (Berkeley: University of California Press, 1980), 174. See also the discussion in Seow, *Ecclesiastes*, 334–35, 342–44.

The Greek word for "tradesman" (*kapēlos*) in this passage might be translated as "swindler" since the author recognizes the frequent tendency for profit seekers to cut corners. One of the reasons for Ben Sira's aversion to commerce here and in other passages is his preference for the life of the scribe over the harsh realities of the marketplace.[19] In his condescending discussion of the various vocations in chapters 38–39, he distinguishes manual laborers and merchants from the one "who devotes himself to the study of the law of the Most High!" (Sir. 38:34). While this belief seems to reflect a preference for the scribal vocation, Ben Sira also witnessed unbridled commercial activity under the Ptolemies and Seleucids (see chap. 4 above), and corruption went against his understanding of the Torah and the wisdom tradition.

Ben Sira's protest against unfairness in the marketplace is an admirable aspect of his ethics; he most likely taught fellow scribes how to interact with the elite (e.g., Sir. 51:23).[20] As a member of the retainer class, he took a risk in publicizing his descriptive views on money within a milieu of wealthy landowners and priestly officials, since he traveled in these same circles. It is a testament to the bravery of this sapiential author that he advises his charges on how to conduct themselves at lavish banquets (31:12–32:13) while also criticizing wealthy persons who benefited from unscrupulous practices.[21] Ben Sira's discourse on wealth and poverty reflects the delicate balance of a figure trying to navigate elite circles, a dynamic marketplace that included questionable practices, and the social-justice expectations of his tradition all at the same time.

His advice for negotiating this tension is cautious enjoyment of one's standing, as long as a person obeys the Torah and does not trample on the rights of others. Ben Sira declares that "riches are good if they are free from sin" (Sir. 13:24). The fact that he does not repudiate money as intrinsically evil indicates his social standing and affirmation of wealth as a reward for virtuous behavior. Yet he does not entertain much hope of individuals combining

---

19. J. Collins, *Jewish Wisdom*, 31.

20. Benjamin G. Wright, "'Fear the Lord and Honor the Priest': Ben Sira as Defender of the Jerusalem Priesthood," in *The Book of Ben Sira in Modern Research: Proceedings of the First International Ben Sira Conference, 28–31 July 1996*, Soesterberg, Netherlands, BZAW 255 (Berlin: de Gruyter, 1997), 195–96, argues that the author is part of the "retainer class" of "scribe-sages" who served the priestly elite and other powerful individuals, including Greek officials. Cf. Richard A. Horsley and Patrick Tiller, "Ben Sira and the Sociology of the Second Temple," in *Second Temple Studies*, vol. 3, *Studies in Politics, Class, and Material Culture*, JSOTSup 340 (London: Sheffield Academic Press, 2002), 74–108.

21. Oda Wischmeyer, *Die Kultur des Buches Jesus Sirach*, BZNW 77 (Berlin: de Gruyter, 1995), 107–8, outlines the relevant passage in Sirach, which is thoroughly Hellenistic in orientation.

financial success with "fear of the Lord" as their baseline principle: "Blessed is the rich person who is found blameless, and who does not go after gold. Who is he, that we may praise him? For he has done wonders among his people" (31:8–9). In conjunction with the appeal for righteous behavior among the wealthy, the sage encourages self-sufficiency, since penury leads to the loss of autonomy and a precarious existence (e.g., 40:28). Like Qoheleth, Ben Sira maintains that kindness to others provides security against future hardship, such as lending to a neighbor (e.g., Sir. 29:3). With such sensible advice, Ben Sira advocates pragmatism, including a belief in alliances with others as a means of ensuring against destitution. This is one of the reasons commentators refer to Ben Sira's advice as reflective of an "ethics of caution": he urges restraint as an operative principle.[22]

The author's adherence to the Torah as a template for social ethics also leads him to call for philanthropy, including the practice of almsgiving. Ben Sira is more persistent in his calls for generosity than are Proverbs and Ecclesiastes, which is a primary reason he advises someone to act as guarantor for a neighbor's loan if the circumstances allow it (Sir. 29:14–20: see chap. 3 above). He appeals to the Mosaic tradition as a rationale for being generous with one's resources: "Help the poor for the commandment's sake, and in their need do not send them away empty-handed" (Sir. 29:9). The likely background for this passage is the call for benevolence in Deuteronomy 15:7–11.[23] With such allusions, the sage acknowledges both his upper-class audience and the plight of the poor. He does not entertain any hope of solving the problem of social stratification, but his belief system demands kindness to those on the margins as a fundamental requirement for faithful living. Ben Sira echoes the commandments by citing the Lord's favor upon the widow and the orphan and their enduring struggles in a patrilocal and patrilineal society (Sir. 35:17–19).

Second Temple Instructions and Question of an Afterlife

In assessing the perspectives on economics in Proverbs, Job, Ecclesiastes, and Ben Sira, it is noteworthy that none of these sapiential works place hope in a beatific afterlife to alleviate earthly struggles. Challenges, including financial struggles, need to be rectified in one's temporal existence or not at all.[24]

22. Jack T. Sanders, "Ben Sira's Ethics of Caution," *HUCA* 50 (1979): 73–106.
23. Benjamin G. Wright and Claudia V. Camp, "Ben Sira's Discourse of Riches and Poverty," *Hen* 23 (2001): 158–59.
24. Statements in Proverbs about leading a righteous life in order to avoid "death" (e.g., Prov. 15:24: "For the wise man's path of life leads upward, in order to avoid Sheol beneath") reflect immediate realities rather than the possibility of future, corrective action in a heavenly realm.

Within the ethical framework of Proverbs, the best one can hope for is plentiful resources, a stable family, and length of days (e.g., Prov. 22:4).[25] Other sapiential voices agree with this understanding but strike a more sorrowful chord about the finality of death and the fleeting nature of life/possessions. Job is despondent over the fact that a person is "few of days and full of trouble, comes up like a flower and withers, flees like a shadow and does not last" (14:1–2). The theological perspective in this text does not allow for an eschatological reversal of fortunes (e.g., 14:1–17).[26] In a similar vein, Qoheleth urges his listeners to soak up the pleasures that life affords: "Whatever your hand finds to do, do with your might; for there is no work or thought or knowledge or wisdom in Sheol, to which you are going" (Eccl. 9:10). Qoheleth's frustration is particularly acute in the area of material belongings. All persons must leave their possessions to someone who did not toil for them, so that death becomes the great equalizer, nullifying any earthly gains (Eccl. 2:18). The author grieves the limits of his framework through the motif of a frustrated accountant: "See, this is what I found, says the Teacher, adding one thing to another to find the sum [Heb. ḥešbôn], which my mind has sought repeatedly, but I have not found" (Eccl. 7:27–28). Such conclusions indicate an honest grappling with the uncertainty of life "under the sun" without benefit of an otherworldly horizon.

Ben Sira arrives at much the same conclusion, although he promises an eternal reputation for the righteous and a painful judgment for the wicked at death. On the first point, his emphasis on a good name seeks to compensate for losing one's family, friends, and possessions. He cites the consolation of the righteous in this regard: "The human body is a fleeting thing, but a virtuous name will never be blotted out. Have regard for your name, since it will outlive you longer than a thousand hoards of gold" (Sir. 41:11–12; cf. 15:6; 37:26; 39:9; 44:8).[27] Previous instructions had utilized this motif of a "good name," but not to the extent of Ben Sira, who offers it up as solace for human mortality. Persons can take comfort that descendants will benefit from

25. James L. Crenshaw, *Old Testament Wisdom: An Introduction*, 3rd ed. (Louisville, KY: Westminster John Knox Press, 2010), 72, explains that "life" in Proverbs means "robust health, an abundance of friends, a house full of children, and sufficient possessions to carry one safely through any difficulty." By extension, "death" is the absence of these features, marking an existence apart from wisdom and "fear of the LORD." According to this logic, a fool has already perished through his idiocy.
26. The famous passage in Job 19:25–27, which includes the declaration, "For I know my Redeemer lives," is a call for a legal vindicator in Job's ongoing defense of himself and not an affirmation of the afterlife.
27. Qoheleth comes to the opposite conclusion: "The people of long ago are not remembered, nor will there be any remembrance of people yet to come by those who come after them" (Eccl. 1:11).

their righteousness, heralding their good works for generations. This promise becomes a response to those with eschatological proposals.[28] In contrast, the memory of the wicked will not survive, and God might force the sinner to experience trauma at the end of life: "For it is easy for the Lord on the day of death to reward individuals according to their conduct. An hour's misery makes one forget past delights, and at the close of one's life one's deeds are revealed" (11:26–27). A few verses earlier, the sage had declared that "it is easy in the sight of the Lord to make the poor rich suddenly, in an instant" (11:21). Yet Ben Sira never explains precisely how the Deity will change the fortunes of the poor or cause a disturbing conclusion for the wicked. In this regard his efforts seek to affirm the character-consequence guarantee he inherited from Proverbs without the benefit of an afterlife.[29] Ben Sira acknowledges the finality of death while at the same time defending the possibility of a lasting reputation (contra Qoheleth). Despite his juggling act to defend the wisdom tradition, his conclusions on death are as absolute as Job and Ecclesiastes: "This is the Lord's decree for all flesh; why then should you reject the will of the Most High? Whether life lasts for ten years or a hundred or a thousand, there are no questions asked in Hades" (Sir. 41:4).

APOCALYPTIC ESCHATOLOGY, ECONOMICS, AND SOCIAL ETHICS

In the late Second Temple period, eschatological proposals emerged as alternatives to such earthly perspectives. Beliefs in the afterlife—whether from Persian (i.e., Zoroastrian) religion, Hellenistic ideas, or the reinterpretation of texts from the Hebrew Bible and beyond—had a profound impact on social ethics.[30] In many respects the promise of a blessed afterlife altered the framework for ethics, including financial matters. If God could "settle accounts" at a final judgment of some sort, the possibility emerged for reversing the effects of present suffering. As an apocalyptic imagination influenced the religious

---

28. Gabriele Boccaccini, *Middle Judaism: Jewish Thought, 300 B.C.E. to 200 C.E.* (Minneapolis: Fortress Press, 1991), 121.

29. The final version of Ben Sira does contain scattered references to the afterlife, but these are later insertions into the text. See Conleth Kearns, *The Expanded Text of Ecclesiasticus: Its Teaching on the Future Life as a Clue to Its Origin*, Deutero and Cognate Literature Series 11 (Berlin: de Gruyter, 2011).

30. John J. Collins, *The Apocalyptic Imagination: An Introduction to Jewish Apocalyptic Literature*, 2nd ed. (Grand Rapids: Eerdmans, 1998), surveys the earliest apocalyptic literature in the Second Temple period and its probable origins.

traditions of early Judaism and Christianity, this development led to new horizons for discussing act and consequence and the possibility for permanent redemption when a person had experienced difficulty.[31] The sayings of Jesus, with their gnomic character, reflect this new paradigm, as do earlier sapiential texts that involve an apocalyptic framework.

4QInstruction and the Dead Sea Scrolls

One early example of this eschatological shift is *4QInstruction* (second century BCE), the longest wisdom text from the corpus of the Dead Sea Scrolls.[32] This is one of the more fragmentary documents found near Qumran, making it difficult to offer definitive conclusions about the perspective in *4QInstruction*. Yet the extant fragments clearly promise heavenly reward to the righteous category of persons: "For he [God] has raised up your head out of poverty, and he has seated you with nobles, and he has placed in your power an inheritance of glory" (4Q416 frg. 2 3.11–12, my trans.). The "nobles" in this fragment probably refer to the angelic host with whom the righteous will enjoy eternal fellowship.[33] *4QInstruction* also commands its listeners to "grasp the birth-times of salvation, and know who will inherit glory and t[oi]l" (4Q417 frg. 2 1.12). The implication in these and similar passages is heavenly reward for the elect category, even if they struggle in their earthly lives. On the other side, sinful persons do not share the same fate: God "passes judgment upon the work of iniquity" (4Q416 frg. 1 lines 10–11), and the ones who have "defiled themselves" through such activity will not enjoy the heavenly rewards of the righteous. As with many apocalyptic texts, *4QInstruction* predicts a period in which "there comes an end to iniquity" (4Q418 frg. 113 line 1) such that sinners will cease to cause misery in the world.

One of the more salient features of *4QInstruction* is that the fragments highlight the lowly social status of the persons receiving this advice, including their economic situation. The audience here is not a closed sect, as we find in some of the other documents from the Dead Sea Scrolls, but the language in both the eschatological discourses and the pithy admonitions implies that the addressees

31. We need to distinguish between (1) the literary genre of apocalypse and (2) literature, worldviews, or social movements that have "apocalyptic" elements. See ibid., 2–14.

32. Unless otherwise noted, translations of the Dead Sea Scrolls are from Florentino García Martínez and Eibert J. C. Tigchelaar, *The Dead Sea Scrolls Study Edition*, 2 vols. (Leiden: E. J. Brill, 1997–98).

33. Matthew J. Goff, *The Worldly and Heavenly Wisdom of 4QInstruction*, STDJ 50 (Leiden: E. J. Brill, 2003), 210–11.

of *4QInstruction* are struggling.[34] References to farming appear in the extant fragments, along with the passages that address the need to stand surety (see chap. 3 above), reflecting a more precarious situation than the audience for Ben Sira's instruction. The young pupil (referred to as a "discerning one," *mĕbîn*) receiving this advice must honor his father "in your poverty" and his mother "in your steps" (4Q416 frg. 2 3.15–16). At several points, this "discerning one" (who represents the entire audience) is told, "You are poor" (4Q415 frg. 6 line 2; 4Q416 frg. 2 2.20; 4Q416 frg. 2 3.2, 8, 12, 19; 4Q418 frg. 177 line 5). This "You are poor" refrain does not seem to indicate metaphorical poverty in most cases, but actual financial challenges.[35] Elsewhere in *4QInstruction*, the author allows that righteous persons might experience economic difficulties, including the need to barter in order to obtain food (4Q417 frg. 2 1.17–18; cf. 4Q416 frg. 2 2.1). An individual should be cautious with what he trades, not giving up more than is necessary, because his situation is difficult. Other statements note struggles in the effort to realize an acceptable standard of living in an agrarian economy. A person who fails to do so might find himself in need of a loan and eventually losing sleep because of his inability to pay it back (4Q417 frg. 2 1.21–24). The target audience here lacks the resources of Ben Sira's charges, who instead receive advice on how to conduct themselves at lavish banquets.

Yet the heavenly consolation of *4QInstruction* transcends the frustrated conclusions of a book like Job or Ecclesiastes. The author declares that God will act "to lift up the head of the poor ones [. . .] with eternal glory and everlasting peace" (4Q418 frg. 126 2.7–8). In this particular fragment, the sapiential author contrasts the "poor" elect with "wicked" persons, upon whom the gates of death will shut (lines 6–7). The audience for *4QInstruction* can take comfort in the promise of "eternal glory and everlasting peace" (lines 7–8), thereby mitigating any current financial distress.

The Epistle of Enoch and the Gospel of Luke

A similar dynamic appears in the Epistle of Enoch (*1 En.* 92–105), and this text specifically identifies the wicked group as "rich."[36] The author lashes

---

34. Much debate has occurred on the status of *4QInstruction* and whether it originates within the same group responsible for such clearly sectarian works as the *Community Rule* (1QS). The addressees of *4QInstruction* can marry and conduct business in the open sphere; the text does not reflect the sectarian identity shown in many other documents from the Dead Sea Scrolls corpus. See ibid., 219–28.

35. See ibid., 151–52.

36. Most commentators date this portion of the Enochic corpus to the second century BCE. See George W. E. Nickelsburg, *1 Enoch: A Commentary on the Book of 1 Enoch*, 2 vols., Hermeneia (Minneapolis: Fortress Press, 2001–12), 1:8.

out at the wealthy for failing to appreciate the responsibility that comes with their status, a failure that will lead to eternal punishment. This section of the Enochic corpus elevates the poor, referring to them as "pious ones," the recipients of a unique eschatological gift. A series of woe statements offers a clear contrast in language that is evocative of Amos and other eighth-century prophets: "Woe to you, rich, for in your riches you have trusted; and from your riches you will depart, because you have not remembered the Most High in the day of your riches" (*1 En.* 94:8).[37] With regard to the elect category, these chapters guarantee heavenly consolation to the righteous. In an address to the "pious ones," the speaker declares, "Take courage, then; for formerly you were worn out by evils and tribulations, but now you will shine like the luminaries of heaven; you will shine and appear, and the portals of heaven will be opened for you" (*1 En.* 104:2). As with *4QInstruction*, the Epistle of Enoch offers a permanent reversal here, with the promise of astral immortality among the stars and angels for those who have suffered hardship during their earthly existence.

We find a similar assessment of poverty and eschatology in certain passages from the New Testament, particularly the Gospel of Luke. Like the Epistle of Enoch and *4QInstruction*, the Lukan author focuses on economics, promising heavenly rewards for struggling persons and eternal punishment for the wealthy.[38] The Sermon on the Plain in Luke (6:17–49) is a famous example of this perspective. The relationship between poverty and election is explicit in the Beatitudes: "Blessed are you who are poor, for yours is the kingdom of God" (6:20).[39] In this verse the "poor" (Gk. *ptōchoi*) refers to those who are actually struggling and not to some metaphorical category. The contrast between the two categories of "rich and "poor" is in the tradition of both the sapiential and apocalyptic texts we have examined throughout this chapter.[40] As with the Epistle of Enoch, Luke claims that the wealthy have misunderstood the ultimate stakes: "But woe to you who are rich, for you have received your consolation." (Luke 6:24). According to this perspective, true discipleship involves repentance, generosity, *and* understanding the eternal consequences of one's decisions. The intent of such passages seems to be didactic in the sense that the Gospel urges benevolence and greater solidarity, with

37. This discussion follows the translation of Nickelsburg and VanderKam, *1 Enoch: A New Translation*.

38. For further discussion on the relationship among these texts on financial matters, see Nickelsburg, "Revisiting the Rich and Poor," 579–605; Goff, "Discerning Trajectories," 657–73.

39. This follows directly in the tradition of the Magnificat (Luke 1:51–53).

40. Betz, *The Sermon on the Mount*, 575–76, also sees traces of Cynic philosophy in this contrast.

eschatological reversal as a motivating factor. The earliest followers of Jesus live into this call in the book of Acts, the sequel to Luke, as they share possessions and thereby alleviate destitution among their small band of disciples (e.g., Acts 2:44–45; 4:32–37).

The most vivid representation of this eschatological dynamic involving social ethics and money is the parable of the Rich Man and Lazarus (Luke 16:19–31). The contrast between the wealthy man "dressed in purple and fine linen" (v. 19) and Lazarus has hortatory value. The audience for this pericope has to understand the import of their earthly behavior, particularly when it comes to oppression of the poor. The antecedents for this description and whether external sources had an impact on the parable have generated debate, but the intention to provide a graphic portrait of the separate destinies of the righteous and wicked based on their conduct is clear enough.[41] Because of his disregard for the social justice that the Torah demands, the rich man faces "agony" in the fiery flames of hell/Hades (Luke 16:24–25), while the poor man "was carried away by the angels to be with Abraham" (v. 22).[42] This emphasis on benevolence as a litmus test for elect status is critical in the parable, especially since heavenly rewards are part of the equation. According to the individualized eschatology of this pericope, God evaluates each person's earthly conduct and then decides where to place them permanently.[43] Repentance, by showing hospitality to the less fortunate, becomes the precursor to heavenly reward, and the parable specifically cites the Torah and the Prophets as the basis for social ethics (cf. Luke 19:1–10; 24:46–47). The heavenly Abraham figure explains to the rich man that his brothers do not need a warning from a heavenly messenger, since "they have Moses and the prophets; they should listen to them" (Luke 16:29). Consequently, the passages from the Pentateuch on fairness, egalitarian social structures, and special attention to

41. Outi Lehtipuu, *The Afterlife Imagery in Luke's Story of the Rich Man and Lazarus*, NovTSup 123 (Leiden: E. J. Brill, 2005), surveys the evidence for influence in the parable, including Hellenistic texts. Among the more convincing parallels are those early Jewish apocalyptic texts such as *1 En.* 22; *4 Ezra* (= 2 Esd.) 7:78–99; and the heavenly journeys of Abraham in the *Testament of Abraham*. The shared themes do not necessarily indicate literary dependence but suggest common traditions.

42. Contrary to certain arguments about this passage, "Hades" is not a temporary holding place for the wicked in this passage (as with *1 En.* 22) but the permanent destination of the rich man, analogous to "Gehenna." This vivid contrast had a considerable impact on the early church, as interpreters utilized this parable to refine their understanding of the underworld as a place of punishment (Lehtipuu, *The Afterlife Imagery in Luke's Story of the Rich Man and Lazarus*, 4).

43. This unit and other passages in Luke (e.g., the Unjust Steward in 16:1–8) imply an immediate accounting for each person upon their death. For the relationship between such parables and language in Luke–Acts that focuses more on the imminent return (Parousia) of Jesus, see Lehtipuu, *Afterlife Imagery*, 250–56.

vulnerable groups remain the blueprint for proper behavior. The account of the Rich Man and Lazarus underscores the permanent repercussions of any mistakes, particularly when conspicuous consumption occurs alongside the desperate struggles of one's neighbor. Earlier prophets and the wisdom writers also railed against such behavior; yet in texts like Luke that affirm eschatological reversal, sinners face more grievous consequences for their callous disregard toward a neighbor in need.

Wisdom and Apocalypticism

The combination of sapiential and apocalyptic motifs in texts like *4QInstruction* and the Gospel of Luke raises the question of the generic relationship between the two categories of wisdom and apocalypticism. The discussion in J. Z. Smith's *Map Is Not Territory* is helpful here: Smith defines apocalypticism as *"wisdom lacking a royal patron."*[44] This definition helps to explain the distinction between sapiential texts that do not have an apocalyptic framework and those that do. The background for *4QInstruction* is not the world of scribal retainers, priests, and members of the more elite classes, as with Ben Sira and Proverbs, but instead an audience that lacks access to the corridors of power. The same is true for the story of the Rich Man and Lazarus. Smith also mentions a "locative" worldview in many wisdom texts where the status quo is affirmed by "scribal elites who had a deep vested interest in restricting mobility and valuing place."[45] Although both the compilers of Proverbs and Ben Sira rail against corruption in the marketplace, the character-consequence sayings in these texts seek to preserve the status quo by promising justice in the present social configuration. *4QInstruction*, the Epistle of Enoch, and similar texts of the Second Temple period do not offer such a guarantee; instead, they present a framework offering heavenly reward as compensation for the righteous individual, especially persons who lack the privileges of elite status.

With the offer of ultimate redemption, this type of eschatological perspective creates solidarity in a stratified society. For example, the defense of a belief in resurrection in Mark (e.g., 12:18–27 and the debate with the Sadducees) or Paul's lengthy discussion in 1 Corinthians 15 has the effect of fostering community. As an alternative to the imperial patronage of Roman society, the presentation of mutual responsibility in 1 Corinthians hinges

44. Jonathan Z. Smith, "Wisdom and Apocalyptic," in *Map Is Not Territory* (Chicago: University of Chicago Press, 1978), 81, does not focus on texts from this period, but his assessment of apocalyptic motifs in ancient Egyptian literature makes this a relevant and helpful study.
45. J. Smith, *Map Is Not Territory*, 293.

on an alternative set of allegiances and associations.[46] Paul encourages self-supporting churches and special concern for the poor as a substitute to the patronage system we discussed in chapters 3–4 (above; e.g., Rom. 15:25–27; 1 Cor. 16:1–4; Gal. 2:9–10). Undergirding Paul's framework is his belief in the power of the resurrection message to build unity. Paul's specific convictions on resurrection and the afterlife—as well as those among the audience for *4QInstruction*, *1 Enoch*, and other groups (such as the Pharisees)—are complex and beyond the scope of the present discussion. What is relevant here is the sense of community that an otherworldly framework engenders, especially for struggling believers. As Claudia Setzer explains, the hope that "death has been swallowed up in victory" (1 Cor. 15:54) is foundational to Paul's efforts with the church in Corinth: "Resurrection allowed the Corinthians to retain the idea of God's power and plan for history, manifested in Jesus' resurrection, and reconcile it with their experience of suffering and insecurity under Roman domination, while beginning to put another society in place."[47]

THE QUESTION OF SOCIAL LOCATION

Although the previous section highlighted the manner in which apocalyptic eschatology transformed the framework for addressing wealth and poverty, the question arises as to the social location for these perspectives. For a study on economic life in the Second Temple period, this is an important consideration. Many commentators have debated whether or not apocalyptic ideas originate from marginal voices in a society. Max Weber and other sociologists of the early twentieth century argued that such ideas and texts often derive from peripheral authors and groups, because dissatisfaction with the status quo prompts some to look beyond temporal events for meaning and hope.[48] These suggestions led to deprivation theory, which held that millennial groups usually form on the periphery, because their constructs function as an alternative to the dominant ethos in a society. For the apocalyptic (and proto-apocalyptic) voices in the Hebrew Bible, the literature of early Judaism, and then among the first Christians, one frequent assumption is that other-

46. Neil Elliott, "The Anti-Imperial Message of the Cross," in *Paul and Empire*, ed. Richard A. Horsley (Harrisburg, PA: Trinity Press, 1997), 167–83. For further discussion on imperial patronage, see chap. 3 above and the discussion of bribery.

47. Claudia Setzer, *Resurrection of the Body in Early Judaism and Early Christianity: Doctrine, Community, and Self-Definition* (Boston: E. J. Brill, 2004), 69.

48. Max Weber, *The Sociology of Religion*, trans. Ephraim Fischoff, 4th ed. (German original, 1922; Boston: Beacon Press, 1963).

worldly perspectives are the products of "outsiders."[49] For the purveyors of this literature, descriptions of visionary journeys and the division of history into periods instill a resolve in the wake of present struggles, precisely because ultimate redemption lies beyond temporal existence. Within this framework, Plöger, Hanson, and others have claimed that apocalyptic ideas are "visionary" as opposed to "hierocratic" in orientation, and therefore the presentation has a more insurrectionist tenor because of its origin.[50] Some have even suggested that pseudonymous authorship (i.e., attributing one's work to a figure from the past, such as Enoch or Daniel) is a function of the precarious social status of those who actually composed these texts.[51]

Yet is the assumption of marginal communities as the locus for apocalyptic literature tenable, especially since sophisticated texts required literate scribes with status in the society?[52] Awareness of emergent apocalyptic ideas would have demanded intricate knowledge, and the ability to build an audience for one's mode of discourse necessitated a certain social standing. The influence and sophistication of apocalyptic writings point to authors with significant exposure to earlier literature from Judea and neighboring cultures.[53] Such awareness required scribal training in priestly, prophetic, and sapiential traditions. Even with his definition of apocalypticism as *"wisdom lacking a royal patron,"* J. Z. Smith links the two categories in his study of texts from ancient Egypt and Babylon: "I would argue that wisdom and apocalyptic are related in that they are both essentially scribal phenomena. It is the paradigmatic thought of the scribe—a way of thinking that is both pragmatic

---

49. Otto Plöger, *Theocracy and Eschatology*, trans. S. Rudman (Oxford: Blackwell Press, 1968); Paul D. Hanson, *The Dawn of Apocalyptic* (Philadelphia: Fortress Press, 1979); Wayne A. Meeks, *The First Urban Christians: The Social World of the Apostle Paul*, 2nd ed. (New Haven: Yale University Press, 2003).

50. Hanson, *The Dawn of Apocalyptic*, 232.

51. Ibid., 252. An influential source for the argument that pseudonymity represents a response to fear is the work of James C. Scott, especially *Domination and the Arts of Resistance: Hidden Transcripts* (New Haven: Yale University Press, 1990). Yet pseudonymity does not necessarily imply caution, but rather a deliberate decision to propagate one's perspective through the authority of an ancient hero. See J. Collins, *The Apocalyptic Imagination*, 39; Portier-Young, *Apocalypse against Empire*, 31–44.

52. This is the argument of Stephen L. Cook, *Prophecy and Apocalypticism: The Postexilic Social Setting* (Minneapolis: Fortress Press, 1995) as he examines Ezek. 38–39; Zech. 1–8; Joel 1–2, and a whole range of millennial movements. He concludes that proto-apocalyptic texts "are *not* products of groups that are alienated, marginalized, or even relatively deprived" (2).

53. Portier-Young, *Apocalypse against Empire*, 309–10, argues that the authors of Daniel and the Enochic literature had significant educational training and influence in the society, such that they belonged to "the class of scribes and sages."

and speculative—which has given rise to both."[54] When considering Second Temple texts in this regard, clues in the Enochic literature suggest a pedagogical setting of some sort for the authors of this esoteric wisdom.[55] Collins cautiously associates authorship of Daniel with the *maśkîlîm*, the "wise among the people" who receive special praise in Daniel 11:33–35.[56] The author responsible for the Lukan material drew from various traditions, including the Q source. The prose in Luke is of a higher quality than most New Testament books, and the Gospel writer combines both early Jewish traditions and an apocalyptic understanding of Jesus and the earliest Christians.[57] These wise teachers required a scribal education of some sort to propagate their apocalyptic worldview and synthesize various traditions. Commentators have rightly argued that such scribes did not necessarily represent a countercultural or populist movement.[58]

Although these helpful qualifications force us to proceed quite cautiously on the question of social location, scribal authorship does not mean that the entire audience for these works came from elite circles. In many cases, language that elevates the poor as recipients of unique eschatological gifts has the hortatory goal of reshaping behavior among the upper classes. Yet apocalyptic literature also transcended such a setting. The oral nature of transmission provided an opportunity for widespread dissemination of ideas.[59] This entire study has highlighted the stratified nature of Second Temple Judea, and the combination of practical advice with apocalyptic eschatology in a text like *4QInstruction* created a discourse that could appeal to a far more diverse audience. The explicit identification of the audience for this text as poor attached a sense of "otherness" to the recipients of this advice, as did the special election of these addressees through their access to "the mystery that is to be" (Heb. *rāz nihyeh*, the central revelatory concept in *4QInstruction*). Poverty is not a desirable state in this text, but eschatological consolation would have appealed to a struggling audience, and *4QInstruction* reflects more of an agrarian context than an urban, scribal perspective. In a different but nevertheless precarious setting, the *maśkîlîm* in Daniel instructed a broader target group during a period of political persecution (i.e., the reign

54. J. Smith, "Wisdom and Apocalyptic," 74.

55. Benjamin G. Wright, "1 Enoch and Ben Sira: Wisdom and Apocalypticism in Relationship," in *The Early Enoch Literature*, JSJSup 121 (Leiden: E. J. Brill, 2007), 159–76, points to didactic elements in such texts as the Epistle of Enoch.

56. J. Collins, *Daniel*, 66–71.

57. John T. Carroll, *Luke*, NTL (Louisville, KY: Westminster John Knox Press, 2012), 2.

58. See Horsley, *Scribe, Visionaries*, 204–5.

59. Susan Niditch, *Oral Word and Written Word*, LAI (Louisville, KY: Westminster John Knox Press, 1996).

of Antiochus IV Epiphanes), and the visions instilled hope into those in a desperate situation. It is true that visionary descriptions do not necessarily lead to widespread rebellions, and millennial movements do not always originate among poor communities. Yet the promise of an afterlife as a means of transcending destitution or persecution frequently has a democratizing effect on believers. Such a guarantee allows for acceptance of present circumstances, and it functions to identify a specific set of people (e.g., Pharisees, Essenes, the first Christians) who have access to an eschatological banquet, while others (e.g., Sadducees) do not. This promise of heavenly fulfillment had the benefit of appealing to a cross-section of believers and providing hope to the marginalized, even if the compilers of texts enjoyed a more lofty status.[60]

SUMMARY

This chapter has surveyed the diverse perspectives on wealth and poverty in much of the instructional literature from this period. Even within individual collections of sayings, conclusions can differ, reflecting a complex agenda in these texts. In certain cases, sources like Qoheleth and Ben Sira indicate the shifting dynamics of the Second Temple period, including social stratification, networks of corruption, and intrinsic challenges for the majority of the population. In the midst of this climate, a fundamental shift occurred in terms of an eschatological vision. Certain instructional texts no longer confined the reward for virtue to social advancement or a lasting name, which for many persons was not a realistic possibility. With the possibility of eschatological reversal, sources like *4QInstruction*, the Epistle of Enoch, and New Testament authors could instead offer heavenly fulfillment as the rationale for uprightness. Such a move made a permanent imprint on the tradition: not only could instructional texts transcend the more pessimistic conclusions of a work like Ecclesiastes, but heavenly rewards also offered a hopeful framework for ethics among those who toiled in a stratified and oppressive system.

---

60. See Meeks, *The First Urban Christians*, 51–73.

Conclusion

Work on this project commenced in the aftermath of the global financial crisis that started in 2008. While researching and writing, it was impossible to ignore the disparity between collateralized debt obligations and the specifics of a preindustrial, agrarian society. The boundaryless, global nature of financial interactions in today's economy differs sharply from the daily concerns of farming households in ancient Judea. The economy of the Second Temple period revolved around the agricultural cycle, bartering, maintaining familial relationships, supporting the priestly establishment and imperial officials, and regional trading. Our modern transportation and communications networks, the massive nature of the global food industry, and an array of medical and scientific possibilities are far removed from the daily transactions and interactions in the ancient world.

Yet even with these contextual differences, there are more similarities than might appear at first glance. These include lending arrangements where a vulnerable borrower faces loss of home and social standing due to exorbitant interest rates. The proliferation of payday lending in the American context is but one example that certain dynamics of human behavior are timeless. Along the same lines, the commonsense advice in the Wisdom literature against standing as guarantor for another person's loan has relevance for both the ancient and modern context. While the status of women and children has changed in many contemporary settings, pay inequities, the demand for early child labor, and the persistent devaluation of domestic tasks continue to play a role in our current global context. In addition, widows still face a myriad of economic and social challenges that limit their ability to recover from the loss of a husband, both in the United States and elsewhere. Vast disparities in wealth between persons in more "professional" vocations and those whose work involves manual labor continue to create class-consciousness and division. The vulnerability of citizens to the revenue demands of the state plays a divisive role in many countries, as evidenced by the rancorous debates in recent years over the fairness of the American tax system.

This study has attempted to show that one cannot separate the economic from the religious all that easily. Ancient authors and the texts they produced did not bracket theological claims from observations about financial matters. One consistent assertion in this regard is that God stands on the side of the most vulnerable members of the society, even becoming their advocate. Anyone whose actions threaten the livelihood of a poor individual has insulted the Creator. From the plaintive cries during the crisis of Nehemiah 5 to the parable of the Rich Man and Lazarus (Luke 16:19–31), texts from this period view financial concerns through the lens of their sacred tradition. Following the theological blueprint in the Torah, Second Temple authors sought to create a society in which swindlers did not prosper and those most susceptible to poverty in a patriarchal context received special protection. Within this framework, it becomes inadvisable to speak of the "religious" aspects of a particular passage or development, as opposed to "economic" or "cultural" factors. These are false distinctions when examining this period.

When studying the Bible and the ancient world, attention to wealth and poverty issues is a welcome and necessary endeavor. With the benefit of archaeological insights, cross-cultural analysis, and close examination of extant texts, it becomes possible to arrive at a greater understanding of a particular period and the economic factors at work. Such study serves as a reminder that life remained precarious for the majority of those who lived in Judea. Most persons experienced difficult conditions, farming the land or pursuing their trades under trying circumstances. Factors such as taxation and more complex financial exchanges contributed to this tenuous situation, with only a small minority attaining significant wealth and social advancement. As analysis of the Second Temple period proceeds, we need to remember that the biblical writers, other ancient sources, and their audiences did not exist in a vacuum. Rather, they lived in a context that tested their resolve on a regular basis. They faced daily challenges that shaped their perspectives about the nature of the Deity, fairness, and how to manage one's resources. We cannot fully understand the God they worshiped or the nature of their faith without also considering the economics of their time.

Bibliography

Ackerman, Susan. "'And the Women Knead Dough': The Worship of the Queen of Hearts." Pages 109–24 in *Gender and Difference in Ancient Israel*. Edited by Peggy L. Day. Minneapolis: Fortress Press, 1989.

Adams, Samuel L. *Wisdom in Transition: Act and Consequence in Second Temple Instruction*. JSJSup 125. Leiden: E. J. Brill, 2008.

Albertz, Rainer. *A History of Israelite Religion in the Old Testament Period*. Vol. 2, *From the Exile to the Maccabees*. Translated by John Bowden. Louisville, KY: Westminster John Knox Press, 1994.

Albright, William F. "The Gezer Calendar." *BASOR* 92 (1943): 16–26.

Alt, Albrecht. "Die Rolle Samarias bei der Entstehung des Judentums." Pages 5–28 in *Festschrift Otto Procksch zum sechzigsten Geburtstag am 9. August 1934 überreicht*. Edited by Albrecht Alt et al. Leipzig: Deichert & Hinrichs, 1934.

Anderson, Nesta. "Finding the Space between Spatial Boundaries and Social Dynamics: The Archaeology of Nested Households." Pages 109–20 in *Household Chores and Household Choices: Theorizing the Domestic Sphere in Historical Archaeology*. Edited by Kerri Saige Barile and Jamie C. Brandon. Tuscaloosa: University of Alabama Press, 2004.

Aperghis, Gerassimos George. *The Seleukid Royal Economy: The Finances and Financial Administration of the Seleukid Empire*. New York: Cambridge University Press, 2004.

Applebaum, Shimon. "Economic Life in Palestine." Pages 631–700 in *The Jewish People in the First Century*. Edited by Shmuel Safrai and Menahem Stern. CRINT 1.2. Assen: van Gorcum, 1974.

———. "The Hasmoneans—Logistics, Taxation and Constitution." Pages 9–29 in *Judaea in Hellenistic and Roman Times: Historical and Archaeological Essays*. SJLA 40. Leiden: E. J. Brill, 1989.

Archer, Léonie J. *Her Price Is beyond Rubies: The Jewish Woman in Greco-Roman Palestine*. JSOTSup 60. Sheffield: JSOT Press, 1990.

Ariès, Philippe. *Centuries of Childhood: A Social History of Family Life*. Translated by Robert Baldick. New York: Alfred A. Knopf, 1962.

Baker, David L. *Tight Fists or Open Hands? Wealth and Poverty in Old Testament Law*. Grand Rapids: Eerdmans, 2009.

209

Balentine, Samuel E. *Job*. SHBC. Macon, GA: Smyth & Helwys, 2006.

Barag, Dan. "The Mint of Antiochus IV in Jerusalem: Numismatic Evidence on the Prelude to the Maccabean Revolt." *Israel Numismatic Journal* 14 (2002): 59–77.

Barstad, Hans M. *The Myth of the Empty Land: A Study in the History and Archaeology of Judah during the "Exilic" Period*. SOFS 28. Oslo: Scandinavian University Press, 1996.

Baumgarten, Albert I. *The Flourishing of Jewish Sects in the Maccabean Era: An Interpretation*. Leiden: E. J. Brill, 1997.

Baumgarten, Joseph M. *Qumran Cave 4.XIII: The Damascus Document (4Q266–273)*. DJD 18. Oxford: Clarendon Press, 1996.

Becking, Bob. "'We All Returned as One!': Critical Notes on the Myth of the Mass Return." Pages 3–18 in *Judah and the Judeans in the Persian Period*. Edited by Oded Lipschits and Manfred Oeming. Winona Lake, IN: Eisenbrauns, 2006.

Bendor, Shunya. *The Social Structure of Ancient Israel: The Institution of the Family (beit 'ab) from the Settlement to the End of the Monarchy*. JBS 7. Jerusalem: Simor, 1996.

Ben-Dov, Meir. *In the Shadow of the Temple: The Discovery of Ancient Jerusalem*. New York: Harper & Row, 1985.

Berquist, Jon L. *Judaism in Persia's Shadow: A Social and Historical Approach*. Minneapolis: Fortress Press, 1995.

Betz, Hans D. *The Sermon on the Mount: A Commentary on the Sermon on the Mount, Including the Sermon on the Plain (Matthew 5:3–7:27 and Luke 6:20–49)*. Edited by Adela Yarbro Collins. Hermeneia. Minneapolis: Fortress Press, 1995.

Beyer, Klaus. *Die aramäischen Texte vom Toten Meer*. Ergänzungsband. Göttingen: Vandenhoeck & Ruprecht, 1994.

Bickerman, Elias Joseph. *Four Strange Books of the Bible*. New York: Schocken Books, 1967.

———. *The God of the Maccabees: Studies on the Meaning and Origin of the Maccabean Revolt*. Translated by Horst R. Moerhing. SJLA 32. Leiden: E. J. Brill, 1979.

———. *The Jews in the Greek Age*. Cambridge: Harvard University Press, 1988.

———. "Une proclamation séleucide relative au temple de Jérusalem." *Syria* 25 (1946–48): 67–85.

Blenkinsopp, Joseph. "A Case of Benign Imperial Neglect and Its Consequences." *BI* 8 (2000): 129–36.

———. *Ezra–Nehemiah*. OTL. Philadelphia: Westminster Press, 1988.

———. "The Family in First Temple Israel." Pages 48–103 in *Families in Ancient Israel*. Edited by Leo G. Perdue, Carol L. Meyers, John J. Collins, and Joseph Blenkinsopp. Louisville, KY: Westminster John Knox Press, 1997.

———. *Judaism, the First Phase: The Place of Ezra and Nehemiah in the Origins of Judaism*. Grand Rapids: Eerdmans, 2009.

———. "Temple and Society in Achaemenid Judah." Pages 22–53 in *Second Temple Studies*, vol. 1, *Persian Period*. Edited by Philip R. Davies. JSOTSup 117. Sheffield: JSOT Press, 1991.

Bloch-Smith, Elizabeth. *Judahite Burial Practices and Beliefs about the Dead*. JSOTSup 123. Sheffield: Sheffield Academic Press, 1992.

Boccaccini, Gabriele. *Middle Judaism: Jewish Thought, 300 B.C.E. to 200 C.E.* Minneapolis: Fortress Press, 1991.

Borowski, Oded. *Agriculture in Iron Age Israel*. Boston: American Schools of Oriental Research, 2002.

———. *Daily Life in Biblical Times*. ABS 5. Atlanta: Society of Biblical Literature, 2003.

————. *Every Living Thing: Daily Use of Animals in Ancient Israel*. Walnut Creek, CA: Altamira Press, 1998.

Boserup, Ester. *Women's Role in Economic Development*. New York: St. Martin's Press, 1970.

Boström, Lennart. *The God of the Sages: The Portrayal of God in the Book of Proverbs*. ConBOT 29. Stockholm: Almqvist & Wiksell International, 1990.

Briant, Pierre. *From Cyrus to Alexander: A History of the Persian Empire*. Translated by P. T. Daniels. Winona Lake, IN: Eisenbrauns, 2002.

Brichto, Herbert C. "Kin, Cult, Land, and Afterlife—A Biblical Complex." *HUCA* 44 (1973): 1–54.

Bringmann, Klaus. *Hellenistische Reform und Religionsverfolgung in Judäa: Eine Untersuchung zur jüdisch-hellenistischen Geschichte (175–163 v. Chr.)*. Abhandlungen der Akademie der Wissenschaften in Göttingen: Philologisch-historische Klasse 132. Göttingen: Vandenhoeck & Ruprecht, 1983.

Brooten, Bernadette J. *Women Leaders in the Ancient Synagogue*. BJS 36. Chico, CA: Scholars Press, 1982.

————. "Zur Debatte über das Scheidungsrecht der jüdischen Frau." *EvT* 43 (1983): 466–78.

Broshi, Magen. "The Role of the Temple in the Herodian Economy." *JJS* 38 (1987): 31–37.

Cameron, George G. *Persepolis Treasury Tablets*. Chicago: University of Chicago Press, 1948.

Camp, Claudia V. "Understanding a Patriarchy: Women in Second-Century Jerusalem through the Eyes of Ben Sira." Pages 1–39 in *"Women like This": New Perspectives on Jewish Women in the Greco-Roman World*. Edited by Amy-Jill Levine. Atlanta: Scholars Press, 1991.

Carr, David M. *Writing on the Tablet of the Heart: Origins of Scripture and Literature*. Oxford: Oxford University Press, 2005.

Carroll, John T. *Luke*. NTL. Louisville, KY: Westminster John Knox Press, 2012.

Carter, Charles E. *The Emergence of Yehud in the Persian Period: A Social and Demographic Study*. JSOTSup 294. Sheffield: JSOT Press, 1999.

————. "The Province of Yehud in the Post-exilic Period: Soundings in Site Distribution and Demography." Pages 106–45 in *Second Temple Studies*, vol. 2, *Temple and Community in the Persian Period*. Edited by Tamara C. Eskenazi and Kent H. Richards. JSOTSup 175. Sheffield: JSOT Press, 1994.

Chapman, David W. "Family." *DEJ* 630–632.

————. "Marriage and Family in Second Temple Judaism." Pages 183–239 in *Marriage and the Family in the Biblical World*. Edited by Ken M. Campbell. Downers Grove, IL: InterVarsity Press, 2003.

Charlesworth, James C., ed. *The Old Testament Pseudepigrapha*. 2 vols. ABRL. Doubleday: New York, 1983–85.

Chirichigno, Gregory C. *Debt-Slavery in Israel and the Ancient Near East*. JSOTSup 141. Sheffield: JSOT Press, 1993.

Clifford, Richard J. *Proverbs*. OTL. Louisville, KY: Westminster John Knox Press, 1999.

Cohen, Shaye J. D. *The Beginnings of Jewishness: Boundaries, Varieties, Uncertainties*. Berkeley: University of California Press, 1999.

Collins, Adela Yarbro. *Mark: A Commentary*. Edited by Harold W. Attridge. Hermeneia. Minneapolis: Fortress Press, 2007.

Collins, John J. *The Apocalyptic Imagination: An Introduction to Jewish Apocalyptic Literature*. 2nd ed. Grand Rapids: Eerdmans, 1998.

———. *Beyond the Qumran Community: The Sectarian Movement of the Dead Sea Scrolls.* Grand Rapids: Eerdmans, 2010.

———. *Daniel.* Edited by Frank Moore Cross. Hermeneia. Minneapolis: Augsburg Fortress, 1993.

———. "Early Judaism in Modern Scholarship." *DEJ* 1–23.

———. *Jewish Wisdom in the Hellenistic Age.* OTL. Louisville, KY: Westminster John Knox Press, 1997.

———. "Marriage, Divorce, and Family in Second Temple Judaism." Pages 104–62 in *Families in Ancient Israel.* Edited by Leo G. Perdue, Carol L. Meyers, John J. Collins, and Joseph Blenkinsopp. Louisville, KY: Westminster John Knox Press, 1997.

Colson, Francis H., and George H. Whitaker, trans. *Philo.* Vol. 2, *On the Virtues.* LCL. Cambridge, MA: Harvard University Press, 1929.

Cook, Stephen L. *Prophecy and Apocalypticism: The Postexilic Social Setting.* Minneapolis: Fortress Press, 1995.

Cotton, Hannah M., and Michael Wörrle. "Seleukos IV to Heliodorus: A New Dossier of Royal Correspondence from Israel." *ZPE* 159 (2007): 191–205.

Cowley, Arthur Ernest. *Aramaic Papyri of the Fifth Century B.C.* Oxford: Clarendon Press, 1923. Repr., Osnabrück: Otto Zeller, 1967.

Crenshaw, James L. *Ecclesiastes.* OTL. Philadelphia: Westminster Press, 1987.

———. *Old Testament Wisdom: An Introduction.* 3rd ed. Louisville, KY: Westminster John Knox Press, 2010.

———. "Poverty and Punishment in the Book of Proverbs." *QR* 9 (1989): 30–43.

Danby, Herbert. *The Mishnah: Translation from the Hebrew with Introduction and Brief Explanatory Notes.* Oxford: Oxford University Press, 1933.

Dar, Shim'on. *Landscape and Pattern: An Archaeological Survey of Samaria, 800 B.C.E.–636 C.E.* British Archaeological Reports Series 308. Oxford: BAR, 1986.

Davies, Eryl W. "Ruth IV 5 and the Duties of the *gō'ēl.*" *VT* 33 (1983): 231–34.

Dixon, Suzanne. *The Roman Family.* Baltimore: Johns Hopkins University Press, 1992.

Doran, Robert M. *2 Maccabees.* Edited by Harold W. Attridge. Hermeneia. Minneapolis: Fortress Press, 2012.

Durand, Xavier. *Des Grecs en Palestine au IIIe siècle avant Jésus-Christ: Le dossier syrien des archives de Zénon de Caunos (261–252).* Cahiers de la Revue biblique 38. Paris: Gabalda, 1997.

Ebeling, Jennie R. *Women's Lives in Biblical Times.* London: T&T Clark, 2010.

Ebeling, Jennie R., and Michael M. Homan. "Baking and Brewing Beer in the Israelite Household: A Study of Women's Cooking Technology." Pages 45–62 in *The World of Women in the Ancient and Classical Near East.* Edited by Beth A. Nakhai. Newcastle: Cambridge Scholars Publishing, 2008.

Eckholm-Friedman, Kajsa, and Jonathan Friedman. "'Capital' Imperialism and Exploitation in Ancient World Systems." Pages 41–58 in *Power and Propaganda: A Symposium on Ancient Empires.* Edited by Mogens Trolle Larsen. Copenhagen Studies in Assyriology 7. Copenhagen: Akademisk Forlag, 1979.

Edelman, Diana. *The Origins of the "Second" Temple: Persian Imperial Policy and the Rebuilding of Jerusalem.* London: Equinox, 2005.

Eisenstadt, Shmuel Noah. *The Political Systems of Empires.* Rev. and enl. ed. New Brunswick, NJ: Transaction Publishers, 1993.

Elliott, Neil. "The Anti-Imperial Message of the Cross." Pages 167–83 in *Paul and Empire.* Edited by Richard A. Horsley. Harrisburg, PA: Trinity Press, 1997.

Erlanger, Steven. "Israel's Top Court Backs Loophole in Farming Laws." *The New York Times,* October 25, 2007.

Bibliography

Bibliography 213

Eshel, Hanan. *The Dead Sea Scrolls and the Hasmonean State*. Grand Rapids: Eerdmans, 2008.

Eskenazi, Tamara C. "Out from the Shadows: Biblical Women in the Postexilic Era." *JSOT* 54 (1992): 25–43.

Fager, Jeffrey A. *Land Tenure and the Biblical Jubilee*. JSOTSup 155. Sheffield: JSOT Press, 1993.

Faust, Avraham. "Household Economies in the Kingdoms of Israel and Judah." Pages 255–74 in *Household Archaeology in Ancient Israel and Beyond*. Edited by Assaf Yasur-Landau, Jennie R. Ebeling, and Laura B. Mazow. CHANE 50. Leiden: E. J. Brill, 2011.

———. "Settlement Dynamics and Demographic Fluctuations in Judah from the Late Iron Age to the Hellenistic Period and the Archaeology of Persian-Period Yehud." Pages 23–51 in *A Time of Change: Judah and Its Neighbours in the Persian and Early Hellenistic Periods*. Edited by Yigal Levin. LSTS 65. London: T&T Clark, 2007.

Feldman, Louis H., trans. *Josephus*. Vols. 9–10, *Jewish Antiquities, Books 18–20*. LCL. Cambridge: Harvard University Press, 1965.

Fiensy, David A. *The Social History of Palestine in the Herodian Period: The Land Is Mine*. Studies in the Bible and Early Christianity 20. Lewiston, NY: Edwin Mellen, 1991.

Fishbane, Michael. *Biblical Interpretation in Ancient Israel*. Oxford: Oxford University Press, 1985.

Fox, Michael V. *Proverbs*. 2 vols. AYB 18A–18B. New Haven: Yale University Press, 2000–2009.

———. "The Social Location of the Book of Proverbs." Pages 227–39 in *Texts, Temples, and Traditions: A Tribute to Menahem Haran*. Edited by Michael V. Fox, Victor Avigdor Hurowitz, Avi Hurvitz, Michael L. Klein, Baruch J. Schwartz, and Nili Shupak. Winona Lake, IN: Eisenbrauns, 1996.

Freyne, Seán. "The Revolt from a Regional Perspective." Pages 43–56 in *The First Jewish Revolt: Archaeology, History, and Ideology*. Edited by Andrea M. Berlin, J. Andrew Overman. London: Routledge, 2002.

———. *Galilee from Alexander the Great to Hadrian, 323 B.C.E. to 135 C.E.: A Study of Second Temple Judaism*. Wilmington, DE: Michael Glazier; Notre Dame, IN: University of Notre Dame Press, 1980.

Gambetti, Sandra. "Seleucids." *DEJ* 1212–15.

García Martínez, Florentino, and Eibert J. C. Tigchelaar, eds. *The Dead Sea Scrolls Study Edition*. 2 vols. Leiden: E. J. Brill, 1997–98.

Garnsey, Peter, and Richard P. Saller. *The Roman Empire: Economy, Society, and Culture*. Berkeley: University of California Press, 1987.

Garnsey, Peter, Keith Hopkins, and Charles R. Whittaker, eds. *Trade in the Ancient Economy*. Berkeley: University of California Press, 1983.

Gauger, Jörg-Dieter. *Beiträge zur jüdischen Apologetik: Untersuchungen zur Authentizität von Urkunden bei Flavius Josephus und im I. Makkabäerbuch*. BBB 49; Cologne: Peter Hanstein, 1977.

Geller, Markham J. "The Elephantine Papyri and Hosea 2, 3: Evidence for the Form of the Early Jewish Divorce Writ." *JSJ* 8 (1977): 139–48.

Gera, Dov. *Judaea and Mediterranean Politics, 219–161 B.C.E.* Leiden: E. J. Brill, 1998.

———. "Olympiodoros, Heliodoros, and the Temples of Koilê Syria and Phoinikê." *ZPE* 169 (2009): 125–55.

Gitler, Haim. "Coins." *DEJ* 479–82.

Goff, Matthew J. "Discerning Trajectories: *4QInstruction* and the Sapiential Background of the Sayings Source Q." *JBL* 124 (2005): 657–73.
———. *Discerning Wisdom: The Sapiential Literature of the Dead Sea Scrolls.* VTSup 116. Leiden: E. J. Brill, 2007.
———. *The Worldly and Heavenly Wisdom of 4QInstruction.* STDJ 50. Leiden: E. J. Brill, 2003.
Golka, Friedemann W. *The Leopard's Spots: Biblical and African Wisdom in Proverbs.* Edinburgh: T&T Clark, 1993.
Goodman, Martin. "The First Jewish Revolt: Social Conflict and the Problem of Debt." *JJS* 33 (1982): 417–27.
———. *The Origins of the Jewish Revolt against Rome A.D. 66–70.* Cambridge: Cambridge University Press, 1987.
Goody, Jack. *The Oriental, the Ancient, and the Primitive: Systems of Marriage and the Family in the Pre-industrial Societies of Eurasia.* Studies in Literacy, Family, Culture and the State. Cambridge: Cambridge University Press, 1990.
———. *Production and Reproduction: A Comparative Study of the Domestic Domain.* Cambridge Studies in Social Anthropology 17. Cambridge: Cambridge University Press, 1976.
Grabbe, Lester L. *A History of the Jews and Judaism in the Second Temple Period.* Vol. 1, *Yehud: A History of the Persian Province of Judah.* London: T&T Clark, 2004.
———. "Hyparchs, *Oikonomoi*, and Mafiosi: The Governance of Judah in the Ptolemaic Period." Pages 70–91 in *Judah between East and West: The Transition from Persian to Greek Rule (ca. 400–200 B.C.E.).* Edited by Lester L. Grabbe and Oded Lipschits. LSTS 75. London: T&T Clark, 2011.
———. *Judaism from Cyrus to Hadrian.* Vol. 1, *The Persian and Greek Periods.* Minneapolis: Fortress Press, 1992.
———. *Judaism from Cyrus to Hadrian.* Vol. 2, *The Roman Period.* Minneapolis: Fortress Press, 1992.
Gropp, Douglas M., and James C. VanderKam. *Wadi Daliyeh II and Qumran Miscellanea.* Part 2, *The Samaria Papyri from Wadi Daliyeh.* DJD 28, Pt. 2. Oxford: Oxford University Press, 2001.
Guillaume, Philippe. "Nehemiah 5: No Economic Crisis." *Journal of Hebrew Scriptures* 10 (2010): 2–21.
Hachlili, Rachel. *Jewish Funerary Customs, Practices, and Rites in the Second Temple Period.* JSJSup 94. Leiden: E. J. Brill, 2005.
Hachlili, Rachel, and Ann E. Killebrew. "Jewish Funerary Customs during the Second Temple Period in Light of the Excavations at the Jericho Necropolis." *PEQ* 115 (1983): 109–39.
Halligan, John M. "Nehemiah 5: By Way of Response to Hoglund and Smith." Pages 146–53 in *Second Temple Studies*, vol. 1, *Persian Period.* Edited by Philip R. Davies. JSOTSup 117. Sheffield: JSOT Press, 1991.
Hamel, Gildas H. *Poverty and Charity in Roman Palestine, First Three Centuries C.E.* Near Eastern Studies 23. Berkeley: University of California Press, 1990.
Hanson, Paul D. *The Dawn of Apocalyptic.* Philadelphia: Fortress Press, 1979.
Harrill, James A. *The Manumission of Slaves in Early Christianity.* Tübingen: Mohr, 1995.
Hartley, John E. *The Book of Job.* NICOT. Grand Rapids: Eerdmans, 1988.
Hayes, Christine E. *Gentile Impurities and Jewish Identities: Intermarriage and Conversion from the Bible to the Talmud.* Oxford: Oxford University Press, 2002.

Hayes, John H., and Sara R. Mandell. *The Jewish People in Classical Antiquity: From Alexander to Bar Kochba*. Louisville, KY: Westminster John Knox Press, 1998.

Hengel, Martin. *Judaism and Hellenism: Studies in Their Encounter in Palestine during the Early Hellenistic Period*. Translated by John Bowden. 2 vols. Philadelphia: Fortress Press, 1974.

Hiebert, Paula S. "'Whence Shall Help Come to Me?': The Biblical Widow." Pages 125–41 in *Gender and Difference in Ancient Israel*. Edited by Peggy L. Day. Minneapolis: Fortress Press, 1989.

Hiers, Richard H. "Transfer of Property by Inheritance and Bequest in Biblical Law and Tradition." *Journal of Law and Religion* 10, no. 1 (1993–94): 121–55.

Hill, Andrew E. *Malachi*. AB 25D. New York: Doubleday, 1998.

Hoehner, Harold W. *Herod Antipas: A Contemporary of Jesus Christ*. Cambridge: Cambridge University Press, 1972.

Hoglund, Kenneth G. *Achaemenid Imperial Administration in Syria-Palestine and the Missions of Ezra–Nehemiah*. SBLDS 125. Atlanta: Scholars Press, 1992.

Hölbl, Günther. *A History of the Ptolemaic Empire*. Translated by Tina Saavedra. New York: Routledge, 2001.

Holladay, John S. "'Home Economics 1407' and the Israelite Family and Their Neighbors: An Anthropological/Archaeological Exploration." Pages 61–88 in *The Family in Life and in Death: The Family in Ancient Israel, Sociological and Anthropological Perspectives*. Edited by Patricia Dutcher-Walls. LHB/OTS 504. New York: T&T Clark, 2009.

Horsley, Richard A. *Galilee: History, Politics, People*. Valley Forge, PA: Trinity Press, 1995.

———. *Jesus and the Spiral of Violence*. San Francisco: Harper & Row, 1987.

———. "Josephus and the Bandits." *JSJ* 19 (1979): 37–63.

———. *Scribes, Visionaries, and the Politics of Second Temple Judea*. Louisville, KY: Westminster John Knox Press, 2007.

Horsley, Richard A., and John S. Hanson. *Bandits, Prophets, and Messiahs: Popular Movements at the Time of Jesus*. Harrisburg, PA: Trinity Press International, 1999.

Horsley, Richard A., and Patrick Tiller. "Ben Sira and the Sociology of the Second Temple." Pages 74–108 in *Second Temple Studies*, vol. 3, *Studies in Politics, Class, and Material Culture*. JSOTSup 340. London: Sheffield Academic Press, 2002.

Horst, Pieter Willem van der. *The Sentences of Pseudo-Phocylides*. Leiden: E. J. Brill, 1978.

Hudson, Michael C., and Marc van de Mieroop, eds. *Debt and Economic Renewal in the Ancient Near East*. International Scholars Conference on Ancient Near Eastern Economics 3. Bethesda, MD: CDL Press, 2002.

Hugenberger, Gordon P. *Marriage as a Covenant: A Study of Biblical Law and Ethics Governing Marriage, Developed from the Perspective of Malachi*. Leiden: E. J. Brill, 1994.

Ilan, Tal. *Integrating Women into Second Temple History*. Peabody, MA: Hendrickson Publishers, 2001.

———. "On a Newly Published Divorce Bill from the Judaean Desert." *HTR* 89 (1996): 195–202.

Kearns, Conleth. *The Expanded Text of Ecclesiasticus: Its Teaching on the Future Life as a Clue to Its Origin*. Deutero and Cognate Literature Series 11. Berlin: de Gruyter, 2011.

Kessler, Rainer. *The Social History of Ancient Israel: An Introduction*. Translated by Linda M. Maloney. Minneapolis: Fortress Press, 2008.

King, Philip J., and Lawrence E. Stager. *Life in Biblical Israel*. LAI. Louisville, KY: Westminster John Knox Press, 2001.

Kippenberg, Hans G. *Religion und Klassenbildung im antiken Judäa*. SUNT 14. Göttingen: Vandenhoeck & Ruprecht, 1978.

Klein, Ralph W. *1 Chronicles*. Edited by Thomas Krüger. Hermeneia. Minneapolis: Fortress Press, 2006.

Knight, Douglas A. *Law, Power, and Justice in Ancient Israel*. LAI. Louisville, KY: Westminster John Knox Press, 2011.

Knohl, Israel. *The Sanctuary of Silence: The Priestly Torah and the Holiness School*. Minneapolis: Fortress Press, 1995.

Koch, Klaus. "Is There a Doctrine of Retribution in the Old Testament?" Translated by Thomas H. Trapp. Pages 57–87 in *Theodicy in the Old Testament*. Edited by James L. Crenshaw. IRT 4. Philadelphia: Fortress Press, 1983. Original, "Gibt es ein Vergeltungsdogma im Alten Testament?" *ZTK* 52 (1955):1–42.

Krüger, Thomas. *Qoheleth*. Translated by O. C. Dean Jr. Edited by Klaus Baltzer. Hermeneia. Minneapolis: Fortress Press, 2004.

Kugel, James L. "Qoheleth and Money." *CBQ* 51 (1989): 32–49.

Lau, Peter H. W. *Identity and Ethics in the Book of Ruth: A Social Identity Approach*. BZAW 416. Berlin: de Gruyter, 2011.

Legaspi, Michael C. "Job's Wives in the *Testament of Job*: A Note on the Synthesis of Two Traditions." *JBL* 127 (2008): 71–79.

Lehtipuu, Outi. *The Afterlife Imagery in Luke's Story of the Rich Man and Lazarus*. NovTSup 123. Leiden: E. J. Brill, 2005.

Lemaire, André. "Administration in Fourth-Century B.C.E. Judah in Light of Epigraphy and Numismatics." Pages 53–74 in *Judah and the Judeans in the Fourth Century B.C.E.* Edited by Oded Lipschits, Gary N. Knoppers, and Rainer Albertz. Winona Lake, IN: Eisenbrauns, 2007.

Lemos, Tracy M. *Marriage Gifts and Social Change in Ancient Palestine, 1200 B.C.E. to 200 C.E.* Cambridge: Cambridge University Press, 2010.

Lenski, Gerhard E. *Power and Privilege: A Theory of Social Stratification*. New York: McGraw-Hill, 1966; repr., Chapel Hill: University of North Carolina Press, 1984.

Lévi-Strauss, Claude. *The Elementary Structures of Kinship*. Rev. ed. Boston: Beacon Press, 1969.

Lewis, Naphtali, Ranon Katzoff, and Jonas C. Greenfield. "Papyrus Yadin 18." *IEJ* 37 (1987): 229–50.

Lichtheim, Miriam. *Ancient Egyptian Literature*. Vol. 3, *The Late Period*. Berkeley: University of California Press, 1980.

Lincoln, Bruce. *Religion, Empire, and Torture: The Case of Achaemenian Persia with a Postscript on Abu Ghraib*. Chicago: University of Chicago Press, 2007.

Lipiński, Eduard. "Marriage and Divorce in the Judaism of the Persian Period." *Transeu* 4 (1991): 63–71.

———. "'ārab, 'ărubbâ, 'ērābôn, 'ārēb, ta'ărûbâ." *TDOT* 11:326–30.

Lipschits, Oded. "Achaemenid Imperial Policy, Settlement Process in Palestine, and the Status of Jerusalem in the Middle of the Fifth-Century B.C.E." Pages 19–52 in *Judah and the Judaeans in the Persian Period*. Edited by Oded Lipschits and Manfred Oeming. Winona Lake, IN: Eisenbrauns, 2006.

———. "Shedding New Light on the Dark Years of the 'Exilic Period': New Studies, Further Elucidation, and Some Questions Regarding the Archaeology of Judah as an 'Empty Land.'" Pages 57–90 in *Interpreting Exile: Displacement and Depor-*

tation in Biblical and Modern Contexts. Edited by Brad E. Kelle, Frank R. Ames, and Jacob L. Wright. AIL 10. Atlanta: Society of Biblical Literature, 2011.

Loewenstamm, Samuel E. "*nešek and tarbît/m*." *JBL* 88 (1969): 78–80.

Ma, John. *Antiochos III and the Cities of Western Asia Minor*. Oxford: Oxford University Press, 2000.

MacDonald, John. "The Status and Role of the *Na'ar* in Israelite Society." *JNES* 35 (1976): 147–70.

MacDonald, Nathan. *What Did the Ancient Israelites Eat? Diet in Biblical Times*. Grand Rapids: Eerdmans, 2008.

Machinist, Peter. "Job's Daughters and Their Inheritance in the *Testament of Job* and Its Biblical Congeners." Pages 67–80 in *The Echoes of Many Texts: Reflections on Jewish and Christian Traditions in Honor of Lou H. Silberman*. Edited by William G. Dever and J. Edward Wright. BJS 313. Atlanta: Scholars Press, 1997.

Magness, Jodi. *Stone and Dung, Oil and Spit: Jewish Daily Life in the Time of Jesus*. Grand Rapids: Eerdmans, 2011.

Maloney, Robert P. "Usury and Restrictions on Interest-Taking in the Ancient Near East." *CBQ* 36 (1974): 1–20.

Marcus, Ralph, trans. *Josephus*. Vols. 6–8, *Jewish Antiquities, Books 9–17*. LCL. Cambridge, MA: Harvard University Press, 1937–63.

Manning, Joseph Gilbert. *The Last Pharaohs: Egypt under the Ptolemies*. Princeton: Princeton University Press, 2009.

Marsman, Hennie J. *Women in Ugarit and Israel: Their Social and Religious Position in the Context of the Ancient Near East*. Leiden: E. J. Brill, 2003.

Martin, Dale B. "Slavery and the Jewish Family." Pages 113–29 in *The Jewish Family in Antiquity*. Edited by Shaye J. D. Cohen. BJS 289. Atlanta: Scholars Press, 1993.

Mason, Steve N. "Jews, Judaeans, Judaizing, Judaism: Problems of Categorization in Ancient History." *JSJ* 38 (2007): 457–512.

Matthews, Victor H. "The Unwanted Gift: Implications of Obligatory Gift Giving in Ancient Israel." *Semeia* 87 (1999): 91–104.

Mauss, Marcel. *The Gift: The Form and Reason for Exchange in Archaic Societies*. Translated by Wilfred Douglas Halls. New York: Norton, 1925. Repr., 1990.

Meeks, Wayne A. *The First Urban Christians: The Social World of the Apostle Paul*. 2nd ed. New Haven: Yale University Press, 2003.

Meshorer, Ya'akov. *Ancient Jewish Coinage*. Vol. 1, *Persian Period through Hasmonaeans*. Dix Hills, NY: Amphora Books, 1982.

Meyers, Carol L. *Discovering Eve: Ancient Israelite Women in Context*. Oxford: Oxford University Press, 1988.

———. "The Family in Early Israel." Pages 1–47 in *Families in Ancient Israel*. Edited by Leo G. Perdue, Carol L. Meyers, John J. Collins, and Joseph Blenkinsopp. Louisville, KY: Westminster John Knox Press, 1997.

———. "From Field Crops to Food: Attributing Gender and Meaning to Bread Production in Iron Age Israel." Pages 67–84 in *The Archaeology of Difference: Gender, Ethnicity, Class and the "Other" in Antiquity; Studies in Honor of Eric M. Meyers*. Edited by Douglas R. Edwards and C. Thomas McCollough. Boston: American Schools of Oriental Research, 2007.

———. "Having Their Space and Eating There Too: Bread Production and Female Power in Ancient Israelite Households." *Nashim: A Journal of Jewish Women's Studies and Gender Issues* 5 (2002): 14–44.

———. *Rediscovering Eve: Ancient Israelite Women in Context*. Oxford: Oxford University Press, 2013.

———. "'Women of the Neighborhood' (Ruth 4:17): Informal Female Networks in Ancient Israel." Pages 110–27 in *A Feminist Companion to Ruth*. Edited by Athalya Brenner. Sheffield: Sheffield Academic Press, 1999.

Meyers, Eric M., and Mark A. Chancey. *Alexander to Constantine: Archaeology of the Land of the Bible*. AYBRL 3. New Haven: Yale University Press, 2012.

Milgrom, Jacob. *Leviticus 23–27*. AB 3B. New York: Doubleday, 2001.

———. *Numbers*. JPS 4. Philadelphia: Jewish Publication Society, 1990.

Moore, Carey A. *Judith*. AB 40. Garden City, NY: Doubleday, 1985.

———. *Tobit*. AB 40A. New York: Doubleday, 1991.

Moxnes, Halvor. "Honor and Shame." *BTB* 23 (1993): 167–76.

Muhs, Brian P. *Tax Receipts, Taxpayers, and Taxes in Early Ptolemaic Thebes*. OIP 126. Chicago: Oriental Institute Publications, 2005.

Murphy, Catherine M. *Wealth in the Dead Sea Scrolls and in the Qumran Community*. STDJ 40. Leiden: E. J. Brill, 2002.

Murphy, Roland E. *The Song of Songs*. Edited by S. Dean McBride Jr. Hermeneia. Minneapolis: Fortress Press, 1990.

Nam, Roger S. *Portrayals of Economic Exchange in the Book of Kings*. Leiden: E. J. Brill, 2012.

Neufeld, Edward. "The Prohibitions against Loans at Interest in Ancient Hebrew Laws." *HUCA* 26 (1955): 355–412.

Newsom, Carol A. *The Book of Job: A Contest of Moral Imaginations*. Oxford: Oxford University Press, 2003.

Nickelsburg, George W. E. *Jewish Literature between the Bible and the Mishnah: A Historical and Literary Introduction*. 2nd ed. Minneapolis: Fortress Press, 2005.

———. *1 Enoch: A Commentary on the Book of 1 Enoch*. 2 vols. Edited by Klaus Baltzer. Hermeneia. Minneapolis: Fortress Press, 2001–12.

———. "Revisiting the Rich and the Poor in *1 Enoch* 92–105 and the Gospel according to Luke." *SBLSP* 37 (1998): 2.579–605. Original, *NTS* 25 (1978–79): 324–44.

Nickelsburg, George W. E., and James C. VanderKam. *1 Enoch: A New Translation*. Minneapolis: Fortress Press, 2004.

Niditch, Susan. "Father-Son Folktale Patterns and Tyrant Typologies in Josephus' *Ant.* 12.160–222." *JJS* 32 (1981): 47–55.

———. *Oral Word and Written Word: Ancient Israelite Literature*. Edited by Douglas A. Knight. LAI. Louisville, KY: Westminster John Knox Press, 1996.

Nongbri, Brent. *Before Religion: A History of a Modern Concept*. New Haven: Yale University Press, 2013.

Oden, Robert A. "Jacob as Father, Husband, and Nephew: Kinship Studies and the Patriarchal Narratives." *JBL* 102 (1983): 189–205.

Olyan, Saul M. *Rites and Rank: Hierarchy in Biblical Representations of Cult*. Princeton: Princeton University Press, 2000.

Pastor, Jack. *Land and Economy in Ancient Palestine*. London: Routledge, 1997.

Pleins, J. David. *The Social Visions of the Hebrew Bible*. Louisville, KY: Westminster John Knox Press, 2001.

Plöger, Otto. *Theocracy and Eschatology*. Translated by S. Rudman. Oxford: Blackwell Press, 1968.

Podechard, Emmanuel. *L'Ecclésiaste*. Études bibliques. Paris: Gabalda, 1912.

Polanyi, Karl. *The Great Transformation: The Political and Economic Origins of Our Time*. Boston: Beacon Press, 1944. Repr., 2001.

Popović, Mladen, ed. *The Jewish Revolt against Rome: Interdisciplinary Perspectives*. JSJSup 154. Leiden: E. J. Brill, 2011.

Porten, Bezalel. *Archives from Elephantine: The Life of an Ancient Jewish Military Colony*. Berkeley: University of California Press, 1968.

Porten, Bezalel, and Ada Yardeni. "Social, Economic and Onomastic Issues in the Aramaic Ostraca of the Fourth Century B.C.E." Pages 457–88 in *Judah and the Judaeans in the Persian Period*. Edited by Oded Lipschits and Manfred Oeming. Winona Lake, IN: Eisenbrauns, 2006.

———. *Textbook of Aramaic Documents from Ancient Egypt*. Vol. 2, *Contracts*. Winona Lake, IN: Eisenbrauns, 1989.

Portier-Young, Anathea E. *Apocalypse against Empire: Theologies of Resistance in Early Judaism*. Grand Rapids: Eerdmans, 2011.

Premnath, Devadasan Nithya. *Eighth Century Prophets: A Social Analysis*. St. Louis: Chalice Press, 2003.

Price, Jonathan J. *Jerusalem under Siege: The Collapse of the Jewish State 66-70 C.E.* Brill's Series in Jewish Studies 3. Leiden: E. J. Brill, 1992.

Rist, Martin. "Caesar or God (Mark 12:13–17)? A Study in *Formgeschichte*." *JR* 16 (1936): 317–31.

Rostovtzeff, Michael I. *The Social and Economic History of the Hellenistic World*. 3 vols. Oxford: Clarendon Press, 1941.

Saller, Richard P. *Patriarch, Property, and Death in the Roman Family*. Cambridge Studies in Population, Economy, and Society in Past Time 25. Cambridge: Cambridge University Press, 1994.

Sanders, E. P. *Judaism: Practice and Belief, 63 B.C.E.–66 C.E.* London: SCM Press, 1992.

Sanders, Jack T. "Ben Sira's Ethics of Caution." *HUCA* 50 (1979): 73–106.

Sandoval, Timothy J. *The Discourse of Wealth and Poverty in the Book of Proverbs*. BInt 77. Leiden: E. J. Brill, 2006.

Satlow, Michael L. *Jewish Marriage in Antiquity*. Princeton: Princeton University Press, 2001.

Schäfer, Peter. *The History of the Jews in the Greco-Roman Period*. London: Routledge, 1983. Repr., 2003.

Schalit, Abraham. *König Herodes: Der Mann und sein Werk*. Berlin: de Gruyter, 1969.

Scherer, Andreas. "Is the Selfish Man Wise? Considerations of Context in Proverbs 10.1–22.16 with Special Regard to Surety, Bribery, and Friendship." *JSOT* 76 (1997): 59–70.

Schloen, J. David. *The House of the Father as Fact and Symbol: Patrimonialism in Ugarit and the Ancient Near East*. SAHL 2. Winona Lake, IN: Eisenbrauns, 2001.

Schuller, Eileen. "Women of the Exodus in Biblical Retellings of the Second Temple Period." Pages 178–94 in *Gender and Difference in Ancient Israel*. Edited by Peggy L. Day. Minneapolis: Fortress Press, 1997.

Schwartz, Joshua J. "Judea." *DEJ* 850–53.

Schwartz, Seth. *Imperialism and Jewish Society, 200 B.C.E. to 640 C.E.* Princeton: Princeton University Press, 2001.

———. *Were the Jews a Mediterranean Society? Reciprocity and Solidarity in Ancient Judaism*. Princeton: Princeton University Press, 2010.

Scott, James C. *Domination and the Arts of Resistance: Hidden Transcripts*. New Haven: Yale University Press, 1990.

Seow, Choon Leong. *Ecclesiastes*. AB 18C. New York: Doubleday, 1997.

Setzer, Claudia. *Resurrection of the Body in Early Judaism and Early Christianity: Doctrine, Community, and Self-Definition*. Boston: E. J. Brill, 2004.

Shargent, Karla G. "Living on the Edge: The Liminality of Daughters in Genesis to 2 Samuel." Pages 26–42 in *A Feminist Companion to Samuel and Kings*. Edited by Athalya Brenner. FCB 5. Sheffield: Sheffield Academic Press, 1994.

Sherwin-White, Susan, and Amélie Kuhrt. *From Samarkhand to Sardis: A New Approach to the Seleucid Empire*. Berkeley: University of California Press, 1993.

Sievers, Joseph. *The Hasmoneans and Their Supporters: From Mattathias to the Death of John Hyrcanus I.* South Florida Studies in the History of Judaism 6. Atlanta: Scholars Press, 1990.

Simpson, William Kelly. *The Literature of Ancient Egypt: An Anthology of Stories, Instructions, Stelae, Autobiographies, and Poetry*. 3rd ed. New Haven: Yale University Press, 2003.

Skehan, Patrick W., and Alexander A. Di Lella. *The Wisdom of Ben Sira*. AB 39. New York: Doubleday, 1987.

Smith, Adam. *An Inquiry into the Nature and Causes of the Wealth of Nations*. London: Strahan & Cadell, 1776. Repr., Oxford: Clarendon Press, 1976.

Smith, Daniel L. "The Politics of Ezra: Sociological Indicators of Postexilic Judean Society." Pages 73–98 in *Second Temple Studies*, vol. 1, *Persian Period*. Edited by Philip R. Davies. JSOTSup 117. Sheffield: JSOT Press, 1991.

Smith, Jonathan Z. "Wisdom and Apocalyptic." Pages 67–87 in *Map Is Not Territory: Studies in the History of Religions*. Chicago: University of Chicago Press, 1978.

Smith-Christopher, Daniel L. "The Mixed Marriage Crisis in Ezra 9–10 and Nehemiah 13: A Study of the Sociology of Post-Exilic Judaean Community." Pages 243–65 in *Second Temple Studies*, vol. 2, *Temple and Community in the Persian Period*. Edited by Tamara C. Eskenazi and Kent H. Richards. JSOTSup 175. Sheffield: JSOT Press, 1994.

Spock, Benjamin M. *The Common Sense Book of Baby and Child Care*. New York: E. P. Dutton, 1946.

Stager, Lawrence E. "The Archaeology of the Family in Ancient Israel." *BASOR* 260 (1985): 1–35.

Stansell, Gary. "The Gift in Ancient Israel." *Semeia* 87 (1999): 65–90.

Stambaugh, John E., and David L. Balch. *The New Testament in Its Social Environment*. LEC 2. Philadelphia: Westminster Press, 1986.

Stern, Ephraim. *Archaeology of the Land of the Bible*. Vol. 2, *The Assyrian, Babylonian, and Persian Periods (732–332 B.C.E.)*. ABRL 2. New York: Doubleday, 2001.

———. *Material Culture of the Land of the Bible in the Persian Period, 538–332 B.C.* Warminster, UK: Aris & Phillips; Jerusalem: Israel Exploration Society, 1982.

Strugnell, John, Daniel J. Harrington, and Torleif Elvgin. *Qumran Cave 4*. Vol. 24, *Sapiential Texts*. Part 2, *4QInstruction (Mûsār lĕ Mēvîn): Q415ff.; With a Re-edition of 1Q26*. DJD 34. Oxford: Clarendon Press, 1999.

Tcherikover, Victor. *Corpus papyrorum judaicarum*. 3 vols. Jerusalem: Magnes Press, Hebrew University; Cambridge, MA: Harvard University Press, 1957–64.

———. *Hellenistic Civilization and the Jews*. Philadelphia: Jewish Publication Society, 1959. Repr., Peabody, MA: Hendrickson Publishers, 1999.

Throntveit, Mark A. *Ezra–Nehemiah*. Interpretation. Louisville, KY: Westminster John Knox Press, 1992.

Toorn, Karel van der. *Scribal Culture and the Making of the Hebrew Bible*. Cambridge, MA: Harvard University Press, 2007.

Trenchard, Warren C. *Ben Sira's View of Women: A Literary Analysis*. BJS 38. Chico, CA: Scholars Press, 1982.

Udoh, Fabian E. "Economics in Palestine." *DEJ* 557–61.

———. *To Caesar What Is Caesar's: Tribute, Taxes, and Imperial Administration in Early Roman Palestine, 63 B.C.E.–70 C.E.* BJS 143. Providence: Brown Judaic Studies, 2005.

VanderKam, James C. *From Joshua to Caiaphas: High Priests after the Exile*. Minneapolis: Fortress Press, 2004.

Waltke, Bruce K. *The Book of Proverbs: Chapters 1–15*. NICOT. Grand Rapids: Eerdmans, 2004.

Weber, Max. *The Sociology of Religion*. Translated by Ephraim Fischoff. 4th ed. German original, 1922. Boston: Beacon Press, 1963.

Weinberg, Joel. *The Citizen-Temple Community*. Translated by Daniel L. Smith-Christopher. JSOTSup 151. Sheffield: JSOT Press, 1992.

Weinfeld, Moshe. *Social Justice in Ancient Israel and the Ancient Near East*. Minneapolis: Fortress Press, 1995.

Weisberg, Dvora E. *Levirate Marriage and the Family in Ancient Judaism*. Waltham, MA: Brandeis University Press, 2009.

Westbrook, Raymond. *Property and the Family in Biblical Law*. JSOTSup 113. Sheffield: Sheffield Academic Press, 1991.

Williamson, H. G. M. *Ezra and Nehemiah*. OTG. Sheffield: JSOT Press, 1987.

Wischmeyer, Oda. *Die Kultur des Buches Jesus Sirach*. BZNW 77. Berlin: de Gruyter, 1995.

Wright, Benjamin G. "1 Enoch and Ben Sira: Wisdom and Apocalypticism in Relationship." Pages 159–76 in *The Early Enoch Literature*. JSJSup 121. Leiden: E. J. Brill, 2007.

———. "'Fear the Lord and Honor the Priest': Ben Sira as Defender of the Jerusalem Priesthood." Pages 189–222 in *The Book of Ben Sira in Modern Research: Proceedings of the First International Ben Sira Conference, 28–31 July 1996, Soesterberg, Netherlands*. BZAW 255. Berlin: de Gruyter, 1997.

Wright, Benjamin G., and Claudia V. Camp. "Ben Sira's Discourse of Riches and Poverty." *Hen* 23 (2001): 153–74.

Wright, David P. *Inventing God's Law: How the Covenant Code of the Bible Used and Revised the Laws Of Hammurabi*. Oxford: Oxford University Press, 2009.

Wright, Jacob L. *Rebuilding Identity: The Nehemiah-Memoir and Its Earliest Readers*. BZAW 348. Berlin: de Gruyter, 2004.

Wunsch, Cornelia. "Debt, Interest, Pledge, and Forfeiture in the Neo-Babylonian and Early Achaemenid Period: The Evidence from Private Archives." Pages 221–55 in *Debt and Economic Renewal in the Ancient Near East*. Edited by Michael C. Hudson and Marc van de Mieroop. International Scholars Conference on Ancient Near Eastern Economics 3. Bethesda, MD: CDL Press, 2002.

Yaron, Reuven. *The Laws of Eshnunna*. 2nd rev. ed. Jerusalem: Magnes Press, 1988.

Yoder, Christine R. *Proverbs*. Abingdon Old Testament Commentary Series. Nashville: Abingdon Press, 2003.

———. *Wisdom as a Woman of Substance: A Socioeconomic Reading of Proverbs 1–9 and 31:10–31*. BZAW 304. Berlin: de Gruyter, 2001.

Index of Ancient Sources

Index follows versification of English Bibles.

OLD TESTAMENT

Pentateuch
6–7, 10, 24

Genesis
24, 41n1

1–2	22, 35
1:28	59–60
2:7	48n24
2:20	22
2:24	35n85
4:1–16	90
5	11n8
12–50	27
12:1	11
16	29
16:1–16	75n94
18:19	108
20:6	70
20:13	11
21:6	59n54
21:9	59, 59n54
23:1–20	73n89
24:7	11
24:11	43n4
24:14–28	68n78
24:22	101
25:1–6	74
26:11	70
27	74

27:1–40	75
28:2	23
29	30n69
29:2–12	68n78
29:10	23
30	75n94
30:3	75n94
34	30, 76n97
34:11–12	30
35:22–26	11n8
37:7	84
38	53–56, 56n49
43:8	60n56
43:9	115, 121
43:11	123
44:32	115, 121
45	123n113

Exodus
41n1

2:6	60n56
2:15–17	68n78
11:5	44
13:2	74n92
20:12	73
20:19–23:33	106n72, 108n78
21:2–6	88n18
21:2–11	78, 78n101
21:22–23	62n63

22:15–16	30n69
22:16–17	69
22:21–23	52
22:21–27	187
22:25	112
22:25–27	106–7, 115, 140
22:26	115n93
23:8	122
23:10–11	88
25:39	101
30:13	135n18
34:16	24
38:26	135n18

Leviticus
6n6, 106n73, 114

11:33	92
17–26	7, 106, 106n73
18	68
18:6–18	19
18:24–30	25
19:19	85
20:24–26	25n57
21:14–15	25n57
24:5–9	49
25	78n101, 79, 89, 107–8, 113, 180
25:1–7	109

Leviticus (*continued*)
25:1–26:2   106
25:20–22   88, 109
25:25–26   108
25:25–55   107–8
25:35   107n75
25:35–37   108
25:35–38   107
25:36–37   111–12
25:40   107n75
26:26   45

Numbers
18:20–21   143n33
18:21–32   143
27   74n93
27:1–11   27
27:2   68n78
27:7   75–77,
                  76nn95–96

Deuteronomy
     12n10, 26n60, 39,
     106n72, 114
5:16   73
5:33   185
7   25
7:3–4   24
7:6   25
11:14   83
14:22–30   143
14:27–29   52
14:29   53
15:1–2   109
15:1–6   88
15:1–8   88n18
15:3   113
15:7–11   194
15:12–18   78, 78n101
16:9   84
16:11–15   52
16:18–20   109
16:19   122, 122n108
17:14–20   109, 130n5
18:1–2   143n33
19:14   190
21:15–17   74, 74n93
22   24
22:4   91
22:19   69n79

22:28–29   30n69, 69
23   24–25
23:8   24
23:19–20   108–10, 112
24:1   38n96
24:1–4   34
24:3   35n83
24:12–13   115
24:17–21   52
25   55n45, 56
25:4   84
25:5–10   53, 55
27:17   190
27:25   122
35:17–19   194

Joshua
2:6   84

Judges
6:11   84
11:1–2   75n94
16:21   44
21:2–23   47n20

Ruth
     2, 7, 7n9, 9, 14, 24,
     27, 39, 53, 57, 62,
     70–71, 80
1:16–17   57
1:22   84
2:5–6   60n57
2:8–9   70
3   57
4   54–56, 55nn44–45;
                  56n49
4:3–5   54n43
4:17   45, 45n13

1 Samuel
8:1–22   130n5
9:22–24   43n6
10:17–19   130n5
12:1–25   130n5
12:17   84
13:21   101
16:11   60n57
17:33   60n57
17:34–35   91
17:42   60n57
17:55   60n57
17:58   60n57

18   33n76
18:25   30n69

2 Samuel
13:8   43n4
13:8–22   68n78

1 Kings
5:2–12   123
5:9–12   123n112
9:16–17   31n69
16:31–33   25n58
21:1–19   108

2 Kings
4:1–7   78

1 Chronicles
     9, 11–12, 12n10, 16,
     31, 62, 64n68
1–9   61n61
2:55   64
4:21   61
4:22–23   48, 91
23:3–5   98

2 Chronicles
     9, 11, 12n10, 16, 31,
     62, 64n68, 98
4:21   14
17:7–9   64
21:1–3   74
21:3   123
36:23   131n9

Ezra
     2, 7, 11, 16–17, 17n36,
     22, 24–29, 26n60, 31,
     35, 50, 61n61, 62,
     64n68, 71, 139n26,
     142, 144
1   142
1:1–4   131n9
2   135
2:36–40   98
2:61   27n62
2:69   102n64
4   137
4:10   135
4:13   137
4:20   137
6:1–12   131n9
7   16n30

7:6	97	5:15	133, 139	40:7	77
7:24	137, 142–43	5:18	144	42:7–17	77
7:28	189n11	6:1–16	134	42:13–16	75
8:25	189n11	7	135	42:15	76, 76nn95, 97
9–10	2, 9, 23, 25–28,	7:5	20n46	45:15	76n96
	28n64, 35, 39, 58	7:39–43	98		

Psalms

9:1	26	10	88	1:1	185
9:1–2	26n60	10:30–31	26	1:4	84
9:2	25–26	10:31	88	68:4	87
9:4	26	10:31–32	108	68:5	52
9:8	25	10:32–33	135n18	78:63	60
9:11	25	10:32–39	143	99:4	105
10:1	60	10:35–39	143	109:11	109
10:3	29	10:36	143n34	119:122	115
10:8	27	10:38	99		
10:44	29	12:11	145n38	**Proverbs**	
		12:22	145n38	2, 4, 7, 9, 22, 51n37,	

Nehemiah
2, 6, 11, 12n10,
16–17, 17n36, 22,
24–25, 27–29, 31, 35,
50, 61n61, 62, 120–21,
139n26, 142

		12:43	60	65, 120–21, 120n106,	
		12:47	99	183–89, 184n1, 188n5,	
		13	28n64	189n11, 194, 195n25,	
		13:4	28	201	
2	16n30	13:5	143–44	1–9	50, 50n34,
2:10	152	13:15	47n20		62, 185n4
2:16	20n46, 63n65	13:16	48n29, 94, 96	1:4	63
3:1–38	61	13:23–24	28	1:10–19	185
3:12	51, 68, 80	13:28–29	28	2:9	185
4:14	20, 20n46			3:10	186
4:19	20n46	**Esther**		3:13–18	120
5	14, 79n104,	31, 57		3:14–15	189n11
	88n18, 89,	1:3	189n11	3:15	50
	108–111, 117–18,	2:12	60n56	4:14	185
	137–40, 138nn22–23;			4:18	185
	140n27, 177, 207	**Wisdom Literature**		5:5–6	185
5:1	79n104, 110	3–4, 6n6, 7, 127, 184		5:12–14	64n67
5:1–19	139n25			6:1–5	116–17, 116n96
5:2	78, 78n103,	**Job**		6:6–9	187
	138n21	4, 189–90, 190n12,		7:6–7	62–63
5:2–7	45	194, 195n26, 198–90		7:21	63
5:4	1, 110n82	1:12–22	189	8:11	50
5:5	66, 68, 78–79	2:3	190	8:18	120
5:7	20, 20n46	2:9	75	10:1–22:16	120n107
5:7–11	109–10	2:11	189	10:5	63
5:7–19	110	5:15–16	190	11:15	115–16,
5:8	110n80	14:1–17	195		115n92,
5:11	79	17:3	115		119, 186
5:11–13	110	21:11	60	11:28	185, 189
5:14–15	140	22:6–9	190	13:21	185
5:14–18	177	24:2–4	190	13:23	186
		24:12	190	14:4	86
		38:3	77, 77n99	14:21	121
		39:19–25	91		

Proverbs (*continued*)

15:16	120
15:17	186
15:24	194n24
16:11	188
16:16	186
17:1	120, 186
17:2	76n96
17:8	124
17:17–18	121
17:18	116, 119
17:23	122, 126
18:1	124
18:11	185
18:16	123
18:22	22
19:4	186
20:10	188
20:16	115–16, 119
20:16–17	120
20:23	101–2, 188
21:14	122n108
22:1	186
22:4	186, 195
22:7	189
22:17–24:22	116n95
22:22	101n59
22:23	187
22:26	117
22:26–27	115–16
23:13–14	63
23:20–21	187
23:25	73
24:30–34	187
24:31	187
25:1	7
26:10	187
27:13	115
27:22	44
28:1	115n92
28:8	107n74, 109
30:17	72
31:10	47, 50
31:10–31	46–48, 47n19, 50n34, 51
31:14	191
31:15	50
31:16	47
31:24	48n29, 96
31:28	51
31:31	50

Ecclesiastes

	2, 4, 153, 191–92, 191nn14, 16; 194, 196n29, 198, 205
1:11	195n27
2:18	195
2:21	191
2:24	191
4:7–9	191
4:7–12	192
5:8	124, 154, 191
5:13–14	191
5:17–18	191
6:1–3	191
7:7	2, 125
7:27–28	195
9:7–10	191
9:10	195
9:13–16	191
9:14–16	21
9:15	191
9:15–16	65
10:5–7	191
11:1	191
11:1–2	191–92
11:9–12:1	59
12:3	44, 44n10

Song of Songs

	70–71
1:3	71
1:5–6	71, 71n81
1:6	47n23
2:15	87
3:3	71n82
3:4	71
3:9	70n80
4:13	70n80
5:7	71n82
6:13	71
8:2	71

Isaiah

	131
1:23	122
5:23	122
28:27–28	84
29:16	48n24
38:14	115
44:8	142
44:28	142
45:1	142
45:9	48n24
45:13	142
47:2	44
50:1	34n80
50:4	64n67

Jeremiah

	39
3:8	34, 34n80
7:18	49
18:1–12	48
27:20	20n46
37:21	101n59
44:19	49

Lamentations

5:13	44

Ezekiel

	106
18:5–9	105
18:5–17	109
18:8	107n74
18:13	107n74
18:17	107n74
22:12	107n74, 122
27	94, 100
27:7	94
38–39	203n52
40–48	76
45:12	101
46:16	74, 76, 76n95

Daniel

	203, 203n53
9:2	97
11:30	164n107
11:31	163
11:33–35	204
11:39	165

Hosea

	130
2–3	34n80
2:2	34

Joel

1–2	110, 203n52
2	87

Amos
  6, 130–31, 130n6

Micah
  130–31, 130n6
  3:11   122

Haggai
  144
  2:20–23   140n28

Zechariah
  144
  1–8   203n52
  3:7   144
  5:10–11   140
  11:7   96
  11:11   96
  14:21   96

Malachi
  24
  2:10–16   22, 35
  2:11   35
  2:15   35n85
  2:15–16   35
  3:5   52
  3:8–9   143
  3:8–10   99
  3:9–12   110

NEW TESTAMENT

Gospels
  179

Matthew
  1:18–19   72
  1:19   69
  3:12   84
  6:12   112–13
  13:1–23   88
  17:24   135n18
  17:25   179n148
  18:23–35   112
  18:24–25   80
  18:28   103
  20:1–16   178
  21:12–17   96n42
  21:33–41   178n145
  22:15–22   103, 178
  22:24–30   56
  25:27   112

Mark
  1:16   14
  1:29   14
  4:1–20   88
  4:4   87
  11:11   96n42
  10:11–12   37
  11:15–19   96n42
  12:1–9   178n145
  12:13–17   103, 178,
  179n148
  12:17   178–79
  12:18–27   201
  12:19–25   56
  12:25   56n48
  12:41–44   103

Luke
  4, 159, 183, 198–201,
    200n43, 204
  1:51–53   199n39
  2:1–3   178
  2:1–5   175
  2:5   72n85
  2:8   91
  3:12–13   179
  6:17–49   199
  6:20   199
  6:24   199
  8:4–15   88
  11:4   112
  15:11–32   76n95
  15:12   75–76
  16:1–8   200n43
  16:19–31   207, 200–201
  16:24–25   200, 200n42
  19:1–10   200
  19:8   180
  19:45–48   96n42
  20:9–16   178n145
  20:20–26   103, 178
  20:28–36   56
  21:1–4   58, 103
  24:46–47   200

John
  2:13–17   96n42

Acts
  200, 200n43
  2:44–45   200

  4:32–37   200
  6:1   58
  9:39   49
  16:14   49
  18   66n73

Romans
  15:25–27   202
  16:1   66n73
  16:3–4   66n73
  16:7   66n73

1 Corinthians
  15   201–2
  15:54   202
  16:1–4   202
  16:19   66n73

Galatians
  2:9–10   202

Ephesians
  5   80

1 Timothy
  2:11–14   66n72

2 Timothy
  4:19   66n73

Philemon
  79–80

APOCRYPHA

Judith
  57, 57n51
  8:2   24
  8:4–8   57
  8:7   52, 57, 75
  10–12   57

1 Maccabees
  165n110, 166, 168
  1:14–15   98
  1:16–19   156n75
  1:29   164
  1:33–42   163
  1:41–63   163–64
  2   165
  2:42   166n113
  3:38–4:23   165
  6:49   88
  6:53   88

1 Maccabees (*continued*)
6:59   166
9:70–73   166
10:31–32   166n114
10:38   166n114
10:89   167
11:65–66   167
13:39   167
13:52   156
14:5   167n115, 170
14:41   167

2 Maccabees
    5, 166, 168
2:21   5n3
3–4   161
3:4–4:1   160
3:6   161n96
3:11   160n95
4:7   161
4:7–17   97
4:9   161
4:12–14   98
4:14–15   161
4:23–24   162
4:30–38   162n102
5   163
5:5   162
5:24   165
5:27   165, 165n110
6:1–2   163
6:2   164n106
6:6–11   163
8:1   5n3
8:1–7   165n110
8:1–17   165
13:23   166
14:38   5n3

Sirach
    2–4, 9, 22, 65, 68, 71,
    120, 159, 159n87, 183,
    189, 192–94, 193n20,
    198, 201, 205
Prologue   97
1:26   192
3:12–13   73
3:17   124
3:31   192
7:29–31   97n46, 99
8:2   63n65

8:13   118
9:13   57
10:30   192
11:21   196
11:26–27   196
13:3–4   63n65
13:3–22   192
13:4   20
13:7   20
13:23   192
13:24   126, 126n121,
                             193
15:6   195
18:25–26   20, 192
19:20   192
20:29   124
22:3   62
22:3–6   63
24:23   97
25:21–22   32
26:14   51n37
26:29–27:2   96, 192
27:1–2   126, 126n121
29:1–7   104
29:3   194
29:9   194
29:14   2
29:14–20   111, 118, 194
29:20   118n101
30:1–13   63
30:3   66
31:1–17   192
31:5–6   192
31:8–9   194
31:12–32:13   193
33:13   48n24
33:20–24   76n95
33:25–27   65
35:17   52
35:18–19   52
36:29   22
37:26   195
38–39   193
38:24   64
38:24–34   65n69
38:25   46, 65
38:29   91–92
38:33   97
38:34   193
39:1–3   97

39:9   195
40:28   63, 194
41:4   196
41:11–12   195
42:11–13   67
42:9   70
44:8   195
50:1   158n86
50:1–4   158
50:1–24   97n46
50:12   159
50:12–16   99
51:23   64, 193
51:28   96n43

Tobit
    2, 7, 14, 39, 80
1:7–8   143
1:8   52, 58
2:11–12   48–49
3:14–15   67n75
6:12   24, 24n53
6:13   24
7:9b   72n86
7:11   24
7:13   24n53, 32
7:16   62
8:21   32
14:4   24n53
14:12–13   75

PSEUDEPIGRAPHA

Ahiqar
81–82   63n64

2 Baruch
84:9   66

1 Enoch
    4, 203–4, 203n53
22   200nn41–42
91–107   159n87
94:6–7   159
94:8   199
96:5–6   159
97:8   159
97:10   159
98:1–3   159
104:2   199
92–105   6, 159, 159n90,
                160n91, 198–99,

198n36, 201–2,
204n55, 205

4 Ezra (= 2 Esdras)
7:78–99   200n41

Jubilees
14, 41n1
4:15   24
7:38–39   66
30:3   72n86
30:18   64
32:10–14   143

Letter of Aristeas
154n74

Pseudo-Phocylides
199–200   32
215–16   67n76

Testament of Abraham
200n41

Testament of Job
77, 77n99
46–53   76n97
46–50   76
46:5   77
46:8   77

Testament of Judah
10:1–6   56n47

Testament of Levi
64

Testament of Zebulun
3:4–5   56n47

RABBINIC WORKS

Mishnah
6, 7n7, 84n5
Baba Batra 1:6   19n41
'*Erubin* 6:7   14
Gittin 9:10   38
Kelim 2:1   92n28
Ketubbot 7:5–10   38
Niddah 5:7   66n71
Šabbat 7:2   46
12:2   44
Ta'anit 1:1–2   87
3:1–3   87
Yebamot 4:4   56

14:1   37–38

Babylonian Talmud
6, 96n44
Baba Meṣi'a 71a   112n86
105b   87n15
Ketubbot 82b   38
Ma'aśer Šeni 33b   169n120
Nedarim 35b   71
Niddah 45a   71
Yebamot 12b   71
100b   71

Tosefta
Berakot 11d   125n119
Nazir 54b   125n119

DEAD SEA SCROLLS (AND RELATED TEXTS)
4, 64, 168, 168n118,
170, 197–198, 198n34

Damascus Document (CD)
170
4Q267   111–12,
111nn84–85;
112n86
4Q267 frg. 2 1.6–7   111

1QpHabakkuk
170
9.4–5   170

Rule of the Community
1QS   198n34
1.11–12   103n65

4QInstruction
118–19, 119nn102,
105; 121, 183, 197–99,
198n34, 201–2, 204–5
4Q415–18   198
4Q415
frg. 2 2.1–9   68
frg. 6 1.2   198
4Q416   72–73, 119, 197
frg. 1 1.10–11   197
frg. 2 2.1   198
frg. 2 2.4   119
frg. 2 2.4–6   119
frg. 2 2.20   198
frg. 2 3.2, 8, 12, 19   198

frg. 2 3.11–12   197
frg. 2 3.15–16   72–73,
198
4Q417   119, 197
frg. 2 1.12   197
frg. 2 1.17–18   119, 198
frg. 2 1.21–24   198
4Q418   119,
119n103, 197
frg. 87 1.7   119
frg. 88 1.3   119
frg. 113 1.1   197
frg. 126 2.6–8   198
frg. 177 1.5   198

4QPesherNahum
168n119

11QTempleScroll
50.17–19   92n28

Wadi Daliyeh
Papyri   102n62, 145n41

Wadi Murabba'at
36n88

Naḥal Ḥever (P.Yadin)
5/6 Ḥev 16.19–32   178
5/6 Ḥev 18   36

Naḥal Ṣe'elim
Papyrus 13   37

OTHER AUTHORS

COLUMELLA

Agriculture
1.7   178n145

CICERO

Consular Provinces
5.10   173

HERODOTUS

Histories
3.90–97   134
3.97   133

JOSEPHUS
4, 50, 64, 86, 94

Against Apion
1.60   93
2.200   33n75

Against Apion (*continued*)
2.202   62n63

Jewish Antiquities
    41n1, 166, 168n118
4.254–256   56
4.266   112–13
5.81   134n16
11.342–43   88n19
11.326–338   145
12.129–53   155
12.138–46   157
12.145–46   158, 158n84
12.154   33n75
12.154–236   21, 125,
                    150, 152
12.158   154
12.172   153n66
12.172–74   153–54
12.186–88   153n68
12.249   169
12.378   88, 88n19
12.384   164n107
13.82   33n75
13.273   168
13.379–83   168
13.380   171
13.404–9   171
14.202–3   88n19
14.203   172–73
15.109   174
15.259   39n98
15.294   177
15.296   177
15.299–316   177
15.300–10   84n7
15.333–34   93n37
16.228   33n75
16.285   177
17.11   33n75
17.23–25   177
17.205   176
17.300–310   176
18.1–2   178
18.23   179n147

Jewish War
    168n118
1.96–98   168
1.154   172
1.483   33n75

1.553   33n75
2.161   71
2.427   113, 180
2.488   14n23
2.574   181

PHILO
    3, 33n76, 64

Against Flaccus
8.55   14n23

Decalogue
107–17   73

Planting
32   86

Special Laws
2.74–78   112–13
2.126   23
3.81   70
3.169   67

Virtues
82   112
85   112–13

PLINY THE ELDER

Natural History
5.70   174
12.11   94n39

PLINY THE YOUNGER

Epistles
3.19   178n145
9.37   178n145

POLYBIUS

Histories
26.1   164n105

PSEUDO-ARISTOTLE

Economics
2.4   133, 157

TACITUS

Histories
5.6   94n39

Varro

Agriculture
1.17.2–3   178n145

**OTHER RECORDS
AND ARTIFACTS**

Aramaic Documents
Ananiah Archive
3.69   110–11
TAD A4.7   144
TAD B2.6   31, 36, 52, 77
See also Dead Sea Scrolls

Baths
    92n29

Coins and Weights
    101–3, 101nn57–58;
    132, 149, 156,
    165n108, 168–69,
    173n129, 179,
    179n149

Eastern Records
    48
Code of Hammurabi
    104
117–19   78n100
Eshnunna Code   104
Nuzi lists   48n28
Persepolis archives   134
See also Inscriptions

Egyptian Texts
    48
Instruction of Amenemope
    116n95, 187
Instruction of Ani
    122n110
Instruction of
    Ankhsheshonqy
19.1   192
Instruction of Duauf
    65n69
Instruction of Ptahhotep
5.10   44
Tale of the Eloquent
Peasant
    122–23n110, 126
See also Papyri Archives

Inscriptions
    66n73, 79n109
Cyrus Cylinder   131n9
Gezer Calendar   84, 84n6
Heliodorus Stela   160–61

Jewelry
38, 101, 148n50

Northern Records
Mari   48n28
Ugarit   114, 114n80

Ostraca and Contracts
85, 85n8, 87, 87n15,
135n18
Arad ostraca 41   102n62

Paintings
93

Papyri Archives
9, 21, 79, 95, 150–52,
124–25, 147, 153–54
Babatha   2, 36–37, 178
Elephantine   2, 5n4, 9,
14, 22, 27,
31, 35n83,
36, 38–39,
50, 50n33, 52,
75, 77, 80,
102n62, 135, 144
Greek   146
P.Cair.Zen. 59003   152

59018   152
59075   152
59076   152
P. Rainer 24552   148n53
See also Dead Sea Scrolls

Tombs, Epitaphs
73, 73n90, 79n109

Vessels
Amphorae   93, 93n35
Pottery   47–48, 91–95,
92n28, 101n56
Stone   92

Index of Subjects

'Ăbar-Nahărâ, (Beyond the River), 135
"abomination that makes desolate," 163,
    163n104
Abraham/Abram
    leaving father's house, 11
    marriage to Keturah, 74
act-consequence relationship, 184,
    184n1, 185–86, 188n7, 190,
    194n24, 196
    afterlife and, 197, 199, 200, 200nn42,
        43
    preserving status quo, 201
Acts, Book of
    care for widows in, 58
    communal ownership in, 200
adulthood in Second Temple period,
    59n55, 66n71
afterlife, 73n91, 196–202
    absent in Wisdom literature, 194–96
    democratizing effect of belief in, 205
agoraia telē (marketplace dues), 133
agrarian economy
    advanced, 129
    stratification in, 21, 129–30, 162n100,
        179, 180–81
    taxation in, 46, 128, 129–30, 138n22,
        140n27, 148, 158, 172–73, 176,
        177, 179
agriculturists. See farming
Akra, 156, 163, 166n114
    coins minted at, 164

Hasmonean control of, 167
    and Jerusalem's loss of autonomy, 165
Alcimus (high priest), 166
Alexander the Great, 88n19, 145, 146
Alexandria
    Diaspora in, 14, 146n43
    as Ptolemaic capital, 146, 146n43
'almānâ (widow), 51, 53
Alt, Albrecht, 135n20
amphorae, 93, 93n35
Ananiah Archive, 110
animals
    husbandry of, 90–91
    labor of, 83, 86, 91
    laws concerning, 158, 158n84
anthropology
    study of cousin marriage in, 23
    study of taxation in, 129–30
    study of women's work in, 46
antichresis, 105, 110, 139
    Jubilee as reversal of, 107
Antioch, citizenship in, 98, 161
Antiochus III, 155, 157–58, 160
    temple decree of, 158, 158n84
Antiochus IV Epiphanes, 88, 88n19,
    155, 160
    edict on cultic observances, 163–64
    as insane, 164, 164n105
    invading Egypt, 162n101
    persecution of Judeans by, 163–65, 205
    selling high priestly office, 161

Antiochus V, 166
Antipater, 171
Aperghis, Gerassimos George, 156n75
apocalypticism, definition of, 201, 203
apocalyptic literature, 159, 197n31,
        201n4
    as scribal phenomenon, 203–4
    social location and, 202–5
    See also eschatology
Apollonius (dioikētēs), 21, 125, 150–51
Apollonius the Mysarch, 163, 164, 165
apostasy, intermarriage leading to,
        25n58, 27n62
Applebaum, Shimon, 167n116, 169n120
Archer, Léonie J., 67n76
Ariès, Philippe, 59n53
Aristobulus I (high priest), 167
Aristobulus II (high priest), 171
Artaxerxes I, 142
assembly (qāhāl), 27–28
assimilation, 98, 125–26
    forced, 164
    and social mobility, 161
athletics, 97, 98

Babatha archive, 36–37, 178
Bacchides (general), 166
baḥûrîm (young men), 60
Balas, Alexander, 166, 167
banditry, 86, 181
Barag, Dan, 165n108
barley, 84
    See also grain
bartering, 3, 100–101, 103
Barzillai clan, 27n62
beer production, 47, 47n21
bĕkōr (firstborn son), 74
Bendor, Shunya, 10n7
Ben Sira. See Sirach, Book of
Berquist, Jon, 11, 140n28
bêt 'āb, 10
bêt 'ābôt, 11–12, 12n10
bêt midrāš (house of instruction), 64
betrothal, age at, 71–72
bĕtûlôt (young women), 60
Betz, Hans D., 199n40
Bible, development of, 97
Bickerman, Elias Joseph, 163n104, 164,
        191n16
birthright. See inheritance

Blenkinsopp, Joseph, 59n54, 65, 131n7,
        143n34
Borowski, Oded, 61n59, 90n23, 91n25
borrowing, 103–26
Boserup, Ester, 46
Boström, Lennart, 185n3
bread, 43
    offerings of, 49
    See also grain
Briant, Pierre, 9n2, 133nn10, 11
bribery, 3, 121–26, 154, 189
    defined, 122, 122n108
    efficacy of, 123–24
    non-Judean teachings on, 122–23n110
    See also corruption
bridewealth, 29–30, 38
    ceasing of custom of, 31, 33, 33n76,
        34, 69
    purpose of, 30
    See also dowry
Brooten, Bernadette J., 66n73
Broshi, Magen, 175
bureaucracy
    flock registration and, 148
    Hasmonean, 173, 176–77
    Persian, 132, 133–34, 139, 139n26
    Ptolemaic, 148, 149–55
    scribes in, 96
    Seleucid, 157
    stratification and, 33, 130, 169n120,
        180
    tax collection by, 21, 45, 89, 128, 132,
        139, 140, 149–50, 149n56, 153,
        157, 172, 173, 178, 179–80
    temple, 99
burial, 73, 73nn90, 91

Caesarea, importance of, 93n37, 95, 103,
        175
"Canaanites" (merchants), 48n29, 96
"capable wife," 47, 47n19, 48, 50–51,
        50nn34, 35; 51nn36, 37
capitalist mentality, anachronism of, 95,
        99, 100n53
capitation tax, 172
    See also poll tax
caravans, 91, 94
careers, 3
Carr, David M., 97n47
Carter, Charles E., 16n30

census taking, 147, 150, 174–75, 178, 179n148
ceramics. *See* pottery
character
  in Ben Sira, 195–96
  in Job, 190
  in Proverbs, 185, 189
children, 3, 58–80
  anachronistic assumptions about, 58–59
  in biblical studies, 41–42, 42n2
  as collateral, 117
  discipline of, 62–63
  female
    as less valuable, 62
    responsibilities of, 65–72
    Hebrew terminology for, 60
  male
    preference for, 62
    responsibilities of, 61–65
  modern injustices facing, 206
  needed for labor, 59–60, 61, 61n59
  roles of, 41, 80
  sent away in Ezra reform, 29
  work of, 59–60
Chronicles, First Book of
  "house of the fathers" in, 12
  Levites in, 98
  potters in, 91
  scribes in, 64
Chronicles, Second Book of
  gifts in, 123
  scribes in, 64
Cicero, 173
circumcision
  assimilation and, 161
  prohibited, 163
  of slaves, 79n109
citizenship in Antioch, 98, 161
"citizen-temple community," 11–12, 108n79
clan, 11
  replaced by "house of the fathers," 12
"clasping of hands," 116, 116n96
class, 20, 20n46
  gender and, 42, 51
classism, 20, 65
cleruchies, 147, 152, 163, 177
coast, wealth concentrated on, 19, 102, 151

Cohen, Shaye J. D., 4–5, 5n4
coinage, 3, 102–3, 102nn62, 64
  Hasmonean, 102–3, 168, 170
  Herodian, 103
  Ptolemaic, 148, 148n52
  at Qumran, 101, 103, 103n65
  Roman, 179
  Seleucid, 156, 164, 165n108
  taxes paid in, 103, 156, 156n76, 168, 179
  Tyrian silver, 173n129, 179
Collins, Adela Yarbro, 179n147
Collins, John J., 5n5, 51n37, 170n123, 204
colonization, 83
  effect on community, 8, 12, 17–18, 21
  impact on household structure, 11
  and morale of the colonized, 140n27
  taxation and, 128, 129, 131
  See also taxation
communal storage, 15, 15n26
compounds, joint family, 18–19
conspicuous consumption, 159, 171
contracts
  divorce, 34
  loan, 104, 110–11, 114n90
  marriage, 22, 32, 31, 35–37, 36nn87, 88; 39, 52, 77
Cook, Stephen L., 203n52
corporal punishment, 63, 63n64
corporate kinship, 33
corporate solidarity, 100n52
corruption
  checks against, 154n70
  leading to downfall, 185
  of officials, 101–2, 120–21, 122n110, 124–26, 138, 153–54, 159–60
  social justice undermined by, 122, 122n108, 154n70, 190, 193
courtyard, common. *See* houses
Covenant Code
  date of, 106n72
  on interest, 106
  on sex with virgins, 30n69, 69
  on widows, 52
Crenshaw, James L., 188n7, 195n25
crown tax, 178
crucifixion, 168

cultic activities
  Hellenistic, 163, 165
  related to farming, 87–89
  shepherds marginalized in, 91
  of women, 49–50
customs duties, 175
Cynic philosophy, 199n40
Cyrus, 131n9, 142
Cyrus Cylinder, 131n9

dairy products, 91n25
Damascus Document, 111–12, 111n85,
    112n86, 170
Daniel, Book of
  authorship of, 203n53, 204
  eschatology in, 204–5
  land seizure in, 165
Darius I, 132, 133, 140n28
dating texts, 7
daughters, dowry and, 33–34
Dead Sea marriage contracts, 36–37
Dead Sea Scrolls
  advice to women in, 68
  afterlife in, 197–98
  dates of, 119n102
  Hasmoneans in, 169–70
  interest on loans in, 111–12, 111n85
  parents in, 72–73
  surety in, 118–19
death
  finality of, 195, 195n27, 196
  as great equalizer, 195
  judgment at, 195, 196, 197, 199, 200,
    200nn42, 43
debt
  burning records of, 113, 180, 181
  cancellation of, 107, 108n78, 109–10,
    112–13, 140
  modern injustice related to, 206
  and seizure of property, 20, 89, 103,
    105, 107n77, 108, 109, 111, 115,
    138, 152
  theological aspects of, 105–10
  and treating debtor as resident alien,
    107n75
debt slavery, 13, 66, 77–80, 78nn100,
    101; 88n18, 107–8, 113, 137–38,
    138n21, 181
  in Elisha cycle, 78
  as opposed to chattel slavery, 77,
    107n76

rape and, 79, 137
as temporary, 78n100, 108
unfair loans leading to, 107, 110
Demetrius I, 166, 166n114
denarius, 103, 178, 179n149
  value of, 173n129
deprivation theory, 202
Deuteronomy, Book of
  on bribery, 122
  on divorce, 34
  on inheritance, 74, 74n93
  on interest, 108–9, 112, 113
  on intermarriage, 25, 26n60
  rain in, 83
  on sanctuary admittance, 24
  on sex with virgins, 69
  on tithing, 143
  on widows, 52, 53, 55n45, 56
Diadochoi, 146
Diaspora, 5n4, 14–15
  divorce in, 36, 39
  Hellenistic culture in, 97, 146n43
  identity and, 14–15
  pilgrimage and, 174
  taxation of, 175–76
Dinah, rape of, 30
dioikētēs (financial administrator), 149,
    149n56, 150–51, 157
dirigisme, 147
divorce
  adultery as grounds for, 36n87, 38
  certificate of, 34, 34n80
  critiques of, 35
  financial aspects of, 34–39, 77
  marriage contracts and, 35–37, 38
  mōhar and, 36n88
  remarriage and, 34n79
  terminology, 34, 34n81
  women initiating, 36–37, 37n92, 38,
    39
Dixon, Suzanne, 73n91
Dorcas, 49
dowry, 23, 31–34
  betrothal and, 71
  class stratification and, 33–34
  end of marriage and, 31–32, 36, 37
  and marriageability, 69–70
drought, 84, 84n7, 85, 86

Ebeling, Jennie R., 47n21
Ecclesiastes. See Qoheleth

economy
  agropastoral, 46, 85–87, 90–91, 95
  scribal role in, 85n8, 96
  subsistence, 19–20, 130–31, 157n80
    food and, 43, 45
  See also taxation; trade
Edict of Cyrus, 131n9
education
  discipline and, 62–63
  for priests, 64
Eisenstadt, S. N., 129, 138, 141
Eleazar (high priest), 155n74
Elephantine
  appeal to high priest from, 144–45,
    145nn38, 39
  Diaspora in, 14
  interest charges at, 110–11
  marriage contracts in, 22, 31–32, 34,
    35n83, 52
    divorce in, 34, 36, 36n86, 39, 77
    widowhood and, 52, 75
  women as merchants in, 50n33
Eliashib, 28
Eliphaz, 190, 190n12
Elisha cycle, debt slavery in, 78
elites, nonagricultural, 11
  See also wealthy class
end-of-life care, 73
endogamy, 14, 23–24
Enlightenment thought, 6
Enoch, Epistle of, 159–60, 159n87,
    160n91, 198n36
  afterlife in, 198–99
  didacticism in, 204n55
Enochic literature
  authorship of, 203n53
  pedagogical setting of, 204
entrepreneurialism. See trade
ephēbeia (training institute), 98, 98n48
Ephesians, Letter to the, 80
epikephalaion (poll tax), 133
'erwat dābār (something objectionable),
    34, 34n80, 38n96
eschatology, 196–202
  and eschatological reversal, 183–84,
    196, 197, 198, 199, 200, 201,
    205
Eshel, Hanan, 170, 170n123
Eshnunna, Code of, 104
Eskenazi, Tamara, 27, 27n62
ethical dualism, 185

ethics of poverty and wealth, 183–205
  See also social justice
ethnographic studies
  on ceramics, 48
  on grinding grain, 44, 44n12
euergetism, 125n119
exile
  Judean identity after, 11, 12
  population and, 16–17
  returnees
    number of, 16n30, 17
    socioeconomic status of, 28
    vs. nonreturnees, 12, 25, 26, 26n60,
      27, 46n18
Exodus, Book of
  bribery in, 122
  date of Covenant Code in, 106n22
  lending in, 106, 108, 115
  on sex with virgins, 30n69, 69
  on widows, 52
exogamy, 24–29, 35, 40
  banned by Ezra, 25–29
  leading to apostasy, 25n58, 27n62
  in Pentateuch, 24–25, 25n57
  of priests, 25n57, 28
  in Ruth, 27, 39
exports, 94–95
Ezekiel, Book of
  oracle against Tyre, 94, 100–101
  on social justice, 105–6
Ezra, Book of
  date of, 7, 17n36
  Edict of Cyrus in, 131n9
  Ezra depicted as scribe in, 64n68, 97
  "foreignness" in, 26n60
  intermarriage banned in, 23, 25–29,
    25n58, 26n60, 27n62
    economic reasons for, 26–29
  number of returnees in, 16n30
  taxes in, 137, 142–43
  on temple reconstruction, 102n64,
    144

family
  defined, 9
  line, 10–11, 11n8, 21, 53–54, 56,
    59–60, 61–62, 74
  occupation, 8n1, 41, 48, 61, 61n61,
    65, 91
  relationships, maintaining, 100
  tombs, 73, 73n90

family life, 8–40
See also patriarchal kinship grouping
famine
    burden of taxation during, 137–38,
        177
    children's vulnerability to, 45
farming, 82–90, 129
    children needed as labor for, 59–60,
        61, 61nn59, 60, 65–66
    and conflict with shepherds, 90–91
    and farm size, 19, 19n41, 147
    "grant land," 147
    Herodian policies threatening, 176
    labor distribution of, 46
    and laws on mixing seeds, 85, 85n10
    Sabbatical Year and, 88–89
    social bias against, 65
    social stratification and, 7
    theological view of, 87–89
    yearly cycle of, 83–84, 84nn5, 6
    yield, 86–87, 87n15
    See also agrarian economy
fasting, 57, 87
Faust, Avraham, 15n26, 17n33
fertility
    deities and, 49, 87
    motifs on coins, 103
"fictive" kin, 10n5
Fiensy, David A., 16
Fifth Syrian War, 155
    aftermath of, 157–58
finance, 99–126
    See also loans; surety, standing
firstborn, 74, 74nn92, 93
flax, 84
flock registration, 148
food
    as central concern of household, 18,
        45
    children preparing, 66
    cult and, 43, 49, 143–44, 177
    importance of grain for, 43–45, 91n26
    shortages, 45, 137–38, 177
    surplus for selling, 41, 45n15, 84, 86,
        87, 91
    widows, allocated for, 52
    women preparing, 3, 43–45
fortification of cities, 137, 141n29, 174
Fox, Michael V., 47n19, 51n36,
        120n106, 188n9

fraud, 120–21
    in tax collecting, 179–80
Freyne, Seán, 177n144
fruit, 84
    See also olive cultivation; viticulture

Gabinius, 173, 173n132
gābōah (payment taker), 124, 124n116,
        154n70
garments as surety, 106, 115, 115n93
Garnsey, Peter, 172n126
gate as center of exchange, 101, 101n59
Gehenna, 200n42
Geller, Markham J., 34
gender reversal, 44
genealogies
    family occupations in, 61n61
    fragmented vs. linear, 11n8
    male dominance of, 62
    priests and Levites in, 64n68, 98
Genesis, Book of
    Abraham's marriage to Keturah in,
        74
    Abram, calling of, 11
    burial sites in, 73n89
    children in, 59
    cousin-marriage in, 23
    Dinah, rape of, 30
    fruitfulness in, 59–60
    Joseph cycle, 60n56, 115, 121, 123,
        123n113
    Tamar, 53, 54, 55
    women in public in, 68n78
gerousia (council of elders), 157
Geshem the Arab, 134
Gezer Calendar, 84
gifts, 122–23, 122–23n110, 125–26
    marriage, 22, 29–34, 30nn67, 69;
        31n72, 33nn75, 76; 123n111
    social status and, 30, 123, 125
goats, 91
God
    as advocate for poor, 187, 207
    as advocate for widows, 52
    ensuring fairness, 184, 184n1, 189
    indebtedness to, 112
    injustice allowed by, 190
    parents' similarity to, 72
    as potter, 48n24
    in Proverbs, 184, 185, 185n3

social justice deriving from, 105, 108, 184, 200
standing surety, 115
gō'ēl (next-of-kin), 54
Golka, Friedemann W., 188n8
Goodman, Martin, 180
Goody, Jack, 33, 46
Grabbe, Lester L., 133n12, 135n20
grain
  and bread preparation, 43–45, 43n7
    as lowly work, 44
  cultivating, 61n59, 83–84
  grinding, 44–46, 44n10
    as lowly work, 44
  needed to feed Rome, 172n126
  as percentage of diet, 43, 43n6, 91n26
  theft, 86
"grant land," 147
greed as leading to failure, 185, 192
Greek culture. See Hellenistic culture
Greek language, 18, 64
guarantors, loan. See surety, standing
guilds
  collecting taxes, 172 (See also publicani [tax gatherers])
  weaving, 48
Guillaume, Philippe, 138n23, 140n27
gymnasiums, 97–98, 161

Hades, 196, 200, 200n42
Haggai, 140n28
ḥăkāmîm (sages), 96n44
halitzah, 56
Hamel, Gildas H., 83n3, 84n5, 85nn10, 11; 87, 87n15
Hammurabi, Code of, 78n100, 104
Hanson, Paul D., 203
haptō (grasp), 70
ḥărēdîm (ones who tremble), 29n66
Hasideans, 166n113
ḥăsîdîm (pious ones), 166n113
Hasmoneans, 165–71
  allies of, 166n113
  bureaucracy of, 173, 176–77
  coinage of, 102–3, 168
  expansion by, 167, 169, 170
  Herod the Great and, 174n134, 177
  internecine warfare of, 171
  land seizure by, 167
  rural support for, 168

Seleucids' treaty with, 166
stratification under, 169–71
taxation by, 167, 168, 169, 169n120, 171, 176–77
Hayes, C., 25
ḥayil (capable), 50, 51n36
heavenly reward, 183–84, 196, 197, 198, 199, 200, 201, 205
Heliodorus Stela, 160, 160n93
Hellenistic culture, 97–98, 133n10, 145, 148, 151, 161, 162n100, 164
  expanded along trade routes, 151
  female modesty in, 51n37
  Hasmoneans expressing, 171
  high priest spreading, 161
Hellenistic period. See Ptolemies; Seleucids
Hellenistic Reform, 161, 164
  stratification intensified by, 162n100
Herod Antipas, 178
Herod Archelaus, 178
Herodian kings, 103
Herodotus, 132–33, 133nn10, 11; 134
Herod the Great, 174–76
  food aid provided by, 177
  leadership void created by, 180
  oppressive taxation by, 176, 176n141, 177n144
  rise to power of, 174n134
  temple reconstruction of, 174, 174n135
  wealth of, 176n142
ḥešbôn (sum), 195
Hiebert, Paula, 52n40
Hiers, Richard H., 74n93, 76n95
high priest
  administrative authority of, 99, 99n50, 144, 155n74
  Alcimus, 166
  Alexander Janneus, 167–68, 168n119, 171
  as ambassador for Judea, 162
  Aristobulus I, 167
  Aristobulus II, 171
  economic role of, 154–55
  Eleazar, 155n74
  as hereditary office, 162, 166
  Hyrcanus II, 171, 173
  Jason, 98, 98n49, 161, 162–63, 163n103

high priest (*continued*)
Johanan, 144, 145n38
John Hyrcanus, 167, 167n116, 168, 169
Jonathan Maccabeus, 166, 167, 170n123
Joseph, 154n73
Joshua, 144
Menelaus, 162, 164, 165
Onias II, 21, 125, 152, 153n66
Onias III, 162n102
purchasing office of, 161, 162
rebellion targeting, 180
Roman control over, 180
Simon Maccabeus, 167, 167n115
Hillel, 38, 113n88
Hiram of Tyre, 123, 123n112
hoe cultivation, 46
Hoglund, Kenneth, 27, 28, 138n22, 141n29
holiness, zones of, 158, 158n84
Holiness Code
date of, 106n73
on interest, 106–8, 108n78
Holladay, John S., 18n39
"holy seed," 25, 25n57
purity of, 26
Homan, Michael M., 47n21
honor/shame, 67, 69, 124, 125–26
ḥōrîm (nobles), 63n65
Horsely, Richard A., 160n91
horses, 91
Hosea, divorce in, 34
household
connected other households, 10
defined, 9–10
as economic mode of production, 13–14
exile's impact on, 11
size of, 15–16
slaves as part of, 15
structures, 10–15
violence in, 68n78
widows outside of, 14, 52, 53
"house of the father," 2, 10, 10n7, 11, 13, 40
inheritance in, 23
"house of the fathers," 11–12, 12n10
"house of the mother," 71
houses, 13n18, 18–19, 19n40, 100

common courtyard of, 13, 14, 18, 19n40, 44, 68
kinship ties and construction of, 19
Hyrcanus, John (high priest), 167, 167n116, 168, 169
Hyrcanus II (high priest), 171, 173

identity
based on household affiliation, 10
status of widows and, 51, 51n39
cultic practices and, 14–15
Diaspora, 14–15
Judean religious, 5–6
post-exilic communal, 11, 12
intermarriage and, 25–26
Idumea, 134–35, 134n16
Ilan, Tal, 37n92
Inaros rebellion, 140, 141n29
inequality. *See* stratification
infanticide, 62, 62n63
infant mortality, 15, 59
inheritance, 3, 74–77
conflict over, 74–75
by daughters, 75–77, 76nn96, 97; 77n99
exogamy and, 27, 29
levirate marriage and, 53, 54, 54n43, 55
mother's role in, 74, 75
spiritualized, 76–77, 76n97, 77n99
by widows, 51, 57, 75
4QInstruction
audience of, 204
context of, 119nn102, 105; 198n34
eschatology in, 197–98
on honoring parents, 72
on standing surety, 118–19
as wisdom text, 201
on women in public, 68
Instruction of Amenemope, 187
Instruction of Ani, 122n110
Instruction of Ankhsheshonqy, 192
Instruction of Ptahhotep, 44
intercultivation, 85n11
interest on loans, 3, 104–14
legislation on, 104–5, 106–9, 114
as modern problem, 206
rates, 104–5, 111, 139, 139n24
theological aspects of, 105–10
intermarriage. *See* exogamy
intersacerdotium, 166

Ioudaios, 5
Ioudaïsmos, 5, 5n3
irrigation, 84, 85–86
Isaiah, Book of
   on Cyrus, 142
   God as potter in, 48n24
   on grinding grain, 44
"Israelite," 4

Janneus, Alexander (high priest), 167–68,
      168n119, 171
   as king, 168, 170
Jason (high priest), 98, 98n49, 161,
      162–63, 163n103
   revolt by, 162–63, 163n103
Jephthah, 75n94
Jerusalem
   captured by Romans, 171
   military garrison in, 156
   as pilgrimage destination, 174
   as *polis,* 161–62
   population, 17
   rebuilding wall of, 137, 139, 141
      women's work in, 51, 68
   tax exemptions for, 157–58, 157n81
   walls destroyed by Antiochus IV, 163
Jesus
   birth narratives of, 69
   on debt forgiveness, 113
   on divorce, 37
   farming imagery in, 88
   gnomic sayings of, 197
   on levirate marriage, 56, 56n48
   on taxes, 178–79
Jesus movement, 171, 200
"Jew," 4–5, 5n2
Jewish Revolt, First, 113, 180–81
   economic causes of, 180
Job, Book of
   character-consequence relationship
      in, 190
   date of, 189, 189n11
   inheritance in, 75–77, 76nn95, 96
   meaning of life in, 195
   redeemer in, 195n26
   skepticism in, 189–90
Johanan (high priest), 144, 145n38
Joseph (high priest), 154n73
Joseph cycle, 60n56, 115, 121, 123,
      123n113

Josephus
   on Alexander Janneus, 168, 168n119
   on Antiochus III, 155, 157
   on banditry, 86
   betrothal in, 71
   on bribery, 125
   on Diaspora, 14, 14n23
   divorce in, 39n98
   dowry in, 32, 33n75
   drought in, 84n7
   on First Jewish Revolt, 180
   geography in, 134n16
   on Herod the Great, 176, 177
   on infanticide, 62n63
   on interest, 112, 113
   on levirate, 55–56
   on Maccabean revolt, 166
   on merchants, 93–94
   on Pharisees, 171
   on Romans, 172, 180
   Sabbatical Year in, 88, 88n19
   on tax protest, 179n147
   Tobiad Romance of, 21, 125, 150,
      152–53, 153n66, 154, 154n73
   women marginalized in, 41n1
Joshua (high priest), 144
Jubilee legislation, 79, 106–8, 107nn74,
      75, 76, 77
Jubilees
   cousin marriage in, 24
   priestly education in, 64
   women marginalized in, 41n1
Judah
   coinage of, 102
   governors of, 135, 135n20, 139–40,
      139n26, 144, 144n36, 145, 154,
      155n74, 172, 178, 180
   Persian fortification of, 141, 141n29
   post-exilic demographics of, 25–26
   rebelling against Persians, 137
Judaism
   as contemporary religious tradition, 5
   conversion to, 167
   "Early," 5n5
   prohibition of practices of, 163–64
Judea, 145, 145n40
   annexed by Romans, 178
   conquered by Pompey, 170
   as military colony, 163
   as part of Mediterranean trade, 174, 175

"Judean," defined, 4, 5, 5n4
Judeans, religious identity of, 5–6
judgment at death, 195, 196, 197, 199, 200, 200nn42, 43
Judith, Book of, 24, 52, 57, 75
Junia, 66n73
justice. *See* social justice

kabbēd (honor), 73
kapēlos (tradesman), 193
kēnson (pay taxes/census), 179n148
Kessler, Rainer, 144n35
ketubbah, 38
kindness
  of guarantor, 118
  as strategic self-interest, 192, 194
  to the vulnerable, 58, 185, 186
King, P. J., 61nn59, 60; 73n90, 85nn8, 9; 91n27
Kings, First Book of, gift exchange in, 123, 123n112
king's tax, 137, 138, 139–40
kinship, 8, 10, 13–14, 19
  corporate, 33
kinship group
  as "clan," 15
kinship groups, 129
  effect of exile on, 17
  as mode of production, 13–14
  property and, 23, 53, 74
  threatened, 56
Kippenberg, Hans G., 138n22
Koch, Klaus, 184n1
Krüger, Thomas, 154n70
Kugel, James L., 124n116, 154n69
Kuhrt, Amélie, 156n75

labor, distribution of, 46, 68
lamps, pottery, 92–93
land
  challenges of retaining, 1, 46
  exilic returnees claiming, 46n18
  fallow in Sabbath Year, 88, 88n18, 89n20, 109
  as gift from God, 89
  Hasmonean resettlement of, 168
  and large landholders, 177–78
  levirate and, 53, 55, 56
  reverting to crown, 151
  royal grants of, 21, 147, 166

seizure, 149, 165, 167, 177–78
  debt leading to, 20, 89, 103, 105, 107n77, 108, 109, 111, 115, 138
  by Herod, 177–78
  prohibited, 107n77, 108
  surveys, 147
  taxation of, 169, 172, 173, 174, 177, 178
  types of, 83, 85–86, 85n11
landlessness, 19–20
language study, scribal, 64
Lau, P. H. W., 7n9
law codes, 78n100, 104–5
laziness, 187
legumes, 84
leḥem (food; bread), 43
Lehtipuu, Outi, 200n41
Lemos, Tracy, 30, 31n72, 33
Lenski, Gerhard E., 83n1, 129–30, 138
levirate, 3, 52, 53–57
  in late Second Temple period, 55–57
  shaming ceremony and, 53, 55, 55n45
Lévi-Strauss, Claude, 23, 23n50
Levites, 64n68, 96, 97n44, 98
  as tithe collectors, 143
Leviticus, Book of
  bread-baking in, 45
  Holiness Code in, 106n73
  on incest, 68
  Jubilee legislation of, 79, 106–7, 108
  on lending, 111
  on tithing, 143
life expectancy, 15, 16, 51, 59
  early marriage and, 72
Lincoln, Bruce, 142
Lipiński, Edward, 37n90, 114n90
Lipschits, O., 17n32
literacy, 64, 97n47
loans, 103–26, 138n23
  changing terms of, 105
  forgiveness of, 107
  interest on, 3, 104–14
  lending as benevolent act, 112, 121
  and speculative lending, 117
  surety on, 2, 3
  See also Jubilee legislation
Lord's Prayer, 112–13
Luke, Gospel of
  authorship of, 204
  census-taking in, 72n85, 175

eschatology in, 199–201, 200nn42, 43
Parable of the Prodigal Son, 75
widow's offering in, 58
luxury goods, 93
Lydia, 49

Maccabean revolt, 5, 159n87, 165–66
Maccabees, First Book of
on Antiochus' persecution of Judeans,
    163, 164
on Maccabean revolt, 165, 165n110,
    166, 167
Sabbatical Year in, 88
Seleucid military in, 156n75
Maccabees, Second Book of, 160n95
on Antiochus' persecution of Judeans,
    163
Hellenistic culture in, 98–99, 161n96
on high priests, 97–98, 160n95, 162
Ioudaïsmos in, 5
on Maccabean revolt, 165, 165n110,
    166
on Seleucid military, 165
Maccabeus, Jonathan (high priest), 166,
    167, 170n123
Maccabeus, Judas, 165, 165n110, 166
Maccabeus, Mattathias, 165n110
Maccabeus, Simon (high priest), 167,
    167n115
MacDonald, John, 60n57
Machinist, Peter, 76, 77n99
Magness, Jodi, 92n28, 93n35, 103n65
Magnificat, 199n39
"maintenance activities," 43
Malachi, Book of
date of, 35n82
divorce in, 35
malqôš (later rain), 83
marbît/tarbît (interest), 107, 107n74, 111
Mark, Gospel of
divorce in, 37
resurrection in, 201
taxation in, 179nn147, 148
marketplace, 3
"marketplace dues," 133
marriage, 2, 22–39
arrangements made by patriarch, 8n1,
    72n86
betrothal and, 71–72
continuation of family line through, 21

contract, 22, 32, 31, 35–37, 36nn87,
    88; 39, 52, 77
of cousins, 23, 24
finding partner for, 22, 23–29
gifts, 22, 29–34, 30nn67, 69; 31n72,
    33nn75, 76; 123n111
property ownership and, 23, 26–29
sacred aspect of, 22, 39
See also bridewealth; divorce; dowry
Marsman, Hennie J., 48n28
Martin, Dale B., 79n109
maśkîlîm (wise), 204
maśśā' (interest, debt), 110, 116, 117, 118
Mason, Steve, 5n3
matrilinearity, 27n62
mattān (gift), 30, 122–23, 122n108,
    123n112
Matthew, Gospel of
birth narrative in, 69, 72
Lord's Prayer in, 112
meat, 91
prepared by men, 43n6
mēbîn (discerning one), 198
Mediterranean, coastal development of,
    18
men
farm tasks performed by, 46
meat prepared by, 43n6
"women's work" done by, 44
Menelaus (high priest), 162, 164, 165
merchants, 93, 94–96, 193
"Canaanites" synonymous with,
    48n29, 96
See also trade
metal, 101, 102n62
coinage, 101, 102, 103, 148, 168, 179
tools, 83
trade in, 94, 101
Meyers, Carol, 42n2, 43, 44n12, 48n26,
    61n58, 83n2
middat hammelek (king's tax), 138,
    138n22
Milgrom, Jacob, 107, 107nn76, 77
military
cleruchies, 147, 152, 163, 177
financing and supplying, 130, 131n7,
    140–41, 140n28, 156, 156n76,
    167, 169, 177
garrisons built for, 141, 156
millennial groups, 202, 203n52, 205

minḥâ (gift), 122
minting. *See* coinage
Miptaḥiah, 31, 36, 36n86
miqvā'ôt (baths), 92n29
mišpāḥâ (clan), 11
mōhar (bridewealth), 30, 30nn67, 69; 31, 33n76, 36n88
monarchy, pre-exilic, 130–31, 130n6
money. *See* coinage; wealth
mourning rites, 73
mō'zĕnāyim (weight balances), 101
Muhs, Brian P., 148n52
Murašu, house of, 139n24
Murphy, Catherine M., 112n86
Murphy, Roland E., 70n80, 71n81

na'ar (child), 60, 60nn56, 57; 62
na'ărōtāy (my young women), 70
naḥălâ (inheritance), 75, 76n95
name. *See* reputation
Negev, farming in, 85n11
Nehemiah, as governor, 144
Nehemiah, Book of
    challenges of food production in, 45
    on charging interest, 108, 109–10, 117
    class and classism in, 20, 63n65, 78, 79, 117, 118
    coastal traders in, 96
    date and composition of, 7, 17n36, 139, 139n25, 141n29
    daughters of Shallum in, 51, 51n38
    debt slavery in, 78–79, 78n103, 108
    exogamy and, 28
    number of returnees in, 16n30
    on Persian rule, 134
    Sabbatical Year in, 88, 88n18, 140
    taxation in, 1, 110n82, 137–39, 138n22
    temple supported by, 143–44, 143n34
nešek (interest), 106, 107, 107n74, 111
networks of productivity, 41, 44–45, 49
Neufeld, Edward, 108n79
Newsom, Carol A., 190n12
New Testament
    betrothal in, 72, 72n85
    dates of, 7
    lending practices in, 112–13
    levirate marriage in, 56, 56n48
    taxation in, 178–79, 179n147

tax collectors in, 179–80
woe oracles in, 159
nomadism, 90n23
nomarch, 149n57
nomes, organization of, 149, 149n57
Nongbri, Brent, 6, 6n6
nōšeh (creditor), 106
Numbers, Book of
    female inheritance in, 76
    tithing in, 143

obligation, theology of, 105, 106
occupation, 82–99
    family, 8n1, 41, 48, 61, 61n61, 65, 91
    farming, 82–90
    pottery making, 91–93
    social status and, 63
    stratification and, 65
oikonomia (household structure and maintenance), 13
oikonomos (leader of nome), 149
old age and end-of-life care, 73
olive cultivation, 61, 61n60, 84–85
    and oil trade, 85n8, 94
Olyan, Saul, 25n57
Olympiodorus, 160, 160n93
Onias II (high priest), 21, 125, 152, 153n66
Onias III (high priest), 162n102
opheilēmata (debts), 112
orphans, 79
ossuaries, 73n90
oxen, 91

parables
    of the Prodigal Son, 75, 76, 76n95
    of the Rich Man and Lazarus, 200–201, 200n41
    of the Sower, 88
    of the Talents, 112
    of the Unforgiving Servant, 80, 113
    Unjust Steward, 200n43
parents
    favoritism towards child, 74
    honoring, 3, 72–73
    instilling discipline, 63
parents, honoring, 50
Pastor, Jack, 43n6, 46n18, 91n26, 147n44, 167n115

pastoralism, 90–91, 90n23
   and conflict with farmers, 90–91
"path" motif, 185
patriarchal kinship grouping, 2, 8, 8n1
patriarchal narratives
   children in, 59, 59n54, 60n56, 74, 75,
      75n94
   gift-giving in, 123
   marriage in, 23, 30, 30n68
   surety in, 115, 121
   Tamar, 53, 54, 55
   women in, 68n78, 75n94
patriarchs, burial sites of, 73n89
patrilinearity, 10–11
   widowhood and, 53
patrilocality, 10
   marriage gifts and, 30
patrimonial household model, 10
patronage, 161
   concern for poor as alternative to,
      201–2
   corruption and, 126
   See also bribery
Paul, 201, 202
payday lending, 206
persecution, 163–65, 176, 204–5
   economic reasons for, 164
   theological implications of, 163, 165,
      204–5
Persepolis archives, 134
Persian period, 8–9, 9n2, 130–45
   lack of inscriptional evidence from,
      9n2
   population and, 17, 17n33, 18
Persians
   cultural tolerance by, 131–32, 141–42
   defeated by Alexander, 145, 145n41
   Ezra reform and, 27, 28, 29
   infrastructure of, 132
   leniency of, 140n27
   satrapies created by, 132, 133
   stratification under, 139
   taxation by, 132–35, 137–43
Pesher Habakkuk, 170
Pesher Nahum, 168
pests, agricultural, 85, 87
pharaonic tradition, 146, 148, 151
Pharisees, 171
   as opponents of Janneus, 168,
      168n119

Philemon, Letter to, 79–80
Philo
   on animals, 86
   on Diaspora, 14, 14n23
   on dowry, 23, 32, 33n76
   on end-of-life care, 73
   on interest, 112
   on seclusion of daughters, 67
   on virginity suits, 70
Phoebe, 66n73
pilgrimage festivals, 143, 174
Plöger, Otto, 203
plow cultivation, 46
Polanyi, Karl, 99, 100, 100nn53, 54
poll tax, 148, 172, 172n127, 178, 179
Pompey, 170, 171
Pontius Pilate, 180
poor and lower class
   apocalyptic texts addressed to, 197–98,
      204
   blessedness of, 199
   God advocating for, 187
   laws marginalizing, 158
   as "pious ones," 199
   suffering of, 130, 138, 138n22, 154,
      159, 186–87, 190, 199–200, 202
population levels, 16–18, 17n33
port cities, 93n37, 95, 148, 151,
   167n115, 174, 175
Porten, Bezalel, 87n16
Portier-Young, Anathea E., 161,
   163n103, 203n53
pottery, 47–48, 48n26, 91–93
   and God as potter, 48n24
   purity laws concerning, 92, 92n28
   Qumran production of, 101n56
   trade in, 93, 93n35
poverty
   God and, 4, 183, 184, 185, 186, 187,
      197, 198, 199, 207
   as sign of disfavor, 190
   See also poor and lower class
prefects, 178, 179, 180
Premnath, Devadasan Nithya, 130,
   130n6
priests
   education of, 64
   exogamy and, 25n57, 28
   land given to, 147
   law interpreted by, 99

priests (*continued*)
  post-exilic prominence of, 98–99
  social status of, 63–64, 128–29
  tithes supporting, 142–43, 143nn32,
      33, 34; 176, 177, 179, 182
  See also high priest; Wicked Priest
primogeniture, 74
Prisca, 66n73
Prodigal Son, 75, 76, 76n95
productivity, character formation and, 63
profit
  coinage and, 101
  from lending, 104–5
    legislation against, 106, 107
  stability more important than, 99–100,
      100nn53, 54
proix (dowry), 33nn75, 76
property ownership
  collective, 12
  and latifundialization, 130n6
  marriage and, 23, 26–29
  women's, 52, 57
  See also inheritance
prophets, eighth-century, 130–31, 130n6
prosbul, 113, 113n88, 180–81
prostagma (decree), 158
prostasia (right to raise taxes), 154
prostitution, slavery and, 79, 149
Proverbs, Book of
  act-consequence relationship in, 184,
      184n1, 185–86, 194n24
  capable wife of, 47, 47n19, 48, 50–51,
      50nn34, 35; 51nn36, 37
  cognitive dissonance of, 185, 188
  didactic material in, 187
  ethics of wealth and poverty in,
      184–89
  farming in, 86
  formation of, 185, 188
  justice and reality in, tension between,
      189
  "life" in, 195, 195n25
  parents in, 72
  pragmatic observations in, 186–87
  "strange woman" of, 62–63, 185n4
  value of wisdom in, 186
Psalms, Book of
  on debt, 109
  justice in, 105
  surety in, 115

Pseudo-Aristotle, 133, 133n12, 157
pseudonymous authorship, 203, 203n51
Pseudo-Phocylides, 32, 32n74, 67n76
ptōchoi (poor), 199
Ptolemies, 20–21, 145–55
  centralization by, 148
  as despots, 148n54
  Greek-speaking towns founded by,
      148
  land seizures of, 89, 147
  pharaonic traditions of, 147, 151
  slave trade under, 148–49
  stratification under, 153–54
  taxation by, 147–48, 149–50, 151,
      152–53, 154–55, 154n73
Ptolemy III Euergetes, 153n66
Ptolemy I Soter, 146
publicani (tax gatherers), 172, 173, 179
punishment. *See* act-consequence
      relationship
purity
  of the "holy seed," 26
  and *miqvā'ôt*, 92n29
  of pottery, 92, 92n28

Qoheleth, Book of, 21, 191–92
  on corruption, 124, 125, 153–54
  date of, 124, 153, 191, 191n14
  on death, 195n27
  enjoyment in, 191, 191n16, 195
  on grinding, 44, 44n10
  on youth, 59
"Queen of Heaven," 49, 49n32
Quirinius, 178
Qumran
  bartering at, 101
  coinage at, 103, 103n65
  pottery produced at, 101n56
  sectarians at, 170

rabbinic texts
  betrothal in, 71
  bribery in, 125–26, 125n119
  dates of, 7n7
  divorce in, 37–38
  on farming, 85n10, 86–87
  household structure in, 14
  lending practices in, 112n86
  levirate marriage in, 56–57, 56n49
  on life stages, 66n71

shedding light on Second Temple
    period, 6, 9
on women's work, 44
rainfall and types of rain, 83, 83n3
rape, 30, 30n69, 69, 69n79
    debt slavery and, 79
    of Dinah, 30
    laws concerning, 30n69, 69, 69n79
    of Tamar, 68n78
rāz nihyeh (mystery that is to be), 204
'rb (surety), 26, 111n84, 114–15, 114n90,
    120
'rb (to be sweet), 120
rēa' (neighbor), 116
rebellion
    anti-Hellenistic, 163n103
    averting, 140–41, 140nn27, 28;
        141n29, 177, 177n144
    of Inaros, 140, 141n29
    by Maccabees, 5, 159n87, 165–66
    against Rome, 180
reciprocity, culture of, 3, 100
    bribery and, 124, 125–26
redemption. See afterlife
Rehum, 137
religion and economics, 6, 207
reputation, 186
    gifts and, 124
    virginity and, 67, 67n75, 69–70, 69n79
    as what survives after death, 195–96
resident aliens, 15, 107n77
responsibility, mutual, 201–2
resurrection, 201–2
retributive justice, 190
rich. See wealthy class
Romans, 66, 171–81
    assimilation under, 125
    increasing stratification under, 113
    Jewish discontent with, 176
    Judea annexed by, 178
    Judean tribute to, 176, 176n140
    stratification under, 180–81
    taxation by, 172–73, 172n127, 178–79,
        180
royal territories, 20
rural settlements, 16, 17n32
Ruth, Book of
    date of, 7, 7n9, 27n61
    exogamy in, 27, 39
    grain-grinding in, 45

household security as theme in, 14,
    57
levirate in, 53, 54–55, 54n43, 55,
    55nn44, 45
women's camaraderie in, 45, 70
women's resourcefulness in, 57, 62

Sabbath, 96
    observance prohibited, 163
Sabbatical Year, 88–89, 88nn18, 19;
    89n20, 108, 109, 172, 180
"sacred land," 147
Saller, Richard C., 15–16, 172n126
Salome. See Shelamzion Alexandra
Samaria, 145n41, 164n106
    Judean control of, 166n113, 167,
        167n116, 174
    as part of Yehud, 135
Sanders, E. P., 143n33, 176
Sandoval, Timothy, 187–88, 188n5
sanhedria (districts), 173n132
Satire on the Trades, 65n69
Satlow, Michael L., 33n76
satrapies, 132, 133
Schloen, J. David, 10, 15, 16, 90n23
Schwartz, Seth, 100, 100n52, 125–26,
    125n119, 157n80
Scott, James C., 203n51
scribes, 96–97
    and apocalypticism as scribal, 201,
        203–4
    Ben Sira on, 64, 97, 119, 193
    education of, 64
    Levitical, 64n68, 96, 97n44
    Proverbs formed by, 188, 188n9
    as retainers, 193, 193n20
sea lanes, 93, 93n37, 94
seclusion of women, 67, 67n76, 68,
    68n77
    class and, 67–68
Second Isaiah. See Isaiah, Book of
Second Temple period, definition of,
    2, 6
sectarianism, 103, 103n65, 111–12,
    198n34
    in Hasmonean period, 167, 168, 170
    in Roman period, 171
    in Seleucid Judea, 162
secular-religious dichotomy, 6, 6n6
"seed." See "holy seed"

Seleucids, 146, 155–66
  charter with Jerusalemites, 157–58,
    157n80
  coinage of, 156, 164, 165n108
  defeated at Magnesia, 160
  empire of, 155
  Hasmonean treaty with, 166
  Ptolemy's struggle with, 146n42
  stratification under, 158, 159–60,
    162n100
  taxation by, 155, 156–57, 158, 160–61,
    165
  as warriors, 155–56, 156n77
Seleucus IV Philopator, 155, 160
self-interest, strategic, 192, 194
separation (bdl), 25n57
Sermon on the Plain, 199
Setzer, Claudia, 202
sexual intercourse, laws governing, 19,
    68, 69
šḥt (damaging), 54
šallaḥ, 35n83
Shallum, daughters of, 51, 68
shame. See honor/shame
Shammai, 38
Shargent, Karla G., 68n78
sheep, 91
shekel (silver, money), 101, 102, 102nn
    60, 61
shekel, Tyrian, 173n129
Shelamzion (wife of Eleazer), 37
Shelamzion (wife of Judah Cimber),
    36–37
Shelamzion Alexandra, 171
Sheol, 195
Shephelah, farming in, 85n11
shepherds, 90–91
  as social outsiders, 91
Sherwin-White, Susan, 156n75
ben Shetach, Simeon, 38
šēbet (tribe), 11
šōḥad (bribe), 122, 122n108
siblings, 11
  sharing house, 14
Sicarii, 113, 113n89, 181, 181n153
Sidon, taxes paid at, 172, 173
Simon I (high priest), 158n86
Simon II (high priest), 158, 158n86
Sirach, Book of, 20
  afterlife in, 196n29

on bribes and gifts, 124, 126
on class, 20, 63n65
on daughters' reputations, 67, 70
dowry in, 32
on gender of children, 62
Hellenistic character of, 193n21
on high priest, 158–59, 158n86
on inheritance, 76n95
on occupations, 64, 65, 91–92, 96,
    96n43, 97, 97n46
reputation in, 195–96
on responsibilities to parents, 73
on scribes, 64, 97, 119, 193
on social ethics, 192–94
on surety, 118, 119
Torah in, 96, 97, 104, 118, 119, 192,
    193, 194
wealth in, 20, 32, 63n65, 96n43, 124,
    126n121, 192–94
on widows, 52
on wives, 51n37
on work ethic, 63
slavery, 79–80, 79n109
  Antiochus IV's participation in, 163
  laws pertaining to, 78, 78nn100, 101
  and manumission of slaves, 79
  prostitution and, 79, 149
  trade in Ptolemaic period, 148–49,
    148n53, 163
  See also debt slavery
slaves
  Ephesians on, 80
  as part of household, 15, 61n61
  publicani made, 173
Smith, Adam, 100n53
Smith, Jonathan Z., 201, 201n44, 203
Smith-Christopher, Daniel, 26, 28
śn' (hate), 34, 35n83, 36
social justice, 105–10, 111–12, 124,
    130n6, 154, 170, 171
  God as origin of, 105, 108, 184, 200
  in Luke–Acts, 199–200
  Torah as template for, 122, 187, 193,
    194, 200, 207
  undermined by corruption, 122,
    122n108, 154n70, 190, 193
social location, 202–5
social status
  assimilation and, 161
  gifts and, 30, 123, 125

occupation and, 63
of traders, 95–96
Song of Songs
date of, 70n80
female initiative in, 70–71
patriarchy reflected in, 71n82
viticulture in, 47n23
women in, 71, 71n81
sōpĕrîm (scribes), 96n44
speculation on next year's produce, 110
spices, 94, 94n39
Spock, Benjamin M., 58n52
Stager, L. E., 61nn59, 60; 73n90, 85nn8,
    9; 91n27
"stranger," 115, 116, 120
stratēgos (governor), 157, 157n79
stratification, 7, 21, 80, 128
    apocalypticism and, 197–98, 204
    dowry practices and, 33–34
    in Hasmonean period, 169–71
    lending and, 117, 120, 139, 180–81
    in modern times, 206–7
    in New Testament, 179, 180
    occupation and, 65
    under Persians, 139
    under Ptolemies, 153–54
    under Romans, 180–81
    in Seleucid period, 158, 159–60,
        162n100
    solidarity and, 201–2
suffering, afterlife as reversal of,
    196–202
surety, standing, 2, 3, 111–12, 111n84,
    114–21
    need for, 114, 118, 121
    negative views of, 115–18, 119, 187
    positive views of, 115, 118, 194
    social context and, 119–20
    usury and, 111–12, 118
synagogues
    female leadership of, 66, 66n73
    as locus of instruction, 64

Tacitus, 62n63
Tale of the Eloquent Peasant, 122–
    23n110, 126
taxation, 3–4, 128–82
    anthropological study of, 129–30
    census-taking and, 147, 150, 174–75,
        178, 179n148

of commercial goods, 148, 148n50,
    156, 172
of Diaspora, 175–76
exemption from, 157–58, 157n81
farming and, 46, 128, 129–30, 138n22,
    140n27, 148, 158, 172–73, 176,
    177, 179
by Hasmoneans, 167, 168, 169,
    169n120, 171, 176–77
by Herod the Great, 174–77,
    176n141, 177n144
on imports and exports, 151, 156, 175
of land, 133, 134, 172, 174, 177, 178
in Nehemiah, 1, 110n82, 137–39,
    138n22, 143–44, 143n34
by Persians, 132–35, 137–43
on produce, 133, 143, 147, 148, 156,
    172, 173
by Ptolemies, 147–48, 149–50, 151,
    152–53, 154–55, 154n73
as punishment for cultic infidelity,
    161n96
relief from, 139, 140, 166n114, 177
rising in crisis periods, 129, 141
by Romans, 172–73, 172n127, 178–
    79, 180
on sales, 176
by Seleucids, 155, 156–57, 158,
    160–61, 165
social unrest interfering with, 162–63
social unrest resulting from, 128, 168,
    179n147
theological aspects of, 179n147
tax farming, 150, 153, 172, 173, 179
    defined, 150
    by local entrepreneurs, 179–80
Tcherikover, Victor, 148n50, 162nn100,
    102; 163n103, 169, 170
Teacher of Righteousness, 170
teachers, 63
temple
    cleansing of, 96n42
    commercial activity around, 174
    communal solidarity based on, 11–12
    dedicated to Zeus, 163
    destroyed by Romans, 171
    as locus of community, 159
    reconstruction, 157–58, 158n86
        by Herod, 174, 174n135
    regained by Hasmoneans, 165

temple (*continued*)
  revenue from, 160, 161n96
  tax, 135n18, 173, 173n129
  theft from, 163
  tithes supporting, 89, 143–44, 144n35, 169
  wealth of, 157n81, 169
  zones of holiness surrounding, 158, 158n84
temptress figure, 62–63
tenant farming, 13, 19–20, 46, 68, 83, 181
  archaeological evidence for, 178
  "people of the land" forced into, 46n18
  unfair loans leading to, 78, 105, 107
  See also debt slavery
terraces, 83n2
Testament of Job, 76–77, 76n97, 77n99
textiles, 47, 48–49, 48n28, 49n30, 61, 94
theology
  of apocalypticism, 196–205
  ethics and, 183–96
  farming and, 87–89
  interest on loans and, 105–10
  and persecution, 163, 165
tithes, 89, 142–44, 144n35, 169
  priests supported by, 142–44, 143nn32, 33, 34; 176, 177, 179, 182
  "secular," 169n120
Tobiad Romance, 21, 125, 150, 152–53, 153n66, 154, 154n73
Tobit, Book of, 24
  cousin marriage in, 24
  date of, 24n53
  dowry in, 32
  inheritance in, 32n73, 75
  virginity in, 67, 67n75
  women's work in, 48–49
van der Toorn, Karel, 64n68, 96n44
toparchies (tax districts), 149
Torah
  in Ben Sira, 96, 97, 104, 118, 119, 192, 193, 194
  as template for social justice, 122, 187, 193, 194, 200, 207
  wisdom and, 119, 192
trade, 93–96, 100–101, 102
  bribery and, 121

coastal, 19, 95, 96, 102, 151, 170, 175
  Judean participitation in, 20, 84–85, 85n8, 93–96, 102, 174, 175
  moral dangers of, 192–93
  in olive products, 84, 85n8, 94
  in pottery, 92–93
  Ptolemaic control of, 148
  routes expanded by Ptolemies, 151
  Sabbath violation and, 96
  sea lanes and, 93, 93n37
  slave, 145n41, 148–49
  and status of traders, 95–96
  in surplus yield, 41, 45n15, 84, 86, 87, 91
  and traders as "Canaanites," 48n29
  See also occupation
tribe, 11
tribute to colonial powers, 133, 133n11, 172, 174n134, 176, 176n140
Tyrian silver, 173n129, 179, 179n149

Udoh, Fabian E., 176nn140, 142; 179n149
usury. *See* interest on loans

VanderKam, James C., 154n70, 158n86, 168n119
villages, post-exilic, 13
virginity, 67
  reputation and, 67, 67n75, 69–70, 69n79
virginity suits, 70
viticulture, 46–47, 47nn20, 23; 61, 61n60, 85, 85n9, 94
  in Song of Songs, 71

Wadi el-Daliyeh fragments, 145n41
wage labor, 13
  See also tenant farming
wealth
  ambiguous nature of, 189
  anxiety of having, 191, 192
  ethics of, 4, 183–205
  oppressive tactics of obtaining, 21, 124, 153–54, 160n91, 170, 176n141, 192, 200
  as reward, 120, 183, 184, 185–86, 193
  seclusion of women and, 67–68
  wisdom as better than, 186, 192
wealthy class, 19, 20

advantages of, 191, 192
enforcing taxation policies, 150, 153
large landholdings of, 19, 177–78
luxury goods and, 93
punishment of, 159, 198–99, 200–201,
200n42
relative independence of, 151–52,
157
taking advantage of poor, 109–10,
139, 160n91, 183, 184, 186–87,
200
virtue as rarity in, 194
as wicked, 198–99
woe oracles against, 159
Weber, Max, 202
weight balances, 101–2, 101n57
Egyptian influence on, 101n58
Weinberg, Joel, 11, 12
Weisberg, Dvora E., 56n49
wheat, 84
See also grain
Wicked Priest, 170
as Jonathan, 170n123
widows, 3, 8, 51–58
and customs of widowhood, 57
inheritance by, 51, 57, 75, 77
laws pertaining to, 52, 52n40
levirate and, 3, 52, 53–57
modern injustices facing, 206
as outside household structure, 14, 52,
53, 58
poverty of, 53
rights of, 56–57, 56n49
wife
as blessing, 22
debt slavery of, 78n100
less-favored, 74, 74n93
rights of, 36–37, 36n88, 37n92
surrogate, 75, 75n94
See also divorce; levirate; marriage
wine making. See viticulture
Wischmeyer, Oda, 193n21
wisdom, 186, 187, 188n5
apocalypticism and, 201, 203–4
death as absence of, 195n25
as more valauable than wealth, 186,
192
Torah as source of, 119, 192
wealth as reward for, 120
Wisdom, Lady, 50, 50n34

Wisdom literature, 3
absence of afterlife in, 194–96
apocalypticism related to, 201–2
bribery in, 123–24
corruption in, 101–2
dates of, 7
ethics of wealth and poverty in,
184–96
self-preservation in, 121
social context of, 120, 120n106
surety in, 115–17, 115n92, 120, 121
woe oracles, 159, 199
women, 2–3
in biblical studies, 41–42, 42n2
childbirth and, 15, 16
as craftspersons, 47–49
cultic activities of, 49–50, 66–67,
66n73
divorce initiated by, 36–37, 37n92,
38, 39
education of, 66, 66n72
food prepared by, 43–45, 43nn4, 43
inheritance rights of, 27
marginalized in Second Temple writings, 41n1, 50
as merchants, 50n33
modern injustices facing, 206
in public settings, 68, 68n78
rights of, 36–37, 36n88, 37n92, 39, 56
roles of, 41, 42–51, 62, 80
synagogue leadership of, 66, 66n73
work
of children, 59–60, 61, 61nn58, 59,
61, 65
ethic, 63, 187
of women, 43–45, 43n4, 44n12,
46–49, 47nn21, 23; 66, 66n73,
68, 72
Wright, Benjamin G., 193n20, 204n55
Wright, Jacob L., 139n25

Yardeni, Ada, 87n16
Yehud, 131, 131n8, 135, 135n20
extent of, 135, 135n20
See also Judah
yĕhûdî, 5, 79n104, 110, 110n80
yeled (child), 60
as military designation, 60, 60n57
Yoder, Christine R., 47n19, 50n35
"yoke" tax, 148

yōnēq (nursing child), 60
yôreh (early rain), 83

zār (stranger), 115, 116
Zelophehad, daughters of, 27, 75, 76
Zeno papyri, 20–21, 95

on coercive financial practices, 147,
    150–51
Ptolemaic bureaucracy in, 124–25,
    147–48, 150–52, 154n70
slavery in, 79
Zerubbabel, 140n28, 144n36

CPSIA information can be obtained at www.ICGtesting.com
Printed in the USA
LVOW13s0840130814

398618LV00005B/45/P